Best Places to Stay in California

THE BEST PLACES TO STAY SERIES

Best Places to Stay in America's Cities
Second Edition/Kenneth Hale-Wehmann, Editor

Best Places to Stay in Asia
Jerome E. Klein

Best Places to Stay in California
Third Edition/Marilyn McFarlane

Best Places to Stay in the Caribbean
Second Edition/Bill Jamison and Cheryl Alters Jamison

Best Places to Stay in Florida
Christine Davidson

Best Places to Stay in Hawaii
Third Edition/Bill Jamison and Cheryl Alters Jamison

Best Places to Stay in the Midwest
John Monaghan

Best Places to Stay in New England
Fifth Edition/Christina Tree and Kimberly Grant

Best Places to Stay in the Pacific Northwest
Third Edition/Marilyn McFarlane

Best Places to Stay in the Rocky Mountain Region
Roger Cox

Best Places to Stay in the South
Second Edition/Carol Timblin

Best Places to Stay in the Southwest
Third Edition/Anne E. Wright

Best Places to Stay in California

THIRD EDITION

Marilyn McFarlane

Bruce Shaw, Editorial Director

HOUGHTON MIFFLIN COMPANY
BOSTON • NEW YORK

To my daughters, who also love California

Third Edition

ISSN: 1048-5422
ISBN: 0-395-65569-2

Printed in the United States of America

Maps by Charles Bahne
Design by Robert Overholtzer
Illustration preparation by Eric Walker

This book was prepared in conjunction with Harvard Common Press.

VB 10 9 8 7 6 5 4 3 2 1

Contents

Introduction viii

Bay Area 1
Central Coast 187
Desert Country 291
North Coast/Mount Shasta 319
Sierra Country 385
Southern California 465

Recommended Reading 575

What's What:
Bicycling 577
Boating 577
Business Services 578
Croquet 578
Fine Dining 579
Golf 579
Historic Hotels 580
Horseback Riding 580
Kitchens/Cooking Facilities 580
Pets Allowed with Permission 581
Restaurant Open to the Public 582
Tennis 584
Wheelchair Access 585

Index 587

Best Places Report 592

Acknowledgments

As I traveled the length and breadth of California in search of the best of lodgings for the third edition of this book, I found helpful assistance and a warm welcome at every turn. My thanks to all those who provided information and suggestions.

I deeply appreciate the help I received from local and regional visitors bureaus, with special thanks to Eric Symons, San Diego Convention & Visitors Bureau; Carol Martinez, Los Angeles Convention & Visitors Bureau; Lucy Steffens, Sacramento Convention & Visitors Bureau; and Kim McNulty, Palm Springs Desert Resorts Convention and Visitors Bureau.

Special thanks go to Brian Garrison, Alison Newman, and my husband, John M. Parkhurst, for his unflagging encouragement, companionship, and resilience.

Introduction

Places to stay in California are as diverse as the state. They range from rustic cabins in the woods to luxurious city hotels, with an astounding variety in between. You can lodge at a luxurious resort, a homey bed-and-breakfast inn, a Victorian mansion, or a romantic retreat in the country. You'll find the best of them all here in this book.

The third edition of *Best Places to Stay in California* is divided by region and, within the region, by the city or town where each hotel or inn is located. There are several new lodgings, a few deletions, and numerous changes. These are the result of months of personally investigating hundreds of inns. Again, the best were selected. That does not mean they're the most elegant or expensive. What I look for are comfortable accommodations, cleanliness, a commitment to hospitality, an interesting setting, and personality. These criteria apply to every lodging in the book.

Although the book's format has changed, the hotels and inns are still listed under the categories that help you decide if this is the type of place you're looking for. In addition, the book has brief descriptions of each region, maps, and a recommended reading list.

The chapter "What's What," at the end of the book, is a handy cross reference to help you select your preferences in sports, dining, business services, and other areas. It indicates which inns are accessible to wheelchairs and which have cooking facilities.

The inns are not rated, as each has its own merits and your choice depends upon the type of place you want. If it's in this book you can assume it is among the best of its kind. *None of the inns paid to be included.*

You may not agree with all the choices. Some fine places were excluded, not as a reflection on their quality, but by necessity (the inn may be changing ownership, for example, with its future in doubt). You won't find many chain hotels in the book because, with a few outstanding exceptions, they differ very little among locales.

Your comments are welcome. If you know of a special

place that is not described here, or if you've had an unsatisfactory experience at an inn listed, please let us know. Your suggestions will help with future editions and allow us to provide you and other travelers with accurate information. Send your comments to:

Chris Paddock
Best Places to Stay in California
The Harvard Common Press
535 Albany Street
Boston, MA 02118

Rates

Please note that all the rates given applied at press time and are subject to change without notice. Taxes are not included (unless so indicated), so total costs may be slightly higher than those listed. Taxes differ in various regions; they may range from 6% to 12% or higher.

Unless otherwise noted, the rates cited are for one night. "Single" is the cost for one person, "double" the cost for two. Be sure to ask about discount packages, corporate and family rates, and off-season and midweek discounts. These are frequently offered, and you may save a substantial amount.

Meals

Breakfasts are described as full, Continental, or expanded Continental. A full breakfast connotes a hot entrée; a Continental meal is a light repast — usually coffee or tea, rolls, and fruit; while expanded Continental falls between the two, often including cereal, yogurt, or an assortment of cheeses.

Children

By law, California hotels may not refuse to accept children. However, young children aren't appropriate at some lodgings. Bringing a lively three-year-old to a quiet, antique-filled, romantic hideaway can be a frustrating experience for everyone. Common sense is your best guide. Some of the larger hotels welcome children, even providing toys and special menus, and many allow children to occupy the same room as their parents at no charge.

Booking A Room

If you explain your needs clearly when you make a room reservation (do you prefer a private bath, a view, quiet surroundings, a firm bed?), they are likely to be met. If you are not satisfied, request a change. Every hotel has less desirable rooms, but you should never have to accept a room you don't like.

The information in this guidebook is as current and accurate as possible, but changes inevitably occur. I recommend asking about rates and policies before you check in. I also strongly urge making reservations ahead. But if you haven't made reservations, try anyway! Innkeepers are delighted to fill rooms that are suddenly empty because of cancellations.

Best Places to Stay in California is the most comprehensive compilation of the state's outstanding lodgings. I hope you enjoy reading and using it as much as I've enjoyed the research and writing. Happy travels!

MARILYN MCFARLANE
Portland, Oregon
January, 1994

CATEGORIES

Intimate City Stops

This category includes small hotels and bed-and-breakfast inns that combine sophisticated urban amenities with personal style and attention to detail. They may have as few as four rooms; none has more than 100.

Grand City Hotels

Famous historic landmarks and hotels of contemporary opulence are included in this category.

Country Inns and B&Bs

When you're looking for a peaceful retreat from city noise and bustle, a country inn or homey bed-and-breakfast is the ideal choice. Those described here are not all in rural areas, but each has a distinct country-inn atmosphere and offers the chance to enjoy a change of pace.

Family Favorites

If you've wondered where to find a vacation spot for the whole family, possibly offering programs for children, these inns, lodges, and ranches are your answer. They fit other categories, too, but they have perfected the art of providing fun for every age, and their rates often favor families.

Inns by the Sea

Resorts, condominiums, lodges, private homes, and old-fashioned beach hotels are the accommodations described here. Most are right on the shore, with views of the broad Pacific, while some are a few blocks inland in seaside towns. Each has a setting that focuses on the ocean.

On a Budget

These inns are included not only for their unusually low rates, but for other appealing qualities such as an outstanding view, a quaint atmosphere, or a prime location.

Resorts

If a resort offers a wide variety of recreational activities and all meals, and if it is a destination rather than a stopover, we consider it a full-service resort that belongs first in this category.

Romantic Hideaways

No matter what your romantic preferences, you'll find a special place among these choices. They all offer privacy and enchanting atmospheres.

Spas

When you're ready for a vacation that combines health, fitness, good food, companionship, and pampering with a tranquil atmosphere, these are the places to try.

Wine Region Inns

Most of these inns are in the Napa Valley or Sonoma County, California's most famous wine-producing regions. These areas have the greatest number of vineyards in the state, although there are other notable grape-growing areas, particularly in Mendocino and Santa Ynez counties.

California

First there were the mountains and the desert, the roaring surf and animals, vast redwood forests and condors wheeling above silent canyons. Then came the Indians, following the sun after crossing the Bering Strait from Asia. Their clans and communities had been deeply settled along the Pacific for untold generations by the time Spanish explorers arrived, seeking a fabled golden island. The English and the Russians laid claim, and in the 18th century the Franciscans established missions, some of them still standing, along the Camino Real (King's Highway). In 1848, after three centuries of Spanish and then Mexican rule, California became a U.S. territory.

In the same year, gold was discovered in Sutter's Mill, near Sacramento. California's future was assured. Thousands of prospectors, struck by gold fever, swarmed in with settlers and merchants on their heels. Immigrants began moving west, dreaming of gold or a new life. Today California is the most populated state in the nation, with an ethnic mix that borders on bewildering.

As a visitor in this state of diversity, you too will find gold. It may not glitter in a creek bed, but you'll see it in other ways: oranges gleaming against glossy green leaves, hillsides aflame with poppies, gold-flecked sands on miles of beaches, the sun-burnished hair of surfers and swimmers, clusters of ripening dates hanging high in palm trees. And the memories you take home will be pure gold, whether you find them in the sun-dappled depths of a redwood forest, on a lively city street, along a sandy beach, or on a white-cloaked mountain.

Because of California's incredible diversity and size, the tourism department divides the Golden State into twelve regions — "The Californias." They are Shasta-Cascade, the Central Coast, the Deserts, the Central Valley, San Diego

County, the Inland Empire, Greater Los Angeles, Orange County, the Gold Country, the North Coast, the San Francisco Bay Area, and the High Sierra.

For maps and information on any or all of the twelve regions, contact the California Office of Tourism, 1121 L Street, Suite 103, Sacramento, CA 45814; phone 916-322-1396.

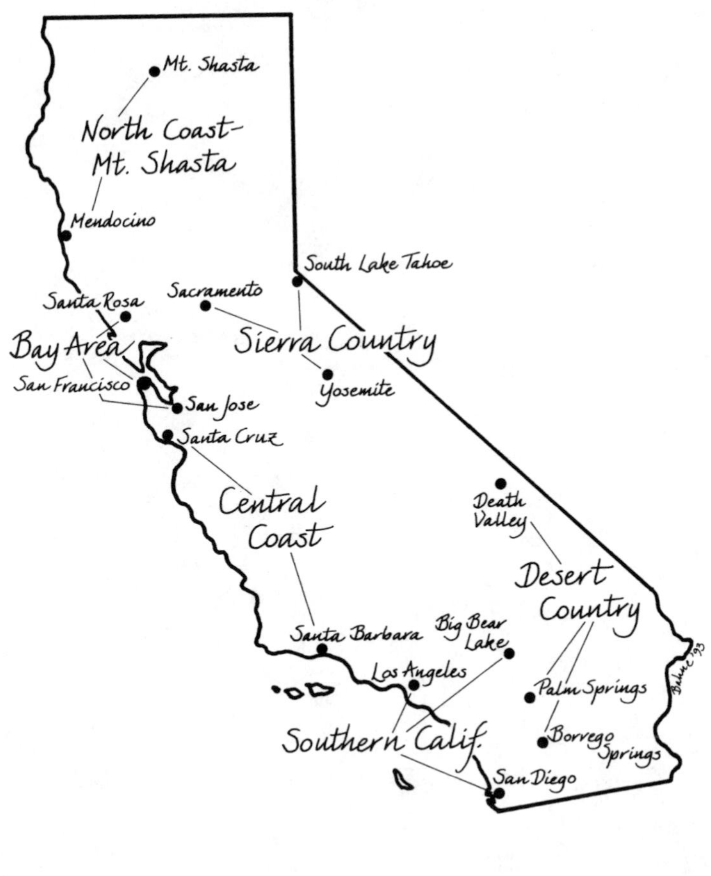
Mt. Shasta
North Coast-
Mt. Shasta
Mendocino
South Lake Tahoe
Sacramento
Santa Rosa
Bay Area
Sierra Country
San Francisco
Yosemite
San Jose
Santa Cruz
Central
Coast
Death
Valley
Desert
Country
Big Bear
Lake
Santa Barbara
Los Angeles
Palm Springs
Borrego
Springs
Southern Calif.
San Diego

Bay Area

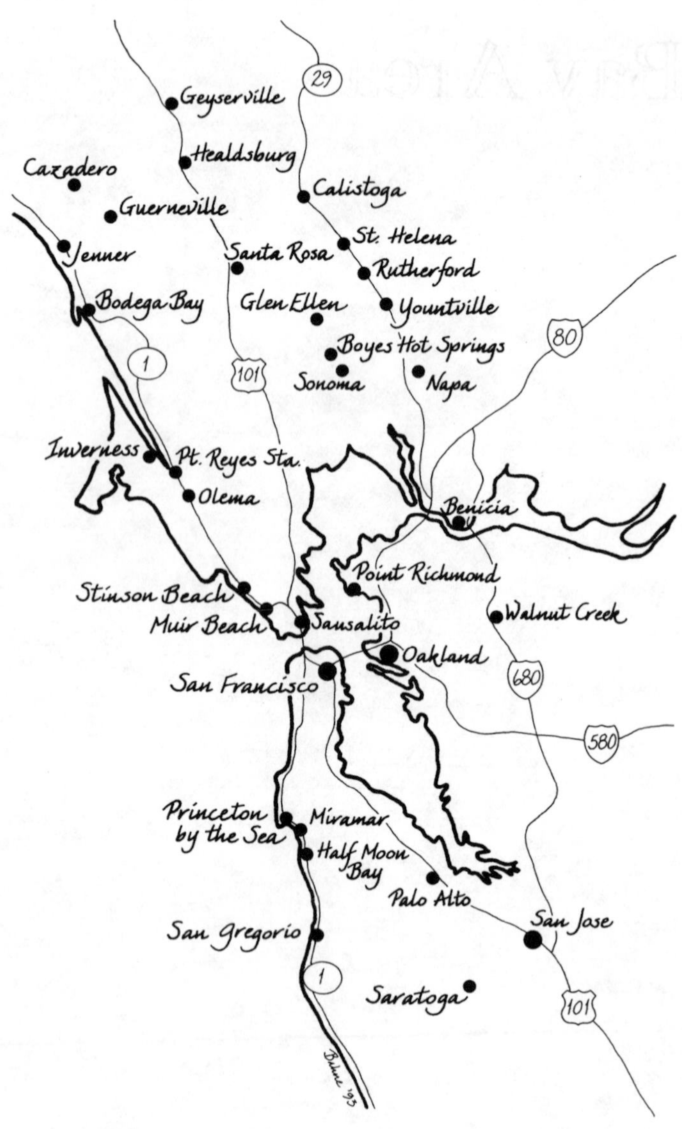

29
Geyserville
Healdsburg
Cazadero
Calistoga
Guerneville
St. Helena
Jenner
Santa Rosa
Rutherford
Bodega Bay
Glen Ellen
Yountville
80
Boyes Hot Springs
1
101
Sonoma
Napa
Inverness
Pt. Reyes Sta.
Olema
Benicia
Point Richmond
Stinson Beach
Walnut Creek
Muir Beach
Sausalito
Oakland
San Francisco
680
580
Princeton by the Sea
Miramar
Half Moon Bay
Palo Alto
San Jose
San Gregorio
1
Saratoga
101

Benicia
Captain Dillingham's Inn, 11
The Union Hotel, 13
Bodega Bay
The Inn at the Tides, 15
Boyes Hot Springs
Sonoma Mission Inn & Spa, 17
Calistoga
Brannan Cottage Inn, 19
Foothill House, 20
Meadowlark, 22
Mount View Hotel, 23
Mountain Home Ranch, 25
Scott Courtyard, 26
Silver Rose Inn, 28
Cazadero
Timberhill Ranch, 29
Geyserville
Campbell Ranch Inn, 31
Hope-Merrill House, 33
Isis Oasis, 35
Glen Ellen
Beltane Ranch, 37
Gaige House, 38
Guerneville
Applewood, 42
Creekside Inn & Resort, 40
Half Moon Bay
Old Thyme Inn, 44
Healdsburg
Belle de Jour Inn, 46
Madrona Manor, 48
Inverness
Blackthorne Inn, 50
Holly Tree Inn, 52
Ten Inverness Way, 54
Jenner
Stillwater Cove Ranch, 56
Miramar
Cypress Inn, 58
Muir Beach
The Pelican Inn, 59
Napa
Churchill Manor, 61
La Residence Country Inn, 63
Old World Inn, 64
Silverado Country Club & Resort, 66
Oakland
The Claremont Resort & Spa, 68
Dockside Boat & Bed, 70
Olema
Point Reyes Seashore Lodge, 72
Roundstone Farm, 74
Palo Alto
Garden Court Hotel, 76
The Victorian on Lytton, 78
Point Reyes Station
Gray's Retreat, 79
Jasmine Cottage, 80
Thirty-Nine Cypress, 82
Point Richmond
East Brother Light Station, 83
Princeton-by-the-Sea
The Pillar Point Inn, 84
Rutherford
Auberge du Soleil, 86
Rancho Caymus Inn, 88
St. Helena
Bartel's Ranch and Country Inn, 90
Deer Run, 92
Meadowood, 93
Villa St. Helena, 97
The Wine Country Inn, 95
Zinfandel Inn, 99
San Francisco
The Archbishops Mansion, 136
Casa Arguello, 102
Campton Place, 101
(continued on following page)

San Francisco (*cont.*)
Country Cottage, 104
The Fairmont Hotel, 138
Four Seasons Clift Hotel, 105
Galleria Park Hotel, 107
Golden Gate Hotel, 109
Harbor Court Hotel, 110
Hotel Griffon, 112
Hotel Juliana, 113
Hotel Nikko, 115
Hotel Sheehan, 117
Hotel Triton, 119
Hotel Vintage Court, 120
Inn at the Opera, 122
The Huntington Hotel, 140
The Inn at Union Square, 124
Jackson Court, 125
The Majestic, 142
The Mansions, 143
The Mark Hopkins Intercontinental, 145
The Nolan House, 127
The Pan Pacific Hotel, 147
Petite Auberge, 128
Prescott Hotel, 149
The Red Victorian, 150
The Ritz-Carlton San Francisco, 152
The San Remo Hotel, 130
Seal Rock Inn, 131
Sheraton Palace Hotel, 132
The Sherman House, 153
Stouffer Stanford Court Hotel, 134
Victorian Inn on the Park, 157
The Villa Florence Hotel, 155
The White Swan Inn, 159

San Gregorio
Pigeon Point Lighthouse Hostel, 161

San Jose
Hotel De Anza, 163

Santa Rosa
The Gables, 165
Vintners Inn, 167

Saratoga
The Inn at Saratoga, 168

Sausalito
Casa Madrona Hotel, 170
Oyama Wildflower Barge, 172
The Phoenix, 174

Sonoma
El Dorado Hotel, 175
Sonoma Hotel, 176
Victorian Garden Inn, 177

Stinson Beach
Casa del Mar, 179

Walnut Creek
The Mansion at Lakewood, 181

Yountville
Burgundy House, 182
Oleander House, 184
The Webber Place, 185

Best Intimate City Stops

Benicia
- Union Hotel

Palo Alto
- Garden Court Hotel
- The Victorian on Lytton

San Francisco
- The Archbishops Mansion
- Campton Place
- Casa Arguello
- Country Cottage
- Galleria Park Hotel
- Harbor Court Hotel
- Hotel Griffon
- Hotel Juliana
- Hotel Triton
- Hotel Vintage Court
- Inn at the Opera
- The Inn at Union Square
- Jackson Court
- The Majestic
- The Mansions
- The Nolan House
- Petite Auberge
- The Red Victorian
- Victorian Inn on the Park
- The Villa Florence Hotel
- The White Swan Inn

San Jose
- Hotel De Anza

Best Grand City Hotels

San Francisco
- The Fairmont Hotel
- Four Seasons Clift Hotel
- Hotel Nikko
- The Huntington Hotel
- The Mark Hopkins Intercontinental

San Francisco (*cont.*)
The Pan Pacific Hotel
The Ritz-Carlton San Francisco
Sheraton Palace Hotel
Stouffer Stanford Court Hotel

Best Country Inns and B&Bs

Benicia
Captain Dillingham's Inn
Calistoga
Meadowlark
Geyserville
Campbell Ranch Inn
Isis Oasis
Guerneville
Applewood
Healdsburg
Madrona Manor
Inverness
Blackthorne Inn
Holly Tree Inn
Ten Inverness Way
Muir Beach
The Pelican Inn
Napa
La Residence Country Inn
The Old World Inn
Olema
Point Reyes Seashore Lodge
Roundstone Farm
Point Reyes
Thirty-nine Cypress
St. Helena
Deer Run
Santa Rosa
The Gables
Saratoga
The Inn at Saratoga
Walnut Creek
The Mansion at Lakewood

Best Family Favorites

Calistoga
Mountain Home Ranch
Point Reyes
Gray's Retreat
San Francisco
Seal Rock Inn

Best Inns by the Sea

Bodega Bay
Inn at the Tides
Half Moon Bay
Old Thyme Inn
Miramar
Cypress Inn
Oakland
Dockside Boat & Bed
Point Richmond
East Brother Light Station
Princeton-by-the-Sea
The Pillar Point Inn
Stinson Beach
Casa del Mar

Best On A Budget

Guerneville
Creekside Inn & Resort
Jenner
Stillwater Cove Ranch
San Francisco
Golden Gate Hotel
Hotel Sheehan
San Remo Hotel
San Gregorio
Pigeon Point Lighthouse Hostel

Best Resorts

Napa
Silverado Country Club & Resort
Oakland
The Claremont Resort and Spa
St. Helena
Meadowood

Best Romantic Hideaways

Cazadero
Timberhill
Point Reyes
Jasmine Cottage
St. Helena
Villa St. Helena
Sausalito
Casa Madrona Hotel
Oyama Wildflower Barge
The Phoenix

Best Spas

Boyes Hot Springs
Sonoma Mission Inn & Spa

Best Wine Region Inns

Calistoga
Brannan Cottage Inn
Foothill House
Meadowlark
Mount View Hotel
Scott's Courtyard
Silver Rose Inn
Geyserville
Hope-Merrill House
Glen Ellen
Beltane Ranch
Gaige House

Healdsburg
Belle de Jour Inn
Napa
Churchill Manor
Rutherford
Auberge du Soleil
Rancho Caymus Inn
St. Helena
Wine Country Inn
Zinfandel Inn
Santa Rosa
Vintners Inn
Sonoma
El Dorado Hotel
Sonoma Hotel
Victorian Garden Inn
Yountville
Burgundy House
Oleander House
The Webber Place

San Francisco, an elegant gem of verve and grace, is everybody's favorite city. Despite earthquakes, fires, and ceaseless change, it remains a place of beauty, from the buttercup-strewn meadows of Golden Gate Park to the chic shops on Nob Hill. The hotels and restaurants in San Francisco are, appropriately, among the best in the world.

The Bay Area has a far wider reach than Marin County and the communities immediately fronting San Francisco Bay. In this context, it extends north as far as **Geyserville** and includes the Russian River region, the **Napa** and **Sonoma** valleys, and down the peninsula to **San Jose** and **Saratoga.** Immediately north of San Francisco are the waterfront boutiques of **Sausalito;** farther north, in the hilly ranch country close to the ocean and Tomales Bay, lies Point Reyes National Seashore, bordered by charming, unpretentious villages — **Inverness, Point Reyes Station,** and **Olema.**

Between Napa and **Healdsburg** some of the state's finest and best-known wines are produced. Vineyards cover the valley floor and climb almost every hillside and grow between farmlands and towns near historic **Sonoma.** Most of the major wineries and a sprinkling of notable restaurants face Highway

29, which is often crammed with traffic and weekend wine tasters. Colorful balloons float overhead, as hot air balloonists get a bird's-eye tour of the valley.

East Bay visitors like to amble by the marina at Jack London's Waterfront in **Oakland** and try the fresh seafood offered in waterfront restaurants. Boaters, joggers, and bicyclists enjoy Lake Merritt, the country's largest saltwater lake within a city.

Up in **Benicia** an artists' colony has formed, and glass-blowing studios sell works of fine quality. The town, which was California's capital from 1853 to 1854, has antiques shops and 19th-century architecture. Not far from here is the famous Marine World Africa USA, with more than a thousand animals.

If you travel west on the peninsula south of San Francisco, you'll come to the charming seaside towns of **Princeton-by-the-Sea** and **Half Moon Bay.** Surrounded by farmland, Half Moon Bay calls itself the pumpkin capital of the world and holds a popular Pumpkin Festival in October. Princeton Harbor offers charter fishing and whale-watching cruises.

Inland from the coast, the Santa Clara Valley — nicknamed Silicon Valley for its electronic technology industry — has California's third largest city, **San Jose.** Its best known attraction is the Winchester Mystery House, a 160-room mansion built by the eccentric heiress of the Winchester rifle fortune. It is said that she believed she would live as long as she kept building — so the house has 10,000 windows and forty staircases, some leading nowhere.

San Jose also has the Rosicrucian Egyptian Museum, with an impressive collection of ancient artifacts from Egypt and Assyria. The San Jose Historical Museum displays items of more recent vintage: buildings and relics from turn-of-the-century California. The Chinese Cultural Gardens are in Overfelt Botanical Gardens, a 37-acre wildlife sanctuary.

Nearby **Saratoga** is known for its fine cuisine; **Palo Alto,** the home of Stanford University, has a collegiate air.

BENICIA

Captain Dillingham's Inn

145 East D Street
Benicia, CA 94510
707-746-7164
800-544-2278 in California

> *A B&B with personality in a historic waterfront town*

Innkeeper: Dennison Demac-Steck **Accommodations:** 10 rooms (all with private bath). **Rates:** $70–$125 single or double, $10 additional person. **Included:** Full breakfast. **Payment:** Major credit cards. **Children:** Under age 10 free. **Pets:** Allowed. **Smoking:** Discouraged.

Captain William Wallace Dillingham was a New England seafaring man who sailed from Massachusetts in 1840 around Cape Horn to Hawaii and, finally, to Benicia, on the Carquinez Strait northeast of San Francisco Bay. Here he married and built a home that remained in the family until the 1980s. It has been a bed-and-breakfast inn since 1985.

Denny Demac-Steck, her husband Roger, and their partner, Harvey Berneking, own the home, with Denny attending to the comforts of guests.

All accommodations include phones, television, and refrigerators, and most have whirlpool tubs. Several enjoy private decks off the colorful English garden. Two rooms may be combined to form a commodious suite. The Captain's Quarters, with a working onyx fireplace and an oversize

Jacuzzi, adjoins the Captain's Suite, a comfortable, sunny room. Wood is supplied for the fireplace.

Four other rooms in the original home are furnished with antiques. Mate's Quarters, under the eaves, is a cozy space. Commodore has double sinks, a bidet, a Jacuzzi, and a balcony above the garden.

Captain Dillingham's is a charming, yellow clapboard Cape Cod–style home on a shady street of exceptionally well-preserved residences in Benicia's Old Town district.

An annex, the Pepper Tree Wing, contains four rooms, each with a separate entrance and private deck. Americana has a colonial decor and two beds, Hemingway is spacious and airy, and Shanghai is decorated in a Far East motif. Casablanca has a Moroccan theme expressed in its colorful wall hanging, dark filigreed screen, paddle fan, and low table of brass and wood. The space for hanging clothes is inadequate; otherwise Casablanca is a room of comfort and charm.

Breakfast, eaten at one long table in the main house, is substantial. The buffet table is laden with fresh fruits, juice, hot and cold cereal, huevos rancheros, quiche, and several cakes. Pots of coffee and tea are kept replenished as guests linger to discuss their plans for exploring the antiques stores, specialty shops, and glass-blowing studios of Benicia.

The Union Hotel

401 First Street
Benicia, CA 94510
707-746-0100

> *A historic hotel in a quaint town on the bay*

President: Stephen Lipworth. **Accommodations:** 12 rooms (all with private bath). **Rates:** $70–$120 single or double. **Included:** Continental breakfast. **Payment:** Major credit cards. **Children:** Welcome. **Pets:** Not allowed. **Smoking:** Allowed.

It's a cheerful, whimsically furnished hostelry today, without a tinge of scandal, but the historic Union Hotel has a risqué past. It was established in 1882 as a 20-room bordello, back when Benicia was a bustling port town on the edge of the Carquinez Strait. You can still see the peephole in one of the doors — just about the only piece left of the original building.

The trim, three-story hotel was restored in 1981, with each guest room decorated individually. Although they are furnished with antiques, the rooms have modern features like television, phones, desks, air conditioning, and whirlpool tubs. The rooms bear names rather than numbers. Mei Ling, on the third floor, has an Oriental decor. Four-Poster, as the name suggests, contains a high antique bed with a curved canopy.

Prism chandeliers sparkle in The Ritz, which has a matching carved bedframe and armoire. This room has a view of the

Carquinez Strait, where the boats head upriver to Sacramento or southwest toward the bay. For the best view in the hotel, request one of the most glamorous rooms, Louis Le Mad.

Benicia served as a U.S. Army arsenal and fort in the mid-19th century, and was the first state capital. Here, in an adobe saloon, the discovery of gold was announced to the world. Here, too, was California's first public school.

Massachusetts Bay hints of Cape Cod, with its spindle bed, wooden rocker, and braided rug. White wicker chairs and fresh flowers give Summer Skies a country garden theme, enhanced by the sky-blue ceiling afloat with white painted clouds. There's an art deco motif in 1932, while Victoriana fits the image of a fine English hotel room of a century ago.

The main floor of the Union contains a noted restaurant. "Everything we serve is fresh. The only thing frozen in our kitchen is the ice cream," says Stephen Lipworth, who has been with the hotel since 1987. The menu offers daily specials and changes seasonally. Diners are served in a room that evokes the hotel's original period, with a stained glass skylight, green lincrusta walls, and historic photographs. A handcarved mahogany backbar dominates the lounge.

In keeping with this step into the past are the antiques shops and historic buildings on First Street. Victorian and false-front western architecture dates from the 1850s to the early 1900s.

Today the quiet little town on the bay, a 45-minute drive northeast of San Francisco, honors its heritage and thrives on old-fashioned celebrations such as a Fourth of July parade and picnic. The Peddler's Fair in August is the largest antiques and crafts fair in northern California.

BODEGA BAY

The Inn at the Tides

P.O. Box 640
800 Pacific Coast Highway 1
Bodega Bay, CA 94923
707-875-2751
800-541-7788

A hilltop resort in a seaside village

General manager: Carlo Galazzo. **Accommodations:** 86 rooms. **Rates:** $110–$140 weekdays, $135–$160 Saturdays, $10 additional person. **Included:** Continental breakfast. **Payment:** Major credit cards. **Children:** Under 12 free in room with a parent. **Pets:** Not allowed. **Smoking:** Allowed.

This luxury resort on six hilltop acres faces the sea some 60 miles north of San Francisco. It offers visitors to the Sonoma coast a quiet, sophisticated retreat with a host of facilities.

The guest rooms are divided among twelve two-story shingled redwood lodges, every one with a view of the harbor. From your window you can watch the fishing fleet come and go and see the sun set over the Pacific, beyond lawns bordered by hardy native plants and blooming annuals.

Most of the rooms have fireplaces and vaulted ceilings. They feature a television with a movie channel, direct-dial phones, clock radios, refrigerators, and terrycloth robes in roomy closets. The baths have custom soaps and gels and, convenient for wet swimsuits, a clothesline that stretches over the tub.

A typical room is furnished with a sturdy oak table and chairs and a gray couch with soft cushions. By the blue ceramic tile fireplace is a basket of wood; more will be brought upon request, at no charge. In this quiet retreat, nighttime sounds fade away until all you hear are the moans of a distant buoy and the crackle of your fire.

A complimentary *San Francisco Chronicle* will be delivered to your door in the morning. When the mood strikes you, you can amble on down to the Bayview Room in the main lodge for a buffet breakfast of croissants, muffins, and fruit. A wall of windows offers fine views of the harbor and Bodega Head, and there's a terrace just outside where you can have your breakfast if the weather is fine.

The restaurant has an à la carte dinner menu that features fresh seafood and local game, fowl, and produce. From January through May, the Dinner with the Winemaker series offers a chance to meet local winemakers and sample their wines.

Bird-watching opportunities abound. Great blue herons, pelicans, cormorants, osprey, sandpipers, and scores more have been sighted here. Movie fans may remember that Alfred Hitchcock's *The Birds* was filmed at Bodega Bay.

On the property are a whirlpool spa, a sauna, and an indoor/outdoor heated lap pool protected from sea breezes by glass walls. For more outdoor recreation you may golf at Bodega Harbour Golf Links, an 18-hole course a mile away, or go whale-watching, charter-boat fishing, clamming, or beachcombing.

The annual Fishermen's Festival in April features a decorated boat parade, the blessing of the fleet, arts and crafts shows, food stalls, and races.

Crabbing season runs from mid-November through April and crab feasts are a Bodega Bay specialty. Try them in restaurants or buy or catch your own and have a feast, accompanied by sourdough bread and chilled Sonoma County wine.

BOYES HOT SPRINGS

Sonoma Mission Inn & Spa

18140 Sonoma Highway 12
Boyes Hot Springs, CA 95416
Mailing Address:
P.O. Box 1447
Sonoma, CA 95476
707-938-9000
800-862-4945 in California
800-358-9022 in U.S.
Fax 707-938-4250

A mission-style hotel with spa facilities

General manager: Peter Henry. **Accommodations:** 167 rooms, 3 suites. **Rates:** $165–$340 single or double, $30 for additional person, suites $395–$650. **Minimum stay:** 2 nights on weekends. **Payment:** Major credit cards. **Children:** Under age 18 free in room with parents. **Pets:** Not allowed. **Smoking:** Nonsmoking rooms available.

In 1895, an enterprising young Englishman, Captain H.E. Boyes, built a bathhouse and a hotel. These later burned to the ground, and in 1927 the present Sonoma Mission Inn was constructed. Typifying the romantic revivalism of the era, the new building was designed as a California mission, complete with arcade and bell tower. The inn's fortunes waxed and waned over the years until, in the 1980s, it was restored and brought to its present state of luxury as a top resort. The rambling pink hotel stands on seven acres of grounds shaded by big maple and eucalyptus trees in the thriving little town of Boyes Hot Springs, two miles north of Sonoma.

The mission motif stops at the front door. Inside, the theme is southwestern in the big open lobby with white walls, a beamed ceiling, and desert colors. Granite tables hold great urns as lamps, and tall palms stand in the corners.

Since the mid-1800s, San Franciscans have been traveling 40 miles north to the Boyes Hot Springs site for the curative mineral waters of its underground springs. The area was long considered a sacred healing ground by Native Americans.

Adjacent to the lobby are a bar and the Grille, a restaurant of soft linens and fresh orchids on the tables, all glowing in candlelight. The Grille features mesquite specialties and California cookery. Fresh local ingredients are emphasized, and the menu includes imaginative and tasty spa cuisine. Another restaurant, the Café, is located at the north end of the property. It has a wine bar and an adjoining market selling wines, gifts, and T-shirts.

The guest rooms are in the three-story main hotel and in newer, separate buildings. The older rooms are smaller but have more charm and character, with half-canopy beds and walk-in closets. Stocked bars hold complimentary wine. The air-conditioned rooms have similar furnishings and contain writing tables, TVs, digital clocks, and phones. The rates reflect the room size. In the Wine Country section of the resort, some rooms have fireplaces and overlook the inner courtyard and landscaped grounds. Carneros Suite, which opens to a patio, is a good choice for small meetings. It has a granite fireplace, comfortable couches, and a wet bar. The rooms closest to the spa are in North Building.

The resort's much-touted spa and fitness facility occupies a smaller space than you might expect, but it's attractively designed and the services seem unending. You can get at least four kinds of massage, a seaweed body wrap, a salt scrub, clay packs, facials, waxings, and numerous hair and nail and skin treatments. There's an extra charge for spa use.

The inn offers two tennis courts, aerobics classes, a weight room, and an Olympic-size swimming pool, heated in winter. Another, smaller exercise pool is for adults only.

CALISTOGA

Brannan Cottage Inn

109 Wapoo Avenue
Calistoga, CA 94515
707-942-4200

A small historic inn close to Calistoga attractions

Innkeepers: Earle Mills, Rick Hernandez. **Accommodations:** 6 rooms (all with private bath). **Rates:** $125 single or double, $20 additional person. **Included:** Full breakfast. **Payment:** MasterCard, Visa. **Children:** Welcome. **Pets:** Welcome with prior arrangement. **Smoking:** Not allowed.

Sam Brannan was one of the first to recognize the commercial potential in the hot springs at the northern end of Napa Valley. In 1859 he purchased 2,000 acres surrounding the hot springs and named the area Calistoga (a combination of California and Saratoga, New York's mineral water spa).

The elaborate resort he built included 25 guest cottages. The only one remaining is now a bed-and-breakfast inn. Its Greek Revival architecture, with intricate gingerbread trim, was intended to bring a sense of civilization to Calistoga in the rugged 1860s. The building has been completely restored.

The house stands behind a white picket fence, roses, and a palm tree that was planted by Sam Brannan. Robert Louis

Stevenson referred to it as a "weedy palm" in *Silverado Squatters.* Now the tree is tall and stately.

The rooms are light and simple, with oak floors, primitive pine antiques, and white wicker furnishings. Each room has a different wildflower stencil: poppies, sweet peas, morning glories, roses, violets, and iris. All have private entrances and air conditioning.

A breakfast that varies daily is served in the dining room, though with the Napa Valley's benign weather, guests can often eat outdoors in an enclosed, lemon-fragrant courtyard.

In the parlor, furnished with pink velvet loveseats near a brick fireplace, stenciled clusters of grapes and leaves decorate the walls, and flowers from the surrounding garden brighten every corner. Sherry and tea are available all day in the parlor.

Brannan Cottage is on the National Register of Historic Places and in 1985 it received the prestigious Napa Landmarks award for its contribution to historic preservation in Napa County.

Foothill House

3137 Foothill Boulevard
Calistoga, CA 94515
707-942-6933

A B&B near wineries and mineral baths

Innkeepers: Doris and Gus Beckert. **Accommodations:** 2 suites plus cottage (all with private bath). **Rates:** $105–$225 single or double, $15 additional person. **Included:** Full breakfast. **Minimum stay:** 2 nights weekends, 3 nights holiday weekends. **Payment:** MasterCard, Visa. **Children:** Not appropriate. **Pets:** Not allowed. **Smoking:** Not allowed indoors.

When guests leave Foothill House, they always rave about the food. Doris Beckert, a longtime culinary student, loves to prepare breakfast specialties and afternoon appetizers and present them artistically for her guests. She serves them in the sun room or on a terrace, in the shade of an immense redwood tree. Some guests like to take their coffee up the grassy slope to the pretty white gazebo.

The innkeepers will arrange for winery and sightseeing tours and make reservations at Calistoga's famed mud and mineral baths. Recommended nearby restaurants include Catahoula's, in the Mount View Hotel, and Showley's.

The small inn also offers well-furnished, attractive, spacious rooms with good reading lamps and stacks of books and magazines. Bottles of valley wine and Calistoga mineral water chill in each refrigerator. Sherry is provided at bedtime, and a teddy bear or other stuffed animal holds freshly made cookies. There are no telephones or televisions in the rooms, but each has a phone jack and the house phone may be borrowed. Wood is laid and the fire is ready to light.

Quail's Roost is a separate hillside cottage with a kitchen, a wet bar, a four-poster bed, and a smaller bed by a bay window. There's a TV and VCR with many videos to choose from, and the fireplace is visible from the living room, bedroom, and bath. A two-person whirlpool tub and double-headed shower are in a very private glass-walled bathroom that faces a rocky slope.

Meadowlark

601 Petrified Forest Road
Calistoga, CA 94515
707-942-5651

A quiet country estate in the Napa Valley

Innkeeper: Kurt Stevens. **Accommodations:** 4 rooms (all with private bath). **Rates:** $100-$135 single or double. **Included:** Full breakfast. **Minimum stay:** 2 nights on weekends. **Payment:** MasterCard, Visa. **Children:** Not appropriate. **Pets:** Allowed by prior arrangement. **Smoking:** Not allowed.

This country home, set on 20 acres of rolling wooded hills outside Calistoga, at the northern end of the Napa Valley, began as a small cabin in 1890. Space was added in the ensuing years, and when Kurt Stevens purchased the property he remodeled it into a light, bright, airy inn that is a pleasure to visit.

After a day spent exploring, sightseeing, and wine tasting, you can relax on the peaceful veranda or enjoy a picnic by the murmuring creek.

Meadowlark's property includes a hill of eucalyptus and oak groves behind the house, bridle trails and walking paths, and a swimming pool off to one side of the driveway. The tan house with white trim is surrounded by perky red geraniums.

The innkeeper welcomes guests hospitably and turns the house over to them. "I treat them as my friends," he says. "I hope they feel that this is their own temporary home." With that aim, he fills the refrigerator with soft drinks, juice, ice, and a basket with fruit. He serves a substantial "California-style" breakfast of fruit, muffins, coffee cake, an egg dish, and coffee on a rustic table in the dining room.

From the big living room, French doors lead to the front veranda, a pleasant spot for relaxing with coffee and enjoying the garden.

All the guest rooms offer views of the forest, garden, or meadow. They're furnished in "eclectic country" — a mixture of antique and contemporary styles done with fine taste and an awareness of travelers' needs for space and amenities.

Each is decorated with objects from Kurt's personal collections. The well-traveled host, who came to California from Germany in the early 1970s, has collected Oriental perfume bottles, old English prints, antique doorknobs, and jade and porcelain horses. He has live horses as well, kept on another part of the estate.

There are no phones in the rooms, but guests may use the house phone (with no charge for local calls). It's turned off at night so sleepers won't be disturbed. Kurt lives in a cottage a few yards down the path and is easy to reach in an emergency.

Meadowlark is a short distance from Calistoga's mineral baths and the valley's numerous wineries and restaurants. Yet it's a retreat from the crowds and traffic that can clog Highway 29.

Mount View Hotel

1457 Lincoln Avenue
Calistoga, CA 94515
707-942-6877

A wine country hotel with deco style

General manager: Mitch Jaffuel. **Accommodations:** 33 rooms. **Rates:** \$85–\$175 single or double, \$15 additional person. **Minimum stay:** 2 nights on weekends, April-November. **Payment:** Major credit cards. **Children:** Under age 10 free in room with parents. **Pets:** Not allowed. **Smoking:** Nonsmoking rooms available.

The first owner of the Mount View was Johnny Ghisolfo, an Italian immigrant with little education but a keen business sense. He became the first mayor of Calistoga, a village at the north end of the Napa Valley known then and now for its mineral waters. In 1917 Ghisolfo built the hotel on the town's main street. Additional wings were added in 1939, and a complete restoration of the Mount View to its original art deco style was completed in 1980. Two years later it was placed on the National Register of Historic Places.

Some of the original furnishings are still in place in the two-story stucco building. Graceful palms stand in the corners of the busy lobby, designed to capture a 1930s European flavor. Overstuffed sofas, a fireplace, and bouquets of flowers make it a pleasant gathering place for conversation and games of backgammon.

On one side of the lobby is a lounge where you can hear jazz or light rock music on Friday and Saturday nights. On the other is Catahoula's, serving California cuisine spiced with a touch of Louisiana. The chef is Jan Birnbaum, formerly of San Francisco's famed Campton Place.

In back of the hotel is a terrace and a swimming pool bordered with fan palms, daisies, and aloe in terra cotta pots. As you swim, you will see silent gliders in the sky above you, dipping and curving like birds with rigid wings.

The guest rooms are in two parallel wings that extend back toward the pool area. In a typical corner room in back you'll have a glimpse of palm trees and the pool and terrace from one casement window, and a hotel wall view from the other. All rooms are air conditioned and have phones and TV. The hotel's owners have spruced up most of the rooms with new furnishings.

The Jacob Schram Suite, named for the founder of Schramsberg winery, is a handsome suite with an ornate carved bed and matching armoire. Flamboyant Sam Brannan, the San Franciscan who founded Calistoga, would likely be pleased with his namesake suite, which is richly furnished in Victorian style.

Most in keeping with the hotel's theme is the Carole Lombard Suite. The actress never stayed at the Mount View, but she would have been comfortable in the large and airy rooms, with their French deco furniture. Framed photographs of the Lombard era hang on pink walls. The bed has a stunning mirror headboard of smoked, beveled glass. Matching end tables hold French porcelain lamps. The tile bath has a shower only, no tub.

The hotel also has a spa offering mud baths, facials, massages, and body wraps.

Mountain Home Ranch

3400 Mountain Home Ranch Road
Calistoga, CA 94515
707-942-6616

A secluded ranch in the Napa Valley hills

Proprietors: George and Joey Fouts. **Accommodations:** 6 lodge rooms, 14 cabins. **Rates:** $49–$165 single or double with breakfast and dinner, $45–$115 single or double with Continental breakfast; varying rates for additional persons, special rates for children. **Minimum stay:** 2 nights during July and August. **Payment:** MasterCard, Visa. **Children:** Welcome. **Pets:** Not allowed. **Smoking:** Allowed, except in dining room. **Open:** February to mid-December.

"Hang on and hope," reads the sign on the long, winding road a mile before you reach Mountain Home Ranch. It's good advice when you're heading deep into the hills between the Napa and Sonoma valleys.

Once you get there, though, life at the ranch is easy, relaxed, and casual. There are a tennis court and two swimming pools with ample decks for sunbathing, but few structured activities. You can walk in the woods and by the willow-shaded creek, or fish in a small, stocked, private lake.

The lodge and cabins are set on 300 acres of wooded land that was homesteaded by George Fouts's grandfather and has been open to guests since 1913. The grand old fir trees and a gnarled, high-climbing wisteria that drops a carpet of lavender petals in spring were planted many years ago, as was the grape arbor above a group of picnic tables.

There are no cooking facilities, though some cabins have refrigerators. Two meals a day are provided; each family is assigned its own table in the big dining room. You may also eat outside on the balcony. George does all the cooking, and he guarantees you'll never go hungry. For breakfast, he'll prepare virtually anything you order — eggs "as you like 'em," hotcakes, potatoes, whatever your preference.

Dinner is equally substantial, with entrées of roast beef or fried chicken accompanied by soup, salad, and dessert. Beer and wine are available, or you can bring your own.

The guest rooms upstairs are not as rustic as the cabins and the decor is simple. Each has a bath with shower, a king-size bed, a dresser, and a couch. At the end of the hall a balcony overlooks a green slope with treed hills beyond. The stillness is broken only by the soft calls of birds.

More rooms are in a building by the pool. The furnishings are basic, designed for tough use. Sliding glass doors open to a balcony above a freeform pool edged with oleander.

George and Joey enjoy their guests, who return year after year to this mountain retreat. They welcome day use and special groups but mostly "we cater to families," they say. "The main idea is to shed your cares and have fun."

The cabins, each with a deck or porch, are clustered on a shady hillside. Some have kitchenettes, woodstoves, and private toilet facilities but share shower houses. The cabins designed for summer use only are simple, unheated, one-room units with double beds and sleeping porches with bunks. You provide your own bedding, linens, and towels.

There's no television reception at the ranch, but a VCR is available, so you can bring movies. The Fouts have several movies to lend and lots of books. The bar in the main lodge has a pool table and jukeboxes.

Scott Courtyard

1443 Second Street
Calistoga, CA 94515
707-942-0948

A secluded inn of suites in a historic town

Innkeepers: Joe and Lauren Scott. **Accommodations:** 6 suites (each with private bath). **Rates:** $125 single or double, $20–$25 for roll-away. **Included:** Full breakfast.

Payment: MasterCard, Visa. **Minimum stay:** 2 nights on weekends. **Children:** Welcome in bungalows. **Pets:** Not allowed. **Smoking:** Not allowed.

Courtyard is an apt name for this complex of four buildings; they surround a latticed courtyard and garden that give guests a sense of privacy and seclusion, though the inn is within walking distance of most of Calistoga's attractions — restaurants, shops, spas, the glider port, and the Sharpsteen Museum.

If you've never stayed at a bed-and-breakfast, this is a good place to try one. You can be as sociable or secluded as you wish. There's plenty to do, with Calistoga's pleasures nearby and the Scotts' art studio seminars, or you can relax in the sauna or in your spacious room.

The Scotts, who came from San Francisco and opened their inn in 1990, have created a relaxing haven with an aviary, garden, pool, three suites in the main house, and three separate bungalows with kitchens suitable for light cooking.

Each one of these cozy, 1930s-era bungalows has its own entrance, a fireplace, and a theme: Tropical, Philadelphia, and Hollywood. All the rooms have queen-size beds and air conditioning. Rose Suite, on the ground floor of the main house, is like an apartment, with a private entrance, rattan furniture, and peach walls. If you take the upstairs suite, you have exclusive use of the upper floor.

The Scotts have furnished their inn with tropical-style art deco antiques selected from curio and antiques shops in the bay area. In the social room they serve evening refreshments and invite guests to enjoy their books and CD player or play chess with an elaborate chess set. This high-ceilinged, airy room has a brick fireplace and French doors that open to the courtyard and swimming pool.

Breakfast, a feast of unusual dishes such as banana-walnut pancakes and Thai chicken sausage, is served at umbrella tables by the pool or in a dining area with bistro-style tables for two.

Silver Rose Inn

351 Rosedale Road
Calistoga, CA 94515
707-942-9581

A top-quality romantic country inn near the vineyards

Innkeepers: Sally and J. Paul Dumont and Derrick Dumont. **Accommodations:** 9 rooms (all with private bath). **Rates:** $115–$195 single or double. **Minimum stay:** 2 nights on weekends. **Payment:** Major credit cards. **Children:** Not appropriate. **Pets:** Not allowed. **Smoking:** Not allowed.

If you want more from the Napa Valley than winery tours, the Silver Rose offers appealing options. Once you're settled in this outstanding bed-and-breakfast inn, you may be reluctant to leave for anything but dinner. It's tempting to sit by the pool all day, or relax on your private balcony and watch the lambs playing and the grapes growing.

The big redwood home on a hill was built as a B&B, with the owners' quarters separate from the side used by guests. The Dumonts' favorite flower, the rose, pervades the inn, from the etched glass rose on the oak front door to the private Silver Rose wine label and, of course, the masses of roses in the garden.

Guests enjoy complimentary wine and cheese in the large living room, which has a stone fireplace, dark beams, and tile flooring. Each guest room has a theme. Most romantic is Turn of the Century, in old rose and lace. Peach Delight, which gets morning sun, has a four-poster bed and calico wallpaper. Cat lovers will appreciate the collection of stuffed cats in this room.

Country Blue has a country motif, and Bears in Burgundy features a collection of some 30 teddy bears. There are bears in a balloon basket, bears made of brass, stuffed bears, and bears in formal dress. The Oriental Suite is the largest and has shoji screens, Oriental rugs, rattan furniture, and Japanese lacquered wood. The four newest rooms have fireplaces and balconies, and two feature double Jacuzzis.

If you decide to venture beyond this lovely enclave, the Dumonts can provide suggestions on places to go. A good restaurant choice in St. Helena is Showley's, in the old Miramonte Hotel, where you can dine in a courtyard under a fig tree that twinkles with lights at night.

Breakfast — a rose-garnished fruit plate with homemade breads and muffins — can be taken to your room or out on the terrace. The inn is well-designed, the hospitality generous, but the grounds are extraordinary. There are many nooks and corners, ideal spots to relax in a chaise and admire the surrounding vineyards and riot of color in the flowerbeds.

CAZADERO

Timberhill Ranch

35755 Hauser Bridge Road
Cazadero, CA 95421
707-847-3258

A luxurious ridgetop ranch and cottages

Innkeepers: Tarran McDaid, Michael Riordan, Barbara Farrell, Frank Watson. **Accommodations:** 15 cottages. **Rates:** $350 double weekends, $296 weekdays. **Included:** Breakfast and dinner. **Minimum stay:** 2 nights on weekends, 3 nights on holiday weekends. **Payment:** MasterCard, Visa. **Children:** Not appropriate. **Pets:** Not allowed. **Smoking:** Restricted.

Timberhill is a mile inland, as the crow flies, from the rugged northern Sonoma coast, 2½ hours from San Francisco. But the road you take to get there twists five miles from the shoreline highway up into the hills. The luxury ranch stands on a ridgetop more than a thousand feet above sea level. If you're in need of a soothing haven with no phone or television or harsh intrusions, the drive is worth it. Add superb meals to the peaceful ambience and pampering Timberhill offers, and you understand why it's in great demand. Hiking trails meander through 80 acres of meadows, ponds, and towering redwoods, leading to wide views of Salt Point State Park and the Kruse Rhododendron Reserve, which together cover 6,000 acres extending to the sea. Tennis courts are tucked away behind a hill overlooking a wooded canyon. A 40-foot swimming pool surrounded by decking is next to the main lodge, with a whirlpool spa in one corner.

If you want to tour the surrounding countryside during the day, the kitchen will pack a picnic basket for you. A good place to enjoy it is Salt Point, a beach park with convoluted lava formations, colorful tide pools, and high bluffs that are good for whale-watching.

In the lodge is an intimate little restaurant where six-course dinners are served nightly to guests in a romantic, candlelit setting. Local products are used to prepare the "California French" cuisine, which features specialties such as pan-grilled salmon with fresh papaya chutney. The wine list has about thirty Sonoma County wines.

Cedar cottages are scattered over the property, some hidden among the redwoods and others on the edge of a meadow overlooking the duck pond. Handmade quilts grace the beds, and tile fireplaces are laid with wood. Fresh flowers are placed in pottery vases, on the pillows, and even atop a stack of fluffy towels in the bathroom.

The innkeepers have added a few unexpected touches such as flashlights for late-night walks, matchbooks and napkins with your name in gilt lettering, and coffeemakers. The flaws are mere annoyances: no towel racks, no place to hang wet swimsuits, and little drawer space.

The skylighted common room in the main building has soft couches facing a big stone fireplace, but privacy is respected in this rarefied atmosphere. The owners are available to answer questions and will show up at your cottage door with a breakfast tray (fruit, muffins, juice, and tea or coffee); otherwise, you're on your own for solitary rambles, tennis, sunning by the pool, or hot-tubbing.

GEYSERVILLE

Campbell Ranch Inn

1475 Canyon Road
Geyserville, CA 95441
707-857-3476

A casual country home in wine country

Innkeepers: Mary Jane and Jerry Campbell. **Accommodations:** 5 rooms (all with private bath). **Rates:** $100–$165 single or double, $25 additional person. **Included:** Full breakfast. **Minimum stay:** 2 nights on weekends. **Payment:** MasterCard, Visa. **Children:** Welcome in cottage. **Pets:** Not allowed. **Smoking:** Not allowed indoors.

This ranch-style home in the Alexander Valley wine country, 75 miles north of San Francisco, provides a quiet, relaxing base for exploring Sonoma County. If you're not interested in wine tasting, the Campbells have provided other options. On their 35-acre ranch there are walking trails, a tennis court, a 40-foot swimming pool, a hot tub spa, bicycles and a horseshoe pit. Lake Sonoma, where you may boat and fish, is four miles away, and you're just three miles from the Russian River.

Breakfast is served on the terrace or at the family dining table next to the open kitchen counter. In this friendly, homey atmosphere, the hosts make it a point to spend time with their guests.

Indoor activities include table tennis, checkers, chess, and reading by the two-sided brick fireplace in the family room or living room. There's always a puzzle in progress.

Guests have the run of the house. You're welcome to use the refrigerator, watch Jerry work on his model train sets, turn on the stereo, or iron your clothes in the laundry room.

There are three spacious, air-conditioned rooms upstairs in the split-level home, all with king-size beds. One has a Baldwin piano. Balconies off the rooms face the hills and Pedroncelli and Gallo vineyards, green-leaved in summer and flaming red in fall. The one downstairs guest room offers the most privacy, though less of a view. The paneled room has a writing table, a tiny TV, and shelves full of books and magazines. There are no antiques here; the traditional furnishings and decor are reminders that you've joined a family in their home. The fifth lodging is a well-furnished two-room cottage a few steps from the main house. It holds four people and has a fireplace and a redwood deck overlooking the vineyards.

The Campbells provide brochures, maps, and menus to help you find your way around. Good-humored Mary Jane is an excellent cook who knows how to make guests feel at home. Even if it's a second dessert, don't miss the delicious pie she serves with coffee or tea at bedtime. Your breakfast choices, which you select the night before, include fruits and juices, cereal, omelettes, and an egg puff filled with sautéed mushrooms or chilis. Breads may be bran or blueberry muffins or sour cream coffeecake, among others.

Hope-Merrill House

P.O. Box 42
21238 Geyserville Avenue
Geyserville, CA 95441
707-857-3356

> *A superbly restored example of Eastlake stick architecture*

Innkeepers: Rosalie and Bob Hope. **Accommodations:** 8 rooms (all with private bath). **Rates:** $95–$140 single or double, $20 additional person. **Included:** Full breakfast. **Minimum stay:** April–November, 2 nights on weekends, 3 nights on holiday weekends. **Payment:** MasterCard, Visa. **Children:** Welcome. **Pets:** Not allowed. **Smoking:** Not allowed indoors.

More than a hundred years ago, J.P. and Martha Merrill settled in Geyserville, a small town 74 miles north of San Francisco. The grand redwood home they built, a striking example of Eastlake Stick architecture, is now an inn.

The Hope-Merrill House opened to guests in 1981. Since then, hundreds of visitors have come to see Rosalie and Bob Hopes' stunning restoration efforts and to enjoy their brand of informal hospitality.

The inn is furnished with treasures collected by the Hopes. Most outstanding are the wallpapers, silk-screened by the designer Bruce Bradbury as replicas of the bold Victorian papers used a hundred years ago. Intricate and fanciful, they cover the walls with exotic designs.

The Victorian Room has an antique double bed, as well as a chaise longue in the bay alcove window and a clawfoot tub. The Peacock Room features a fireplace and a whirlpool tub for two, set in old marble. Briar Rose, Carpenter Gothic, and Bachelor Button all take their names from their motifs. Bradbury and Vineyard View both have fireplaces and double showers. Bradbury has an astonishing array of nine different wallpaper designs swirling around the room in brilliant color. Vineyard View, in colors of plum and wine, has long narrow windows overlooking the vineyard and grape arbor. Sterling Suite is the largest room and has a fireplace, a sitting area, and a queen-size bed.

Geyserville lies in the fertile Alexander Valley, where the vineyards produce some of California's finest wines. Several wineries along the Russian River Wine Trail are open for tours and tastings. From the inn you have a view of Geyser Peak and the steam clouds rising from a geothermal field.

Downstairs in the front parlor is a collection of Victoriana — baskets, eggs, ceramics, plates, tureens. The sun room, by contrast, is casual and light, with wide windows and tables strewn with magazines. Here guests look over restaurant menus and discuss their sightseeing plans.

Rosalie serves a country breakfast of juice, fruit, homemade breads and pastries, and egg dishes. Later in the day, if you want soft drinks or local wine, they're available for purchase. Continuing the Victorian theme, the backyard is fenced with a stone wall and wrought-iron fence. There are raised flowerbeds, a kiwi arbor, rhododendrons, and persimmon and fig trees on the grounds, as well as a deck and swimming pool.

Rosalie and Bob also offer lodging in the Hope-Bosworth House, a historic landmark across the street. Furnished in a sophisticated country style, it is quite different from its impressive Victorian sister and has a cozy atmosphere. The Hope-Bosworth has four rooms and is slightly less expensive. It stands behind tall palm trees and a picket fence covered with roses. Concord grapes grow over the arbor in the backyard; from them, the Hopes make and sell spicy grape jelly.

Isis Oasis

20889 Geyserville Avenue
Geyserville, CA 95441
707-857-3524

A unique and exotic resort in the Alexander Valley

Hosts: Lora Vigne and Paul Ramses. **Accommodations:** 12 lodge rooms (with shared baths), cottage, retreat house, tower house, pyramid, tepees, yurts. **Rates:** $45–$125 (includes tax). **Included:** Full breakfast. **Payment:** MasterCard, Visa. **Children:** Welcome. **Pets:** Allowed with permission. **Smoking:** Not allowed indoors. **Open:** Year round except first 3 weeks in December.

Ocelots, pheasants, an Egyptian shrine, a dinner theater, tepees, stained glass peacocks, workshops in self-exploration — you'll find all these and more at Isis Oasis, an unusual retreat in a quiet village on the Russian River.

Lora Vigne, an artist from San Francisco, opened her multifaceted lodging in 1981 with the intention of providing "a place of inspiration and enlightenment." You'll see evidence of her fascination with ancient Egypt in every building on the ten-acre property. Egyptian symbols and gods and goddesses glow with color in stained glass. A little temple, used as a meditation room, is painted with striking purple and gold hieroglyphics. The Egyptian goddess Isis and her male counterpart, Osiris, are seen in many forms.

Lora herself looks the part, with kohl-lined eyes and a Cleopatra haircut — and an Isis Oasis sweatshirt. She's also a nondenominational minister and often conducts weddings under an immense old fir tree. Her partner, Paul Ramses, is a Gestalt therapist who regularly guides workshops and seminars in self-discovery and past lives.

The wooded grounds were once a Pomo Indian ceremonial site, then a Baha'i school. Isis Oasis continues the tradition of meditation and personal growth based on a belief in the balance of nature's principles.

Meals are taken in a large, bright, open room on the main floor of the Pavilion, where a Swedish fireplace casts warmth on cool mornings. Quantities of fruit, much of it grown on the premises, are served at breakfast, along with fluffy omelettes.

The accommodations vary widely. In the lodge, twelve

rooms have a cheerful country atmosphere, with wicker furnishings, throw rugs, and greenery. A central lounge with a wood-burning fireplace has bay windows that look toward misty Geyser Peak. A dormitory upstairs sleeps ten to twelve.

One of the many intriguing aspects of this retreat is its collection of animals — ocelots, bobcats, and silver and golden pheasants, among others. You may meet Lulu the emu, Dalai the llama, and Isis and Osiris, two serval cats. Black and white swans swim sedately with Egyptian geese and ducks on the pond.

Lodgings with private baths are the three-room cottage with kitchen and hot tub; a secluded two-level tower overlooking plum and pear orchards; and a former farmhouse with two fireplaces, a kitchen, and a hot tub. Vineyard House, with fireplaces, four bedrooms, and cable TV, is a remodeled wide mobile home.

Honeymooners are enchanted with the barrel house, made from an enormous barrel that once was used to age zinfandel wine. It has a skylighted roof and a velvet quilt. For an even more exotic experience, you can sleep in a canvas yurt, a small wooden pyramid, or a tepee. These lodgings are scattered over the grounds and have access to outdoor bathhouses. There's a swimming pool, spa, and sauna.

Isis Oasis is used for four main purposes: seminars for groups, wedding parties, dinner theater, and as a bed-and-breakfast getaway for individuals. The theater is used for productions "of a cultural nature," a broad definition that has included jazz concerts, stand-up comedy, and a German folk-singing troupe. Dinners are mainly vegetarian or Middle Eastern fare.

Isis Oasis is a short walk from the banks of the Russian River and is close to the wineries, vineyards, and fine restaurants of the Alexander Valley.

GLEN ELLEN

Beltane Ranch

P.O. Box 395
11775 Highway 12
Glen Ellen, CA 95442
707-996-6501

A country inn overlooking vineyards

Innkeeper: Rosemary Wood. **Accommodations:** 4 rooms (all with private bath). **Rates:** $95–$120 single or double, $15 additional person. **Included:** Full breakfast. **Payment:** No credit cards. **Children:** Welcome by arrangement. **Pets:** Not allowed. **Smoking:** Not allowed indoors.

This century-old, sunny yellow ranch house with white gingerbread trim and wraparound veranda and balcony stands on a hill above Highway 12, in the Sonoma Valley wine country north of San Francisco.

Built in the 1890s as a bunkhouse when the place was a working ranch, the ranch house was purchased in the 1930s by the present owner's aunt and uncle. They raised turkeys, sheep, and cattle on acreage now growing chardonnay and cabernet grapes.

Rosemary Wood restored the old place in the 1970s and opened it as a bed-and-breakfast for wine country travelers in 1981. In this peaceful country setting she has created a quiet retreat, complete with a tennis court under the oak trees. Behind a low picket fence are the two-story house and the well-tended gardens, where ever-bearing raspberry bushes supply breakfast fruit.

Indoors, there's a dining area by the front door, where breakfast is served in cool weather. On sunny days, breakfast is brought to your own table on the balcony or, if you're traveling with a group, to a table under the trees. Some of Rosemary's specialties are French toast made with Sonoma bread, chili-cheese baked sandwiches, popovers, and homemade jams. And those wonderful red raspberries, just picked.

One room is on the ground floor, the others are upstairs, off the long balcony. One suite, which extends the width of the house, has a daybed in the sitting area and, in the bedroom, a double bed of black iron and gracefully curved brass. Fresh flowers are on the dresser. Books by the noted Glen Ellen author M.F.K. Fisher mingle with travel guidebooks on the table. Works by Jack London, another author who lived in Glen Ellen, are in the opposite corner suite. This suite has a daybed and a settee.

Out on the balcony a hammock swings in the gentle breeze, inviting you to relax while the ranch's cat snoozes on the railing beside you. Or head for the swing on the veranda below, a restful perch for viewing the garden and valley, the orderly vineyards and fields, and the shadowed hills against the horizon.

Gaige House

13540 Arnold Drive
Glen Ellen, CA 95442
707-935-0237

A B&B in a historic home

Innkeeper: Ardath Rouas. **Accommodations:** 9 rooms (all with private bath). **Rates:** $90–$180 single or double. **Included:** Full breakfast. **Minimum stay:** 2 nights on weekends. **Payment:** MasterCard, Visa. **Children:** Welcome by arrangement. **Pets:** Not allowed. **Smoking:** Not allowed.

Glen Ellen is a tree-shaded village in the Sonoma Valley north of San Francisco. The Gaige House is one of its historic homes, set on a rural acre near Calabezas Creek and surrounded by the wooded hills of the California Coast Range. The Italianate Queen Anne home on Glen Ellen's main street was built in about 1890 for A. E. Gaige, the town's butcher. As the years passed, the large Victorian was used as a boarding house and school and was finally restored as an inn in 1980.

Gaige House is a comfortable place to relax after touring the Valley of the Moon. A major attraction is Jack London State Historic Park, about a mile from the inn. The author's former home is now a museum. Also in the park are the ruins of London's fabulous Wolf House and walking and bridle trails.

Jasmine climbs the porch columns, its sweet scent wafting in the front door. On hot summer days, head for the two parlors for complimentary afternoon wine and cheese and the owner's collection of art from around the world. Beyond the parlors is the kitchen, with a big open space where guests eat breakfast at several tables. The menu varies, but always includes a hot dish, fresh juice, fruits, and local products such as Sonoma sausage. The dining area windows overlook a large deck and a lawn and 40-foot pool edged with brick. You can also glimpse another deck built over Calabezas Creek.

The guest rooms are furnished with an eclectic accumulation of antiques and art, reflecting the owner's background in design. They all have air conditioning and two have fireplaces. One street-level room with a fireplace features a brass bed and clawfoot tub. On the third floor — one up from street level, since a lower area was added for more lodging space — the Gaige Suite is popular for its immense blue tile bath with a whirlpool tub. The rest of the large suite is equally well done in wicker and a Balinese theme. Also on the third floor are two rooms with seating by the bay windows and four-poster beds. Up two stairs from the third floor is a cozy room with a fireplace and floors of polished oak. Three rooms on the lower level have private entrances from a backyard deck.

Glen Ellen is a few miles from Sonoma, where you may see

several restored buildings from California's Spanish and Mexican history. The Sonoma area has wineries open for touring and tastings, and there are several excellent restaurants.

GUERNEVILLE

Creekside Inn & Resort

P.O. Box 2185
16180 Neeley Road
Guerneville, CA 95446
707-869-3623

> *A casual resort that's easy on the budget*

Innkeepers: Lynn and Mark Crescione. **Accommodations:** 6 rooms (2 with private bath) and 9 cottages. **Rates:** \$55–\$110 single or double, \$15 less for stays of 2 or more days; cottages \$65–\$150 per day (\$5 less for 2 or more days), \$290–\$500 per week. **Included:** Expanded Continental breakfast in B&B rooms. **Minimum stay:** 1 week in cottages in July and August. **Payment:** Major credit cards. **Children:** Welcome. **Pets:** Not allowed. **Smoking:** Not allowed in B&B rooms.

A stroll away from Guerneville, over the bridge that crosses the Russian River, is the Creekside, an unpretentious resort on three acres. It's bordered by redwood and bay trees and dotted with colorful flower beds.

In the Guerneville area, you can taste local wines, shop at roadside stands, walk in deep redwood forests, rent canoes and bicycles, and browse through shops and galleries.

The homey inn is a lively, busy spot. Its rooms are furnished with simple charm in individual themes. The Victorian Room is a spacious suite with a fireplace, a four-poster canopy bed, and a private balcony. Iron Room, the least expensive, has a bent-iron bedframe and whimsical decorations. The Oak and Walnut rooms are furnished in those woods, while the Wicker Room contains white wicker and has a Victorian motif.

There's a cheerful living room with a fireplace, a deco-style dining room where a breakfast of fruit, cereals, and cheese is set out, and a lounge next to a patio with umbrella tables. Books, TV, and a VCR are available.

The cottages have a rustic appearance. Each has a kitchen and several have a fireplace or private deck. The largest is the Tree House, which accommodates ten. It has a large living room with a fireplace and a sleeping loft under skylights. Packages and special rates are available. At one end of the property there are RV spaces. Creekside has billiards, a swimming pool, barbecue facilities, and pinball and video games. Guests must use public access to reach the river.

The resort's policy of "welcoming well-behaved guests of any age or attitude" draws a mixed clientele and many repeat guests who appreciate the casual atmosphere, reasonable rates, and proximity to the attractions of the Russian River.

Applewood

13555 Highway 116,
Pocket Canyon
Guerneville, CA 95446
707-869-9093

A luxurious mansion near the Russian River

Innkeepers: Jim Caron and Darryl Notter. **Accommodations:** 10 rooms (all with private bath). **Rates:** $115–$185 single or double. **Included:** Full breakfast. **Minimum stay:** 2 nights on weekends, 3 nights on some holidays. **Payment:** Major credit cards. **Children:** Not appropriate. **Pets:** Not allowed. **Smoking:** Not allowed.

The Russian River between Highway 101 and the coast has long been a scenic playground for vacationers. One of the grand homes built during the 1920s was the Belden Mansion, intended to be a "centerpiece of elegant living." Today it's a bed-and-breakfast of great quality and charm. Jim Caron and Darryl Notter brought their experience in business and interior decorating to the venture when they purchased the home in 1985. Their goal was to achieve the ideal country inn, which they have done with style and warm hospitality.

When you enter the stucco, tile-roofed B&B, which sits on a knoll outside Guerneville, you're in a large common room with a stone fireplace, dark woodwork, and comfortable couches. Around the corner is the solarium. Curved walls, lots of glass and views of the trees, leaf patterns against green walls, and tall palms in terra cotta pots give this room an outdoor atmosphere. The stone fireplace and rattan furniture make it cozy. Coffee and tea and the newspaper are provided here in the morning.

In the 1920s, San Franciscans would ferry across the bay and take the train north to Guerneville to fish, swim, ride horses through the redwoods, and dance to swing bands.

All the guest rooms, which are on various levels, have phones, TV, fresh flowers, down comforters, and a harmonious blend of family heirlooms, antique botanical prints, books, and art.

One room has a covered porch, another a walled patio where roses and camellias grow. The largest room, on the ground level, has a secretary desk against apple green walls and a sitting area overlooking the trees.

Dinners are available five nights a week (not on Tuesdays and Wednesdays); Jim and Darryl have gained renown for their cooking as well as their innkeeping. A typical meal might include hot onion rolls; minestrone; a salad of thinly sliced roast beef and capers; lamb Florentine or pasta with bacon, tomato, and basil; and apple tart with crème fraîche. You can purchase wine or bring your own (a corkage fee is charged).

When you return to your room you'll find chocolates, the bedclothes turned down, and your clothing neatly folded or hung in the closet. In the morning, another outstanding meal is served in the dining room.

The inn has a swimming pool behind a wrought-iron gate; beyond is a small vineyard, the garden, and the wooded hills. You can tour nearby wineries, try the region's famous apples, fish for steelhead, taste fresh jam at Koslowski's, or take a Japanese enzyme bath at Osmosis Company.

In Armstrong Park, walk among majestic giants — some of the redwood trees are more than 300 feet high and a thousand years old.

HALF MOON BAY

Old Thyme Inn

779 Main Street
Half Moon Bay, CA 94019
415-726-1616

A bed-and-breakfast in a seaside village

Innkeepers: George and Marian Dempsey. **Accommodations:** 7 rooms (all with private bath). **Rates:** $70–$160 single, $75–$165 double, $10 additional person. **Included:** Full breakfast. **Payment:** MasterCard, Visa. **Children:** Welcome. **Pets:** Not allowed. **Smoking:** Not allowed.

An English herb garden gives this charming bed-and-breakfast inn its name. More than eighty varieties of herbs grow in the garden, spicing the air with their scents and providing dash to breakfast dishes.

The Queen Anne home is a comfortable, relaxing place to visit. The hosts offer afternoon wines, restaurant recommendations, information on the sights of Half Moon Bay, and directions to the nine state beaches nearby, the tide pools at the Fitzgerald Marine Reserve, art galleries, and nearby pumpkin patches.

Old Thyme Inn was built in 1897 and restored as a bed-and-breakfast ninety years later. The guest rooms have antique furnishings and colorful wallpapers, and several contain fireplaces and whirlpool tubs. All but Oregon Room have queen beds; it has an antique French double bed. Rosemary, on the main floor, is furnished with a curved white iron bed, Oriental carpet, wicker chair and rocker, and lace curtains. Behind a stained glass window is a blue and white bath with double whirlpool.

This may be the pumpkin capital of the world. Every October, thousands of people drive here, 30 miles south from the Bay area, to buy their jack-o'-lanterns.

Wild Thyme, also on the main floor, has a coronet canopy bed and down comforter, a gas fireplace, and a double whirlpool in the bathroom. An armoire holds padded hangers for clothing. Lavender, a small room upstairs, is the only one with a detached bath. The Garden Suite offers secluded, quiet, romantic lodgings in a separate building behind the herb garden. Its four-poster pine and oak bed is canopied in violet and blue floral fabric to match the balloon shades and complement the room's rose decor. It has a fireplace, a TV and VCR, a refrigerator with complimentary wine, and a double whirlpool under a skylight.

In the Garden Suite you may have breakfast in bed or join the other guests at a single table in the dining room. Breakfast includes juice, fruit, usually banana bread, and a main dish such as quiche or a frittata. You might also be served Italian bread with herbed cream cheese and tomatoes, a lemon bread, nut bread, scones with marmalade, or a homemade French cherry flan, along with a tray of cold meats and English cheeses.

HEALDSBURG

Belle de Jour Inn

16276 Healdsburg Avenue
Healdsburg, CA 95448
707-433-7892

A romantic bed-and-breakfast near wineries

Innkeepers: Tom and Brenda Hearn. **Accommodations:** 4 cottages. **Rates:** $115–$185 single or double. **Included:** Full breakfast. **Minimum stay:** 2 nights on weekends, 3 nights some holidays. **Payment:** MasterCard, Visa. **Children:** Not appropriate. **Pets:** Not allowed. **Smoking:** Not allowed.

At Belle de Jour an Italianate farmhouse, built around 1873, stands on a hill surrounded by six acres of gardens and fields. This is the owners' residence; a few yards up the slope are the white, rough-hewn guest cottages.

All the rooms have woodstoves or fireplaces with wood supplied and a fire laid. They're decorated in a French country theme and have refrigerators, air conditioning, hair dryers, and robes.

Atelier, once used as a studio, has rattan furnishings and a bed with a muslin canopy. Posters of France hang on the walls. There's a streamlined pedestal sink and a whirlpool tub in the white tile bath. More sophisticated is the Terrace Room, with a fireplace, a brass bed, and colors of mauve, deep green, and rose. The rosy-hued bath has a shower and a whirlpool tub for two. The Caretaker's Suite, which was the caretaker's quarters for many years, is a large, barnlike room in buff, white, and tan. It boasts a bed with a white lacy canopy and a sitting area with a Franklin fireplace. This suite also has an oversize whirlpool tub. Double doors lead to a trellised deck that overlooks rolling hills and vineyards.

The little town of Healdsburg lies in the Alexander Valley wine country 70 miles north of San Francisco. On its outskirts, directly across the road from Simi Winery, is this romantic country getaway.

A favorite among repeat guests for its lovely view is Morning Hill. Green pine walls, dark green shutters, and throw rugs on wood floors add rustic atmosphere to the comfortable room. Floral watercolors above the bed echo the gardens outside. The breakfast menu changes daily. "Guests are at my mercy," Brenda says with a laugh. She may prepare mushroom-chive omelettes, eggs Benedict, or eggs and bacon to accompany her sour cream cinnamon swirl bread, orange juice, fresh fruit, and coffee. Breakfast is served in the farmhouse or on the deck.

Brenda and Tom came to Healdsburg and Belle de Jour in 1986 from Los Angeles. "We had the house, the exotic cars, the toys," says Brenda. "Then one day we were in freeway traffic, talking to each other on our car phones, and we decided we didn't want to live that way anymore."

Now they happily tend vegetable and herb gardens, hang linens to dry in the sun, and welcome travelers looking for a secluded wine country retreat.

Madrona Manor

1001 Westside Road
Healdsburg, CA 95448
707-433-4231
800-258-4003
Fax 707-433-0703

A historic mansion on a wine country estate

Innkeepers: Carol and John Muir.
Accommodations: 21 rooms. **Rates:** $135–$225 single or double, $30 additional person. **Included:** Full breakfast. **Payment:** Major credit cards. **Children:** Welcome. **Pets:** Allowed by prior arrangement. **Smoking:** Allowed in designated areas.

West of the Napa Valley lies the Sonoma Valley, a less touristed wine region with a rural ambience and calm that many visitors prefer. At the north end of the valley, near the village of Healdsburg, an elaborate three-story, seventeen-room mansion was built in 1880 by John Paxton, a wealthy businessman, state legislator, and promoter of Sonoma County's wine industry. The house remained in the Paxton family until 1913. Purchased and restored by the Muirs in the 1980s, the inn and restaurant have been receiving acclaim since they opened. The inn is against a hillside on eight landscaped acres, under eucalyptus and oak trees and the tall madrones that give the place its name. A large garden of vegetables, herbs, roses, and other flowers is overseen by Carol, who arranges bouquets throughout the homey hotel.

Staying at Madrona Manor is like visiting a friend with a country estate — a friend from another century. Victorian antiques fill the spacious rooms. The music room, with ongoing jigsaw puzzle, square rosewood grand piano, and books and scrapbooks, is a genteel gathering place to sip wine before dinner. Next to it is the restaurant, noted for its California cuisine with a Mediterranean flair. The Muirs' son, Todd, is the chef, a graduate of the California Culinary Academy. He prepares such delicacies as veal and sea scallops with mushroom duxelles, fennel timbale, and apricot soufflé. The menu changes seasonally and always makes good use of Sonoma County's fresh products.

A morning newspaper and coffee are set out before breakfast. Then it's fresh orange juice, toast, granola, and an assortment of meats, cheeses, and fruit. Finish it all off with a spoonful of the inn's prize-winning kiwi or dwarf mandarin orange marmalade on deep-fried Spanish pastry (churros).

Nine guest rooms are in the main house. Their fireplaces, antiques, and decor create the atmosphere of an earlier day, while private baths and individual climate control provide modern comforts. The furnishings are impressive: intricately carved four-poster beds, dressing tables with beveled glass mirrors, gilt-framed oil paintings, and tall armoires.

The most popular is Paxton's Room, with a tile fireplace, a curtained alcove with bay windows, and a fine view of Mount St. Helena and Fitch Mountain from the balcony. This is one of two rooms with French doors opening to private balconies.

The third floor, formerly the servants' quarters, has ornate beds and Victorian wallpapers. The other rooms are in separate cottages: nine in the Carriage House, two in Meadow Wood, and one Garden Suite. These are less formal and more "countrified" than those in the main house. The Carriage House was built for the Paxton family's carriages; now it houses visitors in luxury with a Far Eastern touch. The front door and filigreed rosewood interior trim were brought from Nepal, the figures of dancers from Thailand. One room in the Carriage House is furnished with antiques, while the rest are contemporary.

Farther up the hill, near the terraced garden and under oak and ginkgo trees, is the Garden Suite. It has its own deck and yard, a marble fireplace, and a tub for two.

There are phones in all the rooms, but no television at Madrona Manor. The inn has a swimming pool in a grove of orange and lemon trees.

INVERNESS

Blackthorne Inn

P.O. Box 712
266 Vallejo Avenue
Inverness, CA 94937
415-663-8621

A whimsical, handbuilt home on Tomales Bay

Innkeeper: Susan Wigert. **Accommodations:** 5 rooms (3 with private bath). **Rates:** $90–$170 single, $105–$185 double. **Included:** Full breakfast. **Minimum stay:** 2 nights weekends. **Payment:** MasterCard, Visa. **Children:** Not appropriate. **Pets:** Not allowed. **Smoking:** Not allowed indoors.

North of San Francisco, in the wooded hills of the quiet town of Inverness, the Blackthorne Inn offers a unique retreat. It's been called a "carpenter's fantasy" and "an architectural extravaganza," well-deserved labels for a four-story rambling home that resembles an oversize treehouse. It used to be a one-room cabin surrounded by fir, bay, and oak trees. Then Susan and Bill Wigert decided to add a deck. Their plans expanded, local carpenters and woodworkers became involved, and "the project got out of control," says Susan. Now it's a delightfully quirky construction with towers, nooks, balconies, skylights, and a spiral staircase winding to the top.

An interesting shop in Inverness is Shaker Workshops West, which sells handmade boxes, baskets, rocking chairs, and other Shaker furniture and crafts.

Stones from seven counties were collected for the big fireplace in the living room. Local artisans also built fir plank walls and put in rustic beams from San Francisco wharves. In this inviting room are books, games, and a stereo. Alcoves with windows that look into the forest are ideal for curling up with a book and nibbling the brownies and cookies Susan offers in the afternoons. There's also a wet bar with a refrigerator for guests' use. A 3,500-square-foot deck, complete with fire pole to the ground, circles the house on the second level.

In the adjacent dining room, breakfast is served buffet style. Some choices are fresh fruit, baked apples, orange juice, granola and other cereals, quiche, and pastries.

Stairs wind up to two guest rooms on the third level and one at the top. Lupine has a queen-size bed under a gable, a private bath in the room, and an outside deck. From the deck, stairs lead to the upper level and a hot tub under the trees.

Overlook is a light, airy room with a peacock chair and stained glass windows in artful thistle, poppy, and iris designs. Its bath is down the hall. Overlook also has two balconies, one with a view of the treetops and the other above the living room.

Eagle's Nest is the most enchanting (and the most expensive) space. An octagonal room at the top of the staircase, it's enclosed by glass to give you a fine view of the California buckeye trees and the starry sky. Outside, a ladder will take you to a private deck at the uppermost level. Cross a walkway and bridge from your private entrance and you reach the deck, with a hot tub and bath.The drawback to Eagle's Nest (if you don't mind all the climbing) is that you must go outside to the bathroom, and share it with hot tubbers. However, it's a favorite with those looking for a truly special romantic spot.

Two spacious suites on the lowest level each have a private entrance and sitting room. Both are nicely furnished with wicker and pastels; they share a bath with a shower. The advantage of these rooms is their proximity to the parking area, with few stairs to negotiate. The disadvantage is the view of the deck's underside, but you do get forest glimpses as well.

The atmosphere is relaxed and casual, befitting Inverness's homey style. Susan enjoys her guests and is happy to sit down for a chat or discuss the merits of local restaurants and beaches. You'll want to explore Point Reyes for its scenery, flowery meadows, steep headlands, and ocean views.

Holly Tree Inn

3 Silverhills Road
Inverness Park
Mailing address: Box 642
Point Reyes Station, CA 94956
415-663-1554

A wooded retreat near Point Reyes National Seashore

Innkeepers: Diane and Tom Balogh. **Accommodations:** 4 rooms and 1 cottage (all with private bath). **Rates:** $90 single, $100–$150 double. **Included:** Full breakfast. **Minimum stay:** 2 nights weekends. **Payment:** MasterCard, Visa. **Children:** Welcome. **Pets:** Not allowed. **Smoking:** Not allowed indoors.

An abundance of holly trees gives this bed-and-breakfast inn its name. Surrounded by lawns and flowers, it stands on 19 hilly, wooded acres outside Inverness and next to Point Reyes National Seashore, just north of San Francisco.

Holly Tree Inn is a a quietly comfortable dwelling, a place for reflection. The heart of the inn is its spacious living room, where overstuffed chairs and sofas face a copper-hooded brick fireplace. Soft music plays and a fire glows on foggy days, a perfect setting for reading, visiting, or sipping a complimentary glass of wine.

The nearest beach is Limintaur, a 15-minute drive. You can walk for miles on its firm sand. The waters of Tomales Bay are warm enough for swimming in summer. In the winter, watch for gray whales from the lighthouse at the tip of Point Reyes. The entire peninsula is a bird watcher's delight in all seasons.

Each of the guest rooms has its own character. Holly Room features a 1930s bedstead with handpainted flowers on the headboard. A private balcony overlooks the front lawn, creek, and garden of daisies and golden lilies. Mary's Garden, the smallest room, is off the kitchen but has soundproof walls and a private entrance. Its long windows overlook the rose garden. Ivy, decorated in pale green, has a spool bed and ruffled curtains. Laurel's corner windows, hung with white Priscilla curtains, overlook the crab apple tree in the side garden. This spacious blue and white room has a sitting area with a rocking chair and a king-size bed.

Cottage in the Woods — the best room — is a few yards up the driveway from the main house. Built in 1987, it is simple, light, and airy, a wonderfully inviting retreat. Bare wood floors are of warm, polished pine, and walls have a wash of pink-toned white. The Cottage is furnished with pearwood antiques from Austria — note the carved pear baskets on the headboards and armoire — and a gas stove, toaster oven, and refrigerator in the kitchenette. There's a sitting room with a woodstove and a clawfoot tub in the bathroom, where you'll catch a whiff of bayberry and lemon verbena from the soaps on the counter. A greenhouse window by the tub frames a view of the fern-covered hill just outside.

Breakfast is placed in the Cottage refrigerator the night before; other guests eat in the inn's dining room by the brick fireplace. Orange juice, fruit, eggs Benedict, quiche, and French toast are among the dishes Diane prepares.

After breakfast, you might browse through the displays of local crafts for sale or check the array of information on nearby attractions. Point Reyes National Seashore has spectacular scenery and is one of the great hiking areas of the California coast. Diane will give you a map showing various walks. The inn is a mile from the visitors' center, the starting point for trails that wind to the sea over the woodlands and meadows, gold in spring with California poppies. The most popular trail is Bear Valley, a four-mile hike to Arch Rock.

Ten Inverness Way

P.O. Box 63
10 Inverness Way
Inverness, CA 94937
415-669-1648

A turn-of-the-century redwood home on Point Reyes peninsula

Innkeeper: Mary Davis. **Accommodations:** 4 rooms, 1 suite (all with private bath). **Rates:** \$100–\$130 single, \$110–\$140 double, suite \$150. **Included:** Full breakfast. **Minimum stay:** 2 nights weekends. **Payment:** MasterCard, Visa. **Children:** Welcome in suite. **Pets:** Not allowed. **Smoking:** Not allowed indoors.

Mary Davis has written the book on innkeeping — literally. She's the author of a how-to guide for prospective bed-and-breakfast owners. Fortunately for her guests, she follows her own advice, resulting in a delightfully homey, comfortable inn where the energetic hostess knows how to welcome you, provide for your needs, and leave your privacy intact.

Mary's an avid reader who's happy to trade book suggestions; she even publishes a summer reading list of her ten favorites for the year. "This is an inn for hikers and readers," she says.

Inverness, a quiet village on Tomales Bay, was formed a century ago as a resort development by James Shafter, who hoped to recoup some railway investment losses. The family was Scottish, and the town and its streets were given Scottish names such as Hawthornden Way, Dundee Way, and Cameron Street. The promotion wasn't successful at the time, but today the town is a popular tourist destination.

The redwood shingle home that is now Ten Inverness Way was built in 1904. In 1980, Mary Davis bought it, converted it to an inn, and filled it with antiques, Oriental rugs, and handmade quilts. She planted an English country garden of nasturtiums, purple and white cosmos, roses, geraniums, and snapdragons under fruit trees, with paths winding around to the back of the house and the hot tub. Robes are provided for guests to wear to the hot tub.

The suite, entered through a private entrance from the garden, has a kitchen and a sitting area, a queen-size bed in an alcove, and a sofa bed. As a suite guest, you may have breakfast in your room or in the private garden.

In the main part of the house, unusual box windows allow plenty of light. In the big living room, a fire burns on cool evenings. There's a phone here and a sideboard where sherry and hot tea and coffee are always available. Guests enjoy the piano, a guitar, puzzles, and games, but the many books are the main draw.

The common room is upstairs from the inn's entrance, and guest rooms are a flight above that. Each room has something special: a skylight over the bed, an old wicker table, a patchwork quilt, or a daybed piled with pillows. Room 2, at the top of the stairs, is a favorite for its view of the bay from the bed.

At the end of the upstairs hall there's a first aid basket with such items as aspirin, dental floss, and Band-Aids. Other thoughtful touches are the assortment of books in each room and numerous hooks, hangers, and pegs.

The brigh sunroom next to the living room has a cheery red woodstove, original art on the walls, and pots of bright flowers. Breakfast here includes toasted homemade bread with blackberry jam, juice, fresh fruit, and scrambled eggs with basil and cheese, or Mary's specialty, banana buttermilk buckwheat pancakes — and plenty of strong hot coffee.

You can keep very busy on the Point Reyes peninsula. Mary will give you pages of ideas, along with a trailhead guide for hiking in the area. She recommends Heart's Desire Beach in Tomales Bay State Park for swimming and picnics, walking at Abbott's Lagoon on a foggy day, whale-watching from Chimney Rock, and hiking Tomales Point Trail, where you may see Tule elk.

JENNER

Stillwater Cove Ranch

22555 Coast Highway 1
Jenner, CA 95450
707-847-3227

A ranch with inexpensive cottages and an ocean view

Proprietor: Linda Rudy. **Accommodations:** 6 rooms and bunkhouse (some with shared bath). **Rates:** $38–$70, 2-4 people ($5 more per unit on weekends and holidays); bunkhouse $115 for 8, $7.50 additional person. **Minimum stay:** 2 nights on weekends. **Payment:** No credit cards. **Children:** Welcome. **Pets:** Allowed with permission. **Smoking:** Allowed.

On the scenic north coast, 16 miles north of Jenner, a 150-acre ranch once sprawled across the rolling hills that rise from surf-splashed rocks. Now most of that ranch is parkland and belongs to the state, but 50 acres remain as a destination for coastal travelers. Furnishings are simple, but the views of headlands, the kelp-strewn cove, and the ocean are fantastic. And the rates make it an extraordinary value.

In 1931, Clarinel Ione and Paul Rudy founded a boys' school on the site. They had cows, pigs, horses, a barn, and a dairy, and boarded fifty boys at a time until 1966, when the school closed. Now the property is owned by the Rudys' sons and daughter.

Stillwater Cove is near Fort Ross, the historic site of a 19th-century Russian outpost, and Kruse Rhododendron State Reserve.

There are a few animals on the ranch and dozens of peacocks that roam the grounds displaying their colors and dropping gorgeous feathers. Four rooms are in an L-shaped building on a knoll, under eucalyptus and pine trees. The identical East and West rooms, side by side, face the sea. Each has linoleum floors, two beds, a stone fireplace, a bath with a tub and shower, and a kitchenette. They share a long front porch.

Behind them is King Room, a large room with director's chairs, a small desk, and views of the trees and rocky outcroppings. Next to King is the Science Room, with a soft bed, a daybed, a Berber carpet, and a Swedish fireplace. In recognition of the room's original use, there's a microscope on the table.

Teacher's is a separate cottage with two beds, a fireplace, a bath with a tub and shower, and big windows. Cook's Cottage is for romantics who want a private hideaway removed from the rest of the lodgings. This cozy unit has two beds, a stone fireplace, white wicker chairs, and cottage-style windows. The small bath shows signs of wear but is clean. It has a tub only, and with it a rubber ducky.

The Dairy Barn, at the top of the hill, offers the most basic accommodations. The concrete block building is a large bunkhouse with two shower rooms and a well-equipped kitchen. Extra cots are available; bring your own bedding. A woodstove heats the big, open space; wood is supplied for one night's use. The Dairy Barn is a good choice for groups; eight people can cook, sleep, and shower for less than $15 per person per night. It's popular among divers who come to the area for its excellent diving sites.

A low, native stone building was used as a dorm and dining room during the ranch's days as a boys school. Now it's available for seminars, meetings, conferences, and retreats.

MIRAMAR

Cypress Inn

407 Mirada Road
Half Moon Bay, CA 94019
415-726-6002
800-83-BEACH
Fax 415-712-0380

A small seaside inn with a festive atmosphere

Innkeeper: Cindy Granados. **Accommodations:** 8 rooms (all with private bath). **Rates:** $150–$275, $20 additional person, off-season discounts. **Included:** Full breakfast. **Minimum stay:** 2 nights on holiday weekends. **Payment:** Major credit cards. **Children:** Welcome. **Pets:** Not allowed. **Smoking:** Not allowed indoors.

The Cypress Inn's exterior, in quiet browns and greens, gives no hint of the riot of color within. From the yellow parlor to the vividly painted guest rooms, the atmosphere is as bright as an artist's palette. Each room is a different color, but they all have a fireplace, wicker furniture, a deck or balcony, a fluffy comforter and pillow, robes, and tile baths. They're decorated with carved wooden animals from Mexico — colorful folk art that fits the inn's cheery style.

Every room has an ocean view in this light and breezy contemporary inn on a quiet road two miles north of Half Moon Bay. Step out the door and you're facing a five-mile stretch of sandy beach with public access.

The rooms have names from nature: La Estrella (Star), La Luna (Moon), El Viento (Wind), and El Mar (Sea) are examples.

Las Nubes (Clouds) is a third-floor penthouse in white with an oversize whirlpool tub and a panoramic view.

Breakfast, served in your room or in the dining area next to the skylighted parlor, is outstanding. In addition to a granola-yogurt-berry parfait, you'll have juice, fresh croissants, and an entrée such as peaches and cream French toast or an omelette with tomatoes. Consult the inn's information-packed notebook for nearby attractions and restaurant recommendations. One deservedly popular and festive spot is Pasta Moon, which serves wonderful pasta and cheesecake.

MUIR BEACH

The Pelican Inn

10 Pacific Way
Muir Beach, CA 94965
415-383-6000

A touch of old England near the California coast

Innkeeper: Barry Stock. **Accommodations:** 7 rooms (all with private bath). **Rates:** $140–$150 single or double. **Included:** Full breakfast. **Payment:** MasterCard, Visa. **Children:** Welcome ($20 for roll-away bed). **Pets:** Not allowed. **Smoking:** Allowed.

The Pelican nestles among pine and alder trees in the hills a short distance from the ocean (there is no water view). The Tudor-style inn, surrounded by lawns and flowers, looks like a manor house from Elizabethan England though it was built in 1979. Inside it's even more British. Leaded glass windows, heavy beams, worn Oriental carpets on brick flooring, and a menu that includes bangers, cottage pie, and Devonshire chicken would have made Sir Francis feel right at home.

On the ground floor are a restaurant and pub. Benches against dark wood walls, tall candles on trencher tables, and a crackling fire in the fireplace create a cozy atmosphere on the foggiest of nights.

The dining room and pub are open for lunch and dinner daily, except Mondays, and to guests only for a breakfast of toast, marmalade, English sausage, and eggs. There's also a sitting area — the Snug — for guests' use, with a decor that continues the English country theme.

The guest rooms have low doors with wrought-iron hardware. Room 1 features a half tester with a white eyelet quilt, lined tapestry curtains, an upholstered couch, and an old chest so battered it could have been left behind by the crew of the Pelican. Room 5 is smaller, its mullioned windows overlook a balcony. One bedpost is an aged beam into which honeymooning guests often carve their initials; the obliging innkeeper will provide a knife if you ask.

In 1579, when Sir Francis Drake beached the Pelican (later renamed the Golden Hinde) here on the Marin coast a few miles north of the Golden Gate Bridge, there were no country inns offering a warm bed, a mug of ale, and a game of darts. He might have enjoyed this one in Muir Beach, but this bit of Britain arrived four hundred years late.

Room 2 is the smallest, though it has plenty of room for two. Here you ascend a stepladder to the high bed, and fall asleep to the scent of jasmine, which climbs to the roof outside your window.

Barry Stock, who hails from Devonshire, Sir Francis's home port, sees that a decanter of sherry and fresh flowers are placed by your bedside. Ask him about the stone hanging from a ribbon over the bed, and he'll tell you it is to ensure against rickets in case of pregnancy and keeps the evil eye at bay.

Barry's humor and hospitality, the inn's charm, and the proximity to Muir Woods and Muir Beach make rooms at the Pelican in great demand. You'll need reservations far in advance, especially for summer weekends. Spring and fall weekdays are more peaceful — and every bit as beautiful.

NAPA

Churchill Manor

485 Brown Street
Napa, CA 94559
707-253-7733

> *A grand wine country mansion*

Innkeepers: Joanna Guidotti and Brian Jensen. **Accommodations:** 10 rooms (all with private bath). **Rates:** $75–$145 single or double, $15 additional person. **Included:** Full breakfast. **Minimum stay:** 2 nights on weekends. **Payment:** Major credit cards. **Children:** Over age 12 welcome. **Pets:** Not allowed. **Smoking:** Not allowed indoors.

One of the grand old mansions of the wine country has been turned into a bed-and-breakfast that is a wonderful romantic retreat. The stately three-story house, a National Historic Landmark, was built in 1889 and restored with loving care a hundred years later.

Joanna Guidotti's partner, Brian Jensen, is a builder who has recreated the original style of the mansion even while modernizing it. The original gas light fixtures have been rewired and hang in the front parlor. Leaded glass, Oriental carpets, intricately carved woodwork, and Victorian furnishings add period atmosphere to the large (10,000 square feet) B&B. "This is our hobby," Joanna says. Once a tax lawyer in

San Francisco, she moved to Napa to restore and run the inn.

There are fireplaces in all four parlors and in three of the guest rooms. Each room is decorated individually, from cheery little Amy's Room on the third floor to Edward's Room, the original master bedroom, which has an elegant French king-size bed, an armoire with three mirrors, and an oversize clawfoot tub in the bath. Granny's Room has a treadle sewing machine and a mannequin costumed in an antique beaded opera gown. The most unusual (and maybe the most fun for lovers) is the Bordello Room, with its big brass bed, ten-foot carved armoire, Victorian nude painting, and red Jacuzzi tub for two. The phone in this room is the shape of bright red lips. The phones in the other rooms fit their themes: an old-fashioned car, a duck that quacks instead of ringing, Legos in the Children's Room. Children's, on the third floor, also has an antique bed and 19th-century toys.

Thousands of daffodils and tulips bloom in spring. There are rose beds, boxwood hedges, and an herb garden. Guests enjoy playing croquet in the side garden, exploring the area on a tandem bicycle borrowed from the innkeepers, and relaxing on the wide veranda.

A breakfast of muffins, croissants, fruit, and hot dishes such as omelettes or French toast is served in the enclosed sun room, overlooking the colorful garden.

Churchill Manor is in a residential district of Napa, close to restaurants and the valley's wineries.

La Residence Country Inn

4066 St. Helena Highway North
Napa, CA 94558
707-253-0337

> *A country inn with luxurious amenities*

Innkeepers: David Jackson and Craig Claussen. **Accommodations:** 20 rooms (18 with private bath). **Rates:** $85–$190 single or double, $20 additional person. **Included:** Full breakfast. **Minimum stay:** 2 nights weekends. **Payment:** MasterCard, Visa. **Children:** Welcome. **Pets:** Not allowed. **Smoking:** Not allowed indoors.

This sophisticated country inn is one of a growing number of small inns that combine the personal touch of a bed-and-breakfast with the luxuries of a larger hotel.

> **Out the back door, pear trees shade a brick patio. Across the way, on the patio by Cabernet Hall, wine is served in the late afternoon under a 200-year-old oak tree.**

La Residence, north of the city of Napa, is set back from the rush of Highway 29. Its two buildings stand on two acres of fields, vineyards, and oak and acacia trees. One is the Mansion, an 1870 Gothic Revival home. The other is Cabernet Hall, built in 1987 in the style of a French barn. Between them are the parking lot and a heated swimming pool surrounded by gazebos, trellises, brick patios, and pots of flowers.

There are nine rooms in the Mansion, all furnished with

American antiques. On the main floor, left of the entrance, is a suite with a marble fireplace and a Victrola, ready to be wound up for playing the old Decca records. Fruit garlands border the walls, and louvered shutters cover the windows. There's a white iron bed, an armoire, and a bath of white and green tile. Across the hall is a similar room.

All the suites in Cabernet Hall have working fireplaces and access to a balcony or the ground-floor veranda. Comforters, wicker chairs, flowered wallpapers, and painted tiles are in most rooms. Pine antiques from France and England were imported for the inn.

The dining room by the patio is a cheery breakfast spot where David Jackson, who handles the inn's cooking, sees that guests receive their fill of fresh fruit, pastries, and an egg dish, as well as hot coffee or tea and the morning newspaper.

The Old World Inn

1301 Jefferson Street
Napa, CA 94559
707-257-0112

A wine country B&B with distinctive style

Innkeeper: Diane Dumaine. **Accommodations:** 8 rooms (all with private bath). **Rates:** $100–$140 single or double. **Included:** Full breakfast. **Payment:** Major credit cards. **Minimum stay:** 2 nights on weekends, April through November. **Children:** Not appropriate. **Pets:** Not allowed. **Smoking:** Not allowed.

The room rate for the Old World Inn includes much more than a breakfast of crêpes or omelettes, fruits, and freshly baked breads. Guests are treated to a lavish afternoon tea, a wine and cheese hour, and a late evening dessert buffet of homemade treats. This inn is a food-lover's delight.

To showcase the builder's skills, he combined several architectural styles — shingle style in the sweeping roof line, Craftsman in the use of rough cinder brick, Colonial Revival in the porch columns, and Queen Anne in the two-story corner tower. The curly redwood he used in the living and dining rooms glows with the patina of finely finished woodwork.

The innkeeper pampers her guests in other ways, too, including fresh flowers, soft music, restaurant reservations, a bubbling outdoor hot tub in a fenced courtyard, and rooms furnished in fresh Scandinavian style. The Swedish artist Carl Larsson inspired the decor, which is bright with color and unusual designs. Homilies and fanciful bows are painted on the walls above the moldings, and linens and fabrics are all in coordinated colors. Most of the antiques-furnished rooms have Victorian clawfoot tubs, and one has a private Jacuzzi.

The historic inn was built in 1906 by Napa's foremost builder, E. W. Doughty, as his own residence. You can see other examples of Doughty's work on a walking tour through Old Town Napa, where vintage buildings have been restored. Diane will direct you to nearby antiques shops, restaurants, and wineries.

Silverado Country Club & Resort

1600 Atlas Peak Road
Napa, CA 94558
707-257-0200
800-532-0500
Fax 707-257-2867

A gracious golf resort in the wine country

General manager: Kirk Candland.
Accommodations: 289 condominium units. **Rates:** \$130–\$465 spring and summer; \$145–\$380 fall and winter, 1 to 6 people, \$15 additional person under age 12. **Payment:** Major credit cards. **Children:** Welcome. **Pets:** Not allowed. **Smoking:** Non-smoking rooms available.

In an idyllic grove of trees above Milliken Creek, Silverado began as a classic 14-room mansion. Built in the 1870s, it was the estate of John F. Miller, a Civil War general who moved to California and became influential in state politics. He and his wife wanted their house to reflect the Italian and French architecture they had admired on their travels abroad. Now their home, with its Palladian windows, two-story columns, white railings, and flower-filled urns, is the main lodge of a 1,200-acre luxury resort. It's 45 minutes north of San Francisco, just outside Napa in the Napa Valley wine country.

Beyond the small lobby is a lounge with a sunken bar made of polished granite. From the lounge, windows overlook a sun room and a terrace. An 18-hole golf course, one of two on the property, lies across the creek from the terrace.

The 250-foot-long stone wall bordering the terrace is a remarkable example of the masonry skills common when the house was built. Today, trimmed ivy grows over the low wall and roses bloom beside it. This is a spot for lingering over cocktails while you watch the golfers and listen to the birds warbling in the great oak trees that arch over the fairways.

Immense old eucalyptus trees line the road to the entrance, perfuming the air with their pungent oil. Passing a circle of lawn with tall palm trees, you reach a curving driveway where a valet relieves you of your car and smiling bellmen help with your luggage. It's a busy place, as the resort is frequently used for meetings and conferences.

Silverado has 20 tennis courts, three of them lighted, as well as pro shops and instructors. Tennis fees are $13 per person per day. There are eight swimming pools, one of them a lap pool.

Three restaurants offer varying degrees of formality. The casual Bar & Grill serves breakfast and lunch. Royal Oak is a rustic steak house with a mesquite grill. California cuisine is served in Vintner's Court, a pretty salon with white and pink linens and pink roses on a white grand piano. On Sundays, elaborate ice sculptures decorate brunch buffet tables. A seafood buffet is served on Fridays.

The guest rooms, most of them private condominiums furnished and decorated by their owners, are in clusters called Mansion Cottages, Silverado Cottages, and Oak Creek East. They range from standard rooms with no kitchens to three-bedroom units. Studio rooms combine sitting and sleeping areas and have kitchenettes. A typical one-bedroom lodging has rattan furnishings, mirrored sliding doors on a roomy closet, television, phone, and a corner fireplace. The kitchen is fully equipped and the bath has both a tub and shower. The two- and three-bedroom apartments are in Oak Creek East, the most secluded cluster. They border quiet cul-de-sacs and have private patios and balconies overlooking the fairways.

Special holiday packages are available at Silverado. Most include a round of golf and unlimited tennis, along with seasonal festivities.

OAKLAND

The Claremont Resort and Spa

P.O. Box 23363
Ashby and Domingo Avenues
Oakland, CA 94623
510-843-3000
800-551-7266
Fax 510-843-6239

A contemporary spa resort in a convenient East Bay location

General manager: Henry Feldman.
Accommodations: 211 rooms and 28 suites. **Rates:** $155–$195 single, $175–$215 double; suites $295–$720. **Payment:** Major credit cards. **Children:** Under 18 free in room with parents. **Pets:** Not allowed. **Smoking:** Nonsmoking rooms available.

Across the bay from San Francisco, the Claremont has been a hilltop landmark on the Oakland-Berkeley border since 1915. The original castlelike home on the site, built by a farmer from Kansas who struck it rich in the gold mines, burned to the ground in 1901. A sprawling, many-gabled resort hotel was erected in its place, opening in time for the 1915 Panama-Pacific Exposition.

It has undergone several refurbishments, including a $24 million overhaul in 1971. Today the Claremont, now listed on the National Register of Historic Places, reigns over 22 landscaped acres and a lofty view of San Francisco Bay, its bridges, and the glimmering skyline.

Highly recommended for dining are Chez Panisse, as good as its stratospheric reputation, and Santa Fe Bar and Grill, where the chef performs magic with the mesquite grill. Citron and Bay Wolf are also notable eateries.

The location is a plus — it's convenient to the city yet offers resort facilities. There are 10 tennis courts, an Olympic-size pool and an exercise pool, saunas, whirlpools, and a luxurious, European-style health spa, added in 1989. It offers a full program for beauty and fitness, including hydrotherapy treatments, loofah scrubs, herbal wraps, facials, massages, and hair and nail care. There's a spa café offering light fare.

The Pavilion is the resort's showcase restaurant, with a menu that changes daily. The wine selection is extensive and rated highly. The Pavilion is noted for its lavish Sunday brunch. The Terrace Bar offers nightly entertainment and dancing, and there are gift and florist shops, car rentals, and easy parking. A free shuttle is provided to the Oakland airport, BART stations, and the Tilden Golf Course. If you're driving to San Francisco, where parking is at a premium, you'll be given a voucher for three hours of free parking near Union Square.

Because the hotel's owners (the Schnitzers of Harsh Investment Corp.) are art devotees from the Pacific Northwest, the long, wide lobby and halls are filled with superb examples of contemporary art — mostly by Northwest artists. Outside, sculptures are set among the palms, roses, marigolds, and pampas.

The guest rooms at the front of the hotel overlook the city and bay; the back rooms look toward the Berkeley hills and eucalyptus groves. The colors and designs are different in all the rooms, and every six months another block is refurbished.

Suite 606 (with adjoining 605) is the Tower Suite, featuring long, low windows with great views of the bay and city skyline. The secluded suite is reached by a short flight of stairs. More stairs lead to a private balcony in the tower itself, at the top of the hotel, where a sauna awaits. Suite 404 has the widest picture window in the hotel. The view is spectacular. There's a wet bar and, under a skylight in the bath, a tub big enough for two.

The Claremont offers several weekend packages and an array of activities. Other attractions lie close at hand. The East Bay regional park system, with walking and bridle trails, lakes, forests, and panoramic viewpoints, is just out the back door. The campus of the University of California is a few minutes' drive away. Oakland and Berkeley have excellent restaurants and shopping and interesting historic districts to explore. If you're a walker, pick up a guide to walks in the area and you'll find dozens of byways through gardens and residential neighborhoods.

OAKLAND

Dockside Boat & Bed

77 Jack London Square
Oakland, CA 94607
510-444-5858
Fax 510-444-0420

A bed-and-breakfast afloat in the bay

Proprietor: Rob Harris. **Accommodations:** Several private vessels. **Rates:** \$95–\$225 weekdays, \$125–\$275 weekends, single or double; \$25 additional person. **Included:** Continental breakfast. **Payment:** Major credit cards. **Children:** Welcome. **Pets:** Not allowed. **Smoking:** Not allowed indoors.

Hundreds of yachts and sailboats bob at the marina off Jack London Square; a few of them are available to guests looking for unusual lodgings.

From the deck of a sailboat or motor yacht, you can watch the sunset over the San Francisco skyline while you listen to the gulls' cries and water lapping against the hull of the boat.

The vessels Rob Harris handles range from 35 to 68 feet long. All are equipped with showers, television, coffeemakers, and fresh flowers. Arnie's Ark is a 35-foot boat with narrow gangways, a snug salon, a small modern bathroom, and a queen-size bed in the master stateroom. You can prepare snacks and use the microwave oven in the galley, but it's not intended for cooking full meals. Arnie's Ark is available for charter trips; the captain charges $25 per hour per person. Three hours is the suggested minimum time to get a good, exhilarating sail on the bay.

The Sea Burgher is a floating condo with a fireplaces in the spacious salon, a whirlpool tub, and a spiral staircase leading up to two staterooms. Tasha is smaller but has an enclosed flybridge with a good view of the marina. The queen of the fleet is Talisman, a 53-foot motor yacht with a view of the city and the water. There's a large salon with leather chairs, a bar in the galley, a flybridge that seats eight, and three staterooms, two with queen-size beds.

Breakfast — orange juice and a basket of muffins — is brought to your boat in the morning. Rob will also arrange for catered dinners, limousine service, picnic baskets, and massages. He's a Universal Life Church minister, so he can even perform weddings and has done so several times.

Most guests board their yacht-for-a-day looking for relaxation in a romantic setting, but there are other diversions nearby. Jack London Square, a gangplank walk away, has a dozen restaurants and shops such as the Magic World of Disney store and Barnes & Noble, the largest bookstore in Northern California. The *U.S.S. Potomac,* which was formerly used by President Franklin D. Roosevelt, is docked at the marina and is available for charter cruises at $2,500 for three hours.

OLEMA

Point Reyes Seashore Lodge

P.O. Box 39
10021 Coastal Highway 1
Olema, CA 94950
415-663-9000

A country lodge by a magnificent park

Innkeepers: Jeff and Nancy Harriman, Judy and John Burkes. **Accommodations:** 18 rooms, 3 suites. **Rates:** $85–$130 single or double, suites $165–$175, $15 additional person. **Included:** Continental breakfast. **Payment:** Major credit cards. **Children:** Welcome. **Pets:** Not allowed. **Smoking:** Restricted.

The entire Point Reyes National Seashore, 65,000 acres of scenic parkland, abuts the backyard of this attractive luxury lodge. It stands on an acre of landscaped grounds in Olema, 35 miles north of San Francisco. Though the three-story cedar inn resembles a turn-of-the-century country lodge, it was built and opened in 1988. The owners wanted to combine the elegance and comfort of a hotel with the personal warmth of a bed-and-breakfast; for the most part they've succeeded admirably.

You enter to an open lobby of light, natural wood and excessive lighting. Directly above, up a few steps, is a cozy library with books and games; a few steps down is the fireplace room, where a buffet breakfast of fruit, muffins, and croissants is served. You may take a tray to your room if you prefer, or breakfast will be brought to you.

Off to the side is a game room with pool table. Walls are

hung with old photographs of the area, reflecting Jeff Harriman's interest in local history. There are four guest rooms on this lower floor, each with a private entrance from the flagstone terrace. To the west is a lawn sloping down to Olema Creek where willows and eucalyptus trees grow. A bridge across the creek leads to a path to Bear Valley Visitor Center, the park headquarters and starting point for numerous hiking trails.

Everyone at the inn offers a friendly welcome and is happy to tell you about outstanding beaches and viewpoints in the neighboring park. They'll make reservations at restaurants, arrange for horseback rides or bicycle rentals, tell you about the park's nature activities, and help you find shops with special handicrafts.

Other guest rooms are located on two floors in the main lodge and in wings on either side. They all have direct-dial phones, digital clocks, and contemporary colors of mauve, green, blue, and aqua. The quality is excellent, though the mixture of rough woods with European fixtures, shoji screens, and modern brass is occasionally jarring.

Some rooms have a fireplace, whirlpool tub, and superb views of the pastoral surroundings and Mount Wittenberg. An unusual feature is the sliding screen in an arched opening between sitting room and bathroom; from the tub you can see the trees in the park. The three suites have wet bars, refrigerators, and bedroom lofts with feather beds. Birds are the theme of the Audubon Suite. An Audubon egret print hangs above the sofa bed and Roger Tory Peterson's book on the famed ornithologist lies on the fireplace mantel. White walls extend up to a high ceiling and loft. A balcony overlooks the grounds and park.

The Garcia Suite is named for the original owner of the land grant on the hotel's site and contains artifacts that were found in his old barn. The Sir Francis Drake Suite has books on the early sea voyager, a world globe, and a painting of Drake's ship, *The Golden Hinde*. Sir Francis landed on these shores in 1579 and named the area Nova Albion (New England), perhaps because the pale cliffs that rise steeply above the beach reminded him of the coast of Dover.

Roundstone Farm

9940 Sir Francis Drake Blvd.
Olema, CA 94950
415-663-1020

A ten-acre farm with a view near Point Reyes National Seashore

Innkeeper: Inger Fisher. **Accommodations:** 5 rooms (all with private bath). **Rates:** $95 single, $115–$125 double. **Included:** Full breakfast. **Minimum stay:** 2 nights on weekends. **Payment:** Mastercard, Visa. **Children:** Over age 6 welcome. **Pets:** Not allowed. **Smoking:** Not allowed indoors.

Roundstone Farm occupies 10 acres of hilly ranchland above Olema, a village on the Point Reyes Peninsula. From the deck of the cedar board-and-batten farmhouse you can see Mount Wittenberg and Mount Vision, Inverness Ridge, Olema Valley, and Tomales Bay.

The solar home was built in 1987 specifically as a bed-and-breakfast. Inger Fisher used her skills as an interior designer to create a haven for visitors. Each soundproofed guest room is on a different level. The furnishings and color schemes vary, but all have fireplaces, thick carpeting, and white goose-down comforters.

Fresh flowers brighten the understated decor. The quality is first rate, with bathroom fixtures from Copenhagen, Swiss linens, and armoires from England and Denmark providing Old World charm and workmanship. Headboards, patterned after ranch gates, were made by a local craftsperson.

The large living room has a 16-foot ceiling with skylights in the pitched roof and sliding doors along one glass wall that open to a deck and a magnificent view. Guests enjoy reading by the fire, playing board games, listening to the CD player, and admiring the broad expanse of forest, meadow, and ranchland. From here you can see the farm's pond, where waterfowl and red-winged blackbirds nest.

Point Reyes National Seashore is an immense seaside park north of San Francisco Bay. Within its boundaries — Tomales Bay and Sir Francis Drake Boulevard on the east, and the Pacific Ocean on the west — are miles of hiking trails, sand dunes, rolling moors, forests of oak and pine, and far-reaching views of the sea.

A few steps up is the dining area, where a substantial breakfast is served at one seating. Inger believes that part of the B&B experience is getting acquainted with fellow guests over the breakfast table. "People will sit down at 9:15 and not get up until 11, they're so relaxed," she says.

Early morning coffee is on the sideboard; later, Inger comes in with juice, fruit, and an unusual dish such as an apple puff pancake with sausage. "No quiche or croissants," she says. "I try to do things no one else does." The meal is hearty, to prepare you for a day of hiking, bicycling, and exploring the National Seashore. Tea and coffee are available all day.

The farm was named after the village of Roundstone in the Connemara district of western Ireland, where Connemara ponies first lived in the wild. Inger has raised Connemara and Arabian horses for years. There are several on the property now, and guests are welcome to visit them.

The Bear Valley Visitor Center, the headquarters for the Point Reyes National Seashore, is just a few minutes away. It has extensive displays of natural and historic highlights of the park. From here, trails lead over ridges and cliffs to protected beaches.

Inger and her assistant, Barbara Hand, can recommend several good restaurants a short distance from Roundstone Farm. Visitors give the Olema Inn high praise for its light, pleasant atmosphere and excellent food.

PALO ALTO

Garden Court Hotel

520 Cowper Street
Palo Alto, CA 94301
415-322-9000
800-824-9028
Fax 415-324-3609

A small hotel with a Mediterranean atmosphere

Manager: Lorilee Houston. **Accommodations:** 60 rooms and suites. **Rates:** $175–$195 single or double, $15 additional person, suites $200–$400. **Payment:** Major credit cards. **Children:** Welcome. **Pets:** Not allowed. **Smoking:** Allowed.

In cozy little Palo Alto, on the peninsula 20 minutes south of the San Francisco airport, the Garden Court nestles snugly in the heart of the downtown district. The four-story Mediterranean-style building of ochre stucco with dark green wrought-iron trim and curving archways, has a casual, inviting look.

The hotel's residential ambience is apparent in the small second-floor lobby, where soft chairs and a couch face a fireplace, a big bowl of apples sits on a table, and a window alcove has benches filled with pillows. Off to one side are the check-in counter and the concierge's desk. The staff here is unfailingly patient and helpful, always ready to provide directions or lend an umbrella on a rainy day.

Each of the spacious, pastel rooms has a small balcony with just enough room for two chairs and a trellised, potted vine. Palo Alto is quiet at night, but to ensure peace, request an inside room above the courtyard. You'll look down upon an array of colorful flowers and the restaurant terrace. All rooms have phones, minibars, fresh flowers, and four-poster beds, and some include fireplaces and whirlpool tubs. The newspaper of your choice is delivered to the door in the morning.

When you arrive, you're greeted by the parking valet and the fragrance of freshly baked bread wafting from Il Fornaio, a handsome ground-floor restaurant serving fine Italian food.

The Garden Court, which has banquet and meeting rooms that accommodate up to 250, caters to business travelers, visitors to Stanford University, and those looking for a relaxing getaway. It has no exercise facilities, no pool, and no coffee shop: this hotel concentrates only on fine-quality accommodations. Several cafés in the district are open for breakfast — a good excuse for a stroll into the Palo Alto lifestyle.

On a larger scale, the Stanford Shopping Center is a short distance away, along with more typical roadside development.

The Victorian on Lytton

555 Lytton Avenue
Palo Alto, CA 94301
415-322-8555

A Victorian inn with modern style near Stanford University

Proprietors: Maxwell and Susan Hall. **Accommodations:** 10 rooms. **Rates:** \$98–\$175 single or double. **Included:** Continental breakfast. **Payment:** Major credit cards. **Children:** Welcome (no cribs available). **Pets:** Not allowed. **Smoking:** Not allowed.

This pretty Victorian inn in downtown Palo Alto has served many purposes since it was built in 1895 as the home of a schoolteacher. It was a commune, a bookstore, and an apartment house before it became a registered historical landmark and a bed-and-breakfast inn. Susan and Max Hall, who bought the crumbling home in 1985, transformed it into a place of charm and comfort.

Five guest rooms are in the main house and five are in another building behind it, set off by a colorful English garden. Parking spaces are tucked away at the edge of the property.

Each oversize room has down comforters on four-poster or canopy beds, and antiques that reflect the home's Victorian heritage, yet details important to today's travelers — good lighting, modern bathrooms — have not been overlooked. The artistic skills of the proprietor, who was once the art director of an advertising agency, are evident in the stylish, understated decor.

The Halls gutted and rebuilt the interior of the newer building in back, now called the Carriage House. This is where they placed the honeymoon suite, which has a fireplace, botanical prints on the wall, a four-poster bed with embroidered pillows, and a clawfoot tub in an alcove. A breakfast of fruit, croissants, and coffee or tea is brought to each room on a tray. In the evenings, as guests ponder which of Palo Alto's restaurants to try, port and sherry are served.

The first things you notice are the soft strains of classical music and the mouthwatering scent of just-baked cookies; Susan bakes a batch for her guests every day and serves them in the small, homey parlor.

POINT REYES STATION

Gray's Retreat

P.O. Box 56
Point Reyes Station, CA 94956
415-663-1166

A country home for a couple or family

Innkeeper: Karen Gray. **Accommodations:** 1 unit. **Rates:** $115 per night if staying 2 nights; $150 for one night on weekends, weekly rates available. **Payment:** MasterCard, Visa. **Children:** Welcome. **Pets:** Allowed by arrangement. **Smoking:** Not allowed.

If you're bringing the family to Point Reyes Peninsula for a few days of rest, bird-watching, hiking, and enjoying the scenic beauty, Gray's Retreat is an excellent lodging choice. Set in an open pasture and sheltered by a cypress windbreak, the rough cedar home overlooks Inverness Peninsula.

Built as a guest house for the owners' parents, it has an occupied apartment on the upper floor and an apartment on the ground level where overnight visitors stay. Furnished with wicker and assorted wooden chests and chairs, the living room is bright and homey. Sunlight streams through western windows on honey-colored walls, illuminating big bouquets of flowers. Beyond the living room and divided from it by a partition is a full kitchen; beyond that a dining area that opens to an enclosed patio.

The town of Point Reyes Station is within walking distance and has a popular family restaurant, Olema Farmhouse. Another recommended dining spot is Tony's, on the water in Marshall.

Gray's Retreat accommodates six, with a trundle bed, a sofa bed, and a queen-size four-poster. Cribs, high chairs, and laundry facilities are available. Other helpful features for those traveling with children are soundproof walls, fenced front and back patios, shelves with games and puzzles, and a playground across the road.

Jasmine Cottage

P.O. Box 56
Point Reyes Station, CA 94956
415-663-1166

A romantic cottage in the country

Innkeeper: Karen Gray. **Accommodations:** 1 cottage. **Rates:** $115 single or double, $15 each additional person; $650 per week. **Included:** Full make-your-own breakfast. **Payment:** No credit cards. **Children:** Welcome. **Pets:** Welcome with permission. **Smoking:** Not allowed indoors.

Set apart from the innkeeper's home by vegetable, flower, and herb plantings, Jasmine Cottage is for the exclusive use of one group of guests, from one to four people. There are two cabinet beds in the light-drenched sitting room, and a queen-size bed tucked into a cubbyhole. A crib and a high chair are provided.

Hidden behind jasmine-entwined fences and a rustic wooden gate, this cozy cottage is the quintessential romantic hideaway in the country. Private and secluded, it is sequestered in a pretty garden at the top of a hill near Point Reyes National Seashore, one of northern California's most scenic preserves.

The refrigerator in the fully equipped, red tile kitchen contains your breakfast makings: coffee, jam, granola, milk, fruit, cheese, and fresh eggs from the chickens that live in the yard. Flowered quilts, posters of native flora, dried flowers, and Karen Gray's fabric art complete the gardenlike ambience, enhanced by the sweet fragrance of jasmine and window views of fruit trees, geraniums, and roses.

The shed outside is well stocked with wood for the woodstove. Linens and housekeeping supplies are also provided. The shelves are full of books about birds and Point Reyes, and there's an album full of information on local points of interest. There is no telephone and no television to intrude upon the tranquility.

Outside the gate is a brick patio with a hot tub and a view across rolling pastureland to Inverness Ridge. In the cottage you'll find a picnic basket, complete with dishes and a thermos bottle, ready to pack with a lunch to take into the park or to the seashore; but Jasmine's setting is so irresistible you may get no further than the picnic table on your own patio.

Thirty-nine Cypress

Box 176
Point Reyes, CA 94956
415-663-1709

A charming country cottage above Tomales Bay

Innkeeper: Julia Bartlett. **Accommodations:** 3 rooms (all with private half or full bath). **Rates:** $100–$120. **Included:** Full breakfast. **Minimum stay:** 2 nights on weekends. **Payment:** MasterCard, Visa. **Children:** Welcome by arrangement. **Pets:** Allowed by arrangement. **Smoking:** Not allowed indoors.

When you're looking for a rustic hideaway with a pastoral view, lovely gardens, and a cliffside hot tub, book a room at Thirty-nine Cypress. The single-story, weathered gray inn opened in 1981, one of the first in the Point Reyes National Seashore area north of San Francisco. It was Julia Bartlett's home, but now she lives across the neighboring field and comes over in the mornings to fix a hearty breakfast for her guests.

Staying at this B&B is like visiting a friend who has a guest house in the country. There's no television, but you're welcome to use the tape deck, read books, fix popcorn in the kitchen, and light a fire in the fireplace on foggy days.

Wildflowers fill a jar on the table; binoculars hang from a nail by the sliding glass doors. The terrace, bordered by rosemary, overlooks part of a 500-acre ranch near Tomales Bay.

The rooms are furnished in a country style. The north bedroom is the most private. It has a full bath, skylights, and a private patio. The two south rooms each have a tiny half-bath. All the rooms have outdoor showers — step outside your door and there's a protected, sunlit shower. Robes are provided. The house is often taken by three couples; it's ideal for a retreat, a reunion, or a vacation with friends.

Flora Borealis, Julia's friendly Australian cattle dog, will try to accompany you on walks. There are some outstanding hikes in the area, and you can go mountain biking or to the beach.

POINT RICHMOND

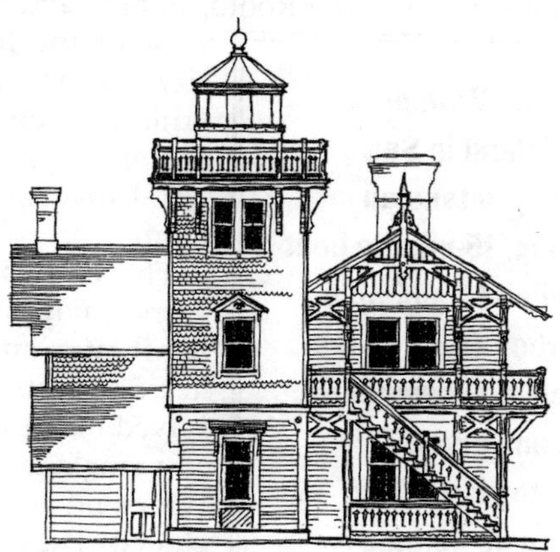

East Brother Light Station

117 Park Place
Point Richmond, CA 94801
510-233-2385

A cozy lighthouse on an island

Managers: John Barnett and Lore Hogan. **Accommodations:** 4 rooms (2 with private bath). **Rates:** $295 double. **Included:** Breakfast and dinner; transportation from harbor. **Payment:** No credit cards. **Children:** Welcome if reserving all rooms. **Pets:** Not allowed. **Smoking:** Not allowed indoors. **Open:** Thursday, Friday, Saturday, Sunday.

When his grandfather was the lighthouse keeper, between 1914 and 1921, Walter Fanning used to come to the tiny island to visit. Today, East Brother Light Station looks just as Walter remembers it — a trim and tidy, well-kept lighthouse of the Victorian era, with carved railings and gingerbread. Volunteers (Walter among them) worked long hours to restore and maintain the lighthouse, which was built in 1873 and automated in 1969. It's owned by the U.S. Coast Guard and is on the National Register of Historic Places.

There are two rooms on the ground floor, each with a brass bed and period furnishings, and a cozy parlor that guests share. The best views are upstairs. The Marin Room faces west toward the Marin County hills and Mount Tamalpais. It's romantic in rose and pink, with lace-edged pillows on the brass bed. The San Francisco Room, in blue and white, has a view of the bay and the city beyond San Pablo Bridge. There's a parlor upstairs, too, which has a woodstove and a nautical theme.

To get to East Brother, a one-acre island in San Pablo Bay, you take an exhilarating, 15-minute boat ride from Point San Pablo Yacht Harbor. Once on the island, you're surrounded by peace and quiet. This is a place to visit when you want to do nothing but watch the cormorants and seagulls.

The enthusiastic managers enjoy showing the lighthouse and preparing hearty meals, which are served in the dining room at a single table for eight. Wine and apéritifs are included. They sell T-shirts and a few gift items in the office, which was once Walter Fanning's grandmother's parlor.

PRINCETON-BY-THE-SEA

The Pillar Point Inn

380 Capistrano Road
Princeton-by-the-Sea, CA
Mailing address:
P.O. Box 388
El Granada, CA 94018
415-728-7377

A New England–style inn on the harbor

Manager: Sarah Woodruff. **Accommodations:** 11 rooms (all with private bath). **Rates:** $140–$150 weekdays, $160–$175 weekends, single or double, $20 additional person. **Included:** Full breakfast. **Payment:** Major credit cards. **Children:** Welcome. **Pets:** Not allowed. **Smoking:** Not allowed.

Halfway between San Francisco and Santa Cruz, facing the only harbor for 75 miles, Pillar Point Inn provides a touch of

Cape Cod on the West Coast. The gray, solidly built hotel trimmed in white and nautical blue sits behind a white picket fence, its curved and gabled windows facing the boats bobbing a few yards away.

The inn has menus for the few nearby restaurants. Across the street is Barbara's Fish Trap, a casual spot by the water. Moss Beach Distillery is a dinner house, and Shore Bird is a favorite for brunch before going whale-watching.

Princeton-by-the-Sea is an unpretentious little town with a livelihood that comes from the sea. It has a waterfront busy with boat building and repairs, charters, fishing and pleasure boats, and whale-watching excursions. There are a few shops, restaurants, and galleries, but this working port has nothing like the tourist activity of its neighbor, Half Moon Bay. It does have a romantic inn offering warm hospitality and luxurious accommodations, however.

In the small living room, guests relax on love seats by the double-sided fireplace and peruse the shelves of books and movies. You can watch old-time favorites such as Robin Hood, Abbott & Costello, and even Hopalong Cassidy on your video player; there's one in every room.

The rooms also have European-style feather beds, radios, telephones, and refrigerators, and ten rooms have views of the water. Themes from local history provide a different decor in each room. El Granada, a second-floor room that faces the road and harbor, holds photographic reminders of 1909, when a developer tried to turn the region into a major resort. Nobody was interested in buying, but many took the offer of a free lunch and a train ride to and from the beach.

El Granada has a brass and white iron bed and a rocker by the high, arched window. A writing table stands in one corner and a tiled gas fireplace with raised hearth in another. Sounds of traffic and restaurant noise from across the street fade in the late evening as the village settles down, until finally all you hear is the moan of the buoy in the harbor. The Whaling Room, also called the Hideaway, is extra large, very quiet, has a view of the mountains, and a partial harbor view.

A full breakfast with egg dishes and homemade granola and muffins is served alongside the fireplace in the dining room.

RUTHERFORD

Auberge du Soleil

180 Rutherford Hill Road
Rutherford, CA 94573
707-963-1211
Fax 707-963-8764

A sophisticated country inn with a valley view

General manager: George Goeggel. **Accommodations:** 48 rooms. **Rates:** $295–$820 double, $40 additional person; cribs $15. **Minimum stay:** 2 nights on weekends. **Payment:** MasterCard, Visa. **Children:** Welcome. **Pets:** Allowed by prior arrangement. **Smoking:** Allowed.

First the inn was a restaurant, set against a steep hillside above Napa Valley's grape-growing heartland. The venture of a renowned San Francisco restaurateur, Claude Rouas, Auberge du Soleil opened in 1981 to great acclaim. It wasn't long before its visitors, impressed with the stunning location and cuisine, yearned for lodgings, as well. So, in the mid-1980s, some of the valley's most exclusive lodgings joined one of its most fashionable eateries.

The views are spectacular from the inn's 33 acres of olive and oak groves, similar to inland country vistas of the French Riviera.

One- and two-bedroom suites combine the sophisticated and the rustic to create a luxurious country French decor.

Each has a fireplace, television, and wet bar. The floors are polished terra cotta tile, the furniture of natural wood and leather. The mood is light, the colors pastel.

Near the villas and below the restaurant terrace is a large swimming pool with lounge chairs. There are three tennis courts. Room service is available, and the restaurant is open for breakfast.

The Auberge du Soleil menu, showcasing locally grown ingredients, is labeled "wine country cuisine." Lunch may be taken inside or out, on the sun-dappled terrace at umbrella tables. Dinners include Peking duck with red cabbage salad, roast poussin filled with wild rice and Sonoma foie gras on roast corn coulis, and grilled bass on fennel and red pepper rouille.

The restaurant, lounge, and terrace all face a panorama of valley and hills that sprawls to the horizon. Terraced against the hillside, reached by winding paths bordered with sweet-scented flowering shrubs, are the guest villas, named for French wine-growing regions.

On weekends, a pianist plays in the bar and lounge across the lobby from the restaurant. The round room has a southwestern flavor, with a single pole in the center reaching to a cone ceiling. A high circular shelf holds firewood for the adobe fireplace. Windows look out on a curving deck and over the treetops to the countryside.

The inn also has meeting and audiovisual facilities. The White Room, lined with mirrors to reflect the light and panoramic view, seats up to eighty. Next to it is the more intimate Club Room, seating up to twenty. A secluded conference room, decorated with light leather, wood, and oil paintings, is off the lower terrace.

Auberge du Soleil retains the chic cachet it has had since it opened. This is not the place to go for cozy warmth. A cool professionalism best characterizes most of the staff, and the well-dressed clientele is here to see and be seen as well as to dine and enjoy the beautiful setting.

Rancho Caymus Inn

P.O. Box 78
Rutherford, CA 94573
707-963-1777

A wine-country inn with eclectic style

Innkeeper: Joyce Bowen. **Accommodations:** 26 rooms and suites. **Rates:** $100–$295 single or double, $15 additional person; winter rates $15–$20 less. **Included:** Continental breakfast. **Minimum stay:** 2 nights on weekends. **Payment:** Major credit cards. **Children:** Not appropriate. **Pets:** Not allowed. **Smoking:** Allowed.

This Spanish-style inn, its walls encircling a courtyard of flowers, vines, and trees, is a showplace for the artists and craftspeople who have created it. Mary Tilden Morton, a third-generation Californian and a professional sculptor, built Rancho Caymus in 1985 to provide lodging for visitors to the Napa Valley and to create a stunning setting for handicrafts she'd collected from California, Mexico, and South America.

The inn stands on part of the original land grant given by the Mexican general Vallejo to George Yount more than a century ago. Rutherford, 60 miles north of San Francisco, is known for its wineries and for Rutherford Square, a complex of cafés and Beaulieu Vineyard's tasting room. Within walking distance of the square are the white stucco buildings and red tile roofs of Rancho Caymus.

All the spacious suites are named for locally famous people and historic places. They contain furnishings that are both beautiful and unusual. Most have plaster beehive fireplaces, and all have wet bars, stocked refrigerators, telephones, television, and a complimentary bottle of wine. Four split-level master suites have whirlpool tubs and full kitchens. Hastings Suite, with two bedrooms, accommodates larger parties.

The dressers, chairs and tables were carved in Guadalajara; the black walnut beds, colorful handwoven bedspreads, llama blankets, and rare leather paintings came from Ecuador. Wrought-iron door straps and railings, tile murals, stained glass windows, stoneware basins, and oaken countertops — all were made by noted regional artists and carpenters. The white oak and pine doors and beams came from an 80-year-old barn in Ohio.

It's easy to understand why Rancho Caymus is popular for wedding receptions. At night, when a guitarist plays and hundreds of lights cast wavering shadows from the shrubbery, this seems one of the most romantic places on Earth.

The General Vallejo Room is a suite with a daybed in the sitting area and a private balcony that views the pine trees of Beaulieu Vineyard next door. The Major Tilden Suite has a kitchen, a sitting area with a fireplace, a private balcony, and the skin of a grizzly bear on the wall. The bed is one of the few antiques in the inn. Beside it stands an elaborate cupboard with spindle columns and arched doors carved with birds, garlands, and a royal crest.

All the rooms are off the ground-floor breezeway or long upper balcony, overlooking the courtyard. Here umbrella tables are grouped near a stone fountain under drooping wisteria, bougainvillea, and pepper trees. The gardens are designed so well, with succulents and cacti, that they were awarded first place in a competition for landscaping with drought-tolerant or native plant materials.

A breakfast buffet of fresh breads, orange juice, and coffee is served in the courtyard or in the Caymus Restaurant, a small restaurant that offers a menu with Costa Rican and South American specialties. Part of the restaurant can be used for group functions.

ST. HELENA

Bartel's Ranch and Country Inn

1200 Conn Valley Road
St. Helena, CA 94574
707-963-4001

A friendly home in the wine-country hills

Innkeeper: Jami Bartels. **Accommodations:** 4 rooms (all with private bath). **Rates:** $150–$275 single or double. **Included:** Expanded Continental breakfast. **Minimum stay:** 2 nights on weekends. **Payment:** Major credit cards. **Children:** Welcome. **Pets:** Not allowed. **Smoking:** Not allowed in guest rooms.

Conn Valley lies four miles east of St. Helena, in the Napa Valley wine country about 60 miles north of San Francisco. Vineyards line the road that winds through oak-covered hills leading to Jami Bartels' 60-acre estate. The sprawling stone ranch house stands on a hilltop that overlooks pastures and sloping fields of grapevines. Its landscaped grounds include fig trees, flowering plums, cypress, and magnificent old oaks.

Jami Bartels is the energetic force who created this unusual inn. She designed all 7,000 square feet of her home, from the formal dining room, where she serves catered dinners, to the 13-sided game room with a brick fireplace and diagonally paneled redwood walls. The huge room holds an amazing array of entertainment possibilities, including table tennis, a pool table, a stereo, a tape deck, and shelves crammed with books and magazines. There are also games, puzzles, an organ, a stationary bicycle, and even a Wurlitzer juke box.

If you want a complete itinerary for your wine country tour, Jami will plan it. She'll make arrangements for hot air ballooning, glider flights, and limousine and helicopter service. You may borrow her bicycles for a ride to Lake Hennessey or just relax by the pool.

Throughout the house are examples of Jami's collections and artwork: butterflies, Chinese perfume bottles, glassware, baskets, and watercolors.

The Blue Valley guest room, overlooking the valley, has a queen-size canopy bed, while the Brass Room features an Empire brass bed dating from the 1850s. Its glass doors open to a terrace by the pool. The Sunset Room has a king-size bed and a sunset theme. The newest room is the lavishly appointed Honeymoon Suite. It has a king-size bed, a sunken heart-shaped Jacuzzi, a huge fireplace, a TV and stereo, and a private deck. The innkeeper's hospitality adds the crowning touch that makes her B&B exceptional. She's an expert at pampering, yet you will never feel stifled by all the attention.

In the laundry room, an ironing board is always set up. "You know the fancy French restaurants around here; you can't show up wrinkled," Jami says. Fresh flowers abound, bubble bath awaits in the bathrooms, wine and cheese are served every evening, and breakfast is any time you like.

Breakfast, often served on the terrace, includes heaping plates of fresh fruit, almond croissants, banana bread, granola, and yogurt. Her specialty is Iowa raisin bread pudding ("I'm from Iowa, can you tell?" she asks with a laugh).

Bartel's Ranch is well known as a superb place to stay in the valley, away from the mainstream of tourism, but everyone who comes here considers it their private find. The inn has attracted the orchestra conductor at La Scala, concert violinists, movie producers, chefs, artists, and the cast from *A Chorus Line,* among others.

Deer Run

3995 Spring Mountain Road
St. Helena, CA 94574
707-963-3794

A quiet, woodsy retreat above the Napa Valley

Innkeepers: Tom and Carol Wilson. **Accommodations:** 3 rooms (all with private bath). **Rates:** $95–$125 single or double. **Included:** Full breakfast. **Minimum stay:** 2 nights on weekends, April 1-November 1. **Payment:** American Express. **Children:** Age 6 months and under welcome. **Pets:** Not allowed. **Smoking:** Not allowed.

Imagine a fifty-year-old cedar bungalow with a stone chimney and a wash porch, back in the hills among tall pine trees. Imagine it with rough paneling, a woodstove, and a king-size bed with a down quilt, and you've pictured the master bedroom in this woodsy bed-and-breakfast on Spring Mountain, in the Napa Valley.

It's quiet here on Spring Mountain. You can hike a one-mile trail, walk to a winery, or swim in the pool. In every nook and corner, strawberry pots overflow with blue lobelia or flame yellow marigolds, and orange and lemon trees glow in sun or shade.

The original cabin is only part of this delightful B&B, however. For the most seclusion, reserve the Cottage. A good honeymooners' choice, it has whitewashed pine, an open beam ceiling in the living room, and Laura Ashley decor. Breakfast is brought to the cottage in the morning. Another private spot is the Carriage Room, an odd-angled building with a large guest room decorated in forest green and burgundy. A vaulted ceiling of bleached pine with green-stained beams covers part of the room. On the other side, sliding glass doors open to a porch where breakfast is served under the trees. It's a quiet place; all you hear are crickets.

But it's not as rustic as you might expect. A lot of expansion has taken place since the home was built in the 1930s. There are large living and dining areas and a wraparound deck that looks right into the treetops. Guests in the main house have breakfast at a round oak table near a buffet set with coffee, fresh fruit, nut breads, quiche or fritatta, granola, and berries from the garden.

In the comfortable, casual living/dining room, collections on display reveal the Wilsons' interests: antiques, silver, German helmets, electric insulators, spoons, and salt cellars. They like the whimsical, too. A cabbage-shaped teapot with rabbit handle perches on the sideboard.

On the deck, along with barrels of flowers and a picnic table, are examples of Tom's work with twigs. He makes baskets and tiny chairs as holders for pots and dried flowers or as ornamentation. The wood comes from hazelnut trees on the four-acre property, which also has walnut and maple trees.

The Wilsons opened Deer Run in 1981; many venturesome travelers have followed the winding, 4½-mile road since then in search of the romantic inn.

Meadowood

900 Meadowood Lane
St. Helena, CA 94574
707-963-3646
800-458-8080
Fax 707-963-3532

An exclusive country resort

Managing director: Maurice E. Nayrolles. **Accommodations:** 99 rooms and suites. **Rates:** $200–$500 single or double, $25 additional person. **Minimum stay:** 2 nights on weekends. **Payment:** Major credit cards. **Children:** Under age 12 free in room with parents. **Pets:** Not allowed. **Smoking:** Allowed.

On 256 acres of oak groves and green meadows in the Napa Valley, outside the village of St. Helena, this luxurious resort welcomes discriminating travelers. Driving up the quiet, shady entrance road is like approaching a country estate, with vineyards on one side and walnut orchards on the other. After the guarded entry, you wind past madrone and oak trees sheltering guest houses, past tennis courts and a swimming pool to the main lodge. The three-story, white and gray gabled building and the clubhouse on a hill above the golf course resemble grand old New England resorts.

Other than winery tours, activities include bicycling on country roads, fishing at Conn Dam and Lake Berryessa, shopping in the boutiques of St. Helena and Yountville, floating above the valley in a hot-air balloon or soaring in a glider, and soaking in the mud baths of Calistoga.

Up in the clubhouse are two restaurants and an executive conference center with 4,000 square feet of meeting space. The formal restaurant serves California cuisine with a Provençal influence and has a wine list that reads like a catalogue of the finest vineyards in the valley. More casual is the Grill, serving light meals indoors and on the terrace.

The guest rooms are in Croquet Lodge and in cottages tucked away in the woods above the pool, near the tennis courts, and by the golf course. Croquet Lodge faces the perfectly manicured English regulation croquet courts. From your balcony or patio you can watch the white-clad players intent on a game or instruction from the resident pro. Beyond the croquet courts, among the cedar, oak, and tall pine trees, are the sweeping fairways of the 9-hole golf course.

Seven championship tennis courts lie on the other side of the property, between the main lodge and the entrance, not far from the swimming pool. Light meals and bar service are available by the pool.

Each cottage has four one-bedroom suites and a studio. They have private entrances, king-size beds, TV, ample closet space, and skylights that open with the press of a button. Cool luxury combined with great comfort is the motif—nothing flowery here. Walls are gray with white woodwork, the vaulted ceilings have rough white beams, and the artwork is minimal (winery maps and wine labels).

Most suites have stone fireplaces with baskets of wood supplied. Other amenities include stocked refrigerators, coffeemakers, terrycloth robes, baskets of fresh fruit, down comforters and lots of pillows, room service, and a daily newspaper at your door.

Wine tastings and classes are an important part of the activities at Meadowood. John Thoreen, a winemaker, writer, and educator, teaches regular courses in wine appreciation. If you wish to go farther afield to explore regional wines, the concierge will arrange tours.

The Wine Country Inn

1152 Lodi Lane
St. Helena, CA 94574
707-963-7077

A comfortable inn with a vineyard view

Proprietors: Jim and Marge Smith. **Accommodations:** 24 rooms (all with private bath). **Rates:** $97–$211 double, $20 less for single, $20 additional person; winter and midweek rates available. **Included:** Continental breakfast. **Minimum stay:** 2 nights on weekends in some rooms. **Payment:** Major credit cards. **Children:** Welcome. **Pets:** Not allowed. **Smoking:** Allowed.

The Wine Country Inn's gray-brown siding has a look of weathered age, and the mansard roof above the central stone section creates the Old World impression the builders, Ned and Marge Smith, wanted. Now the inn is run by Marge and her son, Jim.

The guest rooms are divided among three buildings. Most of them are in the main lodge; six are behind it in Brandy Barn, and four are in Hastings House. Each room is furnished distinctly, with country antiques, handmade quilts, and color schemes reflecting the valley's seasonal changes. Most have patios or balconies. Fifteen rooms have fireplaces that can be used from October to April; plenty of wood is supplied.

All the rooms are comfortable, but those upstairs are preferable if you're bothered by the sounds of drainpipes and footsteps overhead. Also, if you have a downstairs room with patio you must open the doors for ventilation, which could create a privacy problem. There are phones but no TVs in the rooms.

In the 1970s, when the Napa Valley was rapidly becoming the major tourist destination it is today, this inn was built on three acres above a country lane. Its landscaped grounds are bright with roses and other seasonal flowers, and a sweep of lawn descends to a swimming pool and spa.

A breakfast buffet is presented in the large common room in the main house. You can sit at one of several tables here or in a neighboring smaller room by a deck overlooking lawns and vineyards. Coffee, tea, fruit, granola, a choice of juices, pecan rolls, poppy-seed bread, and strawberry bread constitute a typical breakfast, enough to start you on a tour of the countryside. The inn has a refrigerator for chilling your wine purchases and a stock of wine glasses.

In addition to tasting wine at the dozens of wineries nearby, you can visit Bale Grist Mill Historic Park, climb Mt. St. Helena, and see Robert Louis Stevenson memorabilia at the Silverado Museum. Or go shopping in the many boutiques and galleries and, at the top of everyone's list, eat at wonderful restaurants. Some outstanding valley favorites are Tra Vigne, Mustard's Grill, Showley's, Brava Terrace, and Terra.

Villa St. Helena

2727 Sulphur Springs Avenue
St. Helena, CA 94574
707-963-2514

A secluded mansion above Napa Valley vineyards

Owners: Ralph and Carolyn Cotton. **Accommodations:** 3 suites (all with private bath). **Rates:** \$145–\$245. **Included:** Expanded Continental breakfast. **Minimum stay:** 2 nights on weekends. **Payment:** Major credit cards. **Children:** Age 12 and older welcome. **Pets:** Not allowed. **Smoking:** Not allowed in public spaces.

Secluded among California live oaks, bay trees, and madrones in the foothills of the Mayacamas Mountains of the Napa Valley, this expansive villa has a commanding view of vineyards and the village of St. Helena. From the hilltop at the end of a long, winding road, the inn looks over the valley to Mount St. Helena, high in the distance.

The red brick structure was designed in 1941 by the architect Robert M. Carrere. Carrere designed only two California homes, though he created and restored numerous castles, mansions, and châteaux in Europe and the eastern United States.

Villa St. Helena stands on 20 acres of wooded hillside, its three levels blending into the landscape rather than sitting atop it like a fortress. Two wings extend from a central section that contains a stone fireplace and dark beamed ceiling, a pleasing contrast to the white walls and glass and brass table.

Wide, high glass doors lead to a sun room where a buffet breakfast of breads, cheese, fresh fruit, and juice is set out in the morning. The sun room's windows, framed by wisteria and bougainvillea vines, look toward a swath of lawn ending at a 60-foot pool and brick barbecue pit. On either side of this grassy enclave are suites labeled simply A, B, and C. The A Suite, at the end of the west wing, was the original master bedroom. The spacious room has a bed with an antique headboard, a marble fireplace (with a fire laid), a turquoise and white tile bath, and several closets, including one just for shoes. Parquet floors and high-backed red leather chairs lend a sense of traditional dignity, while several windows and French doors leading to a private balcony keep it light and sunny. On one antique table there's a tray with a complimentary bottle of local white wine — replaced daily — and a jar of pickled quail eggs.

This is an ideal retreat for relaxing with a book in the library or under the orange tree by the swimming pool. And when you want to explore the countryside and perhaps taste what Robert Louis Stevenson called "bottled poetry," dozens of wineries are waiting.

B Suite, smaller than A, has a two-poster bed with a tapestry hanging above it, large corner windows, and brass accents. There's no television, but each room has a phone jack and a phone will be provided if you request it.

Most charming, and most private, is C Suite, across the lawn in the east wing. Up a tile staircase from the breezeway, it has two bedrooms, a sitting room with a white brick fireplace, wicker furniture, a wet bar, and a small kitchen. It's a perfectly furnished apartment, complete with fold-down ironing board in the little hall.

There are few lodgings in the Napa Valley that can compare with the Villa St. Helena for peace, quiet, and exclusive privacy.

Zinfandel Inn

800 Zinfandel Lane
St. Helena, CA 94574
707-963-3512

A wine country bed-and-breakfast

Innkeepers: Diane and Jerry Payton. **Accommodations:** 3 rooms (all with private bath). **Rates:** $125–$225 single or double, $25 additional person. **Included:** Full breakfast. **Minimum stay:** 2 nights on weekends. **Payment:** Major credit cards. **Children:** Welcome. **Pets:** Not allowed. **Smoking:** Not allowed indoors.

On the outside, this bed-and-breakfast inn in the heart of the Napa Valley wine country resembles a European manor house, with a stone facade, towers, and a curving driveway with a fountain in the center. Inside, it's a comfortable, casual, family home.

The inn is on a quiet road off Highway 29, south of St. Helena and a 90-minute drive from San Francisco. It was built in the early 1980s on two acres and has been open to guests since 1988.

"I want visitors to feel at home here," says Diane. She encourages guests to relax and watch TV in the big living room and help themselves to ice from the refrigerator.

The Chardonnay Room, on the main floor, has a brass and white iron bed facing an immense stone fireplace. A small TV rests on the corner of the hearth. In shades of blue, Chardonnay has a vaulted beamed ceiling, a curving bay window, and double doors leading to the back deck. The romantic touches include candles on the ledge of the oversize bathtub and a basket filled with fruit, candy, and wine.

Upstairs, past a landing where guests enjoy perching on the curved window seat to watch the hot-air balloons floating over nearby vineyards, are the other two rooms. Petite Sirah is the smallest. It has a 19th-century French feather bed and a view of the vineyards. Zinfandel, which accommodates four, has velvet boudoir chairs, a fireplace, and a private balcony above the well-landscaped yard. As you relax on the balcony, you can enjoy the view of Mount St. Helena and the surrounding hills. The tile bath has a whirlpool tub and double-headed shower.

Diane will book balloon flights, make restaurant reservations, and arrange for mud baths at Calistoga's spas. If you request flowers or champagne for a special occasion, she'll see that they are in your room when you arrive.

The balcony is a pleasant place to enjoy a breakfast of fresh fruits and a hot dish such as waffles, eggs Benedict, or banana pancakes; or you may eat at the formal dining table downstairs. In the back garden, pepper trees grow by a curving lawn, a hot tub, and a lagoon with a fish pond and waterfall.

SAN FRANCISCO

Campton Place

340 Stockton Street
San Francisco, CA 94108
415-781-5555
Fax 415-955-5536

A small central hotel known for its high quality

General manager: Peter Koehler. **Accommodations:** 126 rooms, 10 suites. **Rates:** Rooms $185–$320, suites $395–$800. **Payment:** Major credit cards. **Children:** Welcome. **Pets:** Allowed. **Smoking:** Nonsmoking rooms available.

Campton Place is a jewel. Around the corner from Union Square, in busy downtown San Francisco, it offers extraordinary luxury, superb service, and a fine restaurant.

When you arrive, uniformed doormen usher you into a marble lobby with a theme both French and Oriental. Carved Buddhas, antique jars, and a 16th-century Japanese sumi screen accent the graceful curves of French furniture. An antique Swedish chandelier hangs above a glass table supported by four swans. Off the lobby is a sunken lounge, divided from the dining room by a curving sweep of glass etched with a swan, the hotel's emblem.

Since the restaurant opened in 1983, it has consistently received rave reviews for complex flavors and outstanding cuisine. Both California and European wines are available.

Service throughout the hotel is cheerful, personal, and efficient. There are no VIP floors or differing levels of attention. A valet will unpack your luggage and repack it in tissue paper when you leave. The valet will run your bath at just the right temperature (each tub has a thermometer) and assist you with tours, or, if you prefer, set up your entire visit.

Other routine services include a choice among four complimentary morning newspapers, overnight shoeshine, immediate pressing, same-day laundry and dry cleaning (if you spot your jacket during lunch it will be cleaned and returned to you before the bill for your meal arrives), twice-daily housekeeping, and a full concierge service. Valet parking is also available.

The guest rooms have a residential ambience, with contemporary and traditional furnishings. There are oversize beds with comforters, Henredon armoires housing remote control television sets, Louis XVI writing tables, and limited edition art on the pastel walls. Double-glazed windows keep street noise at a distance, but they open if you prefer the city's sea breezes to air conditioning. Marble baths contain vanities, scales, phones, hair dryers, and terrycloth robes. Luxurious French milled soaps and shampoos and gels by I. Magnin are among the toiletries provided.

In a pastel setting of peach and apricot walls, white Wedgwood china, and Swiss linens, diners feast on foods presented like works of art.

The hotel is actually two buildings, one of 17 stories and the other, eight. On the lower rooftop is a garden with potted petunias and citrus trees and a view of Union Square. This is a pleasant little oasis for enjoying the morning sun, despite the noise from machinery hidden behind a lattice.

Campton Place used to be the Drake-Wiltshire Hotel, dating from the early 1900s. Changed and remodeled several times, it lapsed into decline until 1981, when Ayala International acquired and rebuilt the property. Most recently it was purchased by Kempinski, owners of fine hotels worldwide.

Casa Arguello

225 Arguello Boulevard
San Francisco, CA 94118
415-752-9482

A classic San Francisco home in a city neighborhood

Innkeepers: Emma Baires and Marina McKenzie. **Accommodations:** 5 rooms (2 with private bath). **Rates:** $50–$75 double, $15 additional person. **Included:** Expanded Continental breakfast. **Minimum stay:** 2 nights. **Payment:** Cash or check. **Children:** Over age 7 welcome. **Pets:** Not allowed. **Smoking:** Not allowed.

As you walk and drive the hilly streets of San Francisco, you pass hundreds of stucco rowhouses, each with a bay window and, usually, a trim box of geraniums in front. Casa Arguello is one of them, located in a neighborhood of similar homes, apartments, and shops. Clement Street restaurants and the boutiques on Sacramento are nearby; Golden Gate Park is five blocks away. The beautiful Temple Emmanuel is across the street.

An international clientele comes to Casa Arguello, so you're likely to meet people from all over the world — especially Swiss, German, and English travelers.

This bed-and-breakfast is larger than it seems from the outside, extending back to a courtyard and up some stairs. Owning such an inn was Emma Baires's childhood dream, when her father had a hotel in El Salvador. Emma and her daughter opened their bed-and-breakfast in 1978.

As in many similar homes, the main floor is up a flight of stairs from the entrance. The walls are white, hung with prints of San Francisco scenes. In the living room are lavish floral couches, rosy carpeting, and arched windows. Antique and contemporary furnishings have been tastefully combined. Cove ceilings and the original wall sconces and moldings date the building to the 1920s.

All the guest rooms have TV. Room 1 is a small corner room with a western view; Room 2 has a king-size brass bed. Room 3, overlooking Lincoln and Golden Gate parks, has a king-size bed of white iron. Room 4 is spacious enough to include three armchairs and a refrigerator. Sheer curtains topped by floral swags lend soft color and style to the airy room, which has a view of the University of San Francisco campus. Room 5, for one person, has a twin bed and shares a bath with Rooms 1 and 2.

Breakfast is served family-style in the dining room. Fresh fruit, a choice of cereals, muffins, croissants, scones, and coffee and tea are the usual offerings. The breakfast table is a fine place to meet and talk with other guests, trading sightseeing ideas and restaurant discoveries.

Country Cottage

Mailing address:
Bed & Breakfast San Francisco
P.O. Box 420009
San Francisco, CA 94142
415-931-3083
Fax 415-921-2273

A cozy cottage in the city

Contacts: Richard and Susan Kreibich. **Accommodations:** 4 rooms (2 with private bath). **Rates:** $55 single, $65 double. **Included:** Full breakfast. **Payment:** Major credit cards. **Children:** Welcome. **Pets:** Not allowed. **Smoking:** Not allowed.

You wouldn't expect to find country charm in the heart of San Francisco, but the city is full of surprises. This pretty cottage nestles behind a wrought-iron gate on a cul-de-sac in a quiet, sunny neighborhood near Mission Dolores. It has a parlor with a bentwood rocker beside a brick fireplace and a wicker basket full of pine cones. Muslin curtains hang in the windows. The furnishings are American primitives.

Built in 1791, Mission Dolores is believed to be the oldest structure in the city. It's been completely restored, down to the ornate altar and the hand-hewn redwood timbers lashed with rawhide.

One bedroom, off the parlor, has a pineapple motif and a high four-poster. The skylighted bath is across the hall.

The white tile kitchen, also with a skylight, has a gas stove and refrigerator and is well equipped with dishes, spices, teas, coffee — even a toaster. The cook comes in to make breakfast each morning. Fresh flowers and greenery here and throughout the house add color and charm. Open the casement window and you'll smell the sweet scent of jasmine.

There's a phone for guests' use in a sitting room next to the kitchen, along with an informative letter of welcome. The Kreibiches, who own the cottage and once lived in it, rent several properties in the city. Once professional ice skaters, they are energetic entrepreneurs who like to make visitors to San Francisco feel welcome.

The other bedrooms are downstairs in an area that can be closed off for privacy. One has a brass bed and a door to the flowery little courtyard with a picnic table. Another, darker room has a four-poster, and the third, also with an entrance to the courtyard, has a carved wooden bed and blue ruffled curtains at the windows.

An important piece of San Francisco history is a few blocks away — Mission Dolores (Mission San Francisco de Asis), the sixth of California's 21 missions.

Four Seasons Clift Hotel

495 Geary Street
San Francisco, CA 94102
415-775-4700
800-332-3442
Fax 415-441-4621

A top-quality historic hotel near Union Square

General manager: Kathleen Horrigan. **Accommodations:** 329 rooms and suites. **Rates:** $200–$340, suites $355–$820. **Payment:** Major credit cards. **Children:** Welcome. **Pets:** Small dogs allowed. **Smoking:** Nonsmoking rooms available.

When you want the very best city lodgings — accommodations that are absolutely top quality in every regard — check in at the Four Seasons Clift, two blocks from Union Square. Its atmosphere, furnishings, amenities, and above all its service make the updated Clift one of California's finest hotels.

The 1915 Clift had always been a luxury hotel that attracted the celebrated and the elite. But by the early 1970s, the grand old place seemed a relic of a bygone era. Then Four Seasons, the wizard of modern hospitality, took over. Millions of dollars later, the renamed Four Seasons Clift had retained its sense of history and elegance while its facilities were modernized.

The staff will remember your name, see you quickly through check-in and check-out, provide near-instant 24-hour room service, polish your shoes, bring in a computer, launder your jeans, and place a flower on your pillow at night.

One of the main attractions of the Four Seasons Clift, and of San Francisco, is the Redwood Room. Built in 1934, it is an art deco masterpiece that shouldn't be missed, whether you stay at the hotel or not. The walls of the lounge, reaching 22 feet to a ceiling of pressed metal, are paneled in aged redwood taken from toppled giants that had lain in Northern California streambeds and gullies for years. When polished, this reclaimed wood takes on a deep patina of bronze and topaz. The most striking element, other than the redwood itself, is the mural above the 75-foot bar, a forest scene of inlaid woods.

Lunch is served in the Lobby Lounge, while in the French Room diners enjoy fine Continental cuisine featuring regional foods. California labels dominate the award-winning wine list, which also offers European vintages. In addition to its classic menu, the French Room serves "Alternative Cuisine" — flavorful low-calorie meals.

The guest rooms in the 16-story hotel are large and luxurious. Request a room on one of the higher floors to avoid traffic noise. All have numerous amenities: mini-bars, two-line phones, remote control TV, hair dryers in marble bathrooms, and tiny book lights for bedtime reading. A Petite Suite has a sitting room with Henredon furniture and windows that view Nob Hill on one side and Twin Peaks on the other.

A typical corner Designer Suite has a dining table for eight, potted palms, original artwork, soft robes, and a dressing room that is bigger than many apartments in San Francisco.

The Clift offers unmitigated luxury, but it's the impeccable service that draws the most admiration. Each person seems genuinely glad to be of help.

Children ("Clift dwellers") receive equally happy treatment. The hotel provides supplies for infants, games, comic books, balloons, and treats, as well as babysitting services and a whole program of activities.

Several function rooms provide space for meetings, receptions, and parties of 8 to 800. Many a bride and groom have chosen to be married at the Clift before slipping upstairs to celebrate with champagne for two in a sybaritic honeymoon retreat. The hotel is within walking distance of the shops near Union Square, fine restaurants, Theater Row, museums, and art galleries; and it's a cable car ride away from other San Francisco attractions.

Galleria Park Hotel

191 Sutter Street
San Francisco, CA 94104
415-781-3060
800-792-9639
Fax 415-433-4409

A stylish hotel in the heart of the city

General manager: David C. Smith.
Accommodations: 177 rooms and suites. **Rates:** $145 single or double, suites $165–$400; weekend and corporate rates available. **Payment:** Major credit cards. **Children:** Welcome. **Pets:** Not allowed. **Smoking:** Nonsmoking rooms available.

Urbane and sophisticated, the eight-story Galleria Park is one block from the financial district and two blocks from Union Square. One of the Kimco boutique hotels, it offers incentives designed for the business traveler. There are conference and reception rooms, a full array of support equipment for meetings, and a catering service. A full-time program coordinator will handle arrangements with professional care. Parlor suites are suitable for small and informal meetings.

The hotel offers same-day laundry and valet service and a parking garage. Runners appreciate the track on the rooftop terrace. All the rooms have soundproofed windows, writing desks, direct-dial telephones, television, and clock radios.

Both leisure and business travelers (along with a good many San Franciscans) like Bentley's, an oyster bar and restaurant off the lobby, through etched glass doors. On the street side, windows etched in shell and lobster designs fill the wall. With tile floors, a zinc bar, and brasserie tables, the mood is that of a classic oyster bar — always crowded and usually noisy. A jazz pianist plays most evenings.

The Galleria Park offers several packages and special rates. Ask for the Romantic Rendezvous and you'll stay in a park studio and receive champagne, Godiva chocolates, and a rose, as well as Continental breakfast in bed.

On the carpeted mezzanine, overlooking the curved bar where delectable oysters nestle in their shells, the atmosphere is softer. Bentley's has received superlative reviews for its seafood menu, especially for the shellfish. Other highlights are grilled yellowfin tuna and egg and spinach fettuccini with bay scallops.

The hotel's small lobby has a distinctive art nouveau decor. Beyond the glass and marble entrance are padded green fabric walls and soft couches beneath a skylight; in a corner is a curving, hand-sculpted white fireplace. Complimentary wine is served by the fire on Friday and Saturday evenings.

The guest room configurations vary because a restoration in 1988 worked within the existing spaces. The Galleria Park is an extensive remake of the Sutter Hotel, which was built on the site in 1911. The seven park studios are large rooms with sitting areas. There are seven hospitality suites, plus the popular two-bedroom Grand Suite, with a fireplace and a whirlpool tub. A typical hospitality suite has a sitting room with a large TV (making it a good gathering place for a small group wanting to watch a ball game together) and, in a few, a white brick fireplace on a raised hearth. In the bedroom are a king-size bed and small television.

The suite's comfortable furniture and assortment of potted plants and flowers create the ambience of a city apartment. As in most Kimco suites, the space is in the sitting area.

The hotel is next to Crocker Galleria, three levels of shops and restaurants under a vaulted glass dome. Two rooftop parks in the shopping center have benches and greenery, pleasant sites for a picnic lunch or a rest.

Golden Gate Hotel

775 Bush Street
San Francisco, CA 94108
415-392-3702
800-835-1118

A European-style hotel at bargain prices

Innkeepers: John and Renate Kenaston. **Accommodations:** 23 rooms (some with shared bath). **Rates:** $55–$89 single or double. **Included:** Continental breakfast. **Payment:** Major credit cards. **Children:** Welcome. **Pets:** Allowed with permission. **Smoking:** Discouraged.

In the heart of downtown San Francisco, just north of Union Square, this hotel is more than a terrific bargain. It has several extras you wouldn't expect at these prices. The narrow white Edwardian building trimmed in pink and blue was built in 1913 and has been carefully maintained by the Kenastons, who manage it with warmth and enthusiasm. Half of their guests are experienced travelers from abroad, and many are return visitors.

Golden Gate Hotel is not a luxury establishment, but it offers excellent quality for the price. It's a good San Francisco find.

Geraniums bloom at bay windows in front, where an awning marks the marble entrance. In the little parlor with windows overlooking the rush of Bush Street traffic, coffee (the city's strongest, Renate claims), tea, and croissants are served in the mornings. Afternoon tea and cookies are also offered, at seats near the fireplace. It's a relaxing spot to read, chat, and listen to classical music.

An old-fashioned birdcage elevator, operated by the original drums and relays, connects four floors of guest rooms. The more expensive rooms have private baths; the others have washbasins and share bathrooms. All the rooms have television and several have phones. Renate sees that each has fresh flowers. Though some accommodations are quite small, they're clean, nicely furnished with antiques and wicker, and have a European charm.

The friendly, multilingual (German, Chinese, French, and

Spanish) hosts are delighted to help with sightseeing tours. The hotel is within walking distance of the city's great shops, many of its best restaurants, and Chinatown. The cable car stops at the corner and follows Powell Street to Fisherman's Wharf and North Beach.

Parking garages are available at $14 for 24 hours.

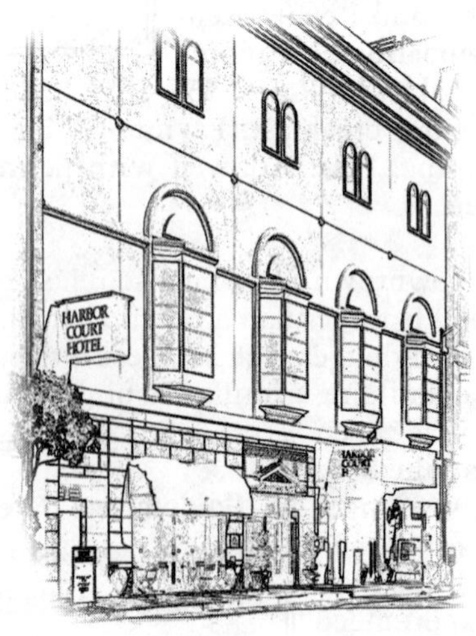

Harbor Court Hotel

165 Steuart Street
San Francisco, CA 94105
415-882-1300
800-346-0555
Fax 415-882-1313

> *A bayview hotel with top-quality fitness facilities*

Manager: Jay Slattery. **Accommodations:** 130 rooms, 1 penthouse suite. **Rates:** $140–$160 single or double, suite $250. **Payment:** Major credit cards. **Children:** Welcome (cribs available). **Pets:** Not allowed. **Smoking:** Nonsmoking rooms available.

At last, the Embarcadero freeway is gone and the view toward East Bay is open again. The Harbor Court Hotel is a prime viewing spot, from half the rooms and from the adjacent Harry Denton's restaurant.

The eight-story hotel, which opened in 1991 as one of the

Kimco group, adjoins a renovated YMCA. Guests may use all the Y facilities, including an Olympic-size pool, weight room, racquetball courts, basketball court, exercise machines, steam room and sauna, and rooftop running track.

Menu offerings at Harry Denton's restaurant are as basic as Yankee pot roast with mashed potatoes and as imaginative as seasonal greens with spiced pecans and goat cheese.

Another plus, especially for business travelers, is the Harbor Court's location, close to the Financial District and Embarcadero Center. The hotel has a business center with fax, photocopying, and typing services and same day valet service. There's also complimentary coffee, tea, and evening wine in the lobby.

There's a nautical hint in the guest rooms, which are on the top four floors. Bayside rooms, decorated in shades of green, are small but adequate — it's the panoramic view that makes them so popular. Space-savers include wardrobes providing closet space, TV, and honor bar, and drawers under the bed. Wide mirrors add the illusion of expanse. Interior rooms, which view a flowery courtyard, are larger.

Harry Denton's, considered a hot spot in the Bay Area, is a festive restaurant open for breakfast, lunch, and dinner seven days a week. It has live music nightly with dancing on Thursday, Friday, and Saturday nights.

Hotel Griffon

155 Steuart Street
San Francisco, CA 94105
415-495-2100
800-321-2201
Fax 415-495-3522

A sophisticated waterfront hotel with a Bay Bridge view

General manager: Alice Morris. **Accommodations:** 59 rooms, 3 suites. **Rates:** $125–$145 single or double, penthouse suite $175–$195. **Included:** Continental breakfast. **Payment:** Major credit cards. **Children:** Welcome (cribs available). **Pets:** Not allowed. **Smoking:** Allowed.

With the dismantling of the Embarcadero Freeway, the view from the back of this small hotel near the waterfront has improved dramatically. Now you can see boats scudding across the water and the Bay Bridge stretching to the East Bay.

The small lobby is a lively spot, divided by a glass partition from one of the city's popular bistros, Rôti. Light jazz plays in the bistro, where country French cuisine is prepared on the rotisserie and grill. Hotel guests partake of pastries and coffee here between 6:00 A.M. and 10:00 A.M.

Upstairs, the fresh, light rooms have custom-carved bedsteads and marble baths. Most suites have a sleeping and sitting area in one room. Lots of style went into appointing these rooms. Rough brick behind the beds contrasts with the smooth white walls and high ceilings, tapestry-covered pillows and window seats. Among the items in the stocked mini-bars are bottles of Sonoma Valley chardonnay with the hotel's own label. The fifth floor suites have private decks with sitting areas.

The hotel is close to the BART system and is a few steps from Embarcadero Center, cable car stops, and ferry service.

The Griffon has become a favorite with business travelers and tourists for its atmosphere, service, and convenient location.

Parking is available, with 24-hour in-and-out privileges.

Hotel Juliana

590 Bush Street
San Francisco, CA 94108
415-392-2540
800-382-8800
Fax 415-391-8447

A small hotel with European charm

Manager: Jan Misch. **Accommodations:** 107 rooms, 28 suites. **Rates:** $140 single or double. **Payment:** Major credit cards.

Children: Welcome. **Pets:** Not allowed. **Smoking:** Nonsmoking rooms available.

During the past several years a number of affordable little first-class hotels have opened in San Francisco, filling a niche between small economy and big luxury hotels. Bill Kimpton, founder of Kimco Hotels, has opened several such European-style hostelries since 1981; one of the best is the charming Hotel Juliana.

On the walls in the lobby and throughout the hotel hang artworks provided by local galleries. The rotating collection showcases contemporary pieces that are available for purchase.

The nine-story beige brick building with burgundy and blue trim is on a busy corner on the Nob Hill side of Union Square. Built in 1903, it has been completely renovated and boasts modern comforts with the atmosphere of a Continental pensione.

The strains of taped viola music play as you enter the small lobby, cheerful and fresh in shades of peach, teal, and green. Soft chairs and couches are grouped by the pink marble fireplace. Against one wall is a table with always-hot coffee, tea, and a tray of fresh fruit. Complimentary wines are served every evening.

The guest rooms have pastel color schemes coordinated with flowered drapes and bedspreads. The atmosphere is that of a nicely furnished private apartment with a French flair, befitting this traditionally French area. The Juliana is across the street from Notre Dame de Victoire, where mass is still spoken in French.

All the rooms have direct-dial telephones, well-lighted desks, honor bars, large baths, and television with HBO. VCRs and movies are available.

Complimentary limousine service is provided to the financial district in the mornings. These and other services, such as same-day laundry and valet service, put the Juliana in the category of the city's better hotels, while its budget-minded aspects (room service is available only part of the day; the bellman doubles as concierge) keep it affordable.

Hotel Nikko

222 Mason Street
San Francisco, CA 94102
415-394-111
800-NIKKO US
Fax 415-394-1106

A touch of Japan near Union Square

General manager: W. Andrews Kirmse. **Accommodations:** 500 rooms and 22 suites. **Rates:** $205–$285 single or double, suites $375–$1,300. **Payment:** Major credit cards. **Children:** Under 18 free in parent's room. **Pets:** Dogs allowed. **Smoking:** Nonsmoking rooms available.

In angular simplicity, the Nikko rises 300 feet above Mason and O'Farrell streets, two blocks from Union Square and four blocks from the Moscone Center. The hotel's sleek, modern look has been modified in recent years with warm jewel tones and sheer curtains in the marble lobby. Cascading water, recessed lighting, and elegant floral arrangements create a soothing effect and a welcoming atmosphere.

Prosperous-looking business travelers, many of them Japanese, patronize the Nikko, which Japan Air Lines opened in 1987. Business and leisure travelers alike receive the best of care, from a computerized key system for security to a fitness center where you can relax under a shiatsu massage. You never have to stand three-deep waiting for an elevator at the Nikko; swift Mitsubishi elevators whisk you to your floor at 700 feet per minute. The ride is said to be so smooth that a nickel placed on end will remain in place throughout the trip.

The hotel has a lounge and two restaurants: Café 222, serving regional cuisine on the mezzanine, and Benkay, an authentic Japanese restaurant on the 25th floor. Benkay offers a sushi bar, traditional Western seating, and private tatami rooms that accommodate from two to sixteen guests.

The guest rooms and suites, serene in shades of gray, are furnished in a contemporary style. Conveniences include a stocked refrigerator that automatically charges your bill when an item is dispensed, a switch by the king-size bed that turns on all room lights, and speedy in-room television checkout.

If you're traveling on business you may prefer one of the four business suites on the sixth floor; they have meeting rooms and the latest audio-visual equipment. Other conference rooms are available — the Nikko offers 18,000 square feet of meeting space.

On the fifth floor there's a health facility with an inviting glass-enclosed swimming pool, whirlpool tub, tanning machine, saunas, massage service, and exercise equipment. The locker rooms are cramped and showers (at least in the women's section) are so limited as to seem an afterthought, without space to hang a swimsuit. Otherwise the center is attractive — and the shiatsu massage refreshing. Outside, on the rooftop, is a sunning area with lounge chairs. The Nikko offers special weekend packages that include deluxe accommodations, use of the fitness center, and free valet parking.

In the Benkay restaurant's tatami rooms you may order a nine-course Japanese dinner that will be brought by kimono-clad servers, or choose from the Benkay menu. You might start with an appetizer of shrimp on green tea noodles and continue with thin slices of beef cooked in the traditional shabu shabu pan and served with the restaurant's original sauces.

Hotel Sheehan

620 Sutter Street
San Francisco, CA 94102
415-775-6500
800-848-1529
Fax 415-775-3271

A comfortable budget hotel in a great location

Proprietors: Pat and William Ferdon. **Manager:** Don Hayden. **Accommodations:** 68 rooms (14 with shared bath). **Rates:** $45–$79 single, $55–$89 double, $10 additional person. **Included:** Continental breakfast. **Payment:** Major credit cards. **Children:** Under 12 free in parent's room. **Pets:** Not allowed. **Smoking:** Nonsmoking rooms available.

It's unusual to find clean, quiet lodgings for two in an excellent downtown San Francisco district for $55 a night — especially when it includes breakfast. Not only are the Sheehan's room rates are a bargain, the hotel has a swimming pool, workout facilities, and a tea room where you can buy snacks and afternoon tea.

Admittedly, the amenities are basic. Most are simple rooms with carpeting, a dresser, a closet, and, usually, a washbasin. Some have cable TV, and a few are as well-appointed as any good hotel. All the shared bathrooms are well-maintained and clean and have several showers.

If you're traveling alone and want to spend the minimum, the $45 room is decent, if small. The most expensive accommodations are larger and have two double beds and a private bath. Breakfast is usually juice, coffee or tea, and scones, muffins, or banana nut bread. Cereal for children is free, for adults it's $1.50.

> **If you'd rather spend your money on San Francisco's wonderful restaurants than on fancy digs, this is a good choice. The location (just two blocks from Union Square) and the price are unbeatable.**

The swimming pool, the largest in the city, dates from the days when this was a YWCA, a favored lodging for many young women in San Francisco. The new owners remodeled the building in 1988.

In the large, open lobby you'll hear a dozen languages spoken as world travelers come and go. At one side of the lobby is a box office selling tickets to the Lorraine Hansberry Theater next door. Parking is available in a garage across the street.

There's nothing luxurious about the Sheehan, but the Ferdon brothers, while planning to keep their hotel in the budget range, have more improvements underway.

Hotel Triton

342 Grant Avenue
San Francisco, CA 94108
415-394-0500
800-433-6611
Fax 415-392-0555

A sophisticated small hotel in a central location

General manager: Steve Salvatore.
Accommodations: 140 rooms. **Rates:** $129–$169. **Payment:** Major credit cards. **Children:** Welcome. **Pets:** Not allowed. **Smoking:** Nonsmoking rooms available.

Whimsical designs and bright colors set the mood at the Triton. It's playful, creative, and sophisticated, but guests' needs for comfort and efficiency come first.

The hotel, which opened in 1991 as part of the Kimco group of small hotels, is conveniently located across from the gate to Chinatown and close to Union Square and the financial district. Entering guests first notice the dramatic curving columns in vivid gold, teal, and purple, and the gold chairs with undulating backs. Soft couches are arranged in conversation nests, one by the fireplace that is built into a purple wall and surrounded with painted flames.

Guest rooms are equally interesting. The smallest, called Salon Rooms, were designed to maximize limited space and appeal particularly to the business traveler. The full-size bed fits into a corner and is used as a couch, covered with a handsome striped spread during the day. There are cleverly angled drawers, mirrors to visually enlarge the space, and theater-style curtains at the windows.

The walls are painted with a dreamlike mythological mural, while seagrass-green stars stud the royal blue carpet.

Other rooms are larger and more traditionally furnished, though they too have unusual elements such as curved fixtures and walls painted with big blue and yellow diamonds or pastel swirls.

Among the services and features are honor bars with reasonably priced items, individual heat control, complimentary wine served in the lobby each evening, and a meeting room (the "Creative Zone") with an adjacent patio. Free limousine service is provided to the design district.

Hotel Vintage Court

650 Bush Street
San Francisco, CA 94108
415-392-4666
800-654-1100
Fax 415-392-4666

A boutique hotel with one of the city's best restaurants

Manager: John Brocklehurst. **Accommodations:** 106 rooms, 1 suite. **Rates:** $109 single or double, suite $229. **Payment:** Major credit cards. **Children:** Welcome. **Pets:** Not allowed. **Smoking:** Nonsmoking rooms available.

A restful environment, reasonable rates, and one of the city's best French restaurants draw increasing numbers of travelers to this attractive downtown hostelry. The Vintage Court is a part of the collection of boutique hotels that have provided a new lodging option in San Francisco in recent years. Bill Kimpton, with his highly successful Kimco Hotels, is a leading figure in the move to renovate old buildings and turn them into distinctive, stylish hotels with rooms at comparatively low prices. The Vintage Court opened in 1983, built in an eight-story hotel originally constructed in 1913. Its wine theme includes rooms named for California wineries, fabrics in muted grape cluster patterns, and impressionistic paintings of vineyard scenes.

In the rooms, cabinets house stocked refrigerators. Additional comforts, many geared to the business traveler, are padded headboards, writing tables with good lighting, direct-dial phones, and digital clock radios. A single corner suite on the eighth floor has a separate living room with working fireplace, views of the city skyline, and an original 1913 stained glass skylight.

Complimentary wines are served every evening in the lobby, near the marble fireplace, while classical music plays in the background.

Complimentary morning limousine service to the financial district is provided, coffee and tea are served on each floor, and same-day laundry service and express check-out are available. A modestly priced breakfast buffet is set up in the restaurant, Masa's, for hotel guests.

Masa's is mentioned in tones of hushed reverence by San Francisco gastronomes. Exquisite food is served in the small, flawless restaurant. Under a cove ceiling with moldings of polished oak, etched mirrors reflect tables set with crisp burgundy and white linens, Christofle silver, and fresh flowers. The lighting is subdued and the music soft.

Chef Julian Serrano, from Spain, follows the tradition established by the late Masataka Kobayashi, the restaurant's founder. He combines fresh ingredients with classic sauces to create dishes that are works of art. Highlights are the seafood and game specialties: grilled Maine lobster with herbed butter and shrimp quenelles, roast breast of pheasant with morels, and quail stuffed with wild rice are examples.

The wine list, with more than 500 fine French and Californian selections, is extraordinary. Desserts include a silky lemon charlotte with raspberry sauce, feather-light puff pastries, thick wedges of chocolate with hazelnuts, and fruity mango sorbet in a praline cone.

Predictably, reservations at Masa's can be difficult to come by — Tuesday or Wednesday night are your best chances of getting a table in the dining room, which seats 100.

Inn at the Opera

333 Fulton Street
San Francisco, CA 94102
415-863-8400
800-423-9610 in California
800-325-2708 in U.S.
Fax 415-861-0821

A small, elegant hotel close to the Civic Center

Managing director: Tom Noonan. **Accommodations:** 30 rooms and 18 suites. **Rates:** \$115–\$160 single, \$125–\$170 double, \$10 additional person, suites \$180–\$220, \$5 less on weekdays. **Included:** Continental breakfast. **Payment:** Major credit cards. **Children:** Under 16 free in room with parent. **Pets:** Allowed by prior arrangement. **Smoking:** Nonsmoking rooms available.

Although San Francisco's Civic Center has long been the cultural and governmental focus for the city — with the Opera House, Davies Music Hall, San Francisco Ballet School, Civic Auditorium, Museum of Modern Art, and City Hall grouped together — the area has lacked a first-class hotel. With the restoration of the 16-story Inn at the Opera, it gained a gem.

The hotel was built in 1927 to house visiting opera performers. After a \$7 million renovation it reopened in 1985, again hosting internationally acclaimed singers and conductors as well as patrons and tourists.

Entering the inn is like stepping into the parlor of a gracious private home. Classical music flows around French armchairs covered in silk and damask, past tall mullioned windows, potted palms, and porcelain jardinieres. At the end of a short hallway lined with Paul Renouard sketches of Paris Opera Ballet dancers is the focal point of the hotel: Act IV. This intimate lounge and restaurant is rich in texture and color. Its dark woods, subdued lighting, and exotic fabric wall coverings patterned with jungle birds create a sensuous, elegant mood. Green velvet sofas facing a fireplace in the bar are favored seats for enjoying post-performance liqueurs or espresso.

A pianist plays every night in Act IV. The restaurant's menu, which changes regularly, features Mediterranean foods and California wines. Act IV is one of the city's few restaurants offering after-theater dinner.

You may choose to have breakfast delivered to your room or to eat in the restaurant, where orchids grace tables with white linens. The buffet includes fresh fruit, yogurt, cereals, muffins, quiche, and a cheese tray.

There's only one elevator, but it takes you swiftly to guest rooms in the boutique hotel. The accommodations include six junior suites, six one-bedroom suites, and six two-bedroom/two-bath suites. All rooms and suites have half-canopy queen-size beds, microwave ovens, stocked mini-bars, and oversize baths. They're furnished with dark mahogany and color schemes of blue, green, and peach that exude a soft and welcoming warmth.

The least expensive and smallest are the Regular rooms; Superiors are larger, but all have the same amenities — a basket of apples, plenty of pillows, fresh flowers, and evening turndown. You'll find a sweet treat (chocolate truffles, strawberries dipped in chocolate, almond marzipan cakes) in your room each night. In the distance, the steady rumble of the freeway never stops, but to light sleepers it's less disturbing than the horns and squealing brakes of downtown traffic.

You may park on the street, but it's not recommended in this urban neighborhood. Valet parking is available.

The Inn at Union Square

440 Post Street
San Francisco, CA 94102
415-397-3510
800-288-4346
Fax 415-989-0529

A small urban hotel of comfort and style

Manager: Brooks Bayly. **Accommodations:** 30 rooms. **Rates:** \$110–\$180, suites \$145–\$400. **Included:** Continental breakfast. **Payment:** Major credit cards. **Children:** Welcome. **Pets:** Not allowed. **Smoking:** Not allowed.

In the heart of downtown San Francisco, half a block from Union Square, this little urban retreat is a delight. Behind the green and white awning that extends over the sidewalk is a narrow lobby, made to appear larger by the *trompe l'oeil* effect of wallpaper resembling open windows and shelves of books. Guests receive two keys — one to their room and the other, for added security, to the single elevator.

Each floor of seven rooms has its own sitting area with fireplace where morning muffins, fresh juices, and fruit are served (or breakfast will be brought to your room if you prefer). Afternoon tea is set out, complete with cucumber sandwiches and delectable cakes, and even as the teapots are whisked away, evening wine and hors d'oeuvres are brought. All this is complimentary, along with a daily paper.

The inn's staff is personable and obliging, and the rooms are attractively furnished with Georgian furniture and colorful fabrics. Ultrasoft sheets, downy pillows, wide windows that open, fresh flowers, a desk, wicker wastebaskets — these are the ingredients of a small and worthy hotel. Bathrooms are not immense marble affairs; they are simple and white-tiled, with brass water taps, shaded lamps, and mirrored medicine chests.

If you like European charm and attention to detail, combined with the atmosphere of old San Francisco, the Inn at Union Square is an excellent choice.

The larger rooms have sitting areas; one has a fireplace. There are two-room suites with fold-out love seats; a large two-room suite with a dining room; and a penthouse suite with a king-size canopy bed, whirlpool bath, sauna, fireplace, and wet bar.

Jackson Court

2198 Jackson Street
San Francisco, CA 94115
415-929-7670

Residential-style lodging in a quiet neighborhood

Manager: Pat Cremer. **Accommodations:** 10 rooms (all with private bath). **Rates:** $108–$150. **Included:** Expanded Continental breakfast. **Minimum stay:** 2 nights on weekends. **Payment:** Major credit cards. **Children:** Not appropriate. **Pets:** Not allowed. **Smoking:** Not allowed.

A mining engineer who made his fortune in Australia at the turn of the century built this solid mansion in fashionable Pacific Heights. It withstood the 1906 earthquake and fire and now offers lodging to San Francisco visitors who prefer a quiet but convenient retreat away from the downtown bustle.

Parking is easy in this hilly neighborhood of lovely old residences. You can leave your car on the street or in a garage two blocks away. Marble stairs under an arch of red stone lead to a courtyard with greenery and a skylight at the entrance to Jackson Court. Inside is an intimate parlor furnished like a fine salon. Velvet couches sit on an Oriental carpet beside the fireplace, which is carved with cherubs, their mouths pursed as if to blow on the hearth. Ceiling beams and wainscoting are of dark woods. Fresh flowers are arranged on the coffee table, an encyclopedia is handy, and game boards are set for dominoes and backgammon. Sherry is served by the fire in the late afternoon.

Jackson Court is more like a home than a hotel because its accommodations are all time-share studios.

The largest rooms are just off the parlor. The Executive Room has a brass bed and a large sitting area with a marble fireplace (nonworking) and built-in bookcases. The Garden Room, originally the dining room, features handcrafted paneling, a bed with a curved brass headboard, a black marble fireplace, and a private patio filled with flowers.

The other rooms, on the second and third floors, convey the ambience of a well-appointed apartment. Two have working fireplaces. Room 1, once the library, is a big favorite for its quiet atmosphere, brass bed, and gray marble fireplace. All the rooms have television and private phones.

Off the wide landing is a breakfast nook where fruit, croissants, and various cereals are available in the mornings. Guests are welcome to use the cooking facilities for heating foods or preparing light snacks.

Jackson Court is managed by the capable Pat Cremer, who will recommend good restaurants, give you a map and the morning newspaper, and answer questions about the city. "It's very informal here," she says. "This is a casual place. No one ever wants to leave."

The Nolan House

1071 Page Street
San Francisco, CA 94117-2218
415-863-0384
800-SF-NOLAN

A spacious urban home in a historic district

Innkeeper: Timothy Sockett. **Accommodations:** 4 rooms (1 with private bath, others share 3 half-baths). **Rates:** $85–$135 single or double, $20 additional person. **Included:** Full breakfast weekends, expanded Continental weekdays. **Payment:** No credit cards. **Children:** Welcome. **Pets:** Not allowed. **Smoking:** Not allowed indoors.

In 1889, Margaret Nolan lived in a quiet, patrician neighborhood that is now known as Buena Vista Historic District, San Francisco's largest historic district. It's near Golden Gate Park and the Haight-Ashbury district. Today, Margaret's Queen Anne home is an outstanding B&B that offers almost everything a city visitor could want. The hard-working innkeeper likes to make guests feel at home, offering afternoon refreshments, evening cordials and mints, and a varied breakfast — juice, fruit, and fresh breads and pastries with an egg dish, French toast and bacon, or Belgian waffles. The meal is brought into the dining room, where a fire burns in the fireplace and candles light the antique table. You may notice a small crack in the French sideboard — it's the inn's only damage from the 1989 earthquake.

The Nolan House has a baby grand piano in the high-ceilinged parlor, six marble fireplaces, luxurious feather beds, antique furnishings, limited off-street parking, and a sunny, protected garden.

A red carpet covers the stairs that lead up to the guest rooms. These are unusually large and light for a late 19th-century home, because the property was five feet wider than most lots of the day. Each room has a special touch. The Green Room has a three-door French armoire in rosewood and a Bufano sculpture on the fireplace mantel. The Garden Room in the back, the only one without a fireplace, is the quietest. The windows in the Master Room, which has a private bath, still have their original wavy glass.

The rooms do not have phones or television, but you're welcome to use the TV in the kitchen, and a portable phone is available for local calls.

Petite Auberge

863 Bush Street
San Francisco, CA 94108
415-928-6000

A city hotel with country charm

Manager: Rich Revaz. **Accommodations:** 25 rooms, 1 suite. **Rates:** \$110–\$160 single or double, \$15 additional person, suite \$220. **Included:** Full breakfast. **Payment:** Major credit cards. **Children:** Under age 5 free in room with parents. **Pets:** Not allowed. **Smoking:** Not allowed.

A French country inn in the heart of San Francisco, between Nob Hill and Union Square, Petite Auberge offers the best of both romantic worlds. It has flower-filled window boxes on every floor, and French and American flags fly over a green awning.

Inside the five-story, narrow hotel, light and breezy pastels, floral fabrics, comfortable antiques, and French landscapes set the tone. The registration desk is just inside the beveled glass front doors, but the gathering place for guests is below-stairs, where couches are pulled up to the fireplace, daily newspapers lie on the tables, and afternoon tea is served.

The inn has a quiet breakfast area where guests have their juice, cereals, egg dish, croissants and coffee at round tables, viewing a little garden full of well-tended shrubs and delicate ferns.

The guest rooms line pale cream halls with paneled wainscoting. The rooms on the first floor tend to be dark; those above are more attractive. They vary in size and are decorated individually, but all the rooms carry through the French country theme with striped and flowered wallpapers, pastel comforters, muslin curtains, handmade pillows, and fresh flowers and fruit. Most have gas fireplaces.

Every room has a teddy bear, one of the signature touches in all Four Sisters Inns. The company, which owns a collection of inns, was begun by Roger and Sally Post in Pacific Grove, when they opened their own 19th-century home to guests. The Posts' four daughters helped make it a family venture and gave the new innkeeping company its name. The sisters are still involved in the operation of the inns. Sally Post, who decorates with flair, worked with other designers to create inns modeled on those in Europe.

Each inn has bits of whimsy. At Petite Auberge they include an antique carousel horse by the front door, floppy-eared ceramic rabbits, and the ubiquitous bears, which may be purchased.

The staff at Petite Auberge is helpful in arranging for dinner reservations or tickets to the symphony or other events. Valet parking is available.

If you're looking for flowery charm, downtown convenience, and warm hospitality, this little inn is an excellent choice.

The San Remo Hotel

2237 Mason Street
San Francisco, CA 94133
415-776-8688
Fax 415-776-2811

A bargain-priced pensione near North Beach and Fisherman's Wharf

Innkeepers: Tom and Robert Field. **Accommodations:** 62 rooms (6 shared baths). **Rates:** $35–$45 single, $55–$65 double; penthouse $85; $10 additional person. **Payment:** Major credit cards. **Children:** Welcome. **Pets:** Not allowed. **Smoking:** Allowed.

The 1906 earthquake left San Francisco in desperate need of hotel rooms, so A.P. Giannini, the founder of the Bank of America, built the New California Hotel. Close to the wharf and Embarcadero, the hotel was convenient for sailors and waterfront workers. Today, after extensive restoration, it's the San Remo, a warm, European-style inn with narrow halls, comfortable rooms, and ferns hanging below stained glass skylights.

The ground floor houses a well-known restaurant, also called the San Remo. The hotel's reception area and rooms are on the floors above. Down the hall, which has walls of white wainscoting and a pressed-paper design, are a phone, laundry room, and soft drink machine. The guest rooms, each one different, have two twin beds or a twin and a double, white walls, flowered quilts, tables, and extra touches such as an interesting piece of art, a wicker chair, or throw rugs. Each has a washbasin.

The shared tile bathrooms are immaculate. The separate

shower room has black and white tile and corner sinks painted with flowers.

The shingle-sided penthouse has a private bath, television, refrigerator, and a rooftop deck with a view of Coit Tower and Telegraph Hill. If there are no guests in the penthouse, others may use the deck.

The San Remo, renovated with taste and loving care by two brothers, is a block from a cable car stop and within walking distance of Fisherman's Wharf and North Beach.

Seal Rock Inn

545 Point Lobos Avenue
San Francisco, CA 94121
415-752-8000

A family motel on a hill near the ocean

Proprietors: Larry and Barbara Elam. **Manager:** Cecilia Downer. **Accommodations:** 27 rooms. **Rates:** $76–$97 single, $80–$102 double, $8 additional adult, $4 children. **Minimum stay:** 2 nights on weekends. **Payment:** Major credit cards. **Children:** Welcome. **Pets:** Not allowed. **Smoking:** Allowed.

This three-story hotel with free covered parking is in San Francisco's northwest corner, across the street from Sutro Heights Park. It overlooks Seal Rocks, famous for their sea lions, and is just two blocks up the hill from a venerable name in restaurants, Cliff House.

Seal Rock Inn is a wise lodging choice when you're bringing children to the city. It's removed from the downtown hubbub (though the street does get a lot of city and tourist buses) and has a casual atmosphere. Some rooms have a kitchenette, which you can use for an additional $4; it comes in handy when you want a snack or when the kids tire of restaurants. Dishes and utensils are supplied, along with a refrigerator and two-burner stovetop.

The furnishings are plain and serviceable. You won't worry about rambunctious youngsters destroying fragile antiques here, yet the comfortable sitting areas, earth-tone carpeting, and grasscloth walls are attractive and clean. Each room has a television, a direct-dial phone, refrigerator, and complimentary coffee. Many include fireplaces with gas starters; oak logs are supplied. These units are the most popular and should be reserved far in advance. The rooms with ocean views are also big favorites.

Ideal if you're traveling with children is a unit with queen-size bed and two studio twins. A folding vinyl wall can be pulled out to separate the two sleeping areas. Other rooms contain two double beds.

Sutro Heights Park, overlooking Cliff House and the ocean, was once the estate of Adolph Sutro. Now the buildings are gone, but you can see bits of statuary among the groves of eucalyptus, cypress, and pine. It's a pleasant place to stroll and watch the sunset.

The coffee shop at the inn can be crowded and steamy but is known for its omelettes and pancakes. It's open for breakfast and lunch only. The inner patio is set up for table tennis and badminton and has a small swimming pool.

In addition to Sutro Heights Park, a nearby attraction that intrigues kids and adults alike is Musée Mécanique, down the street at Cliff House. It's a collection of antique amusement machines, including coin-operated musical instruments. Golden Gate Park, one of the world's great urban oases, is four blocks south of the hotel.

Sheraton Palace Hotel

2 New Montgomery Street
San Francisco, CA 94105
415-392-8600
800-325-3535
Fax 415-543-0671

A glamorous old hotel near the convention center

General manager: Donald N. Timbie. **Accommodations:** 552 rooms, includes 36 suites. **Rates:** \$205–\$265 single, \$225–\$285 double, suites \$400–\$2,000, \$20 additional person. **Payment:** Major credit cards. **Children:** Under 18 free. **Pets:** Not allowed (though actress Sarah Bernhardt brought her pets, a tiger and a parrot, in 1887). **Smoking:** Nonsmoking rooms available.

After a 27-month, $150 million restoration, the historic Palace opened again in April, 1991. The grand hotel that was built in 1875 as the first hotel west of the Mississippi, and rebuilt after burning in the 1906 earthquake and fire, was returned to its former glory — with a few additions. Now it has a conference area and business center, a health spa, and a skylighted swimming pool.

The Garden Court is a beloved lunch, tea, and Sunday brunch spot for San Franciscans who remember the old days, as well as for awed newcomers.

The glamour has returned, with the lovely Garden Court its centerpiece. A magnificent stained glass dome covers the famous restaurant, where ten chandeliers sparkle above the potted palms, gilded marble columns, and linen-covered tables.

Another restaurant, Maxfield's, features steaks, seafood, and pasta. It, too, has a stained glass ceiling, uncovered during the hotel's restoration. Maxfield's is named for Maxfield Parrish, who was commissioned to paint the beautiful mural that adorns the Pied Piper Bar. Kyo-Ya is the Sheraton Palace's third restaurant. Named for the company that now owns the hotel, it offers award-winning Japanese cuisine for lunch and dinner.

Acres of marble, high ceilings, polished woods, and numerous amenities characterize the guest rooms and suites. There are hair dryers and magnifying mirrors in the baths, refrigerators, TVs with movies, robes, and hook-ups for personal computers. Overnight valet service, nightly turndown, and 24-hour room service are offered. Business travelers like the telephones with custom message, conference call, voice mail, and call waiting features.

The hotel's location is convenient for both business and pleasure. It's adjacent to the financial district and within walking distance of Moscone Center and the Embarcadero Center. Theaters and shops are nearby.

Stouffer Stanford Court Hotel

905 California Street
San Francisco, CA 94108
415-989-3500
800-227-4736
Fax: 415-391-0513
Telex: 34-0899

A historic luxury hotel on the Nob Hill cable car line

General manager: Christian J. Mari.
Accommodations: 402 rooms. **Rates:** $195–$295 single, $225–325 double, $30 additional person; suites $450–$2,000. **Payment:** Major credit cards. **Children:** Under 18 free in room with adult. **Pets:** Allowed by arrangement. **Smoking:** Nonsmoking rooms available.

The Stanford Court has been a Nob Hill landmark for years, with its stained glass domes above the entry courtyard and lobby, its collection of antiques and art, and its outstanding restaurant. Recent improvements have enhanced the hotel's appeal, adding warmth and style to its previously somewhat dated look. Now it has a sepia-toned mural encircling the lobby with scenes of San Francisco history and a snazzy International Bar displaying vintage travel posters — in addition to a view of the city skyline, tastefully decorated rooms, and a million-dollar presidential suite.

The hotel was built as a fashionable apartment building,

constructed in 1912 on the site of Leland Stanford's 1876 Italianate mansion (which went up in flames in 1906). The apartment building was remodeled in the early 1970s as an elegant hostelry overlooking the city and the bay. In 1989 Stouffer Hotels purchased the property and began a major refurbishment program.

Unusual and thoughtful touches in the rooms at the Stouffer Stanford Court include dictionaries, prethreaded sewing kits, and heated towel racks.

Inside the marble and wood-paneled lobby are Baccarat chandeliers, Oriental carpets, and fine antiques such as ornately framed 18th-century mirrors and a grandfather clock that was a gift from Napoleon Bonaparte to his minister of war in 1806.

The guest rooms in the eight-story hotel are comfortable and for the most part spacious, with a blend of 19th century European reproductions and antique or Oriental pieces. Each room has television, two or more phones with call-waiting feature, clock radios, and desks. Rooms facing the street get traffic noise, so if you want quiet and are willing to forego the spectacular views, request an inner courtyard room.

Business travelers appreciate the hotel's complimentary limousine rides to the financial district and downtown, the 24-hour room and laundry service, and an array of business services — including typists, computers, translators, free fax receipt, and a multilingual staff. Guests have health club privileges across the street at the Nob Hill Club.

Fournou's Ovens is the Stanford Court's award-winning restaurant, featuring contemporary cuisine with a Mediterranean flair. It serves three meals a day. There are little dining alcoves, private rooms, and a section by the 54-square-foot roasting ovens covered with Portuguese tiles. The other main area has conservatory-style windows overlooking the cable cars and city skyline. The wine cellar is remarkable, with more than 20,000 bottles.

The hotel has several meeting and reception rooms, and a 5,000-square-foot grand ballroom.

The Archbishops Mansion

1000 Fulton Street
San Francisco, CA 94117
415-563-7872

> *A romantic, historic home on Alamo Square*

Owners: Jonathan Shannon and Jeffrey Ross. **Manager:** Kathleen Austin. **Accommodations:** 15 rooms (all with private bath). **Rates:** $115–$285 single or double. **Included:** Continental breakfast. **Minimum stay:** 2 nights on weekends. **Payment:** Major credit cards. **Children:** Welcome. **Pets:** Not allowed. **Smoking:** Not allowed in public spaces.

If you want lodgings in San Francisco that remind you of home, don't stay at this inn unless you live in an opera set! The opulence of The Archbishops Mansion is best enjoyed by those who revel in the lavish, the lush, and the extravagant — all carried off with great taste and a sense of humor.

The inn is across the street from Alamo Square, a hillside park eight blocks from Golden Gate Park and six blocks from the Civic Center, Davies Symphony Hall, the Opera House, and the Museum of Modern Art. The Alamo Square area, its streets lined with lovely Victorians, has been designated a City Historic District, thanks in large part to the efforts of Jeffrey Ross and Jonathan Shannon. They have also worked to preserve other parts of the city. In 1980, they began the painstaking task of restoring their time-battered mansion.

The three-story home, built in 1904 as a residence for Archbishop Patrick Riordan, was based on Second Empire French styling, so the new owners gathered furnishings from around the world to reflect that period. When they were through, they had created a belle époque French château and, because it is so grand (and so close to the Opera House), they named the rooms after romantic 19th-century operas.

The rooms, all with impressive antiques or reproductions, are furnished with comfort and flair. The smallest is La Bohème, which has a partial canopy above a bed that is as elaborate as the tent of a fabled sheik. Romeo and Juliet is another elegant little room, with flowers and garlands.

Cosi Fan Tutti is a suite with antique lace, gilded molding, and French pine doors separating the bed and sitting areas. Don Giovanni is an expansive suite with cherubs carved in the four-poster bed. There's a dramatic fireplace (one of several in the inn), and in the bath a seven-headed shower.

La Traviata, on the main floor, features a sitting room with a glazed tile fireplace, head-high wainscoting, and a gilded chandelier hanging from a high, coffered ceiling. In the white tile bathroom are robes, a shower, a pedestal sink, and a lighted makeup mirror.

The owners have been careful to encourage a lively, friendly ambience. "I've been in historic inns where you're afraid to sit on the sofa," says Jonathan Shannon. "Antiques are wonderful, but I want people to be comfortable. I like to see them in jeans and shorts, being casual."

Breakfast is brought to your room in a picnic basket and includes juice, croissants, granola, and eggs, with tea or coffee. You may have breakfast in the formal dining room if you prefer.

The main hall is another example of the owners' sense of atmosphere. It has chairs inlaid with mother of pearl, a gilt-framed mirror from Abraham Lincoln's home in Illinois, and columns of polished redwood and mahogany. At one end is a grand piano — playable, but also computerized, so you may hear a tune without a piano player. A pair of 17th century Venetian figures guard the wide staircase; above the stairs is a large stained glass dome. Morning coffee and complimentary newspapers are offered in the front parlor, and wine in the evening.

The innkeepers will make restaurant reservations and help with tour ideas. The only drawback is the tiny parking area beside the house; it's less than convenient, as cars must stack up and then be moved.

The Fairmont Hotel

950 Mason Street
San Francisco, CA 94106
415-772-5000
800-527-4727
Fax 415-772-5086

A Nob Hill classic, overlooking the city and bay

General managers: John Unwin and John Ceriale. **Accommodations:** 535 rooms and 65 suites. **Rates:** $129–$285, $30 additional person, suites $450–$6,000. **Payment:** Major credit cards. **Children:** Under age 13 free. **Pets:** Not allowed. **Smoking:** Nonsmoking rooms available.

Opulence on the grand scale in a historic building at the top of one of the world's great cities — that's the Fairmont. When it opened in 1907 (after a delay caused by the 1906 earthquake and fire), the community was impressed by its resemblance to a European royal palace. It's still impressing locals and visitors alike with its ornate facade, magnificent lobby, fine accommodations, and panoramic views of the city and San Francisco Bay. The Fairmont, long known for its luxury and upper-income clientele, was used as the location of the television series *Hotel.* Television and film celebrities show up regularly, both as guests and performers.

The Fairmont has several restaurants. Off the lobby, the plush Squire features seafood and an extensive wine list. Masons is downstairs, as is Bella Voce, where you'll listen to operatic arias as you dine on pizza, pasta, and seafood. From Chinese food in the Polynesian-style Tonga to chocolate sundaes in the Sweet Corner, you can find just about anything your tastebuds yearn for within the hotel's walls. The Fairmont Crown, reached by a glass-enclosed elevator, is noted for its stunning views as well as its lavish buffets.

> **Guests were entertained in the darkly rich Venetian Room from 1947 until 1989, when Tony Bennett sang "I Left My Heart in San Francisco" for the last time in that room and the supper club closed. Now it's used for private banquets.**

If it's people-watching you want, just sit in the lobby for a while. Fascinating crowds come and go between the gold marble pillars that soar to an ornamented ceiling.

Ten of the suites overlook the rooftop garden and terrace, a green oasis of palm trees and flowers. There is no pool, but a fitness center with weight machines, sauna, whirlpool, steam room, and massage service is available.

The guest rooms feature simple, elegant furnishings. Down pillows, fine cotton sheets, a TV with a movie channel, and daily maid and turndown service are some of their luxuries. To assist corporate travelers, multiline modem phones are in each room. Voice mail and a business center are available.

The rooms in the main building vary, but in general they are larger and have more spacious baths and closets than those in the adjoining 23-story tower. The architecture of the tower, erected in 1963, is outlandishly inappropriate to the imposing original building, but there's no denying the beauty of the views it affords. Some suites feature balconies that overlook the garden or downtown to the Financial District.

The suites vary in decor. You may see a classical Roman theme with off-white colors and low tables made to resemble temple columns, or a more traditional look with dark woods and antique reproductions. For the ultimate in luxury, reserve the penthouse, probably the most expensive hotel suite in the nation. The eighth-floor, eight-room suite, reached by a private elevator, rents for $6,000 a night, which includes an around-the-clock butler, maid, and private limousine to and from the airport.

The Huntington Hotel

1075 California Street
San Francisco, CA 94108
415-474-5400
800-652-1539 in California
800-227-4683 in U.S.
Fax 415-474-6227

Luxury and elegance on Nob Hill

Managing director: Micarl T. Hill. **Accommodations:** 100 rooms and 40 suites. **Rates:** \$165–\$215 single, \$185–\$235 double, suites \$250–\$685. **Payment:** Major credit cards. **Children:** Welcome (infants free). **Pets:** Not allowed. **Smoking:** Allowed.

This dignified, twelve-story red brick hotel at the top of Nob Hill thrives on tradition and a reputation for excellence. Since it opened in 1924 as an apartment building, it has been owned by the same family. John Cope, president of the ownership company, is the great-grandson of the developer who bought the property the year it was built. Many members of the staff have been with the Huntington for years. Whether you're a repeat guest or a newcomer, you are greeted by name, and the concierge always calls to make sure you're settled in.

Off the gracious lobby is the hotel's dining room, the Big Four. It's named for the early San Francisco railroad tycoons Collis Huntington, Leland Stanford, Charles Crocker, and Mark Hopkins, and a collection of railroad memorabilia is on display This impressive room has dark woods, etched mirrors, and reflective walls. The menu, under the skilled direction of Gloria Ciccarone-Nehls, offers innovative American and Continental dishes, with seafood and game specials. The chef's spectacular chocolate creations give new meaning to dessert. Wines are California and French vintages. A pianist performs nightly in the Big Four's lounge.

Understated elegance, unobtrusive service, and assurance of privacy make this San Francisco landmark a romantic retreat and a favorite with a demanding clientele that includes many famous names.

The guest rooms and suites are all larger than average, a legacy from their former years as residential apartments. Each was individually decorated by Anthony Hail, Lee Radziwill, Elizabeth Bernhardt, and Charles Gruwell, using differing color schemes and furnishings that include a generous smattering of antiques and original art. Suites have refrigerators and wet bars, and some contain kitchenettes.

Every room has large windows that open to gorgeous views of San Francisco Bay, the city, or Huntington Park and stately Grace Cathedral. Accouterments include fluffy down cushions, hair dryers, plush bath towels and linen hand towels. Twice-daily housekeeping, overnight laundry service, valet parking, and your choice among three daily newspapers are some of the services provided. The Nob Hill Club fitness center, which guests may use, is one block away.

The hotel has several handsome meeting rooms suitable for board meetings and receptions. The concierge is on duty all day and will arrange for tours, theater and restaurant bookings, secretarial services, and babysitters. A Cadillac limousine will take you to the financial district and Union Square at no charge. And the cable car stops at the front door.

The Hungtington is a member of Small Luxury Hotels of the World and Preferred Hotels and Resorts.

The Majestic

1500 Sutter Street
San Francisco, CA 94109
415-441-1100
800-869-8966
Fax 415-673-7331

A restored landmark, the essence of old San Francisco

General manager: James O'Donnell. **Accommodations:** 50 rooms and 9 suites. **Rates:** \$115–\$205 single or double, \$15 additional person, midweek and group discounts. **Payment:** Major credit cards. **Children:** Welcome (no charge for use of a crib). **Pets:** Not allowed. **Smoking:** Nonsmoking rooms available.

San Francisco's turn-of-the-century golden era is brought to life at the Majestic, a beautifully restored five-story Edwardian structure. It's just outside the bustling downtown area, about six blocks from Union Square.

Entering the glass-paned double doors of the hotel takes you even farther from the modern rush and city noise. Wide stairs of green marble lead to a carpeted lobby where a chandelier with torch globes gives a warm glow to the antiques-filled room. A fire burns in the fireplace and Oriental vases hold sprays of golden lilies. Fringed lampshades and cushions, lace curtains at narrow windows, and glass-fronted bookshelves add atmosphere. To the left of the lobby are the Café Majestic and bar, the latter a clubby spot with a 19th-century mahogany bar from France.

Some of the guest rooms have four-poster canopy beds, boudoir chairs, and velvet or plush couches. It's easy to imagine yourself in an old San Francisco residence — an updated one, however, with TVs, clock radios, and direct-dial telephones. Several rooms have gas fireplaces. If you'd like to step into a long-gone era, you'll enjoy the charm of the Majestic. Soak in the clawfoot tub or sit at your desk in the bay window overlooking the trees and strollers on Sutter Street, and you might be a guest visiting in 1902, when the hotel was built. The Majestic has received state recognition for historic and architectural preservation.

The Café Majestic — actually a full-scale dining room with a pleasantly French ambience — is noted for its combination of classic San Francisco dishes with California nouvelle cuisine. Among the memorable desserts are orange crème brûlée and chocolate cake with jalapeño chilies.

Today's services include valet parking, limousine service to the financial district and Union Square, afternoon sherry in the library, and nightly turndown service. The concierge will arrange for restaurant reservations and wine country tours. During the off-season (November through March) the Majestic offers special packages at lower rates.

The Mansions

2220 Sacramento Street
San Francisco, CA 94115
415-929-9444
800-826-9398

A pair of mansions featuring luxurious style and a sense of fun

Owner: Robert C. Pritikin. **Accommodations:** 21 rooms. **Rates:** rooms $89–$159, $15 additional person, suites $169–$350. **Included:** Full breakfast. **Payment:** Major credit cards. **Children:** Welcome. **Pets:** Allowed. **Smoking:** Allowed.

Two long-time San Francisco hotels, side by side in a neighborhood of apartments, homes, and a medical center, form an unlikely lodging combination. The Mansion Hotel, a twin-towered Queen Anne structure, is known for its sense of fun and eclectic mixture of whimsy and Victoriana. The Hermitage House is a serene, urban refuge. Connected by a hallway, they are The Mansions.

With all its trappings, the hotel has a lighthearted atmosphere. Even the ghost seems to have a good time, concluding her evening concerts with a rousing march or ragtime tune while bubbles float to the ceiling. A magic show is presented nightly.

Robert Pritikin is a hotelier of boundless energy and many interests. He writes books *(Christ Was an Ad Man)*, collects sculpture (he has a major Benjamin Bufano collection), keeps a macaw in the hotel parlor, and plays the musical saw. A few of his original hotel's features are a "hauntress" named Claudia who plays the piano, a billiards room with a wall-size mural of pigs, caged white doves, and priceless Joseph Turner and Joshua Reynolds paintings.

One of the world's largest examples of stained glass stands in the dining room. The colorful mural, first created for a villa in Spain, is nine feet high and stretches the length of the room. Prix fixe dinners are served nightly.

The grand home was built in 1887 by a senator from Utah, Charles Chambers, who earned a fortune in silver. It's a historic landmark now, filled with museum-quality art and antiques. Accommodations, divided among three floors, are sumptuous, with four-poster beds, potted palms, and elaborately trimmed wardrobes. They have piped-in classical music, fresh flowers and candy, velvet quilts, and red carpets. The Lillie Coit Room, once a third-floor hideaway, has been combined with the DeYoung Room to form a small suite with windows that look out on the Golden Gate Bridge and Mount Tamalpais. Tom Thumb, on the second floor, is the smallest room, good for a single traveler or a cozy twosome. Breakfast is served in the country kitchen or brought to your room with the morning paper: cereal, fruit, crumpets, eggs, English sausage, and potatoes are on the wide-ranging menu.

The west wing (formerly Hermitage House) has a different

flavor. Laura Ashley fabrics grace most rooms with a French country decor. High coffered ceilings, mullioned windows, antiques, and flowers give this side of the hotel a European flavor. Most rooms have fireplaces. This building houses the Bufano Conference Center, the hotel's meeting space.

The Mark Hopkins Intercontinental

999 California Street
Number One Nob Hill
San Francisco, CA 94108
415-392-3434
800-327-0200
Fax 415-421-3302

A 1920s landmark on the crest of Nob Hill

General manager: Sandor Stangl. **Accommodations:** 361 rooms, 30 suites. **Rates:** \$180–\$275 single, \$200–\$305 double, suites \$375–\$1,775. **Payment:** Major credit cards. **Children:** Under 14 free in room with parents. **Pets:** Not allowed. **Smoking:** Nonsmoking rooms available.

In the devastating fire that followed the earthquake of 1906, the fabulous Mark Hopkins mansion at the top of Nob Hill burned to the ground. The more modest structure that followed was moved in 1925 by a mining engineer, George D. Smith, who then began building the luxury hotel that stands today.

The 19-story Mark Hopkins, a combination of French château and Spanish Renaissance architecture, has been a world-famed city landmark since it opened in 1926 and was proclaimed "perfect, flawless." Ownership has changed several times (in early 1989 it was acquired by a Japanese firm), but its traditional style and quality of service remain. A recent major renovation updated the tired lobby, restaurant, and all the guest rooms and suites, so the hotel is again a place of grandeur, with marble floors and Persian carpets in the light-filled lobby. Off the lobby is the Lower Bar, where cocktails, high tea, and light meals are served under a Tiffany-style skylight.

The Top of the Mark is obligatory on every San Francisco tourist's must-see list. As a result, the rooftop lounge is crammed every night with imbibers trying to glimpse the breathtaking views. Everyone is in a celebratory mood.

Because the hotel comprises a central tower and two wings, every room has a view of San Francisco Bay and the city skyline. Even the lowest rooms, on the second floor, overlook machinery-screening flower boxes to the city below. The public spaces are grand and gilded, befitting a hotel of such prestige. Only its neighbor, the Fairmont, vies with the Mark Hopkins for compelling views and an air of festivity.

In the Nob Hill Restaurant, Andre Zotoff prepares creative Continental cuisine. Among his specialties are sauteed escalope of foie gras with lentils, apple puree and olive oil and roast loin of lamb in a fresh herb coulis. The herbs come from what is probably the most expensive herb garden in the world: a little plot of land the hotel owns on nearby Mason Street, valued at $4,000 a square foot. The wine list includes labels from 34 out of 41 wine-producing states.

The guest rooms have been redone in a neoclassic style in gray or khaki and gold. The quilted chintz bedspreads, thick carpeting, and damask wall coverings were all designed for the hotel. The nightstands have tortuma tops made with crushed South American gourds in black resin. The televisions and mini-bars are encased in cherrywood armoires.

The best of the preferred accommodations are the corner terrace suites. Each features an enclosed solarium with a close-up of the hotel's elaborate architectural ornamentation and the spectacular panorama beyond. Each suite has three phones, a desk, and a white marble bath with pedestal sink, hair dryer, oversize towels, robes, and assorted toiletries.

The service at the Mark Hopkins is excellent, and the presence of groups (the hotel has a conference capacity of 750) does not seem to detract from it for the individual traveler. The concierge will handle most requests. An additional level of service, Guest Relations, provides for special needs — language interpreters, VIPs, group assistance. Several seasonal and honeymoon packages and special rates are offered.

The Pan Pacific Hotel

500 Post Street
San Francisco, CA 94102
415-771-8600
800-533-6465
Fax: 415-398-0267

A contemporary hotel of cool elegance

Managing director: Donald Dickhens. **Accommodations:** 311 rooms, 19 suites. **Rates:** $185–

$310 single or double, suites $335–$1,500. **Payment:** Major credit cards. **Children:** Under 18 free in room with parents. **Pets:** Allowed by arrangement. **Smoking:** 8 nonsmoking floors.

The Pan Pacific rises 21 stories above the corner of Post and Mason streets, a block west of Union Square. Famed for its elegant, contemporary style, the hotel was designed by architect John Portman, who is known for introducing the open atrium to large convention hotels. This is a smaller, more opulent version of the Portman trademark.

The hotel is noted for its impeccable service, a continuation of the tradition established by the Portman Hotel when it opened in 1987.

You are met in the porte-cochere by a white-gloved attendant who welcomes you warmly and whisks your car away. Inside, in the third-floor lobby, a 17-story glass and brass atrium soars above a dazzling array of lights and an Elbert Weinberg sculpture, *Joie de Danse.*

At one side of the large, open lobby is an attractive lounge with Oriental carpets and potted palms. Near it the Pacific Grill menu offers Asian-influenced California cuisine. Room service features dishes on the restaurant's menu.

The floor below the entry level has an executive conference center, the only one like it in downtown San Francisco, containing four conference suites and a dining room. There's a large ballroom on the second floor.

Each floor has a valet who is responsible for the comfort of the guests on that floor. He unpacks luggage, delivers newspapers, presses clothing, shines shoes, and tidies your room every time you leave. He knows when the room is empty because he's placed a broom bristle against the door; if it has fallen, he'll come in to empty ashtrays, straighten the bed, and restock your refrigerator.

The guest rooms include 16 Pacific Suites and three specialty suites: the Penthouse, the Olympic, and the California. The Penthouse occupies 3,000 square feet on the 21st floor. It has two bedrooms with canopy beds, two baths (and a huge whirlpool tub), powder room, living room with working fireplace, dining room, study, access to an open-air terrace, valet's room, and pantry.

The rooms have television, phones with call waiting and voice mail features, Swiss milled soaps, and terry robes in lavish bathrooms of Portuguese marble (though counter space is lacking). Decorated in gray on gray with accents of pale mauve, the rooms are reminders of the sea fog that swirls through this coastal city's streets.

There are no fitness facilities, but you can arrange to use nearby clubs, and the valet will deliver an exercise bicycle to your room if you ask. The check-out system is flexible, and the hotel will provide airport and in-city transportation in a Rolls Royce. Semicircular windows, lavish lighting, Oriental art objects, and an extensive use of rosewood and glass create intense visual interest in this unusual hotel. They don't soften the cool, corporate tone, however. If you like a clean-edged, high-tech look, you will enjoy the Pan Pacific.

Prescott Hotel

545 Post Street
San Francisco, CA 94102
415-563-0303
800-283-7322

A sophisticated hotel with an urban mood

Manager: Patrick Sampson. **Accommodations:** 167 rooms, 34 suites. **Rates:** Rooms \$155–\$175, suites \$165–\$225, penthouse $525. **Included:** Continental breakfast on Club Level. **Payment:** Major credit cards. **Children:** Welcome. **Pets:** Not allowed. **Smoking:** Nonsmoking rooms available.

Here's another boutique hotel with the winning Kimco Group combination: small but attractive rooms, reasonable rates, and a top-quality restaurant. Curved copper awnings mark the entrance to the hotel, which is close to Union Square. Inside you'll find a quiet sitting area with couches and wingback chairs in the lobby, and curving staircases leading to the mezzanine's meeting rooms and guest rooms above.

When the hotel opened in 1990, Postrio earned immediate raves. Lavish bouquets, Robert Rauschenberg paintings, and hand-blown light fixtures hung with copper spirals create a bright and whimsical setting for the outstanding California cuisine.

The smartly appointed rooms, more elaborate than the other Kimco hotels, have hair dryers and robes in the modern, well-lighted baths. The compact suites make efficient use of the space and are more like urban apartments than hotel lodgings. On the Club Level (the fourth through seventh floors), guests have their own concierge and lounge where appetizers — catered by the Prescott's restaurant, Postrio — are served in the evenings. A complimentary buffet breakfast is provided, along with the morning papers.

Pizza is a specialty at Postrio, but you won't go wrong ordering anything on the menu. Reserve a dinner table when you make your room reservation; Postrio is usually booked weeks in advance, but a few tables are held for hotel guests.

The Red Victorian

1665 Haight Street
San Francisco, CA 94117
415-864-1978

An offbeat inn in the heart of the Haight

Owner: Sami Sunchild. **Manager:** Sue Stone. **Accommodations:** 18 rooms (4 with private bath, others share 4 baths).

Rates: $55–$130 double in winter, $65–$135 double in summer; $5 less for single, $15 more for additional person). **Included:** Expanded Continental breakfast. **Minimum stay:** 2 nights on weekends. **Payment:** Major credit cards. **Children:** Welcome. **Pets:** Not allowed. **Smoking:** Not allowed.

Exuberant colors, good-humored hospitality, and touches of whimsy characterize this delightful turn-of-the-century hotel in the famous Haight-Ashbury district. Sami Sunchild's paintings, which incorporate affirmations and positive thoughts, hang in the halls and guest rooms and are for sale. You'll see them on display in the art gallery/breakfast room on the ground floor, next to the Global Village Center, where products that help environmental causes are sold.

It wouldn't be Haight-Ashbury without the Flower Child Room and the Peace Room, reminiscent of the district's renown in the 1960s.

The hotel rooms range from modest to luxurious and are filled with creative artworks and furnishings. The Rainbow Room, where bay windows overlook Haight Street, has a bed swathed in netting of rainbow hues; the Conservatory is like a garden with its fresh greenery and white wicker. The Peacock Suite has stained glass windows, a moon window between the tub and sitting room, and a king-size bed with an exotic canopy. Others include the Japanese Tea Garden Room, the Sunshine Room, the Butterfly Room, the Redwood Forest Room, and the Skylight Room. Each room has a washbasin. The shared baths are artistic ventures of their own, with walls of mirrors, an aquarium, skylights, and colored lights.

In tune with the times, the Red Victorian has Macintosh computers available for rent. There's a café where light fare is available. German, French, and Spanish are spoken in this European-style, friendly hotel just two blocks from Golden Gate Park.

The Ritz-Carlton, San Francisco

600 Stockton Street
San Francisco, CA 94108
415-296-7465
800-241-3333
Fax 415-291-0147

A luxury hotel in a historic building

Hotel manager: Mark DeCocinis. **Accommodations:** 292 rooms, 44 suites. **Rates:** Rooms \$205–\$335, suites \$315–\$3,500. **Payment:** All major cards. **Children:** Welcome. **Pets:** Not allowed. **Smoking:** Nonsmoking rooms available.

One of the city's best examples of Neoclassical architecture has joined the Ritz-Carlton group of luxury hotels. Built in 1909 for the Metropolitan Life Insurance Company, the stately structure on Nob Hill was restored and opened in 1991. Like other Ritz-Carlton hotels, it offers sumptuous accommodations in a conservative setting. The walls are adorned with museum-quality 18th- and 19th-century paintings.

However, this being San Francisco, there's a lighthearted quality that keeps pretension at bay. Heavy, dark woods have been kept to a minimum.

The hotel bustles with activity, as many functions take place here, but the halls, padded in gray damask, are quiet. Guest rooms are handsomely furnished in classic residential style. The marble bathrooms are lovely, down to the orchids on the counter, though you may notice minor flaws such as no shelf in the oversize shower and a single hook on the door.

Rooms and suites on the eighth and ninth floors are designated the Ritz-Carlton Club. Guests have the use of a concierge, a private lounge with subdued atmosphere, and complimentary snacks and cocktails. All rooms have many useful features: remote control TVs (VCRs and a video library are available), stocked honor bars, plush robes, clock radios, safes. Some have bay views, but if you prefer a quiet room, follow the example of frequent visitors and request one on the courtyard side.

One of the most appealing places in the imposing hotel is its sunny outdoor terrace, with a fountain and umbrella tables. You may also dine in the intimate, elegant Dining Room, where Continental cuisine is served and the wine list is lengthy.

Services offered by the multilingual staff include twice-daily maid service, valet parking, a 24-hour concierge, child care, and newspaper delivery. Disposable sweatsuits and swimwear are available in the fitness center, where you'll find a swimming pool, whirlpool, sauna, and weight machines.

The Sherman House

2160 Green Street
San Francisco, CA 94123
415-563-3600
800-424-5777
Fax 415-563-1882

An elegant mansion with views of the bay

Owners: Manouchehr and Vesta Mobedshahi. **General manager:** Gerard Lespinette. **Accom-**

modations: 8 rooms, 6 suites. **Rates:** $235–$375, suites $550–$750. **Payment:** Major credit cards. **Children:** Welcome. **Pets:** Not allowed. **Smoking:** Allowed in designated areas.

This intimate, exclusive hostelry in one of the city's most fashionable districts is an 1876 French-Italianate mansion. Once the home of Leander Sherman, founder of the Sherman Clay Music Company, it now caters to a discriminating clientele. The rich and famous find it a haven, as do those looking for service far above the ordinary.

> **In the Music Room, where finches trill in a bird cage that is a miniature of Château Chenonceau in France, it's easy to imagine Paderewski playing the grand piano in the corner, as he did in years past.**

Manou Mobedshahi, an Iranian economist turned San Francisco entrepreneur, bought the historic landmark in 1981 and with his wife, an art preservationist, carefully restored the house and its formal gardens.

Wine is served in the Music Room in the afternoon, and occasionally there's a wine tasting or a music recital. The gallery above the Music Room provides a pleasant sitting room, with cushioned seats at five bay windows, a fireplace, and French provincial armchairs and sofa.

The guest rooms are in the main house and former carriage house. One of the suites has its own garden with a deck and arbor. Furnishings in all rooms are antique or custom-made. Hand-loomed carpets, Coromandel screens, Belgian tapestries, marble fireplaces, brass fixtures, crystal chandeliers, and original art fill the interiors, planned by the late great designer, William Gaylord. Most rooms adhere to a French Second Empire theme, popular in Leander Sherman's day, with a few in a Biedermeier or Jacobean motif. All have a sense of solidity and permanence.

Some rooms have sweeping views of the bay, Golden Gate Bridge, and Alcatraz. The Garden Suite, set among the multilevel lawns and cobblestoned pathways, is the largest. It has a spacious living room with freestanding fireplace, lattice walls, and wide windows overlooking shrubs and flowers, a gazebo, and a pond. Hollow core rattan wraps the four-poster bed. The suites upstairs in the carriage house are equally light and bright. The top-floor suite features a sunken living room with French doors to a balcony overlooking the bay.

Canopied and draped beds have down comforters. Each elegant black marble bath has a small TV and second telephone, thick white towels and robes, and imported toiletries.

Three meals a day are served in the intimate dining room, which is open to the public for special-occasion dining. French cuisine with California accents is served, under the direction of Maria Helm.

Needless to say, the service and attention to detail at this hotel are impeccable. Whether it's room service at any hour, immediate shoe repairs, secretarial services, a tour of the Napa Valley, or a ride to the airport in a vintage automobile, Sherman House will oblige. This is a lodging of polish, privilege, and ease.

The Villa Florence Hotel

225 Powell Street
San Francisco, CA 94102
415-397-7700
800-243-5700
Fax 415-397-1006

A boutique hotel with an Italian flavor

General manager: Jim Dowling. **Accommodations:** 177 rooms, 36 suites. **Rates:** $119 single or double, suites $139–$189. **Payment:** Major credit cards. **Children:** Welcome. **Pets:** Not allowed. **Smoking:** Nonsmoking rooms available.

The Villa Florence is one of the city's distinctive small hotels, offering stylish lodgings in a historic building to cost-conscious travelers. Bill Kimpton helped to lead the way for these boutique hotels when he saw a niche to be filled and began renovating a few of San Francisco's rundown but usable structures.

Formerly the Manx Hotel, built in 1916, the Villa Florence was remodeled with an Italian Renaissance theme and opened as one of the Kimco Hotels in 1986. In the busy lobby are a marble fireplace and a gauzy mural depicting 16th-century Florence. Indirect lighting on the marble columns highlights ceiling detail.

Separated from the lobby by etched glass walls is Kuleto's Restaurant, which is known for its Italian food with a California perspective. Baked goods and desserts such as pumpkin tarts and rich chocolate decadence on raspberry sauce are made daily on the premises.

Highlights in Kuleto's are the pastas, innovative salads, and grilled fish and meats. A specialty is the excellent antipasto bar.

The restaurant's ambience combines an aura of old San Francisco with Italian vitality. Dark wood, warm lighting, and strings of peppers, herbs, sausages, and garlic hanging above the bar add to the atmosphere. Ficus trees grow to the ceiling under three stained glass skylights in the light and airy dining section. The guest rooms, which include junior and deluxe suites, have a pastel decor, with flowered fabrics and pale furniture. All include honor bars, concealed televisions, direct-dial phones with long cords, and soundproofed walls and windows. Desk space is on the skimpy side — adequate for writing postcards.

Some bathrooms are very small. Much roomier are those in the junior suites, which also have sitting areas, though not divided rooms. The deluxe suites have two rooms.

The hotel offers morning and evening room service, complimentary limousine service to the financial district, valet service, and same-day laundry service. There are three meeting rooms and a full range of audiovisual equipment. Room keys are coded for security.

Villa Florence is just south of Union Square on the main cable car line, not a poor location but highly touristed, with many trinket shops and hordes of people. With new developments such as the snazzy shops of San Francisco Centre, the tenor of the neighborhood may change.

Victorian Inn on the Park

301 Lyon Street
San Francisco, CA 94117
415-931-1830
800-435-1967
Fax 415-931-1830

A Queen Anne mansion overlooking Golden Gate Park

Innkeepers: Lisa and William Benau. **Accommodations:** 12 rooms and suites (all with private bath). **Rates:** $94–$154, suites $154–$300. **Included:** Expanded Continental breakfast. **Minimum stay:** 2 nights on weekends. **Payment:** Major credit cards. **Children:** Welcome. **Pets:** Not allowed. **Smoking:** Allowed in guest rooms and parlor.

Directly across the street from the Panhandle of Golden Gate Park, in an area of noble Victorian homes, the hospitable Benaus welcome guests to this Queen Anne mansion. It was built in 1897 for Thomas Jefferson Clunie, a prominent lawyer and legislator, who piled on the gingerbread and fretwork and added an open belvedere tower. Only two homes in the city still boast such towers. After the Clunies were gone, the gray brick house underwent a steady stream of changes, going from private residence to a haven for '60s flower children and rock bands, to a rebirthing center. Finally, in the early 1980s, Shirley and Paul Weber took over and began a handsome restoration. Shirley's daughter and son-in-law now run the inn with casual, good-humored style.

Marble steps lead to a front door with stained glass side panels and a foyer beautifully paneled in mahogany. Up the carpeted stairs, past 19th-century opera posters, you come to six guest rooms on the second floor and four on the third. Each bedroom has special characteristics — a brass bed, a freestanding mirror, a fireplace, a sunken tub. Each has a phone, and television and a fax machine are available upon request.

A cozy fire burns in the parlor's white tile fireplace on foggy afternoons, and a game table with a backgammon set stands by the curved windows. A tapestry-covered fainting couch, baskets of flowers, fringed lamps, and a red settee make this a period piece of comfort and charm.

The tower room has French doors that open onto the belvedere porch overlooking the bay and eucalyptus trees of the Panhandle. In the pleasant little room you can lie in the bathtub and watch flames flicker in the marble fireplace, their reflections dancing in stained glass. The tower room connects with the larger one next to it to form a suite.

The rooms on the garden level, below the main floor, face the sidewalk and passersby through curved, lace-curtained windows. One large room, which has a brass bed and a working fireplace of ceramic tile, combines both antique and contemporary furnishings.

The inn's location is ideal for jogging — it's both flat and scenic. You can run without interruption through the Panhandle and Golden Gate Park, all the way to the ocean.

After your morning jog, you'll be served breakfast in the bay-windowed dining room — baskets of scones, croissants, and freshly baked poppyseed or strawberry bread, along with juice and platters of fresh fruits and cheeses. It all comes with full pots of coffee or tea and the morning paper.

The innkeepers know the local restaurants and will steer you in the right direction for sightseeing, dining, and recreation. Limited parking is available. Two bus lines run within one or two blocks, leading downtown or to the Marina district, near the Golden Gate Bridge.

The White Swan Inn

845 Bush Street
San Francisco, CA 94108
415-775-1755

An English garden theme in a city hotel

General manager: Rich Revaz. **Accommodations:** 23 rooms, 3 suites. **Rates:** \$145–\$160 single or double, \$15 additional person, suites \$195–\$250. **Included:** Full breakfast. **Payment:** Major credit cards. **Children:** Under age 5 free in room with parent. **Pets:** Not allowed. **Smoking:** Not allowed in public areas.

Once this four-story hotel with a marble facade and bay windows was the Hotel Louise, built after the great earthquake of 1906. Renovated in 1986, it now provides a tranquil downtown retreat from the busy city. This is one of the more expensive of the Four Sisters inns and has the most amenities.

Beveled glass doors open to a large reception area with granite floors, an antique carousel horse, and English art. Downstairs is the guests' lounge where breakfast and a full afternoon tea, with scones, cheeses, fondues or other hearty snacks, are served. In the parlor and library are inviting chairs before the granite fireplace, shelves full of books, and a decorative freestanding globe — a peaceful setting with a manor house motif.

> **Parquet floors and dark green woodwork provide contrast to an alcove and garden court that reflect the inn's English garden theme.**

The terrace outside, shaded by an avocado tree, is next to a conference room that can accommodate up to thirty people. The White Swan also does catering upon request. A few of the hotel's special services are one-day laundry and pressing, complimentary cookies and fruit all day, business equipment, and complimentary wine and roses in every guest room.

All rooms have wet bars, a television, fireplaces, and phones. The hotel's two-bedroom suite has two fireplaces. Four-posters, antique reproductions, and books in the rooms lend a residential ambience. The baths are modern, with basins set in granite counters, but contain some original tiles.

Valet parking is available, and the front desk provides concierge services, booking restaurant tables and tickets to events. Several fine restaurants are close to the hotel. Recommended are Fleur de Lys, L'Epic, and Café Mozart. Kuleto's and Trattoria Contadina serve excellent Northern Italian cuisine, and Fratelli's is noted for its dishes of Southern Italy.

SAN GREGORIO

Pigeon Point Lighthouse Hostel

Pescadero, CA 94060
415-879-0633

> *An inexpensive place to stay in a spectacular setting*

Manager: Janice Keen. **Accommodations:** 53 beds. **Rates:** $9 per person for American Youth Hostel members, $12 non-members, $5 additional for private room. **Maximum stay:** 3 nights. **Payment:** MasterCard, Visa. **Children:** Half-price in room with parents. **Pets:** Not allowed. **Smoking:** Not allowed.

Between San Francisco and Monterey Bay on scenic Highway 1, where the rocky shore curves into the sea, the lighthouse at Pigeon Point stands at the edge of a steep, rugged cliff. Below it, breakers crash and foam against the rocks, and seals bob in the surf. American Youth Hostels operates this and other hostels in California, which are open to travelers of all ages.

The accommodations are next to the lighthouse, in four low white bungalows surrounded by geraniums and ice plant. Each building has a carpeted living room, kitchen, two bathrooms, a couple's bedroom, and dorm rooms with six bunk beds each. Furnishings are basic: plain pine beds with covered mattresses, lamps, closets, and carpeting. But the rooms and baths, which have showers, are well maintained.

Bring your own food to cook in the worn but clean kitchen. The view from the window over the sink is a knockout, placing this hostel far above the simple category of no-frills, low-cost lodgings.

At the edge of the bluff is the former Fog Signal Building, now a recreation and meeting room with table tennis, a piano, battered couches, and a woodstove. Here you'll find brochures on area attractions and other hostels. There's also an outdoor hot tub that can be rented in the evening. A boardwalk and steps extend over the cliff to a fenced viewpoint where you gain a closer look at the Pacific panorama.

At Año Nuevo State Reserve, six miles south of Pigeon Point, you can see elephant seals. This is the only mainland breeding colony of the 3,500-pound mammals.

When you stay at a hostel, you're assigned an easy cleanup chore (vacuuming, dusting, etc.) and you bring your own bedding and food. Alcohol is not allowed. The hostel is closed from 9:30 A.M. to 4:30 P.M.; check in after 4:30 in the afternoon.

This is open coastal country, and there are no facilities or shops nearby, though in Pescadero, five miles north and two miles inland, there are gift and clothing stores, a gas station, and a restaurant, Duarte's, that serves lunch.

Pigeon Point Lighthouse, 115 feet tall, has been guiding mariners since 1872. It's open for tours on Sundays, May through August. A small donation is requested.

Watch for migrating whales and explore tide pools along the coast, or you can drive six miles inland to Butano State Park, where you may hike through redwood forests.

SAN JOSE

Hotel De Anza

233 W. Santa Clara Street
San Jose, CA 95113
408-286-1000
800-843-3700
Fax 408-286-0500

An updated historic hotel in Silicon Valley

General manager: Judy Young. **Accommodations:** 94 rooms, 6 suites. **Rates:** $120–$250 single or double, $15 additional person (special packages available), penthouse suite $750. **Payment:** Major credit cards. **Children:** Under age 18 free with parent. **Pets:** Not allowed. **Smoking:** Allowed on 1 floor only.

Originally opened in the 1930s, this art deco landmark fell into decay. Restored and reopened in 1990, the De Anza again offers fine accommodations with a sophisticated flavor. This architectural classic, a few blocks from the Convention Center, the Center for the Performing Arts, and the Civic Arena, is a part of San Jose's revitalized downtown area.

You won't find resort amenities here — there's no pool, the health club is tiny and seldom used, and the views are mainly of freeways and buildings. But the distinctive character and in-room conveniences make up for any deficiencies. In keeping with its Silicon Valley location, state-of-the-art technology is provided. Each room has two TVs, a VCR (movies are complimentary), three phones, a two-line desk phone and fax, and voice mail message service. Other services include the use of a computer, a portable cellular phone, a video camera, and a beeper and pager.

Business is the mainstay on weekdays, but romance takes over on weekends at the De Anza. With the Remember the Romance package, you'll receive champagne, a red rose, dinner for two at La Pastaia, chocolates, a night in a standard room or suite, and a generous breakfast.

Meeting more leisurely needs are honor bars, ice machines on every floor, terrycloth robes, turndown service, and an unusual offering called Raid Our Pantry. Your room key opens a fully stocked bar on the second floor where you can help yourself to drinks and snacks (salads, fruits, muffins) at any time. Most of the rooms are unusually large for a city hotel and have king-size beds. In a small suite you'll find a foyer with wet bar, a cozy sitting area with puffy cushions on the couch, and a green granite and tile bath with a whirlpool tub. Most elaborate is the penthouse suite. Furnished in an Egyptian theme and featuring two rooftop patios, it has a black tile fireplace, a glass-topped bar, and a luxurious bathroom.

Off the lobby on the main floor are La Pastaia, a restaurant noted for its Italian food, and the Hedley Club lounge. The lounge, named for an architect who was influential in South Bay building design, is an inviting spot to enjoy cocktails and listen to opera on Sundays. The Hedley Club's painted ceiling is one of the few pieces remaining from the original hotel.

The De Anza has several meeting rooms and an enclosed outdoor patio, the Patio Court Terrace.

SANTA ROSA

The Gables

4257 Petaluma Hill Road
Santa Rosa, CA 95404
707-585-7777

A Victorian country mansion

Innkeepers: Michael and Judy Ogne. **Accommodations:** 6 rooms and cottage (all with private bath). **Rates:** $95–$135 single or double; cottage $175. **Included:** Full breakfast. **Minimum stay:** 2 nights on weekends. **Payment:** Major credit cards. **Children:** Welcome. **Pets:** Not allowed. **Smoking:** Not allowed.

In 1877 William and Mary Jane Roberts built one of the most interesting homes in Sonoma County — a Gothic Revival mansion with 15 gables above keyhole-shaped windows. Inside there are 12-foot ceilings, marble fireplaces, and a spiral staircase of mahogany.

The Roberts' home is now a bed-and-breakfast, a graceful combination of formal elegance and country comforts. It's only 3½ miles from downtown Santa Rosa, but with wooded acreage, a 150-year-old barn, a creek, and chickens providing breakfast eggs, its atmosphere is one of rural tranquility.

Leaving the parlor, where tea is served in the afternoon, you climb the curved staircase to reach the spacious guest rooms. They have antique furnishings, brass beds with down comforters, and literary classics to read in bed or by the windows that overlook the countryside. No two rooms are alike, and there's a gable at every angle. Sunrise is filled with light from bay windows; Sunset has a view of the the hills and lights of Sebastopol in the distance, and on the south overlooks the pasture.

In the dining room, a fire burns on cool mornings while guests enjoy a breakfast that varies daily — it might include apricot cobbler with cream or a frittata, as well as coffee cake, muffins, and fruit.

Meadow, crisp in blue and white, is furnished in bird's-eye maple. Garden View is a favorite for its flowery decor, clawfoot tub in an arched alcove, and sunset view. The newest and most luxurious room is the Parlor Suite. It has a king-size four-poster, an Italian marble fireplace, and a clawfoot tub.

Behind the main house is a separate, romantic cottage with a roomy living room, a woodstove, a wet bar, and a Jacuzzi for two. In this trim little home, built in the 1850s, the Robertses raised seven children and worked to build their estate. Now completely restored, it's a cozy spot for a honeymoon or a small family. It has a loft with just enough space for a queen-size bed and a trunk. The loft has a pitched ceiling, so the only place you can stand upright is in the center of the room.

Michael and Judy are gracious innkeepers, happy to make suggestions for dining and sightseeing. They'll direct you to award-winning wineries, antiques shops, the Luther Burbank gardens, and the coast. Recommended restaurants in Santa Rosa include La Gare, Mixx, and John Ash & Co.

If you'd like to take a cup of coffee to the inn's back deck and join the snoozing cats, you're welcome to do so. You'll have a view of the rose garden, lilacs, grapevines, the weathered barn, and the old outhouse, now covered with roses.

Vintners Inn

4350 Barnes Road
Santa Rosa, CA 95401
707-575-7350
800-421-2584 in California
Fax 707-575-1426

A Mediterranean village in California wine country

General manager: Cindy Young. **Accommodations:** 44 rooms. **Rates:** $118–$195 single or double, $10 additional person. **Included:** Expanded Continental breakfast. **Minimum stay:** 2 nights on weekends, mid-March to November. **Payment:** Major credit cards. **Children:** Under 6 free in room with parents. **Pets:** Not allowed. **Smoking:** Not allowed in dining room.

Santa Rosa is a sprawling town 60 miles from San Francisco, between the vineyards of Sonoma on the south and Alexander Valley on the north. Just north of town and adjacent to Highway 101, Vintners Inn stands in the center of 45 acres of pinot blanc, French colombard, and sauvignon blanc grapes. Some of the vinifera grapes are sold to local wineries, while some are bottled under the inn's own label.

Like a luxury complex transplanted from the south of France, the country inn is composed of stucco buildings centered around lawns and a fountained courtyard. Red tile roofs, arched doorways and windows, and wrought-iron railings add to the Mediterranean theme. Because the owners want an authentic village atmosphere, there are no swimming pools or tennis courts. However, nearby country clubs and health clubs are accessible to guests. The rooms, divided among three two-story buildings, are furnished with European antiques. They all have air conditioning and French doors that open to a patio or balcony. In a typical mid-range room, you will find wingback chairs by tall windows overlooking the landscaped grounds, an armoire concealing a television set, phones, pine nightstands, and a desk. The well-lighted bath has an oversize tub and shower. Five junior suites are larger and have wet bars, refrigerators, and fireplaces.

John Ash is a talented, award-winning chef who works culinary magic with fresh local produce, the bounty of regional ranches and vineyards, and herbs grown just outside the window.

Beer and wine will be delivered to your room upon request; beverages are also available in the library. The library is a comfortable place to relax. Across the lobby is the breakfast room, where croissants and occasionally waffles are served. In the lobby itself, sun streams through high windows to light walls and tiled floors, creating a welcoming entrance.

Next to the inn is John Ash & Company, a restaurant that is one of the best reasons for lodging at Vintners Inn. An after-dinner stroll among the vineyards, a soak in the whirlpool tub by the sun deck, and you may be ready for a book or movie from the library. VCRs are available for a $6 rental fee; there's no charge for videotapes.

SARATOGA

The Inn at Saratoga

20645 Fourth Street
Saratoga, CA 95070
408-867-5020
800-543-5020 in California
800-338-5020 in U.S.
Fax 408-741-0981

A contemporary inn in the Santa Cruz Mountains

Manager: Jack Hickling. **Accommodations:** 39 rooms, 7 suites. **Rates:** $145–$245 single or double, suites $295–$495.

Included: Continental breakfast. **Payment:** Major credit cards. **Children:** Welcome. **Pets:** Not allowed. **Smoking:** Allowed.

Saratoga is a special place. A hidden village tucked away among the redwoods on a hillside south of San Jose, Santa Clara, and Silicon Valley, Saratoga offers a retreat from high tech, an escape from high rise.

This historic resort area in the Santa Cruz Mountains first began to lure visitors in the 1860s because the waters of its hot springs were said to be as therapeutic as those in Saratoga, New York. For nearly fifty years the springs (long since abandoned) attracted city-weary Bay Area residents for a few days of relaxation and rejuvenation.

In this shady spot you feel miles from anything remotely resembling a city. Yet you're just a few steps from Saratoga's main street, Big Basin Way, which is lined with excellent restaurants, chic boutiques, and galleries.

Today, Saratoga has become a fashionable dining spot, with an array of award-winning restaurants, and it's a good base for exploring some of California's most interesting wineries. Outdoor enthusiasts enjoy Big Basin Redwoods State Park and its miles of hiking trails. Via Montalvo and Hakone Gardens invite visitors to stroll their manicured pathways.

When the Inn at Saratoga opened on the site of the old Toll Gate in 1987, it fit in well with this relaxing environment. Intended as a retreat for the executives of Silicon Valley, the inn offers quiet, privacy, proximity to fine dining, and rooms appointed to meet the needs of business travelers.

Nestled in a glen overlooking Saratoga Creek, the inn is surrounded by elm, sycamore, and eucalyptus trees and colorful gardens, giving it a sense of seclusion.

All the guest rooms are spacious, with separate sitting areas, balconies, and views of Saratoga Creek and the gardens. The appointments include two phones, robes, double sinks, hair dryers, cable television, and honor bars.

The suites serve as midweek meeting sites for businesspeople as well as romantic weekend retreats. These elegant two- and three-room arrangements have separate living rooms with a wet bar, refrigerator, and a television with VCR. The bathrooms are large, with double whirlpool baths and European towel warmers. Two of the suites, named for sisters Olivia de Havilland and Joan Fontaine, include formal dining rooms that can accommodate up to six people for private dining.

The Inn at Saratoga places a premium on personal service. A light breakfast is served in the lobby. Tea, complimentary wine, and hors d'oeuvres are also set out there every evening. The newspaper is delivered to your room, and the inn offers nightly turndown service. Secretarial and valet services are available.

SAUSALITO

Casa Madrona Hotel

801 Brideway
Sausalito, CA 94965
415-332-0502
800-288-0502
Fax 415-332-2527

A romantic inn with a bay view

Proprietor: John Mays. **Accommodations:** 35 rooms (all with private bath). **Rates:** $105–$225 single or double, $10 additional person. **Included:** Continental breakfast. **Minimum**

stay: 2 nights on weekends. **Payment:** Major credit cards. **Children:** Welcome **Pets:** Not allowed. **Smoking:** Not allowed in restaurant.

Few inns are as romantic in atmosphere and style as the lovely Casa Madrona. Terraced on a hillside above the chic resort town of Sausalito, just across the Golden Gate Bridge from San Francisco, the hotel offers comfortable accommodations, excellent food, and superb views. Every room has a view, sometimes breathtaking, of the harbor, San Francisco Bay, and the city, or of the bridge and headlands. Brick paths and stairs separate the rooms (there are elevators, too) winding up the hill to a Victorian mansion, the oldest building in Sausalito.

During the day you can watch the boats come and go over the moody bay waters; at night the lights of the city sparkle against the horizon or are diffused by drifting fog.

Built in 1885 by William Barrett, a wealthy San Franciscan, the Italianate villa later became a boarding house, an inn, a '50s crash pad, and a fine country inn and restaurant. In the late 1970s, the now-historic landmark was purchased by John Mays, a lawyer with a vision. He renovated and expanded on the property, creating an exceptional hotel.

The retreats range from a Parisian artist's loft, complete with easel, paints, and brushes, to a tribute to Hollywood, which has a harbor view from the elevated canopy bed, epic movie prints, a neon flamingo, and classic films.

Kathmandu is a regal room of paisley fabrics, huge cushions, and alcoves. It has a fireplace, a deck, and tub for two. A 19th-century English merchant would feel at home in Lord Ashley's Lookout, where he could keep an eye on the ships in the harbor from this oak- and brass-filled room.

In the gardenlike Renoir Room, an inviting window seat is ideal for gazing at the sails in the bay below. Summer House, with its wicker furniture, white oak walls, high bed, and array of books, is reminiscent of a New England vacation home.

Cottages with kitchenettes are Calico Cottage, cozy with a rocking chair by the fireplace; English Gate House, which has two bedrooms and a sun porch; and La Tonnelle, a little hideaway with a panoramic view. It has a tiled tub for two and a garden deck.

In the main house, rooms have period decor, with brass beds, flowered quilts, greenery, and wicker furniture. Perhaps most romantic is the soft blue Belle Vista Suite, two rooms divided by a partition. It has a tub for two near a window overlooking Angel Island and the San Francisco skyline.

In the hillside restaurant, you may eat indoors or on a deck with retractable glass walls and roof. A buffet breakfast of fruit, cheese, scones, and juice is served here.

Dinner specialties are rack of lamb with roasted garlic glaze and minted gremoulata, striped sea bass with citrus, gravlax with spicy cucumber, and New York steak with caramelized onions.

Oyama Wildflower Barge

B-61, Issaquah Dock
Sausalito, CA 94965
415-332-2270

A floating home with a view of the bay

Owner: Bill Jones. **Accommodations:** 2 rooms. **Rates:** \$50–\$75 single, \$75–\$110 double. **Payment:** No credit cards. **Children:** Not appropriate. **Pets:** Not allowed. **Smoking:** Allowed on deck only.

Along the waterfront of the picturesque village of Sausalito, houseboat dwellers have moored their floating homes for decades. Until 1971, when the county ordered them brought up to code, many were primitively outfitted health hazards at makeshift docks — not without an eccentric charm, but a growing problem.

Now that has changed. The Bohemian lifestyle is gone, for the most part, and money has moved in, bringing its own eccentricities. One houseboat (now they're called floating homes) looks like a Moorish fantasy; another has a rooftop heliport.

In 1978 Wesley Oyama commissioned a lavish home at Issaquah Dock, the most elite address on the water. The three-story houseboat is one of the largest in the bay. The Oyama home, now owned by Bill Jones, is a six-minute drive from the Golden Gate Bridge and then a four-minute walk from the parking lot at Waldo Point Harbor. The long boardwalk is lined with flowering plants and deluxe homes.

A bridge of a few steps leads to the front door and large living room, which has a beamed ceiling and a wall of glass overlooking the water. Bill has furnished the room with a gray sectional sofa with bright cushions and a grand piano that guests are welcome to use. Against one wall is a fireplace with a black stone hearth. "Rolls Joyce," wearing a perpetual smile and flashy costume, stands across the room. Found in a junk shop, she's the life-size figure of a tap dancer, rather like a hood ornament with wings.

Some floating homes have greenhouses, wine cellars, whirlpool tubs, elevators, and rooftop gardens.

Upstairs, a Japanese theme has been retained with a low bed on tatami mats behind shoji screens. Sliding doors lead to a sitting area with low cushions. A rich red and gold kimono graces one wall; otherwise, the decor is serene and simple. Outside on the deck where flags whip in the wind, the view is spectacular, over the choppy bay to the towers of San Francisco and the fog-shrouded bridge. Great blue herons, snowy egrets, pelicans, and mallards fly by, and almost every day you'll see fishing boats, sails, and yachts.

A big blue and green tile bath has a whirlpool, a deep tub, and a shower with sliding glass doors that open to a small deck covered with flowers and vines.

Downstairs, below the main level, is the second bedroom, a dimly lighted hideaway with no outside view. This room shares a bath, which includes a sauna, with the owner.

Guests may use the kitchen; the refrigerator is stocked with wine, juice, and beer. Bill's guests are mostly gay couples, but the outgoing, hospitable host welcomes everyone. He's happy to offer suggestions for sightseeing and local restaurants.

Sophisticated and whimsical, filled with the owner's numerous interests (such as an extensive model car collection), the houseboat is often used for fund-raising parties for the Floating Homes Association, AIDS support groups, and other charities.

The Phoenix

Sausalito, CA
Mailing address:
Bed & Breakfast San Francisco
P.O. Box 349
San Francisco, CA 94101-0349
415-931-3083

A spacious houseboat for private use

Contact: Richard and Susan Kreibich. **Accommodations:** 1-bedroom houseboat. **Rates:** $125 single or double. **Included:** Expanded Continental breakfast. **Minimum stay:** 2 nights. **Payment:** No credit cards. **Children:** Welcome (room for 1 child on futon). **Pets:** Not allowed. **Smoking:** Not allowed indoors.

The Phoenix is a roomy houseboat at the end of a pier edged with bright flowers in pots and a string of charming, stylish, floating homes. From the deck and walls of windows on the Phoenix you can see the harbor, the million-dollar homes on Strawberry Point, and windsurfers skimming over the waves while cormorants, pelicans, egrets, and herons fly overhead. Ducks paddle below, hoping for handouts. It's a peaceful setting that provides visitors with a different view of San Francisco Bay and Sausalito.

The owners, Alicia and Roy Law, have provided menus for Sausalito restaurants and useful material such as a *Field Guide to Western Birds*.

There's a sitting room with a fireplace, couches, television, VCR, and assorted books and magazines. The spacious bedroom is downstairs.

You'll find coffee and tea in the little kitchen, and a breakfast of croissants, pastries, cereal, and fruit in the refrigerator. There's a gas stove, or you can use the barbecue grill on the deck.

You may not see the Laws, as they are usually at their home in Glen Ellen, but Alicia leaves a letter of welcome that explains the houseboat and mentions a few of the area's attractions.

SONOMA

El Dorado Hotel

405 First Street West
Sonoma, CA 95476
707-996-3030
800-289-3031
Fax 707-996-3148

A historic hotel in a historic wine-country town

General manager: Craig Clark. **Accommodations:** 27 rooms. **Rates:** $115–$145 single or double in summer, $85–$115 in winter. **Included:** Continental breakfast. **Minimum stay:** 2 nights on weekends. **Children:** Under age 7 free. **Pets:** Not allowed. **Smoking:** Allowed.

Old Mexico meets contemporary California, with a colorful dash of Italy, at the El Dorado in historic Sonoma. The two-story mission revival hotel, overlooking the town's shady plaza, has an interesting past. Built in 1843 as a home for Don Salvador Vallejo (brother of the Mexican commandante), it was a refuge during the Bear Flag uprising of 1846 and became a hotel in 1851. Later it was a literary college, a winemaking shop, a home, and finally a hotel again.

The restaurant has a latticed courtyard with an old fig tree in the center. Here you can sit at umbrella tables, swim in the heated lap pool, or have a party for a hundred people.

Each pale taupe room is simply furnished with a steel four-poster bed, a peach duvet, and a dresser. There are no curtains, and the walls are plain except for one mirror, artfully framed with twigs. A throw rug lies on the tile floor; a TV is on the dresser. White louvered doors slide open to reveal a balcony (too narrow to be useful, with no room for a chair) above the street.

A breakfast of orange juice, Italian cheese, fruit, and fresh breads and muffins is served in a lounge off the white, open lobby. Each guest also receives a split of Sonoma Valley wine. The hotel's acclaimed restaurant, Ristorante Piatti, is noted for its innovative Italian cookery. Artichokes, asparagus, and other foods are painted on the walls in this casual setting.

The obliging staff at the El Dorado will advise you on winery tours and nearby attractions.

Sonoma Hotel

110 West Spain Street
Sonoma, CA 95476
707-996-2996

A historic Old West hotel by a shady plaza

Innkeepers: John and Dorene Musilli. **Accommodations:** 17 rooms (5 with private bath). **Rates:** $75–$120 single or double. **Included:** Continental breakfast. **Payment:** Major credit cards. **Children:** Not appropriate. **Pets:** Not allowed. **Smoking:** Allowed.

More than a century ago, a bar and dance hall were built across the street from the plaza in Sonoma, a town of significance in California history. This was where the state's wine industry was founded, where the short-lived Bear Flag Revolt took place, and where the northernmost (and last) of the twenty-one missions was built in 1823. Part of the adobe mission still stands.

In the early 1900s, the two-story dance hall gained a third floor and was converted to a hotel. The Sonoma Hotel has been providing rooms and meals to travelers since then, in an atmosphere that is still turn-of-the-century. The Musilli family works hard to keep it that way.

The rooms are furnished in antiques such as brass or intricately carved wooden beds, carved armoires, dressers with beveled mirrors, and marble-topped nightstands. The grandest is the Vallejo Room, which boasts a bedroom suite of carved rosewood once owned by General Vallejo's family. Many rooms are quite small, often with an antique bed angled against a corner. Only five rooms have private baths; the others, on the two upper floors, have washbasins but share baths down the hall.

Mexican-era adobes surround the grassy, shaded plaza, which was laid out by General Vallejo in 1835 and is now the largest in California. It has flower gardens, picnic tables, a playground, a duck pond, and an outdoor theater.

A breakfast of juice, croissants, and coffee is served in the small lobby/parlor, a bit of frontier elegance with Victorian settees and a rough stone fireplace.

Adjoining the lobby is a saloon with genuine Old West flavor. It has wooden floors, a battered piano, a gleaming old oak and mahogany bar, and even a bullet hole in the mirrored back bar to add authenticity. Ask the friendly bartender to tell you about the hotel's ghost. Some guests and staff members swear they've seen a Chinese spirit — perhaps from the days when there was a Chinese laundry on the back patio.

A pleasant three-room restaurant, Regina's, offers local ingredients and herbs from the garden on a dinner menu that changes seasonally. During the summer months you can dine on the patio under shade trees.

Victorian Garden Inn

316 East Napa Street
Sonoma, CA 95476
707-996-5339

A stylish Victorian home in town

Innkeeper: Donna Lewis. **Accommodations:** 4 rooms (3 with private bath). **Rates:** $79–$139 single or double, $20 additional person. **Included:** Full breakfast. **Minimum stay:** 2 nights on weekends, 3 nights on holiday weekends. **Payment:** Major credit cards. **Children:** Discouraged. **Pets:** Not allowed. **Smoking:** Discouraged.

Follow the path past lavish flower gardens and you'll come to this charming Victorian home. It's on a comparatively busy street in Sonoma, but because it is set back the atmosphere is one of seclusion.

Donna will organize winery tours, pack a picnic basket, and recommend Sonoma's best restaurants. She serves breakfast on the patio or in the dining room, or brings it on a wicker tray to your room.

Donna Lewis, once an interior decorator, has furnished and decorated the rooms with flair. The most popular is Top o' the Tower, with its own entrance. Done in blue and white and wicker, it has the country charm of painted floors and braided rugs. The tower overlooks the maze of gardens and the swimming pool. Below it, with a door to the garden, is the Garden Room, which has a high bed, wicker rocker, and splashy floral decor.

Woodcutter's Cottage, next to the pool and brick patio, is cool and dark in green with peach accents. It has a fireplace, country antiques, a brass bed piled with pillows, and a skylight in the pitched roof. This room can accommodate three.

The least expensive accommodations are two antiques-furnished rooms in the main house; together they are called the Classic. You have a choice of a room with twin beds or one with a queen-size bed. A basket of towels is provided to use in the adjacent bathroom.

Laundry facilities and a refrigerator are available.

STINSON BEACH

Casa del Mar

P.O. Box 238
37 Belvedere Avenue
Stinson Beach, CA 94970
415-868-2124

A hillside villa near the shore

Innkeeper: Rick Klein. **Accommodations:** 6 rooms (all with private bath). **Rates:** \$100–\$200. **Included:** Full breakfast. **Minimum stay:** 2 nights on weekends. **Payment:** MasterCard, Visa. **Children:** Age 6 and older welcome. **Pets:** Not allowed. **Smoking:** Not allowed.

Like a Mediterranean villa, this peach stucco home with a red tile roof rises above a blue sea and masses of flowers in a terraced garden. This hillside, though, is on the Pacific shore, in a village north of San Francisco. It's a 35-minute drive from the Golden Gate Bridge to Stinson Beach, which lies at the foot of Tamalpais State Park.

Casa del Mar is slightly inland from the beach. Wooded trails extend from the back door up Mount Tamalpais, through meadows of wildflowers to wide ocean views. Rick Klein moved to the area in the mid-1980s, planning to settle down after a checkered background as a restaurateur, fisher, treasure hunter, builder, and attorney. Gardening was to become his next passion, along with rebuilding the house he purchased and turning it into a bed-and-breakfast. His efforts have created a work of art and a lovely sanctuary.

Light streams through windows in the open, white interior, where Rick's collection of works by Marin County artists is displayed. Guests share two breakfast tables in the informal, sun-splashed dining area, getting acquainted as they feast on fresh fruit, granola, yogurt, pastries, and a main dish.

Meandering the rocky paths of the Casa del Mar garden, with the sound of the surf in the background, is a special pleasure. Herbs and wisteria scent the air, while jacarandas, palm trees, and cacti lend exotic appeal.

The guest rooms vary in size. Each is named for the hand-painted ceramic design in the shower: Hummingbird, Shell, Passion Flower, and Heron. Each has a queen-size bed covered with a duvet, fine cotton linens, and a private balcony with a view of the woods or the ocean. The penthouse on the third floor contains an additional single bed. Decorated in blue and white, this skylighted room has a big bathroom with a two-person tub. The Garden Room, below the kitchen, has its own entrance and patio.

The softspoken, hospitable innkeeper has numerous suggestions for things to do during your visit. You're close to Point Reyes National Seashore, the giant redwoods in Muir Woods, and Audubon Canyon Ranch, where in spring you can watch herons nesting in the treetops. Stinson Beach has three miles of white sand to stroll.

WALNUT CREEK

The Mansion at Lakewood

1056 Hacienda Drive
Walnut Creek, CA 94598
510-945-3600
800-477-7898

> *A historic estate in East Bay*

Innkeepers: Sharyn and Mike McCoy. **Accommodations:** 7 rooms (all with private bath). **Rates:** $125–$250 weekends, $20 less midweek, $15 additional person. **Included:** Continental breakfast. **Payment:** Major credit cards. **Children:** Discouraged. **Pets:** Not allowed. **Smoking:** Not allowed.

The oldest home still standing in Walnut Creek is on a three-acre estate that is a tranquil oasis in the fast-developing East Bay area. This 1860 manor home is on the site of a Mexican land grant, a 50-minute drive from the Oakland airport.

After the electric gate is opened, you enter landscaped grounds with a fountain, a lush lawn, and flowers (the property has its own well, so even in times of drought the gardens remain green).

The rooms are large and cool, with high ceilings and windows. There are four rooms on the main floor, each decorated individually. The Terrace Suite has an antique bed, a fireplace, and lace at the windows. Country Manor contains a heavy four-poster and a double-headed, white tile shower.

The Estate Suite is lavish and romantic, with a white fireplace and white carpet, padded fabric walls, and a high brass bed. There's a private deck overlooking the lawn and gazebo, and a Jacuzzi for two. Upstairs is the Attic Hideaway, a cozy retreat in winter, when you can hear rain pattering on the roof. It has antique furniture and puffy pillows on the window seat.

The well-furnished library and parlor are open to guests in this lovely, romantic place. It's a popular spot for weddings and as a getaway for area residents.

A Continental breakfast can be served in the dining room, on the verandah, or in your suite.

YOUNTVILLE

Burgundy House

P.O. Box 3156
6711 Washington Street
Yountville, CA 94599
707-944-0889

A picturesque stone inn

Innkeepers: Dieter and Ruth Back.
Accommodations: 5 rooms (all with private bath). **Rates:** $95

single, $110 double, $20 additional person. **Minimum stay:** 2 nights on weekends. **Payment:** MasterCard, Visa. **Children:** Over age 14 welcome. **Pets:** Not allowed. **Smoking:** Not allowed indoors.

Like an old stone house in the French countryside, this Napa Valley inn has 22-inch thick walls, hand-hewn posts and lintels, and rustic masonry. Originally a brandy distillery, it also housed a winery, a hotel, and a warehouse before becoming a bed-and-breakfast.

When you arrive, perhaps after a day of touring the wineries that make the valley famous, you'll find fresh flowers and a decanter of wine in your room.

There are five guest rooms, all of them named for cities in Burgundy: Beaune, Autun, Dijon, Pommard, and Cluny. Although they've been recently remodeled, you can see traces of the old stone walls in each. The rooms are quiet, as the inn is off the main highway.

Beaune and Autun occupy the front corners of the inn. Dijon, in a back corner, has a cozy window seat with a view of the lovely rose garden. Pommard, with its own entrance off the garden, has a fireplace, a white iron bed, and white walls and rustic beams. Outside the door is a patio under a sweet-scented orange tree.

The ebullient innkeeper, Dieter Back, serves breakfast in the comfortable little parlor or on the patio. He'll assist you in planning winery tours and balloon and glider rides and in selecting one of the many highly rated restaurants in the area.

Oleander House

7433 St. Helena Highway
Yountville, CA 94599
707-944-8315

A B&B within walking distance of wineries

Innkeepers: Louise and John Packard. **Accommodations:** 4 rooms (all with private bath). **Rates:** $115–$160 single or double. **Included:** Full breakfast. **Minimum stay:** 2 nights on weekends and holidays. **Payment:** MasterCard, Visa. **Children:** Not appropriate. **Pets:** Not allowed. **Smoking:** Not allowed indoors.

Bordered by the oleander hedges that give the place its name, this bed-and-breakfast inn offers numerous amenities and (despite facing the heavily used Highway 29) a fine location. It's set back from the road, behind a garden of strawberries, herbs, and roses, and is within walking distance of two wineries and one of the Napa Valley's best restaurants, Mustard's Grill.

In the evening, you can watch the sun set from the patio and sample your wine purchases as you enjoy the romantic fragrance of star jasmine and the tempting scents that waft over from Mustard's.

The Packards, who have owned the inn since 1989, have created a haven for their guests. The rooms are furnished in a contemporary style, each with a fireplace, a balcony, Laura Ashley wallpaper and fabrics, and a basket of brochures and chocolate kisses. The quietest rooms, in the back of the house, have brass beds and views of the hills and Carmelite monastery.

On the second-floor landing there's a sitting area with a TV, wet bar, bookshelves, and refrigerator. You can help yourself to soft drinks or chill your wine. Guests are welcome to use the spa on the back patio.

Breakfast is served at a long table in the dining room, which has items the Packards brought home from their two-year stay in Japan. Among them are a Nakayama painting and an antique kitchen ton-su, used as a sideboard. Strawberries from the garden are used in a sauce for the baked pancakes and French toast; breakfast dishes vary daily and are served along with juice, coffee, and fruit.

The Webber Place

P.O. Box 2873
6610 Webber Street
Yountville, CA 94599
707-944-8384

A classic farmhouse close to valley vineyards

Innkeeper: Diane Bartholomew. **Accommodations:** 4 rooms (2 with private bath). **Rates:** $69–$119 single or double. **Minimum stay:** 2 nights on summer weekends. **Included:** Full breakfast. **Payment:** Major credit cards. **Children:** Over age 12 welcome. **Pets:** Allowed by arrangement. **Smoking:** Not allowed.

If you've ever longed to visit Grandma's house in the country, where you're welcomed with a smile, a cup of tea, and an invitation to rest in the rocker on the veranda, you will be happy at the Webber Place.

The old-fashioned red farmhouse stands on a quiet corner, behind a flower garden marked by a white picket fence and rose-covered trellis. Built in the 1850s by early settlers, the house was moved from a ranch site east of town to its present location by John Lee Webber. Reconstruction began in 1971, with careful attention paid to details in the woodwork, wallpapers, brass fittings, and porcelain fixtures. The original tongue-and-groove redwood paneling had been painted many times; it was simply removed, turned over, and replaced.

Diane Bartholomew, a painter and sculptor, has furnished

her home for simple comfort. "Classic Victorian is too elegant and formal for this country farmhouse," she says, arranging a big bouquet of sweet peas on the coffee table. "I want the style to fit the place."

A nice place to end an afternoon of touring wineries, bicycling, or ballooning is at the picnic table in the front yard. Pick up a snack at a deli to enjoy with the wine you have purchased or the complimentary beverage Diane provides.

Diane lives in a cottage next door, where she has a studio, and is back and forth regularly. Between the houses is her "art yard," with sculptures and other works of art. On the main floor is a cozy living room with a brick hearth and woodstove, a small dining area, and one guest room with a private entrance off the side veranda. The Veranda Room has a white wicker rocker, a clawfoot tub, and a down duvet on the bed. Double doors lead to a latticed porch where a big hammock sways, perfect for lazing away an idle afternoon.

The three rooms upstairs contain double beds. The East Room has its own bath; Redwood and the Sun Room share a white tile bath. Rose café curtains hang at long windows in the Sun Room. Fluttering leaves on the valley oak outside cast intricate shadows on the bare wood floor. None of the rooms has television or a phone, but guests may use the phone in the living room.

If you visit at harvest time, you'll see an amazing array of jack-o'-lanterns at the Webber Place. They perch on posts, grin from railings, and peek out from cornstalks and piles of hay. Each October, Diane invites all the children in town to carve pumpkins. For every twelve faces, she gives the carver a T-shirt commemorating the occasion. You're welcome to join in the fun.

Central Coast

Davenport
Soquel
Capitola
Gilroy
Santa Cruz
Aptos
Pacific Grove
Pebble Beach
Monterey
Carmel Valley
Carmel
Big Sur
1
101
Cambria
Shell Beach
Arroyo Grande
Los Alamos
Ballard
Solvang
Montecito
101
Ojai
Goleta
Santa Barbara

Aptos
Apple Lane Inn, 194
Mangels House, 196
Arroyo Grande
Rose Victorian Inn, 198
Ballard
The Ballard Inn, 200
Big Sur
Deetjen's Big Sur Inn, 202
Post Ranch Inn, 203
Ventana, 205
Cambria
Beach House, 207
Capitola
The Inn at Depot Hill, 209
Carmel
Cypress Inn, 211
Happy Landing Inn, 213
Highlands Inn, 214
La Playa Hotel, 216
The Sandpiper Inn, 218
The Stonehouse Inn, 220
Sundial Lodge, 222
Vagabond's House, 223
Carmel Valley
Carmel Valley Ranch Resort, 225
Quail Lodge, 227
Robles del Rio Lodge, 229
Stonepine, 230
Davenport
New Davenport Bed & Breakfast Inn, 232
Gilroy
Country Rose Inn, 234
Goleta
Circle Bar B Guest Ranch, 236
Los Alamos
The Union Hotel, 238
Victorian Mansion, 240
Montecito
San Ysidro Ranch, 243
Monterey
The Jabberwock, 245
Monterey Plaza Hotel, 247
Old Monterey Inn, 249
Spindrift Inn, 250
Ojai
Ojai Valley Inn & Country Club, 252
Pacific Grove
The Centrella, 254
Gatehouse Inn Bed and Breakfast, 255
The Green Gables Inn, 257
The Martine Inn, 259
Seven Gables Inn, 261
Pebble Beach
The Inn at Spanish Bay, 263
The Lodge at Pebble Beach, 265
Santa Barbara
The Bayberry Inn, 267
Blue Quail Inn, 268
El Encanto, 270
Four Seasons Biltmore, 272
The Old Yacht Club Inn, 274
Simpson House Inn, 276
The Upham Hotel, 278
Villa Rosa, 280
Santa Cruz
The Babbling Brook Inn, 281
Chaminade, 283
Shell Beach
The Cliffs at Shell Beach, 285
Solvang
The Alisal Guest Ranch, 286
Soquel
The Blue Spruce Inn, 288

Best Intimate City Stops

Santa Barbara
The Upham Hotel

Best Country Inns and B&Bs

Aptos
Apple Lane Inn
Mangels House
Arroyo Grande
Rose Victorian Inn
Ballard
The Ballard Inn
Carmel Valley
Robles del Rio Lodge
New Davenport
New Davenport Bed & Breakfast Inn
Gilroy
Country Rose Inn
Los Alamos
The Union Hotel
Montecito
San Ysidro Ranch
Soquel
The Blue Spruce Inn

Best Family Favorites

Goleta
Circle Bar B Guest Ranch

Best Inns by the Sea

Big Sur
Deetjen's Big Sur Inn
Post Ranch Inn
Ventana
Cambria
Beach House

Carmel
- Cypress Inn
- Highlands Inn
- La Playa Hotel
- The Sandpiper Inn
- Stonehouse Inn
- Sundial Lodge

Monterey
- The Jabberwock
- Monterey Plaza Hotel
- Spindrift Inn

Pacific Grove
- The Centrella
- Gatehouse Inn Bed & Breakfast
- The Green Gables Inn
- Seven Gables Inn

Santa Barbara
- Four Seasons Biltmore
- The Old Yacht Club Inn

Shell Beach
- The Cliffs at Shell Beach

Best Resorts

Carmel Valley
- Carmel Valley Ranch Resort
- Quail Lodge

Ojai
- Ojai Valley Inn & Country Club

Pebble Beach
- The Inn at Spanish Bay
- The Lodge at Pebble Beach

Santa Cruz
- Chaminade

Solvang
- The Alisal Guest Ranch

Best Romantic Hideaways

Capitola
- The Inn at Depot Hill

Carmel
Happy Landing Inn
Vagabond's House
Los Alamos
The Victorian Mansion
Monterey
Old Monterey Inn
Pacific Grove
The Martine Inn
Santa Barbara
Bayberry Inn
Blue Quail Inn
El Encanto
Villa Rosa
Santa Cruz
The Babbling Brook Inn

From Santa Cruz to Santa Barbara, the California coastline is a constantly changing panorama of ocean vistas. With the spectacular 90-mile exception of Big Sur, the shore is less rugged here than in the northern part of the state. Numerous public parks along the way make broad sandy beaches and gentle waves easily accessible. Around the long crescent of Monterey Bay is some of the world's most celebrated scenery — wind-twisted cypress trees, hidden coves, and inviting towns with sophisticated shops and restaurants. World-class golf courses, grand estates, and a forest of pine cover the southern peninsula to the resort town of Carmel.

South of quaint Carmel and the resorts and pastoral landscape of Carmel Valley, past the wooded bluffs of Point Lobos State Reserve, is Big Sur. Here Highway 1 winds through the western slopes of the Santa Lucia Mountains as they tilt toward the Pacific. Streams rush down ravines, tawny cliffs drop steeply to the sea, and spindrift plumes above waves that rush to break against jagged rocks far below. Under the glare of the sun, a silvery sea glints, occasionally turning a brilliant green in the eddies of a shallow cove.

The mountains move inland as you near San Simeon and Cambria, and the crumpled ridges soften to grassy rolling hills, green in winter, seared dry in summer. On a hill above San Simeon is the Hearst Castle, a state historic monument open to the public. The palatial estate is filled with fabulous antiques and art treasures. Development crowds the shoreline as you continue south to Shell Beach and Arroyo Grande, then fades to miles of ranches and vineyards as the main highway travels inland toward the Santa Ynez valley.

The city of Santa Barbara lies beside the sea and climbs the steep slopes of the Santa Ynez Mountains, which form a dramatic backdrop to one of California's loveliest communities. The white walls of the city's Spanish mission style architecture gleam in the ever-present sun, palm trees wave in gentle breezes, and a civilized attitude prevails. Every visitor plans to tour the beautifully restored mission. Fewer see the county courthouse, but it's well worth a visit for its outstanding architecture, colorful tiles, and artwork reminiscent of Old California.

Inland from Santa Barbara, near the Topatopa Mountains and Los Padres National Forest, are vineyards, sprawling horse ranches, and the small town of Ojai.

APTOS

Apple Lane Inn

6265 Soquel Drive
Aptos, CA 95003
408-475-6868

A 19th-century farmhouse close to Santa Cruz

Innkeepers: Douglas and Diane Groom. **Accommodations:** 5 rooms (3 with private bath). **Rates:** $70–$125 single or double, $15 additional person. **Included:** Full breakfast. **Payment:** Discover, MasterCard, Visa. **Children:** Welcome by arrangement. **Pets:** Not allowed. **Smoking:** Not allowed indoors.

Three acres of fields and gardens surround this Victorian farmhouse just south of Santa Cruz. The house was built in the 1870s, and though it's now close to a busy town and you can hear traffic in the distance, it retains the sense of seclusion and quiet you'd expect from a country home of decades past.

Velvet ties hold back the parlor drapes, a red settee faces the fireplace, and a player piano stands against the wall. Shelves filled with books on art and local history reach to the ceiling. A mantel clock chimes the hour. A bay window overlooks the garden, wisteria vines, and gazebo.

The guest rooms are furnished with antiques, many of them Groom family heirlooms. Blossom has a ring-patterned quilt on a 14th-century French canopy bed and a flowery bathroom as big as the bedroom. It has a wicker lounge, a rocker, and a clawfoot tub with hand shower. Uncle Chester's room contains a 260-year-old Spanish mahogany four-poster. The Pineapple room is dominated by a four-poster pineapple bed and features a pineapple motif. Arbor and Orchard, in the attic, share a bath.

After driving up the hillside lane from the highway, you park under the grape arbor and walk a brick path bordered by jade plants and rosemary to the front porch. Inside, the present day recedes; you've entered the Victorian era.

There is little space for hanging clothes in the small rooms, but they're comfortable, light, and quiet. On the second floor landing there's a sitting area with a phone, a television, and a little refrigerator with juices. Morning coffee is set out here for early risers to take back to their rooms. Breakfast, served in the dining room, includes fresh fruit, a pitcher of juice, homemade granola, Diane's blue-ribbon baked goods, and a hot dish with eggs from the farm's chickens.

Apple Lane Inn has a wine cellar, too, where you might play a game of darts. When you leave, take an apple from the basketful in the front hall to feed the horses, Celeste and Camelot.

Mangels House

P.O. Box 302
570 Aptos Creek Road
Aptos, CA 95001
408-688-7982

A country home by a forested park

Innkeepers: Jacqueline and Ron Fisher. **Accommodations:** 5 rooms (all with private bath). **Rates:** $96–$120 single or double, $15 additional person. **Included:** Full breakfast. **Minimum stay:** 2 nights on weekends. **Payment:** American Express, MasterCard, and Visa accepted; check or cash preferred. **Children:** Over age 12 welcome. **Pets:** Not allowed in rooms. **Smoking:** Allowed in sitting room.

Aptos is a small community just south of Santa Cruz, in the northern curve of Monterey Bay. It was here, in the woods along Aptos Creek, that Claus Mangels built his vacation home in the 1880s. Mangels and his brother-in-law, Claus Spreckels, founded the sugar beet industry in California. The country estate stayed in the family until 1979, when the Fishers purchased it and turned it into a bed-and-breakfast.

The two-story white frame house bears some resemblance to an imposing antebellum mansion, but it's neither opulent nor lavishly furnished. Rather, it is a large country home with a veranda, four acres of lawns and gardens, and two creeks nearby.

Victorian and contemporary decor are combined to pleasing

effect. In the immense living room, beside high windows, a rough marble fireplace stands eight feet wide and reaches from floor to ceiling. Books fill the built-in shelves and there's a grand piano at one end of the room.

Once the canyons and ridges were covered with redwoods, but by 1923 the last stand of old-growth forest was gone. When the loggers left Aptos Canyon, the forest gradually began to heal. That process continues today as new redwoods grow and wildlife returns. There are thirty miles of hiking and biking trails in this peaceful refuge.

The dining room has a long table where breakfast is served if the house is full, but if only a few guests are present, they eat in the kitchen. Juice, scones, muffins, persimmon bread, fruit, and an egg entrée are a few of the dishes Jackie likes to serve her guests. Coffee is always out early, on an antique oak sideboard on the upstairs landing.

The large upstairs guest rooms have views of the orchards, the garden, or the wooded canyon. The smallest is the cozy Nursery, decorated in bright red, blue, and green prints. Nicholas's Room, named for the Fishers' son, is exotic with African artifacts, mementoes of Nicholas's two years in Zaire. Mauve Room, with a daybed, sleeps three people. It has a marble fireplace, stencils on the pink walls, and tall windows.

In the Guest Room, you can raise one of the floor-to-ceiling windows to get to the balcony overlooking the English garden. This room has a cheery country look, with a wicker couch, white lattice headboard, and fresh roses on the table.

Mangels House is on a quiet road on the edge of the Forest of Nisene Marks State Park, 9,600 acres of wooded wilderness. The park was donated to the state by the Marks family in memory of their mother in 1963.

ARROYO GRANDE

Rose Victorian Inn

789 Valley Road
Arroyo Grande, CA 93420
805-481-5566

An ornate pink home a mile from the sea

Innkeepers: Diana and Ross Cox. **Accommodations:** 5 rooms (1 with private bath, 4 share 2 baths), plus 2 cottages and 4 suites. **Rates:** $130–$175 single or double, $40 additional person. **Included:** Full breakfast and dinner. **Minimum stay:** 2 nights on weekends. **Payment:** MasterCard, Visa. **Children:** Under age 16 not appropriate. **Pets:** Not allowed. **Smoking:** Not allowed in rooms.

Rose is the theme of this inn on the coast halfway between San Francisco and Los Angeles. The four-story home is painted in four shades of pink, each guest room is named for a type of rose, and the garden is full of roses that are picked to adorn every room.

The ornate house, built in 1885 as a homestead for a walnut farm, is surrounded by farmland, with a sprinkling of houses here and there. Development is encroaching, but for now the fields of green beans, lettuce, and celery provide a rural context. The ocean is a mile away, as the crow flies. You can see the sand dunes from the upper floors of the Rose Victorian.

In addition to entertaining guests and growing roses, Diana Cox runs a successful restaurant, open for dinner on weekends. In the garden-level restaurant, pink and white linens grace the tables and windows overlook the gazebo and rose arbor. Dinners are included in the room rate or, for outside guests, are reasonably priced. They include soup or salad, fresh wheat bread, garden vegetables, and seafood, chicken, or lamb. Desserts are such decadent items as white chocolate and raspberry divine, Victorian cream with apricot sauce, and a rich chocolate mousse.

Breakfast is served in the restaurant if the house is full, in the dining room upstairs if it's not. Hot biscuits, croissants with ham and Parmesan cheese, eggs Benedict, and fresh fruit are among the dishes often served, along with coffee or tea and fruit juice laced with champagne.

At the front of the mansion is a parlor with a fireplace, a pump organ, and a bay window. Another sitting room is a favorite of guests for its square grand piano and table with an ongoing jigsaw puzzle.

There are more than forty wineries in San Luis Obispo County, many of them open for tours and tastings. Lopez Lake, the valley's water source, is ten miles inland and a popular site for water sports.

The guest rooms are furnished with antiques, most of them carved mahogany, rosewood, and oak pieces. One room, Olé, named for a red rose, is on the main floor. Four more rooms are upstairs, with views of the gardens and fields. Designed to keep noise at a minimum, their closets act as buffers between the rooms. The upper rooms share two large baths.

Summer Sun, light and floral, contains a white iron bed, country furniture, and a small prism chandelier. Sterling Silver, a spacious room done in soft grays and silvers, sets off the Sterling Silver rose to advantage.

Behind the house are the cottages. The rooms are small, a good choice if you prefer cozy, secluded lodgings. The newest suites are in the former carriage house. The honeymoon suite, done in pink and burgundy, has a private balcony. Garden Party is like a gazebo, with its white lattices, arches, and multitude of flowers.

BALLARD

The Ballard Inn

2436 Baseline
Ballard, CA 93463
805-688-7770
800-638-BINN

> *A peaceful retreat in a frontier village*

Owners: Steve Hyslop and Larry Stone. **Accommodations:** 15 rooms. **Rates:** $160–$195 single or double. **Included:** Full breakfast. **Minimum stay:** 2 nights on weekends. **Payment:** Mastercard, Visa. **Children:** Welcome. **Pets:** Not allowed. **Smoking:** Not allowed.

Some forty miles east of Santa Barbara, in the scenic Santa Ynez Valley, is a village with a frontier history. It's the valley's oldest town, with a quaint church and an 1883 red schoolhouse still in operation.

On the main road, behind a white picket fence bordered with roses, is the Ballard, the image of a genteel country inn. From a long porch with white rocking chairs, double doors lead to a foyer with a vaulted white ceiling and a three-sided green marble fireplace. On the right is a dining room where a sumptuous breakfast is served. Omelettes, French toast with cinnamon and sautéed bananas, muffins, and fruit are a few of the morning offerings. If you're musically inclined, you may play the black grand piano in the corner.

The Vineyard Room is on the other side of the lobby. A carved cabinet holds games and puzzles, local wines are on display, and wines and hors d'oeuvres are set out in the evening. In keeping with the wine theme are the burgundy wallpaper in a trellis pattern, an oak bar with legs carved in grapevines, and displays of wine labels.

If you really want to get in the spirit of the place, go to the antique trunk in the corner of the Stagecoach Room and pull out a hat with trailing boa, a coonskin cap, or a shawl, and imagine yourself just stepping off the stage.

Sofas by the fireplace and a case of books and antiques make the living room an inviting place to relax and contemplate the portrait of William Ballard. The bearded patriarch built and operated a stagecoach stop here for the two-day run from San Luis Obispo to Santa Barbara. His adobe home has been preserved and is still in use.

The Stagecoach Room, dark with black leather chairs and a braided rug on a polished floor, is done in the colors of the original stage: burgundy, black, and gold. A painting of the Ballard Stage Station and coach hangs on the wall, along with coach lanterns and photographs of other valley coaches.

All the rooms, named for places and people important in Ballard's history, have phone jacks, air conditioning and soundproof walls. Oak bathroom cabinets are stocked with wine soap, wine hand lotion, and champagne shampoo. Welcoming baskets of fruit, cheese, and wine are provided.

Western Room is a tribute to the cowboys who worked the cattle ranches. It has a log cabin quilt, old-fashioned rockers, a fireplace, and a collection of Western hats. Davy Brown's Room, in honor of a rugged frontiersman who rode with the Texas Rangers, also has a rustic charm. It has a fireplace made of native stone, a wagon-wheel quilt, and American antiques.

Quite different is the Valley Room, commemorating five little valley towns with scenes from each on walls bright with California poppies. There is a Belgian armoire and matching dresser and a friendship quilt made by local quilters. Jarado's Room takes its theme from a Chumash Indian who helped construct the Ballard Station. It contains the red, white, and black designs of Chumash cave paintings. Pine furniture and arrowheads add to the atmosphere.

Cynthia's Room recalls a pioneer who came west to marry her sweetheart, William Ballard, on his deathbed. Ballard's last wish was that she marry his friend George Lewis, which she did. The room holds a portrait of the youthful widow; the handmade quilt on the bed is, appropriately, in a double wedding ring pattern.

When you wish to explore the picturesque countryside, with its highly regarded wineries and thoroughbred horse ranches, the innkeepers can help you plan your route. They'll also arrange for a hot air balloon ride, a romantic way to see the valley. To the south is Solvang, a tourist-oriented village in quaint Danish style. Los Olivos, north of Ballard, has numerous art galleries.

BIG SUR

Deetjen's Big Sur Inn

Highway 1
Big Sur, CA 93920
408-667-2377

> *A rustic group of cabins among the trees*

Manager: Andy Gagarin. **Accommodations:** 19 rooms (14 with private bath). **Rates:** $66–$121 single or double, $11 additional person (includes tax). **Payment:** No credit cards. **Children:** Under age 12 not appropriate. **Pets:** Not allowed. **Smoking:** Allowed.

In the early 1930s, when the coastal highway was a dirt road, Helmuth Deetjen, a Norwegian immigrant, built a homestead by the road in Castro Canyon. There he and his wife, Helen, welcomed overnight guests. They gradually added more simple frame buildings until the home became the Big Sur Inn.

There is no real town of Big Sur, though there is a post office, but you feel a sense of community in the group of homes and shops that extends for six miles along the highway. Its heart is the Big Sur Inn, where locals and tourists alike come together for coffee, good meals, and spirited conversation. The restaurant is in Helmut Deetjen's original house. With dark walls and rustic charm, it has a woodstove and several rooms where excellent breakfasts and dinners are served. The morning menu offers pancakes, oatmeal, eggs Benedict, French toast, and other dishes at reasonable prices. Dinner, by reservation, is served by candlelight with classical music in the background.

Big Sur is an 80-mile stretch of wild coastline that runs from Carmel south to San Simeon. Rugged cliffs and wooded ridges rise steeply from the shore, and every curve of the snaking road presents another astounding view of green coves, blue ocean flecked with white, and rocky headlands and beaches.

The guest rooms are back among the trees in five buildings lining a dirt path that extends above the canyon creek. They have unpainted plank walls, rough-hewn doors, and fireplaces. Despite the rustic environment, the beds are firm and cozy under down comforters. In Grampa's, across from the restaurant, an old radio rests on the big desk and an antique pump organ stands against a wall.

Not all the rooms have a backwoods atmosphere; in fact, no two are alike. Faraway, perched at the edge of the canyon, has a redwood interior, a small porch, and a private fenced area with ferns and fuchsias. On a hillside across the small parking lot from the restaurant are four rooms that share two baths. They're simple but comfortable and clean.

Post Ranch Inn

P.O. Box 219
Big Sur, CA 93920
408-667-2200
800-527-2200
Fax 408-667-2824

A unique contemporary inn above the Pacific

Manager: Jim Pawling. **Accommodations:** 30 suites. **Rates:** \$245–\$475. **Included:** Expanded

Continental breakfast. **Minimum stay:** 2 nights on weekends. **Payment:** Major credit cards. **Children:** Welcome (though resort is adult-oriented). **Pets:** Not allowed. **Smoking:** Not allowed in restaurant.

Tucked against a cliff 1,200 feet above the spectacular Big Sur coast, this is the resort that critics have raved about since it opened in 1992. Imaginative and whimsical, yet filled with the practical comforts travelers appreciate, Post Ranch deserves all its accolades. Great care was lavished on the planning and construction, and it shows in almost every detail.

In building this resort, only one tree went down, an example of a concern for the environment that is apparent at every turn. Some call the construction politically correct; more astute observers note that this commitment to protecting the land is more than merely politic.

Five of the redwood guest units are Ocean Houses, overlooking the Pacific, and have sod roofs covered with grass and wildflowers. Others, round as the giant tree trunks, are Coast Houses and Mountain Houses. The seven Tree Houses stand on stilts designed to protect the roots of the surrounding redwood trees. When they're wreathed in the mists that often move along the coast, the houses seem to float in the branches. One building, the Butterfly House, has six units.

Inside, the rooms have character and style, as well as the usual luxury hotel features: coffeemakers, minibars, phones, music systems, fireplaces, whirlpool tubs. The floors are of slate and the angled and curved walls of natural wood. The decor is spare, with nothing to detract from the dramatic views. Quiet and privacy are paramount.

Also on the 98-acre property, once part of a 1,600-acre cattle ranch, are groves of madrone and oak trees, trails, grassy meadows, and a fish pond.

Guests are invited to enjoy the panorama from the outdoor basking pool, swim in the lap pool, have a massage or tarot card reading, select a book from the little library, and, especially, dine in the exquisite Sierra Mar restaurant. Perched at the edge of a cliff, it seems to be made mostly of windows focused on the riveting ocean view. Raised sections allow every table to have a view. A buffet breakfast is set out here (or breakfast will be brought to your room if you prefer). Sierra Mar serves lunches and memorable dinners.

Wendy Little, the chef, came to Sierra Mar from the renowned Mustard's Grill in Napa. Her fresh California cuisine features simple but interesting dishes on a fixed-price menu that changes regularly, but might include sautéed baby abalone with almonds and basil; rack of venison with chanterelles and smoked bacon; or albacore with sesame, shiitake, and wasabi butter. The restaurant's organic garden provides much of the produce. The broad wine list offers more than 2,000 selections.

Ventana

Highway 1
Big Sur, CA 93920
408-667-2331, 408-624-4812
800-628-6500

A contemporary inn with a grand view and a quiet location

General manager: Robert Bussinger. **Accommodations:** 59 rooms and suites, and 3 houses. **Rates:** $155–$475 single or double, $50 additional person; house $775. **Included:** Expanded Continental breakfast. **Minimum stay:** 2 nights on weekends. **Payment:** Major credit cards. **Children:** Discouraged. **Pets:** Not allowed. **Smoking:** Not allowed in restaurant.

A thousand feet above the sea, where the Santa Lucia Mountains rise in steep folds and ridges along the dramatic Big Sur coast, Ventana's weathered cedar buildings blend with their environment of rocky canyons, meadows, and redwood groves. The inn, built in 1975, is 150 miles south of San Francisco; rental cars are available at Monterey Peninsula Airport, 35 miles north.

This is country lodging at its best, offering relaxation and tranquility in a setting of stunning beauty. There are no tennis courts or golf courses for miles; Ventana is a place to relax, unwind, go for walks, and read in the sun or by the fire.

Contemporary buildings, latticed against the sun, are dispersed among groves of redwood, oak, and bay laurel. In the main lodge is an airy glass and cedar lobby with a large stone fireplace. Every afternoon complimentary wine and cheese are presented, and breakfast with pastries made on the premises is served here or delivered to your room.

The guest rooms are decorated tastefully in Swedish country style, all light woods and wide windows. Most of them have fireplaces and hot tubs or dining alcoves with wet bars. All are furnished with wicker and rush chairs, natural wood paneling, handmade quilts, fine pastel linens, honor bars, and televisions and VCRs. Every room has a private balcony or patio with ocean or mountain views.

A library and a lounge which serves as another breakfast room are near the second swimming pool and a Japanese hot tub complex. With a casual, European attitude toward sunbathing, nudity is allowed in some areas and swimwear is optional in the coed hot tub.

Ventana's dining room, a delightful walk up lighted paths from the inn, is noted for its extraordinary cuisine. With the much-acclaimed Joachim Splichal as consulting chef and Kurt Grasing the executive chef, many travelers come just for the imaginatively prepared food. The menu features fresh local fish, herbs and vegetables grown on the grounds, wild mushrooms and berries, and breads from the inn's own bakery. There's an extensive wine list of California and imported labels.

The food may be exceptional, but the setting is incomparable. The 50-mile view of the Big Sur coast from above is breathtaking, worthy of hours of admiration from the restaurant windows or the broad, flowery terrace where lunch and cocktails are served.

Ventana, which means "window" in Spanish, offers many vistas of mountains, sea, and sky; given its peace and serenity, it can also be a window to renewed inner perspectives.

CAMBRIA

Beach House

6360 Moonstone Beach Drive
Cambria, CA 93428
805-927-3136

A bed-and-breakfast by the sea

Innkeepers: Penny Hitch and Kernn McKinnon. **Accommodations:** 7 rooms (all with private bath). **Rates:** $100–$135 single or double. **Included:** Full breakfast. **Payment:** MasterCard, Visa. **Children:** Welcome (limit of 2 persons per room). **Pets:** Not allowed. **Smoking:** Not allowed.

Beach House, outside Cambria, is on a quiet road by the shore. The sound of rumbling breakers can be heard from every room. The modern blue house with angles and tall windows and dormers opened as a bed-and-breakfast in 1986. Penny Hitch and her daughter operate the little inn, though the rest of the family helps, too. They provide such hospitable touches as umbrellas in the entryway, wine and cheese in the evenings, and bicycles to lend if you'd like to ride the level roads in the area. The village of Cambria is best known for its proximity to the San Simeon Historical Monument, often called the Hearst Castle.

Hearst Castle, near Cambria, is a magnificent estate that is a major tourist attraction. Daily tours allow visitors to see the opulence and fine art that William Randolph Hearst and his friends enjoyed in the '20s and '30s.

The guest rooms are spread over three floors and a two-room bungalow in back. All have television with a cable movie channel. They're decorated in a contemporary country style, with white wicker furnishings and light shades of plum, gray, and blue.

From the common room on the second floor, sliding glass doors open to a large deck and an expansive ocean view. Binoculars and a telescope are provided for spotting birds and boats and deciding whether that black shape in the water is a rock or a whale.

It's an inviting space, with bentwood rockers by a tile fireplace, books, games, and a long table where breakfast is served. Fruit, quiche, French toast, muffins, and granola are some of the morning choices. Guests have the use of a microwave oven and a coffeemaker.

Above the common room on the third floor loft, and closed off by smoked glass sliding doors, is a large room that is everybody's favorite. It has a king-size platform bed, great views on three sides, a cavernous walk-in closet, and a wall-length mirror in the bathroom. You might have a noise problem here, as the common room is just below, but Penny says no one has complained so far.

Another favorite is in the back cottage. This light and airy room has only a partial ocean view, but the white walls flood with morning sun. There's a small bath and a wicker lounge. Family photos create a homey atmosphere.

Guests enjoy perusing menus by the upstairs fire, for Cambria has several good restaurants. Recommended are Ian's, Rigdon Hall, Robin's, and Sow's Ear.

CAPITOLA

The Inn at Depot Hill

250 Monterey Avenue
Capitola, CA 95010
408-462-3376
Fax 408-458-0989

An opulent hillside inn near the sea

Innkeepers: Suzanne Lankes and Dan Floyd. **Accommodations:** 8 suites (all with private bath). **Rates:** $155–$250 single or double. **Included:** Expanded Continental breakfast. **Minimum stay:** 2 nights on weekends. **Payment:** Major credit cards. **Children:** Welcome. **Pets:** Not allowed. **Smoking:** Not allowed indoors.

Sumptuous and sophisticated, the Inn at Depot Hill is one of the most romantic lodgings on the coast. It's come a long way from its origins as a 1901 train depot on a hill above Capitola, a charming seaside village south of Santa Cruz.

Each suite has been painstakingly furnished and decorated to evoke the mood of a train destination. The Paris room is an elegant study in black and white. It has fabric walls, a double fireplace, French doors to a patio, and a bath in black and white marble. Sissinghurst is like a garden room in a traditional English country inn, with a canopy bed and raised fireplace.

Delft is exquisite in blue and white; Stratford-on-Avon is cozy with a window seat and trellis wallpaper; Portofino has the frescoed walls of an Italian villa; and Côte d'Azur, once the depot's baggage room, has a Mediterranean theme with tile floors, whitewashed columns, and an iron bed draped in gauze.

Capitola Beach is casual and contemporary, with a metal four-poster. The Railroad Baron's Room, in red, is the grandest — with ornate moldings, thick draperies, a domed ceiling, and damask and silk fabrics.

The inn holds a few reminders of turn-of-the-century rail travel. The original columns and ticket windows are here, and the dining room, once the ticket office, is decorated with a rack of old-fashioned baggage and a trompe l'oeil scene that creates the illusion of countryside seen from a train window. The depot lobby is now a parlor with a baby grand piano.

Each room has television with VCR, a stereo system, phones with modem and fax capability, a marble bath with a two-person shower, and such luxurious extras as a hair dryer, clothes steamer, robes, fresh roses, and embroidered Egyptian linens. Some rooms have private brick patios and entrances.

Breakfast is served in the dining room, on the terrace, or in your own room. For other meals, Santa Cruz and Capitola have several excellent restaurants. The inn provides afternoon tea or wine, after-dinner dessert, and off-street parking.

CARMEL

Cypress Inn

P.O. Box Y
Lincoln & 7th
Carmel, CA 93921
408-624-3871
800-443-7443
Fax 408-624-8216

A small hotel with a light, bright atmosphere

General manager: Sarah Moon. **Accommodations:** 33 rooms. **Rates:** $94–$192 single or double, $15 additional person, off-season rates available. **Included:** Continental breakfast. **Minimum stay:** 2 nights on weekends. **Payment:** Major credit cards. **Children:** Welcome (no cribs or roll-aways available). **Pets:** Allowed with permission. **Smoking:** Nonsmoking rooms available.

In the heart of quaint Carmel-by-the-Sea, on the Monterey Peninsula, the Cypress first captures your eye with its white, Moorish, Mediterranean facade and red Spanish tile roof. When the hotel opened in 1929 it was hailed as a landmark for its classic exterior and stately interior. That charm has been restored, and it is again a fine and quiet place to stay, gracious in its tasteful simplicity. With the updated accommodations are hints of the hotel's origins in ceramic tiles, arched windows, oak flooring, and a few antiques.

The Cypress abuts the sidewalk on Lincoln Street (there's

no number — Carmel doesn't allow street addresses), facing the Church of the Wayfarer and its garden across the street.

A few brick steps lead to the reception area. On the right is a sitting room, light with peach walls, a large white fireplace, and white beamed ceiling. Tall windows face the street on one side; on the other are three sets of double glass doors leading to a serene courtyard with blooming fuchsia and morning sun. Garden furniture is placed among the shrubs and topiary ivy.

This is one of the few hotels where pets are welcome, thanks to the influence of one of the owners, the actress and animal lover Doris Day. The hotel will even provide pet food if it's requested.

Breakfast is served in the courtyard, in your room, or in a skylit room off the lobby where hanging plants help create a gardenlike atmosphere. The sunny theme continues in two floors of guest rooms decorated in pastels and whites. Each room has fresh fruit and flowers, sherry, a telephone, a television, and a tile bath. Some include fireplaces. Six specialty rooms are noted for their size and amenities — sitting areas, wet bars, balconies, and ocean views.

There's no concierge, but the staff is uniformly obliging about providing information on nearby attractions and restaurants. Menus are available to help you choose.

Happy Landing Inn

P.O. Box 2619
Carmel, CA 93921
408-624-7917

A quaint, relaxing inn with a garden setting

Innkeepers: Carol and Robert Ballard. **Accommodations:** 5 rooms and 2 suites. **Rates:** $90, $15 additional person; suites $145. **Included:** Expanded Continental breakfast. **Minimum stay:** 2 nights on weekends. **Payment:** MasterCard, Visa. **Children:** Welcome. **Pets:** Allowed with prior arrangement. **Smoking:** Discouraged.

The focus of this pretty inn is its central garden. If you like ponds and fountains, lush vines, and pots overflowing with geraniums and fuchsias, you'll love this spot. It's a beautiful retreat where you can sit under a white trellis with hanging plants or watch the goldfish dart among the water lilies.

Most of the guest rooms are in three pink, one-story buildings that form a U around the garden; their private entrances are blue doors under curved arches, each painted with birds and vines — quintessentially quaint Carmel. On the fourth side of the garden, the street side, is the main building with the office and common room. Here guests may relax, read, or have tea and cookies.

The rooms are furnished individually with antiques and modern comforts such as hair dryers and thick pink towels. There are brass beds, balloon shades or cottage curtains, iron latches on the built-in drawers, casement windows, and fresh flowers.

Whenever you're ready for breakfast, you part the curtains or raise the shades, and the innkeeper will bring your tray. You'll have fresh fruit, fresh orange juice, muffins or scones, and quiche.

> **Although it is a few blocks from the sea, and you can glimpse the water from some windows, Happy Landing is not the place to go for panoramic views of the Pacific. Says Robert Ballard, "Carmel is really an urban forest, full of trees."**

Happy Landing keeps menus for nearby restaurants. Among those recommended are Flaherty's for good seafood and a casual atmosphere and Piatti's for flavorful Italian cookery.

Highlands Inn

P.O. Box 1700
Carmel, CA 93921
408-624-3801
800-682-4811 in California
800-538-9525 in U.S.
Fax 408-626-8105

> *A contemporary resort with an ocean view*

General manager: David Fink. **Accommodations:** 142 rooms and suites. **Rates:** $225–$295 single or double, $25 additional person; suites \$300–\$600. **Payment:** Major credit cards. **Children:** Under 18 free in room with parent. **Pets:** Dogs allowed if 10 pounds or less. **Smoking:** Allowed.

Terraced against the hillside, above the rocky, rugged cliffs south of Carmel, this contemporary inn of stone and wood offers grand views, fine food, and luxurious accommodations. Completely transformed in the 1980s from a humbler lodging, it now has a skylighted promenade, bleached oak floors, a big lobby with a beamed ceiling and two granite fireplaces, and a snazzy restaurant, Pacific's Edge. It's a curious blend of formal (jackets and ties are requested in the restaurant) and casual (the friendly parking valets wear shorts), and of natural beauty and corporate sleekness.

Although the views of the Monterey pines and the ocean are striking, there is no immediate access to the shore. The action is at the resort itself. There are three whirlpool tubs, a swimming pool, a VCR library of movies, board games, and dancing to the music of a jazz combo in the lounge. Mountain bikes are available and tennis, golf, and horseback riding are nearby.

In the lounge, wide windows overlook spectacular vistas of sea and sky. Around the corner is the two-tiered restaurant, known for its outstanding wine list, Continental cuisine, and fresh seafood. There's an à la carte menu or you can order the Sunset Dinner, a four-course, fixed-price meal with or without wine. You can eat more casually on the terrace at the California Market, a combined deli, tavern, and boutique.

The Highlands' guest rooms are scattered among 22 buildings and the main lodge. They're all furnished in a contemporary style, and most have fireplaces and kitchens. Some are equipped with spa baths. Sizes and views vary; you can get a single room or a two-bedroom townhouse, a view of the road or a panoramic ocean view. Generally, the higher up the hill you go, the better the room. Some of the rooms close to the pool are good choices, too.

La Playa Hotel

P.O. Box 900
Camino Real & 8th
Carmel, CA 93921
408-624-6476
800-582-8900 in California
Fax 408-624-7966

A Mediterranean hotel with ocean views

Owner: Newton A. Cope, Sr. **General manager:** Tom Glidden. **Accommodations:** 75 rooms and 5 cottages. **Rates:** $115–$210 single or double, $15 additional person; suites and cottages $210–$495. **Payment:** Major credit cards. **Children:** Under 12 free in room with parents. **Pets:** Not allowed. **Smoking:** Nonsmoking rooms available.

Two blocks from Carmel's beach is a hotel that is a lovely find. La Playa has a classic Mediterranean look, with pink walls, red tile roofs, and terraced gardens. In the gardens are a heated swimming pool, a fountain, a filigreed black iron gazebo, and a brick patio. There are hundreds of colorful flowers and beds of pungent herbs, many used in the kitchen.

The hotel grew from a rockwork mansion built in 1904 by artist Chris Jorgensen for his bride, a daughter of San Francisco's Ghirardelli family. Later, the property was turned into a hotel and in 1983 sold to the Cope family and completely restored. Newton Cope is a historian who concentrates on turn-of-the-century California and the Old West. Photographs and memorabilia from his collections hang in La Playa's public spaces.

The staff at La Playa is small-town friendly and the service exemplary. "Our concierges are human encyclopedias," the desk clerk declares proudly, citing a few of the requests they fill with ease — from getting postage stamps or a recipe to assisting you with golf reservations.

Parts of the original mansion still exist — mainly the rockwork at the entrance of the L-shaped building and the curving staircase that leads up from the lobby.

The hotel's Terrace Grill is open for three meals a day and Sunday brunch. Continental cuisine, using local seafood and produce, is served in this room above the gardens. The wine list includes California, French, and Italian labels and several rare old ports and sherries. If you wish to eat outdoors while you watch the sunset, the terrace is a romantic spot.

About a third of the guest rooms have ocean views, three are beside the pool, and nine have private walled patios. Those without an ocean view overlook the fragrant garden, the patio, or residential Carmel. The hotel's mermaid motif is seen in unexpected places — embroidered on the towels, carved into the driftwood-like headboards. The decor includes heavy, Spanish-style furniture, plain white walls, and louvered shutters. Porcelain lamps, rawhide chairs, and brass tables mingle to create an effect that works best in the larger rooms; the smaller ones feel crowded. The views, especially from the upstairs rooms that face west, are stunning.

In a separate building on Camino Real, the executive suite is a good choice for entertaining a group. It has a meeting room, a kitchen, a living room with a gas fireplace, and an angled glass wall that opens to broad patios. There's a large bedroom with solid carved furniture, a vaulted beam ceiling, and two closets.

La Playa's five cottages are a block away from the hotel, toward the beach. The largest, a good choice for a family, contains four bedrooms. Four cottages have kitchens.

The Sandpiper Inn

2408 Bay View Avenue
Carmel, CA 93923
408-624-6433

An ocean view home with warm hospitality

Innkeepers: Graeme and Irene MacKenzie. **Accommodations:** 16 rooms (all with private bath). **Rates:** $90–$170 single or double, $20 additional person. **Included:** Expanded Continental breakfast. **Minimum stay:** 2 nights on weekends, 3–4 nights on some holidays. **Payment:** Major credit cards. **Children:** Age 12 and older welcome. **Pets:** Not allowed. **Smoking:** Not allowed indoors.

Sixty yards from Carmel Beach, the Sandpiper has some of the best ocean views in town. The white stucco house with brown shutters and green awnings stands on a residential corner, surrounded by green hedges and pots of bright flowers. It's a welcoming place, and the innkeepers take care to keep it that way.

The MacKenzies, who have owned the house since 1975, had a strong background in the resort business when they opened the Sandpiper. Originally from Scotland, they worked in the Orient and Bermuda before settling in Carmel. Memorabilia from their travels is displayed throughout the house, along with traditional and contemporary furniture and some rare antiques.

A dark-beamed ceiling and small chandeliers grace the living room, where a fire is usually crackling in the stone hearth. A breakfast of cereal, muffins, croissants, and fruit is served here, by windows that overlook the front garden and glimpse the sea.

The Sandpiper is close to a path that winds above the shore. If Carmel Beach is crowded, go south to Carmel River State Beach, which is much less used. It has a lagoon and natural preserve where you may see herons, brown pelicans, and other wildlife and birds.

Graeme and Irene are well aware of travelers' preferences; their expertise has pleased visitors from seventy countries. They have numerous menus from nearby restaurants and will make reservations for dinner, tennis, and golf. Guests may make tea in the kitchen and use the refrigerator to store drinks and snacks. Sherry is served every evening.

The furnishings in the guest rooms vary, ranging from standard contemporary to European antiques and reproductions. Fresh flowers, walk-in closets in the largest rooms, and modern baths with hair dryers and makeup mirrors are among their features. Some have wood-burning fireplaces, and kindling is provided. Several rooms have views of the ocean and Pebble Beach. None have television or phones, but there's a pay phone in the hall for guests.

Behind the fragrant garden are three charming cottage rooms with skylights.

Among Carmel's noted restaurants are Flaherty's, serving good fresh seafood, Rio Grill in Crossroads shopping center, and Sans Souci.

The Stonehouse Inn

P.O. Box 2517
8th below Monte Verde
Carmel, CA 93921
408-624-4569

A bed-and-breakfast retreat a few blocks from the beach

Innkeeper: Loretta Rolleri. **Accommodations:** 6 rooms (share 3 baths). **Rates:** $90–$135 single or double. **Included:** Expanded Continental breakfast. **Minimum stay:** 2 nights on weekends. **Payment:** MasterCard, Visa. **Children:** Age 12 and older welcome. **Pets:** Not allowed. **Smoking:** Not allowed.

This handsome stone inn, built in 1906, offers a peaceful retreat in a residential neighborhood of quaint Carmel-by-the-Sea. Its first owner was Josephine ("Nana") Foster, an eccentric and beloved patron of the arts, and her many guests included important artists and writers of the day.

In recognition of this history, the guest rooms are named for her notable visitors, as well as for Nana herself. Jack London, one of the larger rooms, has a daybed as well as a white iron and brass bed. Another large room, and the most expensive, is George Sterling, which has an unusual king-size canopy bed, a distant view of the ocean, a walk-in closet, and a reading area with an antique desk.

Lola Montez is quaint, with a high antique four-poster bed under the eaves. Nana's room is quite small — a good choice for one person. It's a hideaway with an antique armoire and a cotton duvet on the double bed. Natural light floods the room through a skylight. This room has a tiny washbasin in one corner.

In the European style, all the rooms share three baths. One, done in white tile, has a pedestal sink, a shower, and a skylight with a view of the dark green branches of a Monterey cypress tree. Another also has a skylight and a shower, as well as a clawfoot tub.

Soft colors, fresh flowers, and cozy quilts make the guest rooms welcoming havens. Some of the woodwork is scuffed and the carpeting worn, but otherwise the accommodations are fine.

Loretta Rolleri sets out a buffet breakfast of homemade breads, granola, juice, and coffee. You can eat in the small, sunny dining room or on the patio. The living room is a big, informal gathering place where hors d'oeuvres — hot in winter, cold in summer — are available every evening and a fire burns steadily in the big stone fireplace (ask about the secret hiding place in the stone).

Recommended restaurants are Giuliano's for Italian food and Flaherty's Fish House. For the best clam chowder on the peninsula, local residents will refer you to the Monterey Aquarium, which you'll undoubtedly want to see anyway. Just schedule your visit for lunchtime.

Loretta has added more greenery and flowers, but for the most part the inn remains unchanged, with antiques that include a baby stroller holding menus for nearby restaurants. Homemade cookies and port are provided in the evening.

Sundial Lodge

P.O. Box J
Carmel, CA 93921
408-624-8578

A small hotel surrounding a flower-filled courtyard

Manager: Carol Weir. **Rates:** $105–$170 single or double, $15 additional person. **Included:** Continental breakfast. **Minimum stay:** 2 nights on weekends. **Payment:** Major credit cards. **Children:** Welcome. **Pets:** Not allowed. **Smoking:** Not allowed in common room.

Two hours south of San Francisco, the little town of Carmel lies on a long, gradual slope between Highway 1 and the Pacific. Sundial Lodge is on Monte Verde Street, a few blocks above the beach. The two-story building with gray shutters and a red awning has tidy boxes of privet in front. Red geraniums tumble from window boxes, and bright yellow marigolds bloom against the wall. The flowery entrance hints at what you'll see as you step through a vine-covered trellis to a central brick courtyard. It's a bower of daisies, fuchsias, begonias, ferns, and honeysuckle with a rusty, old-fashioned sundial in the center. Peeking from among the flowers and ivy are Chinese animal sculptures. White chairs and glass-topped tables are set about the two-level terrace; in warm weather, you might enjoy having your breakfast here.

The guest rooms surround the courtyard and have garden or ocean views over the rooftops. They all have cable television and direct dial phones. Ten rooms include kitchens, useful for preparing light snacks. Silverware and dishes are provided; ask at the office for pots and pans.

Despite its heavily congested tourist traffic in summer, Carmel-by-the-Sea retains its charm. The shops are a delight, the restaurants excellent, and the beaches inviting.

The guest rooms, in French country or Victorian styles, are furnished in wicker. Room 17, on the ground level, has a garden view and a four-poster bed with a canopy. An armoire serves as a closet and a curtained alcove holds an extra bed. In the trim little kitchen there's a fold-down ironing board and a table for two. A breakfast of juice, toast, muffins, and coffee or tea is served in the small lobby, or you can take your repast to an outdoor table.

Sundial Lodge has no off-street parking, but you can easily find long-term parking on the street within two blocks.

Vagabond's House

P.O. Box 2747
4th & Dolores
Carmel, CA 93921
408-624-7738

A quiet inn surrounding a courtyard garden

Proprietor: Dennis LeVett. **Accommodations:** 11 suites (all with private bath). **Rates:** $79–$204 single or double, $20 additional person. **Included:** Continental breakfast. **Minimum stay:** 2 nights on weekends. **Payment:** Major credit cards. **Children:** Over age 12 welcome. **Pets:** Allowed with permission. **Smoking:** Allowed.

This cluster of half-timbered, shingled cottages blends perfectly with the quaint ambience of Carmel-by-the-Sea, as the village of Carmel is often called. The main building, which was a private home in the 1940s, and the one- and two-story guest accommodations face a flagstone courtyard with a waterfall. Centered by an immense old oak tree, the courtyard is lush with color and greenery: camellias, rhododendrons, and trailing vines fill every nook; ferns grow against the oak tree and fuchsias hang from its branches. On December nights, the tree twinkles with hundreds of tiny white lights. The effect is magical.

Vagabond's House is a five-minute drive from Carmel's beautiful mission, which dates from 1793 and is one of only two Basilicas in the western U.S. The annual Carmel Bach Festival is held at the mission during the summer.

Vagabond's House was named for a poem written by Don Blandings in 1928, in which the poet, who stayed at the inn in years past, describes his dream house. Several copies of a book of Blanding's poetry are on display in the parlor, where you may also see the owner's intriguing collections of British lead soldiers and Big Little Books.

All the guest rooms have fireplaces with wood supplied, and most have kitchens. Those rooms without full kitchens have small refrigerators.

Most of the guest rooms have been redone in the past few years. A few still have individual themes, such as a nautical decor and an English hunt motif, but most are now in a comfortable residential style, with flowered comforters, easy chairs, and balloon shades. They have roomy closets, luggage racks, full baths with tubs and showers (or showers only), and good reading lamps. Some have white wicker furnishings and beds with a partial canopy. Breakfast (coffee or tea, muffins and croissants) is delivered to your room within minutes after you call the office.

Treasure-filled shops, art and antiques galleries, and restaurants are within a short walk of the inn, and a long curve of surf-lapped sandy beach lies at the bottom of the hill.

CARMEL VALLEY

Carmel Valley Ranch Resort

One Old Ranch Road
Carmel, CA 93923
408-625-9500
800-4-CARMEL

A hillside golf resort with grand valley views

General manager: Cal Jepson. **Accommodations:** 100 suites. **Rates:** $235–$700 single or double, $20 additional person. **Payment:** Major credit cards. **Children:** Welcome. **Pets:** Not allowed. **Smoking:** Allowed.

Carmel Valley Ranch Resort is 6 miles east of Carmel, on the Monterey Peninsula. The only resort in the area with a private, guarded gate, it is sequestered on 1,700 hilly acres above the valley. Once admitted, you drive up a hillside, past fairways and greens, to the main lodge and 23 buildings of suites clustered among the oak trees. You immediately notice the striking display of color. Hundreds of flowers — geraniums, dahlias, roses, petunias, zinnias — maintained by the chief gardener and artist, Doris Ewing, surround the contemporary ranch-style lodge. Her creative skills are also evident in the resort's floral arrangements and in the watercolors which hang in the suites and lodge.

The lobby and lounge have gray-stained redwood walls and a blend of antiques and early California furnishings. Floor-to-ceiling windows overlook the golf course on one side and a terrace and freeform swimming pool on the other. Tucked against one corner of the terrace is a whirlpool spa, one of five on the property. The intimate, formal dining room (jackets required for men) is warm with earth tones, a natural wood ceiling, and a rough stone fireplace. Bruce Silverblatt, the executive chef, uses regional foods prepared with traditional French techniques. There's a varied wine list. A pianist plays light jazz here every evening. The kitchen will pack a picnic basket if you request it, and room service is available 24 hours a day (though it will cost you a $2 tray charge plus 18 percent gratuity).

The 18-hole golf course, designed by Pete Dye, is known for its challenges and beauty. Five fairways climb the mountainside, offering wide views of the valley floor. Three manmade lakes, the Carmel River, and numerous sand and grass bunkers provide opportunities to test all levels of skill.

Some suites are near the lodge; the rest are above it, in buildings with sweeping views of the valley. The commodious suites are decorated in Santa Fe, French country, or traditional style. Standard features include a stocked wet bar, two TVs (VCRs are available), three two-line phones, robes, and gas fireplaces. Some suites have two fireplaces and private spas.

Each of the one- and two-bedroom accommodations has a large deck with a view of the oak groves, golf course, gardens, or valley. Amish quilts cover the beds, and when they're turned down at night, cookies are left beside them. Coffee, tea and cocoa are in every room. A luxury master suite, with a dining room often used for business hospitality or executive conferences, has an Oriental decor. There are granite fireplaces in both bedroom and living room, a pink granite bar between the dining room and kitchen, and a deck on two sides jutting into the tops of oak trees.

Country club facilities are open to resort guests. The clubhouse restaurant is down the hill from the main lodge and overlooks the front nine holes of the golf course.

The resort has twelve hard-surface tennis courts, along with a pro shop and instructors who will arrange matches, lessons, special events, and tournaments.

For a luxurious golf or tennis vacation in a serene setting, Carmel Valley Ranch Resort is an excellent choice. The security of a guarded entrance is important to many guests, who like knowing that the only visitors who wander around uninvited are the deer that come to nibble the begonias hanging from oak tree branches by the front door.

Quail Lodge

8205 Valley Greens Drive
Carmel, CA 93923
408-624-1581
800-538-9516
Fax 408-624-3726

A luxurious resort on a golf course

General manager: Csaba Ajan. **Accommodations:** 100 rooms and villas. **Rates:** $195–$1,720 single or double, $25 additional person. **Payment:** Major credit cards. **Children:** Under 12 free in room with parents. **Pets:** Allowed with permission. **Smoking:** Nonsmoking rooms available.

A few miles east of Highway 1, off Carmel Valley Road two hours south of San Francisco, this serene, luxurious resort stands on ten landscaped acres of a private country club. Ten small lakes, the habitat of wildlife and waterfowl, dot the grounds, and an 18-hole golf course sprawls across the valley floor.

You drive down a road lined with pepper trees to a scattering of buildings behind winding paths. Inside the main lodge, there's a two-story atrium with dark beams and skylights above the mezzanine. Around the corner are the Covey restaurant and a cocktail lounge. A few steps down from the lounge, in the plant-filled sunroom, the glass walls offer views of the lake and lush grounds.

Breakfast and lunch are available at the Club, a casual restaurant overlooking the driving range just across the Carmel River, which divides Quail Lodge from the country club.

The guest rooms are beside walks with trellises that bloom with trumpet vines. Fragrant blossoms and expensive perfume scent the air as you walk or ride in a golf cart to your well-furnished room. Every room has either a patio or a balcony. All have phones and television. A typical room will have a four-poster bed, a dressing area, and a tile bath with a lighted makeup mirror. The colors are in neutral blonds and tans; only the quilts provide a bright touch.

Candlelit and romantic, with dark, polished woods, rose upholstery, and ivory linens, the Covey restaurant's two-level dining room overlooks Mallard Lake and its lighted fountain. A pianist plays in the small bar five nights a week.

The light cottage suite has a sitting-bedroom combination with a wet bar, gas fireplace, and vaulted ceiling with track lighting and skylights. The windows overlook the curving lakeshore, and from the patio you see ducks swimming on the lake and the arching bridge under graceful trees.

The California Suite is dramatic in a dark, shadowy mood. Black tables, brass lamps, indirect lighting, an Oriental cabinet, and a bed set on a platform accentuate the striking decor. All the rooms have stereo systems; this one has a VCR as well. A pocket door leads to a bath in deep red tile, with tub and shower. On the private deck, behind vine-covered walls, is a wooden hot tub. The suite has a dining room, which can be rented separately if you wish to host a meeting or dinner for eight. It, too, has dramatic flair, with its dark bamboo chairs, an Oriental screen, and low couches.

Most of the guests at Quail Lodge are repeat visitors, a tribute to the high quality of service and superb accommodations. Among the recreational diversions are four tennis courts, two swimming pools, and guest privileges on the golf course. The generally well-heeled patrons make occasional use of the helicopter landing next to the country club's driving range.

Robles del Rio Lodge

200 Punta del Monte
Carmel Valley, CA 93924
408-659-3705
800-833-0843
Fax 408-659-5157

A casual country lodge

Proprietors: Adreena and Glen Gurries. **Accommodations:** 27 rooms, 4 cottages. **Rates:** $80–$120 single or double, $10 additional person; cottages $150–$160; weekday and winter discounts available. **Included:** Expanded Continental breakfast. **Minimum stay:** 2 nights on weekends. **Payment:** MasterCard, Visa. **Children:** Welcome (infants free). **Pets:** Not allowed. **Smoking:** Allowed.

Oak trees stud the rolling hills around Carmel Valley, 13 miles inland from coastal Highway 1, and centuries-old oaks shade the flagstone terrace of Robles del Rio. Hence the lodge's name, which is Spanish for "oaks of the river." The lodge, the oldest in the area, covers nine acres of a hillside off a winding road above the valley.

The lodge was built in 1928 as a private golf club and turned into a public resort in 1939. Now run by the Gurries family, it's a casual, low-key place far removed from the busy, shop-lined streets of Carmel.

A swimming pool lies behind trimmed hedges, oak trees, and beds of daisies. Potted pink geraniums add color to the lovely terrace, where dozens of tiny birds in the trees keep the leaves fluttering.

In the low main building are the Cantina bar and The Ridge, a restaurant with a view of the valley. The Continental menu includes seafood, chicken, and beef. The avocado soup, fresh salmon, and rack of lamb are commendable. Also overlooking the valley is a lounge with a stone fireplace, where a buffet breakfast of fresh fruit, cereals, boiled eggs, and juice is set out.

Accommodations are in one- and two-story buildings (Oak Leaf, Cypress, Cherry, Knotty Pine, and El Roblar) and cottages set against the hillside below the lodge. The cottages are rustic, and the standard rooms have thin walls and outmoded decor, but the suites offer excellent lodging for the price. Roblar Suite C, for example, is a second-floor apartment in crisp blue and white. The living room holds a sofa bed, TV, several chairs and tables, and a white cabinet decorated with painted flowers. Trim curtains frame a fine view. There's a clean, well-equipped kitchen and a bedroom with two white iron queen-size beds. Double doors open to a private deck above the lawn and slope covered with painted daisies. With the use of a kitchen and breakfast included, the suite is well-priced at $180 for four people.

Stonepine

150 East Carmel Valley Road
Carmel Valley, CA 93924
408-659-2245
Fax 408-659-5160

An exclusive inn in the country

General manager: Daniel Barduzzi.
Accommodations: 14 suites. **Rates:** $225–$750 single or double, $50 additional person. **Included:** Expanded Continental breakfast. **Minimum stay:** 2 nights on weekends, 3 nights on holidays. **Payment:** Major credit cards. **Children:** Welcome (age 12 and older in main château). **Pets:** Not allowed. **Smoking:** Allowed.

This luxurious retreat began in the 1930s as a throughbred racing farm in the hills east of Carmel. Called the Double H Ranch by its owners, Helen and Henry Potter Russell of the Crocker banking family, it covered 22 square miles of the valley. No effort was spared in creating the perfect estate, from the Mediterranean main house to the carefully designed gardens and orchards.

By 1983, when it was purchased by Noel and Gordon Hentschel, the property had dwindled to 330 acres. Its new owners renamed the place after the Italian pines that Helen Russell had planted as saplings and began an extensive restoration that would turn the estate into an opulent inn and equestrian retreat.

Eight suites are in Château Noel, a pink French country mansion with a tower, black ironwork, and red tile roof. The château is at the end of a mile-long road that winds up a hill past meadows and trees and over a creek to a circular gravel drive punctuated with oak trees and low stone walls.

The living room is furnished in a combination of contemporary and traditional styles. Its seven-foot carved limestone fireplace is from 19th-century Italy; the French tapestries above it date from the 1700s. The theme is light and restful, and the mood tranquil. French doors lead to a loggia with stone arches supported by carved columns from ancient Rome. Tall stone pines edge the sheltered lawn and garden beside it. Flowering shrubs scent the air, and vines and gnarled olive trees cast leafy shadows over the chairs and tables where breakfast may be served. Around the corner, below walls cascading with white wisteria and purple bougainvillea, is the pool level, reached by descending broad stairs.

Enter through the triple-arched porch and you're greeted by a gracious staff member who will invite you to have cognac in the living room after dinner, or perhaps attend the performance of a string ensemble on a summer afternoon.

Indoors, in the dark, elegant dining room, guests who choose to dine here sit at a single table set with fine china, crystal, and sterling silver. The oak paneling is from 19th-century France — a wedding gift to Helen Russell from her family. The same burnished paneling is in the library, a comfortable nook for reading, chess, and conversation by the marble fireplace.

The only lodging on the main floor is the Don Quixote Suite, which has a private patio garden. Up time-worn stairs are the other suites, all lavishly appointed with antiques, down comforters, and luxurious baths. Each room has cable television and a VCR, fresh flowers, lounging robes, and shelves of books. Several have fireplaces laid with wood and ready to light.

Wedgwood, in blue, has a king-size bed and Wedgwood china on display. The big bathroom contains a two-person whirlpool tub. Chanel is a favorite of many guests, with its soft gray satins, a fireplace, antiques, and a whirlpool tub. The bedroom has two double beds. Taittinger is the largest and most expensive suite. A chilled bottle of Taittinger champagne awaits your arrival, and a champagne satin decor sets the tone. There are two bathrooms (one with a whirlpool tub and bidet) and dressing rooms.

Four more suites are down the hill in the Paddock House, an old-fashioned green and white country ranch house with a large veranda and lawn. If you bring young children, this is where you'll stay. Guests in the informal but well-furnished inn can use its kitchen and dining room.

A third building is Briar Rose Cottage, which has two suites, a kitchen, a fireplace, and a garden with a gazebo. It's a good choice to two couples traveling together.

Horseback riding lessons and trail rides are offered at the equestrian center. Stonepine also has a soccer field, an archery range, a croquet lawn, tennis courts, and a horseshoe pitch. There's also an exercise room, and mountain bikes are available.

DAVENPORT

New Davenport Bed & Breakfast Inn

31 Davenport Avenue
Davenport, CA 95017
408-425-1818
408-426-4122

A seaside inn with artistic flair

Innkeepers: Bruce and Marcia Mc-Dougal. **Accommodations:** 12 rooms (all with private bath). **Rates:** $60–$115.50 single or double, $10 additional person. **Included:** Full breakfast. **Payment:** MasterCard, Visa. **Children:** Over age 12 welcome. **Pets:** Not allowed. **Smoking:** Not allowed.

The seaside community of Davenport, halfway between San Francisco and Carmel on Highway 1, was an active port at the turn of the century. When a cement plant went up in 1906, it grew into a town with a general store, and half a dozen hotels. Over time, Davenport declined, but in recent years new homes and businesses have sprung up. On the site of the former Cash Store, which burned down, Bruce and Marcia McDougal built the New Davenport Cash Store and opened it in 1978 as a pottery gallery, restaurant, and guest lodging. The present gallery, on the ground floor of the inn, has become a center for folk art, textiles, pottery, and jewelry from around the world.

Within walking distance are several studios and showrooms where local craftspeople display their works. The historic St. Vincent de Paul Church and the restored jail are interesting photographic subjects.

Across the room is the rustic restaurant, with brick walls hung with masks and carvings. Here you may sit at wooden tables on mismatched chairs or benches — there are even a few church pews — and lunch on pasta, seafood, soups, and sandwiches. Hotel guests are given a $5 credit for breakfast on weekdays; on weekends, breakfast is served in the cottage.

Above the Cash Store and Restaurant are eight guest rooms with a sheltered balcony that stretches around two sides of the building, overlooking the highway and, beyond it, a bluff above the ocean. Wide doors open to rooms furnished with antiques and ethnic art from the McDougals' extensive collection. The rooms have telephones but no television, and armoires or pegs rather than closets.

China Ladder has an Oriental theme. Pigeon Point is small, cool, and blue, decorated with a New England flavor. Captain Davenport's Retreat, on the corner, is the largest room. It has a sitting area with four double doors opening to the balcony, peacock wicker chairs, and an ocean view.

If you're willing to sacrifice the view for quiet (Highway 1 can be noisy, though it's usually peaceful at night), request one of the four rooms in the cottage around the corner. It has a common area decorated with Indian wall hangings, where guests may relax, read, and visit. There are games, a sideboard with coffee, tea, mugs and plates for breakfast, and a small kitchen. As one visitor wrote in the guest book, "All the comforts of home — or the home you'd like to have — and yet you're on a holiday."

The decor in the cottage is light and bright, with country furnishings. Grandma's Room, small and serene, has a white iron bed and eyelet curtains at a high window. It faces east to a small garden and patio. The other three — Nellie's Sewing Room, The Guest Room, and Mike's Room — are also furnished in white wicker and have cotton quilts on white iron beds. You may find scuff marks and peeling paint, but the inn is clean and comfortable and generally well maintained.

Across the highway there's a secluded beach to stroll, and from the ocean cliffs you may see migrating gray whales spouting just offshore.

GILROY

Country Rose Inn

P.O. Box 1804
Gilroy, CA 95021-1804
408-842-0441

A serene home in garlic-growing country

Innkeeper: Rose Hernandez. **Accommodations:** 5 rooms (all with private bath). **Rates:** \$79–\$169. **Included:** Full breakfast. **Minimum stay:** 2 nights on summer weekends. **Payment:** Major credit cards. **Children:** Welcome (rooms accommodate two persons only). **Pets:** Not allowed. **Smoking:** Not allowed.

Roses dominate this charming inn, from the flowers in the rooms to the innkeeper's name. Carefully tended gardens and shade trees grow by the white Dutch Colonial home, which was built in the 1920s on a chicken ranch. The chickens are gone, but the sense of rural tranquility remains on these five acres surrounded by farmland. Gilroy, the garlic capital of the world, is a few miles away, and San Jose is a 30-minute drive.

Rose, a former teacher, is a conscientious hostess. She will offer information on accessible attractions, such as San Juan Bautista and Pinnacles National Monument, and recommend good restaurants. One of her favorites in Gilroy is Station 55, whose menu emphasizes garlic, of course.

There are two parlors in the simply furnished inn. One has a brick fireplace, another a baby grand piano. The dining room has a view of the front veranda and rosebed. Also on the main floor is the Garden Room, the home's original living room. It reflects Rose Hernandez's interests and her family, with its carved antique bed and trunk, a photograph of her parents' 1916 wedding, and her mother's treasured wedding dress in the armoire.

The upstairs rooms have views of the big valley oaks and, in the distance, the Gabilan Hills. Double Delight is secluded behind two doors; Sterling Rose is a corner room with a window seat and a view of the magnolia tree and its birds' nests. Usually the magnolia blooms in time for Rose's annual Valentine tea.

Imperial Rose has a window seat, a white wicker settee, and a walk-in closet. Rambling Rose is a large suite with French doors between the sleeping and sitting areas. Its balcony extends to the branches of a 300-year-old oak tree.

GOLETA

Circle Bar B Guest Ranch

1800 Refugio Road
Goleta, CA 93117
805-968-1113

A family ranch for relaxing and horseback riding

General manager: Pat Brown. **Accommodations:** 13 rooms (all with private bath). **Rates:** $128–$225 double, $50–$75 additional person. **Included:** All meals. **Minimum stay:** 2 nights on weekends, 3 nights on holidays. **Payment:** MasterCard, Visa. **Children:** Under 3 free in room with parents. **Pets:** Not allowed. **Smoking:** Allowed.

The Circle Bar B, 20 miles north of Santa Barbara, combines a rustic atmosphere with contemporary comforts. Tucked in a wooded canyon in the Santa Ynez Mountains, the ranch has stables, a chicken coop, and assorted animals, including peacocks that wander the grounds and peer from the branches of the walnut trees. The atmosphere is down-home casual, befitting a place that opened fifty years ago as a children's camp.

On nearly 1,000 acres of hilly, coastal countryside, the ranch offers great scenery and good food and lodging, but for many guests its major appeal is the horses. Experienced wranglers take riders of all levels of ability on daily rides. They'll give individual instruction, too.

Yet along with the rusticity are rooms with down comforters on the beds and freestanding fireplaces. Five are small, attached rooms; the rest are in separate cabins. All are set against a hillside of olive trees and reached by brick baths bordered by large jade plants.

A typical cabin resembles a spacious hotel room with a raised brick hearth, high beamed ceiling, white walls, and Southwestern art. It has a king-size bed with padded headboard, a dresser and closet, good reading lamps, and a bath with a tiled shower stall. A recent addition is a two-bedroom cabin, useful for families. The kids' favorites, though, are the two cabins with pull-down stairs that lead to lofts with double beds. Linens are changed daily, and full cleaning is provided on alternate days.

The ranch, begun by the Brown family in the 1930s, is still a family operation. Pat Brown runs the stables, and Jim, his father, handles maintenance and the Friday and Saturday night cookouts. Weekend barbecue buffets feature country-style ribs, steak, chicken, baked beans, three kinds of salad, garlic bread, and carrot cake. Afterward, those who've come for the dinner theater mosey down to the Old Barn to watch a Circle Bar B production. The theater, which has been operating since the early 1980s, presents comedies, mysteries, and musicals that are usually (though not always) suitable for the whole family.

Meals are eaten at common tables in the dining room of the main ranch house, or under the grape arbor. Breakfast is hearty country fare — fruit, eggs from ranch chickens, pancakes, potatoes, and strong coffee. After breakfast, you may want to take a picnic lunch on a hike to the swimming hole beneath a waterfall, or on a trail ride to a scenic vista above the coast. The ranch is 3½ miles inland from Refugio State Beach.

When you return you can wash off the trail dust with a dip in the pool, or play croquet or table tennis, or soak in the hot tub. The living room — also the lobby, office, and game room — has books and games.

LOS ALAMOS

Union Hotel

P.O. Box 616
362 Bell Street
Los Alamos, CA 93440
805-344-2744

An Old West hotel with frontier hospitality

Proprietor: Dick Langdon.
Accommodations: 13 rooms (3 with private bath). **Rates:** \$80–\$100 single or double. **Included:** Full breakfast. **Payment:** Major credit cards. **Children:** Welcome. **Pets:** Not allowed. **Smoking:** Allowed. **Open:** Friday and Saturday.

It took the wood from twelve old barns to restore the original appearance of the Union Hotel. That was just a part of the work that was done to turn it into an exaggerated version of a 19th-century lodging. With the potted palms and Victorian furniture in the lobby are a fireplace mantel taken from a Pasadena mansion, a clawfoot copper bathtub topped with beveled glass, a pair of 200-year-old Egyptian burial urns, and a *Gone with the Wind* lamp.

Saloon doors swing open to a 150-year-old mahogany bar. Headlights from a 1914 Oldsmobile hang on the side wall, along with washboards, saws, boots, well-used tools, horseshoes, and a moose head. There are two jukeboxes, an upright piano, and a pay phone encircled by a red velvet curtain. The ceiling was once the wall of the oldest store in town.

Each room has something special: a bearskin rug, an unusual Murphy bed, a curtained alcove, a fireplace. There's even a secret passage. Ask Dick to show you the hidden room behind a retreating bookcase.

The dining room has chandeliers made from gaslights and an oak dining set that once graced a Mississippi plantation home. Dinner is served on Friday, Saturday, and Sunday evenings. The menu includes swordfish, filet mignon, chicken, and lamb.

The first Union Hotel was built in 1880 as a stagecoach stop. It went up in flames in 1886 and was rebuilt of 18-inch-thick adobe and renamed Los Alamos. When the current owner found a picture of the hotel as it was in 1884, he determined to restore it. So the old barns were dismantled to create the dark facade it has today.

The hotel stands behind an old-fashioned boardwalk on the main street of tiny Los Alamos, 14 miles from Solvang, a Danish-style village. The hotel is open on weekends only (or midweek for private parties and receptions). "If we were open every day, it wouldn't be fun anymore. And I do this because it's fun," says the irrepressible owner. Formerly from Los Angeles, Dick Langdon was in the meat business when he dreamed of escaping the city's fast pace. In 1972 he stumbled upon the hotel and found a master craftsman, Jim Radhe, who constructed the entire front of the building by hand.

Upstairs, you can while away an evening in the large, skylighted parlor at the 1880 Brunswick pool table, game tables, and shelves filled with books. The guest rooms contain antique furniture, handmade quilts, pedestal sinks, and authentic Victorian wallpapers.

In this quiet place your sleep will be undisturbed. Come morning, the scent of freshly brewed coffee will lure you downstairs to breakfast. As you linger over bacon and eggs, you can chat with other guests and plan the day. Not that there's much to plan in Los Alamos (which is Spanish for "the cottonwoods"). This is a sleepy agricultural town, with no resort activity or nightlife. "There's nothing to do here but enjoy the tranquility," as Dick puts it.

However, he may take you for a ride in a 1918 White touring car, first used in Yellowstone National Park. And you may be given a tour of the Mansion, Dick's amazing Victorian house next door (see Victorian Mansion, below).

Lounging on the brick terrace by the swimming pool and soaking in the hot tub, which sits in a gazebo entwined with night-blooming jasime, are probably the favorite pastimes. Dick is also putting in a squash court, a privet maze, and a railroad tunnel.

Victorian Mansion

P.O. Box 616
Los Alamos, CA 93440
805-344-2744

A one-of-a-kind hotel with fantasy themes

Proprietor: Dick Langdon. **Accommodations:** 6 rooms. **Rates:** $200 double. **Included:** Full breakfast. **Payment:** Major credit cards. **Children:** Not appropriate. **Pets:** Not allowed. **Smoking:** Allowed.

From the outside, this yellow Victorian with white gingerbread trim looks like a perfectly preserved, quaint example of a 19th-century home. Step inside and you enter a unique world that is far from anything remotely Victorian. It bears no resemblance to the rest of Southern California, either, or the little agricultural town of Los Alamos.

> **"This whole house is an illusion," says Dick. "It lets you step into another world for a day." The place could be hopelessly hokey, but because of the exceptional quality of the workmanship, the clever ideas, and the playful approach, it's successful.**

Each room is a fantasy, a dream brought to life by Dick Langdon's fertile imagination and the 200 artisans who turned his ideas into reality.

For starters, there's the Drive-In Movie room. Enter through the black leather padded door and you see a yellow 1956 Cadillac convertible. That's the bed, facing a screen where a movie from the '50s will be shown later. The rear of another Cadillac forms a magazine table, and the trunk of yet another holds a black porcelain wash basin. In the room is a sunken tub, operated by remote control. A neon sign reads "Snack Bar."

There are no visible windows — here or in any of the rooms. The walls are meticulously painted with scenes of the Hollywood hills and Mickey and Minnie Mouse dancing to a jukebox. In the cedar closet, hidden behind the scenery, are Mickey and Minnie robes.

That's just the beginning. In Ancient Rome, you sleep in a silver Ben Hur chariot that holds a queen-size bed. You're surrounded by paintings of arbors, arches, busts, ruins, and Rome burning in the distance. The bathroom, behind a bookcase, has ancient battle scenes hand-painted on the tiles. A remote control operates the lights, television, fireplace, and Roman tub. Wide marble stairs lead to the sunken tub. The robes are togas.

Desert Gods, behind a stone door, is a sheik's oasis with a canopy bed on a platform, a fabric ceiling, Oriental carpets, and a tile fireplace. A low table, set with silver teapots from Arabia, is surrounded by plush cushions. Pull the beard of a life-size King Tut, and the mummy pulls from the wall to reveal a bathroom with an Egyptian motif.

If you've ever wanted to be a swashbuckling buccaneer, Pirate is the room for you. Shaped like the interior of a Spanish galleon, it has a bed tucked into a corner, an open treasure chest full of sparkling booty, a low table set on a 700-pound cannon, and a stone fireplace carved with dragons. Best of all is the small leaded glass window, with scenes of battling ships behind it. Open the window and you hear the sounds of creaking masts and a stormy sea. In the tiled bathroom, painted parrots watch pirates at work, and Blackbeard hides in the shower.

Artist's Loft is Dick's idea of an 18th-century Parisian artist's studio. It includes a spiral staircase leading to a curtained bed, an alcove with a view of the French countryside, a tiny French fireplace, and a partially completed canvas of a nude. The walls are painted with views of Paris; in the bath it's a mural of kicking cancan dancers. Each dancer has the face of one of the artists who helped create the hotel's elaborate scenes.

Picture a gypsy encampment in the forest, and you have Gypsy Wagon. Portières hang over the bed, which appears to be a Gypsy wagon, embellished with carved mythological horses. Every season in the woodland is painted on the walls, from the blossoms of spring to the snow-clad trees of winter. There's a stone fireplace, a sunken pool, and a bear rug. At the touch of a button, a hidden TV swings out; another button operates the whirlpool tub.

Guests are offered champagne on arrival, and on the weekends they can dine at the Union Hotel, where the menu offers entrées geared to the themes of the rooms. Among them are Roman chicken, Egyptian shish kebab, Gypsy stew, and '50s Rock 'n' Roll (cheeseburgers or hot dogs and french fries).

MONTECITO

San Ysidro Ranch

900 San Ysidro Lane
Montecito, CA 93108
805-969-5046
800-368-6788
Fax 805-565-1995

An exclusive cottage resort in the coastal hills

General manager: Janice Clatoff. **Accommodations:** 44 cottages. **Rates:** $195–$695 2 to 4 people. **Minimum stay:** 2 nights on weekends, 3–4 nights on holidays. **Payment:** MasterCard, Visa. **Children:** Welcome. **Pets:** Allowed. **Smoking:** Not allowed.

This cottage resort in the hills above the sea has been like a second home to famous names and discerning travelers since it opened in 1893. Somerset Maugham, Sinclair Lewis, and John Galsworthy stayed in bungalows and wrote; Laurence Olivier and Vivien Leigh were married in the garden. John Huston stayed for three months, writing the screenplay for *The African Queen*; John F. and Jacqueline Kennedy honeymooned here; and celebrities from Jean Harlow to Julia Child have lauded the breathtaking views.

Once the 550 acres just south of Santa Barbara served as a way station for Franciscan friars. It was later a cattle ranch and citrus tree farm, and now a resort that attempts to preserve San Ysidro's traditional calm, beauty, and history while providing contemporary luxury.

The single-story white cottages with peaked roofs are spread across the hillside under stately palms, eucalytpus, oak, and sycamore trees. Most of the cottages contain one, two, or three units; one has eight. They all have views of the distant sea or wooded foothills of the Santa Ynez mountains.

Each room is decorated differently and with traditional good taste. One, in Sycamore Cottage, has a brass bed, a TV, a phone, and a desk. Wood is laid in the fireplace and the refrigerator is well stocked. The bathroom has a tub and shower, a washbasin set in an antique sideboard, numerous toiletries, and a lighted makeup mirror. French doors lead to a deck under the sycamore trees.

All the rooms have fireplaces, wet bars, coffeemakers, and

terrycloth robes; several feature private outdoor Jacuzzis. Canyon Cottage, surrounding an oak-shaded terrace, has some of the smallest rooms and best views. Behind it is Lilac, highest on the hill and closest to the tennis courts and heated swimming pool. Geranium is one of the original cottages. It's been refurbished with a country flavor in white and natural wood and has an outdoor Jacuzzi tub under flowering vines.

A part of San Ysidro's history is an 1825 adobe building, once the home of a pioneer family. Another is a former citrus-packing house that is now Stonehouse, an award-winning restaurant.

Many guests come for the horseback riding. If you're planning to ride and want the most secluded lodging on the property, ask for Forest Cottage, a one-bedroom suite near the stables. San Ysidro's lodgings are attractive and comfortable, and the adobe-walled restaurant terrace has a stunning view, but most admired are the grounds. Scarlet-blooming bottlebrush trees, brilliant lantana, natal plum, and roses grow in profusion around lawns and paths. Vines cover a trellis in the wedding garden, and the air is fragrant with honeysuckle, jasmine, and orange blossoms. Tidy herb and vegetable gardens keep the Stonehouse kitchen well stocked.

The Hacienda Lounge is in the main building, next to the registration office. Here you'll find complimentary morning coffee and newspapers and an honor bar. There's a stone fireplace and pool table, and chess and backgammon are set up for play. Groups and small conferences are welcome at the ranch. Catering and audiovisual and meeting materials are available.

MONTEREY

The Jabberwock

598 Laine
Monterey, CA 93940
408-372-4777

A well-located bed-and-breakfast with warm hospitality

Innkeepers: Jim and Barbara Allen. **Accommodations:** 7 rooms (3 with private bath). **Rates:** \$100–\$180 single or double. **Included:** Full breakfast. **Minimum stay:** 2 nights on weekends, 3 nights on some holidays. **Payment:** MasterCard, Visa. **Children:** Older children welcome (rooms accommodate two persons). **Pets:** Not allowed. **Smoking:** Outdoors only.

"'Twas brillig, and the slithy toves did gyre and gimble in the wabe." So begins "Jabberwocky," Lewis Carroll's poem in *Through the Looking Glass.* The Allens decided that it provided the perfect theme for their bed-and-breakfast. Every room has a Jabberwocky name, and bits of Lewis Carroll whimsy are found throughout the house. It's not overdone, however; the decor is charming but never precious.

The pleasant home, on a residential corner away from seaside tourist traffic, was built in 1911. Used as a convent for years, it was purchased by the Allens and opened to guests in

1982. Jim, a retired firefighter and a skilled gardener, landscaped the property, putting in ponds, waterfalls, a sundial, and red gravel paths traversing green lawns — as well as a brick parking lot.

Recommended restaurants in Monterey are Domenico's for its view (it's on the wharf) and bouillabaisse, Gianni's for the best pizza in town, and the nearby Gallery, known for its Continental menu.

Barbara, formerly in the hotel business, is the cook, and her breakfasts are noteworthy. You'll find early morning coffee on the dining room table, and later dishes with such names as "snarkleberry flumpsious" and "razzleberry flabjous" are served by the fireplace in the dining room or on the sun porch. Sherry and hors d'oeuvres are served on the sun porch at 5:00 P.M. Bedtime cookies and milk are the final treats of the day.

Soft drinks and juices are always available in the refrigerator (called the Tum Tum Tree) on the upper stair landing, and you may store your own snacks and wine there.

The comfortable living room is available for relaxing, reading, listening to the stereo, and looking through local menus and other guests' restaurant critiques. Beyond is the cheerful sun room, filled with plants, overlooking the side gardens.

The Toves, the only guest room on the main floor, has an eight-foot carved walnut Victorian bed, a private bath with a clawfoot tub and shower, and a little patio. High on the third floor are two garret rooms, the Mimsey and the Wabe, which share a bathroom and sitting room with an ocean view. Mimsey is a hideaway overlooking the bay and town. Peach-toned Wabe gets afternoon sun and has an Austrian carved bed.

The other rooms are on the second floor. Each is furnished distinctively and includes thoughtful accents such as fresh flowers, sachets, bathrobes, and fruit liqueurs. You may feel that you, like Alice, have stumbled through the looking glass when you see the card on your bedside table. It must be held to a mirror to be read.

Brillig is a small room, but its large closet and cupboards offer plenty of storage space. The antique rolled oak bed with crocheted afghan gives it an old-fashioned country atmosphere. Borogrove is the largest and best room, running the width of the house and overlooking Monterey Bay and the garden through three walls of windows. It has a white brick fireplace, a king-size bed, and a bath with a shower. Despite its classic elegance, Borogrove has not escaped the Allens' lighthearted touch. A stuffed wool goose stands in one corner, a book of gnomes lies on the table, and a Victorian children's book reminds you of the era you've briefly joined.

Barbara and Jim go out of their way to assure that you have a good time in their home and in Monterey. They'll give you lists of sightseeing suggestions, sell admission tickets to the aquarium so that you won't have to wait in line, introduce you to their lovable English bull terrier, and provide you with dozens of restaurant recommendations.

Monterey Plaza Hotel

400 Cannery Row
Monterey, CA 93940
408-646-1700
800-334-3999 in California
800-631-1339 outside California
Fax 408-646-5937

An elegant hotel above the bay

General manager: Daniel E. Kelly. **Accommodations:** 290 rooms and 20 suites. **Rates:** \$150–\$280 single or double, \$20 additional person. **Minimum stay:** 2 nights on holiday weekends. **Payment:** Major credit cards. **Children:** Age 17 and under free in room with parents. **Pets:** Not allowed. **Smoking:** Nonsmoking rooms available.

This is the snazziest hotel of size in Monterey, so grand and sophisticated it seems slightly out of place on Cannery Row, where seedy remnants of John Steinbeck's colorful stories still cling. Fish processing was the main activity here until the bay was fished out and the sardine canneries deserted. Now they house art galleries, shops, and restaurants, and tourism brings in new life.

Like a transplant from San Francisco, 120 miles to the north, the Monterey Plaza boasts white-uniformed valets who greet you in the porte cochere, take your car, and open the doors to the marble lobby. The exterior is Spanish Colonial in style, but inside, all is Oriental and Mediterranean luxury. Sweeping staircases, custom carpets, 18th-century Chinese and Italian Empire furnishings, and dramatic flower arrangements create an elegant mood.

The hotel is not merely close to the ocean, it's virtually on it. Waves crash, the surf splashes, and sea lions bark right below your balcony and beside the terrace where lunch and cocktails are served.

Directly across the lobby is a wall of windows framing the water and mainland mountains across from this western hook of the bay. Downstairs, the Duck Club restaurant has an even closer proximity to the kelp-covered surf. The menu features duck, grilled meats, pasta, and seafood.

Some guest rooms are in another building across Cannery Row, but since the main attraction here is the stunning view, the oceanside rooms are far superior. The best are the "02" rooms on the corners. The rooms and suites have carpeting and light walls, brass lamps by the beds, round tables with rattan chairs by the windows, and television with HBO. You can rent VCRs and movies. A deluxe suite with a view offers a spacious, light-filled sitting area and two balconies from which you can watch the ducks, seagulls, kayakers, fishing boats, and sailboats. As you sniff the salt air, watch the sea otters cracking oyster shells, and listen to the sea lions beg for sardines at Fisherman's Wharf, you'll know this is unmistakably Monterey Bay.

Old Monterey Inn

500 Martin Street
Monterey, CA 93940
408-375-8284
800-350-2344

A tranquil bed-and-breakfast in a luxurious setting

Innkeepers: Ann and Gene Swett. **Accommodations:** 8 rooms, 1 cottage, 1 suite. **Rates:** $160–$220 single or double. **Included:** Full breakfast. **Minimum stay:** 2 nights on weekends. **Payment:** MasterCard, Visa. **Children:** Not appropriate. **Pets:** Not allowed. **Smoking:** Not allowed.

Tucked away on a side street in a residential district of Monterey is Old Monterey Inn, a world removed from the crowds of Cannery Row.

Brick paths wind past bird baths under oak trees, ferns, a trickling fountain, blooming begonias, and drought-resistant succulents. Outside the dining room window, fuchsia baskets hang from the branches of an immense oak tree. Around the corner are painted carts from Costa Rica and other pieces of folk art collected during the Swetts' travels. The fragrant rose garden is Gene's labor of love; he has duplicated the garden planted by the home's original owner, Carmel Martin, and dedicated it to him.

In the large common room, tea and cookies are set out in the afternoon. They're replaced by hors d'oeuvres in the evening, when the gracious hosts encourage mingling and getting acquainted. This is a good time to check through an assortment of local restaurant menus, consult with other visitors, or ask the Swetts for a recommendation.

On the other side of the foyer is the dining room, which still has its original metal fireplace, built in 1929, and a stucco ceiling with handpainted designs. A gourmand's breakfast is served here at one 9 A.M. seating. The dishes are different every day. You may feast on California quiche with chilies and pimentos, poached apples, crêpes, or Belgian waffles with Gene's special syrups. Takahashi china, painted with delicate birds and flowers, graces the table, centered by flowers from the garden.

The romantic rooms have no TV or phone to interrupt the mood. The beds are puffy with down comforters and pillows, and handcrafted natural woods and family antiques furnish the rooms. Most have wood-burning fireplaces, skylights, and stained glass windows.

The most spacious is the Ashford Suite, once the master bedroom. The sitting area has a tile fireplace, an antique pine daybed, and bay windows overlooking the gardens. In the bedroom is a king-size bed and more windows above the flowers.

For years the big, half-timbered house was the Swett family home, where they raised six children. In 1977, it opened to guests and now is one of the gems of the Monterey Peninsula, a thoroughly charming, peaceful retreat set on more than an acre of lovely grounds and gardens.

Appropriately named, the Library Room boasts walls of books and a stone fireplace. It also has a private sun deck. Third-floor hideaways are Dovecote, with an oak rocker and a built-in loveseat by the hearth, and Rookery, a sunny room with a skylight and wicker chairs.

Some rooms are in a cottage with private entrances behind the house. Shuttered windows, wicker furniture, and colors of white and green complement the inn's English country garden theme. The most secluded is wisteria-vined Garden Cottage, a suite with three skylights for stargazing, a private patio, and bay windows. Soft yellows and greens and a bed with a partial canopy of antique lace add to the romantic mood.

Offstreet parking is available.

Spindrift Inn

652 Cannery Row
Monterey, CA 93940
408-646-8900

A romantic retreat on the bay

General manager: Jayne Decker. **Accommodations:** 41 rooms. **Rates:** \$149–\$269 per room December–May, \$169–\$289 June–November, \$299–\$319 special weekends and holidays. **Included:** Continental breakfast. **Minimum stay:** 2 nights some weekends. **Payment:** Major credit cards. **Children:** Welcome. **Pets:** Not allowed. **Smoking:** Allowed.

Built in the mid-1970s, Spindrift Inn stands between Cannery Row and the Pacific, aloof from the souvenir shops, its focus on the rumbling sea. The elegant four-story hotel possesses residential charm in a turn-of-the-century environment. Fine reproductions of period furniture are enhanced by Italian and French influences.

There's an additional romantic retreat in the rooftop garden. Flower boxes and lounges under umbrellas provide a relaxing place to enjoy the sun and Monterey's blue sea and sky.

Valet parking takes care of your car, and you step into an atrium lobby with a skylight above. Just past it is an intimate, carpeted sitting area with soft chairs and a couch facing a fireplace. The concierge desk is nearby, where you can obtain information about sightseeing, restaurants, and tickets to peninsula attractions.

Upstairs, the guest rooms are romantic and inviting, with walls in soft peach, wood-burning fireplaces, feather mattresses, marble baths with brass fixtures, and Chinese carpets. The majority have queen-size beds with full or partial canopies.

Plush terrycloth robes, nightly turndown service with Swiss chocolates, and breakfast on a tray in your room are a few of the special touches. A television and a mini-bar stocked with soft drinks are in the armoire.

Your room is likely to have a cushioned window seat piled with pillows, an ideal spot for contemplating the bay in sun and fog and watching for whales, sea lions, and the endlessly fascinating sea otters. The corner rooms are the largest and have the best views, but none lacks for space.

If you purchase a special-occasion package, you'll receive champagne, a fruit and cheese basket, and, on weekdays, tickets to the renowned Monterey aquarium.

OJAI

Ojai Valley Inn & Country Club

Country Club Road
Ojai, CA 93023
805-646-5511
800-422-OJAI
Fax 805-646-7969

A golf resort in a tranquil valley

General manager: John A.V. Sharp. **Accommodations:** 212 rooms and suites. **Rates:** $195–$260 single or double, $25 additional person, suites $345–$850. **Payment:** Major credit cards. **Children:** Free in room with parents. **Pets:** Allowed with prior permission. **Smoking:** Allowed.

In 1923, glass manufacturer Edward Libbey began turning a long-held dream into reality: building a private club in the idyllic Ojai Valley. Libbey commissioned Pasadena architect Wallace Neff to design a classic resort that would harmonize with the tranquil valley's oak and orange groves and the encircling mountains. The result was an enduring example of southern California architecture — a low, rambling, adobe hacienda with a red tile roof and flagstone terrace.

Over the years the inn and country club expanded, changed hands several times, and had a $35 million renovation. Now, spread over half a mile of the property's 200 hilly acres, it offers modern luxury accommodations, four dining areas, a bar, and many kinds of recreation.

An eighteen-hole golf course plays 6,252 yards across green hills edged with oak trees. There are eight hard-surface tennis courts, four of them lighted; clinics and private lessons are available. The two swimming pools are appealing on summer days that often reach 100 degrees in Ojai, 15 miles inland. Breezeways, arcades, and a fountain in the circular entrance freshen and cool the air during the day. In the evening, fireplaces in some rooms and in the lounge ward off the chill.

The finish materials used in the inn's renovation are of indigenous materials, with the strong influence of Southwest Indian art. Rose and lavender touches are in the shades of the valley's remarkable "pink moment," when sunset hues bathe the mountains in color.

The original lobby is now the lounge, where a ceiling of heavy, rough beams and white walls give it a southwestern flavor. It's a relaxing place for conversation, a game of chess, or snacking from the cookie tray.

The new lobby is open and light, with a beamed ceiling three stories high and palms in terra cotta pots. Vista, the main dining room, emphasizes light, healthy fare, with a special focus on fish of the central California coast and wines from small nearby vineyards. Steaks, Mexican and southwestern dishes, and classic Continental cuisine are also on the menu. In the formal restaurant jackets are recommended, while the Oak Grill & Terrace is more casual.

The larger-than-average guest rooms have sofa beds and private patios or balconies. New suites have two working fireplaces. One section's four connecting rooms make it a good choice for several couples traveling together.

If you're looking for the romance of the past, the oldest rooms, which are smaller and cozier, are the most appealing. Arched ceilings over the halls, solid doors, and baths in blue and white tiles of the period give these rooms character.

The Honeymoon Suite, in the old section, has just one room but is popular for its view and its private terrace. Shangri-La is a good choice for a family. It has three bedrooms, each with a king-size bed, and room for roll-away beds in the large parlor. It's named after the Shangri-La mountain view, filmed in the Topa Mountain Range for the 1937 movie, *Lost Horizon*. The same spectacular view of the rocky massif can be seen from the terraces of the ballroom in the Topa Center, which accommodates groups and meetings.

PACIFIC GROVE

The Centrella

612 Central Avenue
Pacific Grove, CA 93950
408-372-3372
800-233-3372

Comfort and character on Monterey Peninsula

Manager: Canan Bariman.
Accommodations: 21 rooms and suites (19 with private baths) and 5 cottages. **Rates:** $90–$185 single or double, $15 additional person. **Included:** Expanded Continental breakfast. **Minimum stay:** 2 nights on weekends. **Payment:** Major credit cards. **Children:** Welcome in cottages. **Pets:** Not allowed. **Smoking:** Not allowed.

Once a boarding house, this attractively restored inn on the Monterey Peninsula, a two-hour drive south of San Francisco, adds personal, homey touches to its hotel amenities.

In the reception area and parlor bright flames burn in the fireplace and trays of afternoon cookies, sherry, and hors d'oeuvres sit on an old oak table. Against a wall, a framed stitchery project is in progress. It's a design of the hotel, and any guest so moved may add a few stitches to it; eventually it will join a similar picture on the corridor wall.

Up the open, skylit staircase are the guest rooms. Furnished with antiques, down comforters, and armoires, they have starched lace curtains at the windows and baths with showers or tubs with hand-held showers. Preferred rooms are the ones overlooking the lovely gardens abloom with camellias and gardenias. These are also the quietest rooms.

Take the historic walk through old Monterey, play golf on some of the world's best courses, or go to the monarch preserve to marvel at the thousands of butterflies that return every year.

In the Attic Suite on the third floor, you may watch the stars through a skylight above the white iron and brass bed. The suite has a television, wicker chairs, a standing full-length mirror, and a tub with a brass hand shower. From the window, you may catch a peek of the ocean two blocks away.

The cottages are reached by brick paths that wind through the courtyard gardens of calla lilies, palm trees, and Norfolk pines. Their rooms are furnished with a mixture of antiques and modern pieces. Each has a fireplace, wet bar, television, and phone.

A buffet breakfast of fresh fruit, juice, pastries, eggs, yogurt, and granola is presented in the parlor. Sometimes the old-fashioned waffle iron is put to use and you'll have crisp, buttery waffles to enjoy at an alcove table by the garden.

The Centrella is close to many of the Monterey Peninsula's attractions. You can stroll two blocks to Lover's Point for a view of the bay or drive to Monterey to meet sea creatures face to face in the highly acclaimed aquarium.

Gatehouse Inn

225 Central Avenue
Pacific Grove, CA 93950
408-649-1881
408-649-8436
800-753-1881

A historic home within walking distance of Monterey Bay

Managers: Kristi and Doug Aslin. **Accommodations:** 8 rooms (all with private bath).

Rates: $95–$170 single or double, $20 additional person. **Included:** Full breakfast. **Minimum stay:** 2 nights on weekends. **Payment:** Major credit cards. **Children:** Over age 12 welcome. **Pets:** Not allowed. **Smoking:** Not allowed indoors.

The Gatehouse has an interesting history. It was built in 1884 by a state senator, Benjamin Langford, as a seaside retreat for his family. In those days, Pacific Grove was a religious meeting ground surrounded by a white picket fence. If the senator came home late the gate was locked, and he had to hunt up the keys and then return them. One night in 1885, tired of this ordeal, he chopped the gate down; it was never rebuilt.

In the kitchen of the main house, coffee, tea, cookies, and fruit are always available. The informal buffet breakfast may be taken to your room or eaten in the dining room or parlor, or some guests choose to eat at the table in the kitchen.

There's no barrier now to this lovely old home on the corner of a residential street. Guests are welcomed into the parlor, which retains the atmosphere of a Victorian summer house with its white wicker, pale green walls, stained glass windows, and ferns.

Several of the rooms have views of Monterey Bay, which is a short walk down the hill from the inn. The Langford Suite, which has a fireplace and a sitting room, has the best water view. The small Sun Room, cheery in white and green, is flooded with morning sun through two walls of windows. The most intriguing room in the main house is the spacious Turkish Room, with its Middle Eastern hangings and brass. On the ground floor are the Steinbeck Room and Italian Room. Each has its own entrance and latticed patio.

Behind the main house, in a separate building, are the Hollywood and Wicker rooms. Hollywood has a deco motif — black and white designs, paneled mirrors, a skirt of silver sequins in the bath. Wicker has a Victorian garden theme, with a white lattice fence on the wall and exuberant flower displays.

The only drawback to this charming inn is the noise. In the main house you're likely to hear traffic from the busy street, early morning street cleaners, the clatter of dishes, and footsteps. If you're a light sleeper, the rooms in the back building are preferable.

The Green Gables Inn

104 Fifth Street
Pacific Grove, CA 93950
408-375-2095

A restored Victorian with contemporary comfort

Manager: Shirley Butts. **Accommodations:** 11 rooms (7 with private bath). **Rates:** $100–$160 single or double, $15 additional person. **Included:** Full breakfast. **Payment:** Major credit cards. **Children:** Welcome in Carriage House. **Pets:** Not allowed. **Smoking:** Not allowed.

This half-timbered Queen Anne mansion, built in 1888, stands on a corner across the street from beautiful Monterey Bay. Soft music plays as you enter the house, and colors dance against the wall from the stained glass window in the front door. Flowered carpeting, pale peach walls, and carved molding create a warm setting in the living room. Here guests sit by the white fireplace and play chess, or retire to the alcove window to browse through restaurant menus. There are numerous reading lamps, but, oddly, no books or magazines.

Through double doors is the dining room, where a buffet breakfast is set out. After helping yourself to juice, fruits, cereal, a hot egg dish, muffins, and coffee, you may sit at the main table under a crystal chandelier or at a table for two by the window overlooking the sea.

The five upstairs rooms are furnished with antiques, soft quilts, and ruffled curtains. They all feature typical Four Sisters Inns decor: coordinated fabrics and wallpapers, fresh flowers, lavish greenery, and the occasional ceramic rabbit, teddy bear, or stuffed goose. Most of the rooms have ocean views, and six have fireplaces. Chapel Room is reminiscent of a chapel on a private estate, with its mullioned windows, heavy woodwork, beamed ceiling, and straight-backed benches. The room is full of cupboards and nooks, and the bed is a hand-carved antique.

Pacific Grove is a fine place to relax, walk, and enjoy the sea views and tidepools. At Natural Bridges State Beach, you may see thousands of wintering monarch butterflies in the Monarch Natural Preserve.

The Lacey Suite can accommodate four people. It has a sitting room with a fireplace and an antique tub in the bath. Balcony Room, which has the best ocean view, accommodates three and shares a bath.

In back, behind the main house and a tiny garden, is the Carriage House, with five rooms on three levels. All have fireplaces, king-size beds, televisions, and private entrances.

The staff at Green Gables seeks to please and enjoys the extras that make a stay memorable. Holiday celebrations, birthday and honeymoon specials, and arranging reservations at golf courses, concerts, theatrical events, and restaurants are among the services they provide.

Recommended restaurants in Pacific Grove include Fandango's, Taste Bistro, the Old Bath House, and, for Victorian atmosphere, Gernot.

The Martine Inn

255 Ocean View Boulevard
Pacific Grove, CA 93950
408-373-3388
800-852-5588
Fax 408-373-3896

A castlelike home overlooking the sea

Innkeepers: Don and Marion Martine. **Accommodations:** 20 rooms (all with private bath). **Rates:** $125–$230 single or double, $35 additional person. **Included:** Full breakfast. **Minimum stay:** 2 nights on weekends, 3 nights on holidays. **Payment:** MasterCard, Visa. **Children:** Welcome. **Pets:** Not allowed. **Smoking:** Allowed in fireplace rooms.

Like a little Mediterranean castle, this rose-colored stucco mansion stands on a cliff above Monterey Bay. The first thing you notice when you enter the parlor is the irresistible view; from the picture window you see a panorama of surf and rocks, sea and sky. You may catch glimpses of the sea otters, seals, and whales that frequent these waters.

The next eye-catcher is the gleam of silver from the innkeepers' collection of ornate teapots, trays, vases, and other museum-quality pieces. The Martines have myriad interests, as a quick glance around their home reveals. Their antiques collection fills the common rooms and guest rooms.

The home was built in 1899 and purchased in 1901 by Laura and James Parke, of Parke-Davis Pharmaceuticals. Many dignitaries were entertained here over the years, and some major remodeling took place. Eventually the cupola and dormers were removed and the house was converted from a Victorian to a Mediterranean style. Don Martine and his parents bought it in 1972.

Later, Don and Marion fully renovated the mansion, adding modern plumbing and heating but replacing the fixtures, wallcoverings, colors, and furniture with turn-of-the-century pieces. Some are particularly outstanding: a mahogany suite from the 1893 Chicago World's Fair, an Eastlake suite from the estate of C. K. McClatchy (it's in the McClatchy Room, which also has a seven-headed original shower), Edith Head's bedroom suite, and an 1860 Chippendale revival four-poster bed with a canopy and side curtains.

The four-poster is in the original master bedroom, the

Parke Room, now the most expensive and most popular at the inn. It has a spectacular bay view, a white brick fireplace, a ceiling-high armoire with a beveled mirror, and bathroom doors that open to an iron railing above a banana tree and immense Australian tree fern.

Don says the Martines' goal is "to recreate the experience you would have had ninety years ago if you'd been a personal guest of the Parkes."

The Early American Room has a rope bed of solid burled walnut dated 1800. Behind the main house, on the other side of a courtyard with a dragon fountain, is the Carriage House, which has six rooms. The Captain's Room is furnished with a carved, inlaid, American bedroom set, a rare standing mirror from 1840, peacock wallpaper, and a view through double doors to the breezeway and courtyard.

Guests gravitate to the courtyard, bright with potted flowers, to see the marble bar with stained glass windows and the Coinola player piano. There's a pool table behind the bar, and a whirlpool tub around the corner.

Intriguing collectibles are only part of what makes the Martine Inn superior. The service and hospitality are exceptional, drawing visitors back again and again.

The Martines offer hors d'oeuvres with wine and sparkling cider and will bring champagne in a silver ice bucket to your room upon request. Breakfast, which is served on Sheffield china with sterling silver and crystal, is different every day. Fresh orange juice, muffins, quiche, eggs with artichoke sauce, and fruit in a spicy sauce are a few of the dishes.

A page of suggestions of things to see and do on the Monterey peninsula is given to each guest, and the Martines will arrange for tours and restaurant reservations. They also handle conferences, seminars, and weddings.

Seven Gables Inn

555 Ocean View Boulevard
Pacific Grove, CA 93950
408-372-4341

A Victorian mansion overlooking Monterey Bay

Innkeepers: Nora and John Flatley and family. **Accommodations:** 14 rooms (all with private bath). **Rates:** $105–$205 single or double. **Included:** Full breakfast. **Payment:** MasterCard, Visa. **Children:** Not appropriate. **Pets:** Not allowed. **Smoking:** Not allowed.

When this showy, yellow and white Victorian was built in 1886 it was one of a series of mansions fronting Monterey Bay. Few are left today, but the panorama of sea and surf and rocky bluffs remains much the same. Lucie Chase, a wealthy widow and civic leader, owned Seven Gables at the turn of the century; she added the sun porches and gables that give the home such distinctive style.

John and Nora and their children restored the old home and opened it as a bed-and-breakfast in 1982, and maintain it with loving care. It's a gingerbread delight on the outside and a treasure chest within, full of fine antiques. Chinese carpets, ornate chandeliers, marble pedestals, gilded tables and armoires mingle in tastefully furnished rooms. A mirror with a gilded frame reaches to the ceiling in the dining room, where a silver bowl filled with roses rests on the table. Tea is served here in the afternoon, and in the morning guests get acquainted over a generous breakfast.

Off the dining room is a sun room with a wall of lace-curtained windows and a view of the bay and coastal mountains to the north. The guest rooms are divided among four buildings: the main house, a guest house, and two cottages, one a separate unit and the other with rooms on two levels. All are furnished with antiques and a romantic but not fussy decor.

Anyone at the inn will make golf reservations for you, recommend restaurants and entertainment, and tell you about nearby attractions such as Cannery Row, the Monterey Bay Aquarium, and Lover's Point Beach, a sheltered stretch of white sand just a two-minute walk from the inn.

The Gable Room is tucked under a high gable in the main house. With windows on four sides, it has views from the village streets to the horizon of sea and sky. The room is at the top of narrow, steep steps and has a low ceiling and slanted walls — cozy, but not for tall visitors.

The guest house in back, off the flowery courtyard, has four rooms, all with refrigerators. There's a pay phone in the hall, and television in a sun room. The Cypress Room, one of the most expensive and most elaborate, is in a corner with wide windows and a window seat, a gilded couch, fabric walls, and Oriental pillows.

Spacious Ocean Mist has inlaid wood antiques, stained glass, and a bay window; Mayfair views the brick courtyard and cottage and catches a glimpse of the sea. Baskets of candies and fruit are provided in every room.

Despite all the gilt and marble elegance, you won't feel surrounded by formality at Seven Gables. The Flatley family is eager to see that you're comfortable. "We want to keep things homey," says white-haired, motherly Nora, with a pat on your arm.

PEBBLE BEACH

The Inn at Spanish Bay

2700 Seventeen-Mile Drive
Pebble Beach, CA 93953
408-647-7500
800-654-9300
Fax 408-647-7443

A seaside resort with a world-class golf course

General manager: John Chadwell.
Accommodations: 270 rooms and suites. **Rates:** $245–$350 single or double, $25 additional person; suites $550–$1,650. **Payment:** Major credit cards. **Children:** Under 18 free in room with parents. **Pets:** Not allowed. **Smoking:** Allowed.

The Inn at Spanish Bay and its 18-hole, par 72 golf course opened in late 1987, at the northern end of the sand dunes of Spanish Bay. The low-profile, red-roofed buildings of the complex blend with the setting, their walls the color of the dunes around them. Accommodations, located in two wings off the central lobby area, are spacious and well-appointed, with blond woods, gas fireplaces, wall-to-wall carpeting, and small decks or balconies that overlook the forest, golf course, or ocean.

Stocked refrigerators, television, large baths with deep soaking tubs, terrycloth robes, and assorted toiletries (including sewing kits and clothes steamers) are among the amenities. Typical of today's California luxury lodgings, the colors are in off-white and neutral tones. Abstract paintings and landscapes add a dash of color.

The resort has eight tennis courts, two with lights for night play, as well as a swimming pool and spa, but the main attraction is the golf course. The Links at Spanish Bay was modeled after the demanding seaside courses of Scotland and Ireland, with the game played close to the ground to avoid the wind. Fescue grasses, native to Scotland, provide a hard, fast surface. There's even a kilted bagpiper who plays at dusk as he strides across the fairway.

Several meeting rooms and a ballroom big enough to hold a banquet for 400 give the resort a conference orientation. When a group here, the lobby is filled with nametagged crowds, all enjoying the country club atmosphere.

Past the large, busy lobby is a lounge where musicians play nightly and appetizers and cocktails are served in the evenings by the stone fireplace. Just outside is the Terrace Grill, open in summer. The Dunes is Spanish Bay's two-level dining room, offering California cuisine in a light, bright, casual atmosphere. The crab cakes and the lamb noisettes are especially commendable in this restaurant of noteworthy food and service. More intimate and elegant than the Dunes is the Bay Club, featuring a Mediterranean menu and fine wine list.

Monterey Peninsula, 120 miles south of San Francisco, boasts some of the world's most spectacular coastal scenery. Winding above its rugged headlands, the renowned Seventeen-Mile Drive is contained entirely within the Del Monte Forest Preserve, which covers some 5,300 acres.

Several shops are off the breezeway by the entrance. Elan displays sequined gowns, Italian leather belts, and furs with discreetly hidden price tags. Breezes sells artworks, wines, and fashionable sportswear.

One of Spanish Bay's greatest attractions, after its location and golf course, is its service and attention to detail. A concierge and thirteen assistants are on hand to help you register, escort you to your room, and deal with special needs, such as finding a dentist, making tour reservations, or dressing up as elves for your group's Christmas party.

A $15 gratuity is charged each day. Room service is available 24 hours a day. You'll receive twice-daily housekeeping and a morning newspaper. Convenient racks are available to store your golf clubs, and you may have one-hour shoe shines and pressing and same-day dry cleaning. A complimentary airport shuttle from Monterey is provided.

The Lodge at Pebble Beach

P.O. Box 1128
Seventeen Mile Drive
Pebble Beach, CA 93953
408-624-3811
800-654-9300 in California
Fax 408-624-6357

A classic golf resort overlooking the Pacific

Manager: Gary Davis. **Accommodations:** 155 rooms, 6 suites. **Rates:** $295–$375, $25 additional person, suites $800–$2,000. **Payment:** Major credit cards. **Children:** Under 18 free in room with parents. **Pets:** Allowed with permission. **Smoking:** Non-smoking rooms available.

Since 1919, the Lodge at Pebble Beach has catered to travelers seeking luxurious accommodations in one of nature's most spellbinding, magnificent settings. Some 120 miles south of San Francisco, in the heart of the Del Monte Forest Preserve along the rocky coast, the sprawling resort stands on a bluff, under towering pines and gnarled cypress trees. Between the main lodge and the sea lies hallowed ground to golfers: the famed Pebble Beach fairways.

Until 1977 the hotel was known as Del Monte Lodge, after Charles Crocker's original resort; the name was changed, but the superior hospitality and accommodations remained. Eleven guest rooms are in the original lodge. The rest are in rambling, low-rise buildings laced throughout the six acres of grounds and golf links. Guests receive preferential tee times at other Pebble Beach golf courses: Spyglass Hill, the Links at Spanish Bay, and Del Monte Golf Course.

Each room has its own patio or balcony with a view of the gardens, fairways, or the surf-pounded shore. The traditional, residential furnishings feature natural fabrics and light woods. There are fireplaces ready to light, stocked bars, televisions, and gracious accents such as flowers and original art. The one- and two-bedroom suites are lavishly decorated and have grand views of the golf course and the sea. Most in demand are the 18th fairway suites, with their marble fireplaces and unobstructed, spectacular ocean vistas.

A $15-per-night gratuity is added to all room rates. This is intended, say staff members, to cover housekeeping, baggage handling, shuttle transportation, and airport pickup. So tipping in these areas is not expected.

If you prefer other sports, the lodge has some options. There are 14 tennis courts, and games and lessons can be arranged. You may swim in a pool above the surf, hike or jog the trails in the Del Monte Forest, play polo or soccer, bicycle, sail, or fish. Horseback riding on 34 miles of scenic trails is offered; the Pebble Beach Equestrian Center is considered one of the finest on the West Coast. There is no good beach at the resort. For strolling on the sand, go next door to Stillwater Cove.

The Pebble Beach Golf Links is often called the premier golf course in the world open to the public; you'll need a reservation far in advance to play. The site of many tournaments, it is both challenging and beautiful, perched at the edge of a cliff over the sea.

Four restaurants give you a choice of cuisine. In the glass-walled Cypress Room the menu favors California creativity and mesquite-grilled meats and seafood. The Tap Room is an informal spot for sandwiches and pub specials while you check the display of golfing memorabilia and photographs. Club XIX overlooks the golf course and sea. During the day it's an al fresco café, serving sandwiches and salads at outdoor tables hedged by cascading flowers; at night you dress up and dine by candlelight on classic French cuisine. The Gallery, above an arcade of a dozen shops across from the main lodge, is a bar and grill serving breakfast and lunch. It accommodates early birds eager to head for the first tee.

The Terrace Lounge is the place for cocktails, conversation, and gazing through wide windows at the seascape framed by cypress trees. A pianist plays during the day, and jazz artists or guest combos perform evenings and weekends. In this calm room, with its glass chandelier, two fireplaces, and soft couches in neutral colors, there's a sense of stability and tradition — an atmosphere that permeates the resort. It's too sporty for elegance, but the Lodge at Pebble Beach has been catering to elite crowds for some time and it clearly intends to maintain the quality it takes to continue doing so.

SANTA BARBARA

The Bayberry Inn

111 West Valerio Street
Santa Barbara, CA 93101
805-682-3199

A tranquil B&B with an atmosphere of luxury

Innkeepers: Keith Pomeroy and Carlton Wagner. **Accommodations:** 8 rooms (all with private bath). **Rates:** $85–$135 single or double. **Included:** Full breakfast. **Minimum stay:** 2 nights on weekends. **Payment:** Major credit cards. **Children:** Not appropriate. **Pets:** Dogs occasionally allowed with permission. **Smoking:** Not allowed.

Pure enchantment is what you'll find at the Bayberry. From the cherub fountain in the entrance to the fresh flowers in every room, not a detail has been overlooked in creating an inn of beauty and comfort.

The innkeepers' backgrounds in art, catering, psychology, and interior design help them to create a fantasy home in a residential neighborhood. They have filled the restored, 1886 house with imported antiques, beveled mirrors, lush fabrics, and glistening crystal.

The dining room probably draws the most immediate admiration. From a ceiling of shirred pink silk hangs an elaborate chandelier, its prisms reflected in the room's crown of mirrors. Antique walnut chairs covered with hand-loomed tapestry from Italy sit at a long table set with sterling silver, Royal Doulton china, tall candlesticks, and colorful flowers. Your first glimpse tells you that breakfast will be interesting.

And so it is. Keith and his helpers prepare different dishes daily, sometimes with a Mexican accent. Orange juice and a fresh fruit bowl are always included. Early morning coffee, tea, and newspapers are available in the sun porch, where Letitia and Lawrence, the resident zebra finches, greet your arrival with soft chirping.

Beyond the light and sunny porch is a deck with glass tables, where breakfast may be served in warm weather. The deck faces an expansive lawn (fine for croquet and badminton) with an orange tree standing against a white lattice fence.

All of the guest rooms, five upstairs and three down, have queen-size beds, some with romantic canopies. Down comforters, fine linens, and opulent furnishings make these retreats luxurious. The inn is on a busy street corner, but outside sounds have been muted by upholstering the halls. There are no common walls between bedrooms; closets or baths divide them, keeping neighboring noise to a minimum.

Several eating places are within walking distance, and the innkeepers are happy to make recommendations. They'll also lend bicycles, provide maps for walking and shopping tours, and share their knowledge of Santa Barbara.

Each room is named for a berry. Bayberry, the largest, has a brick fireplace and a tiny bath in green and white. Hollyberry is the quietest room and is cozy with a small, wood-burning fireplace. On a platform in the green tile bath is an old weight scale from a long-gone hotel. Learn your weight for a penny (a tray of pennies has been provided).

Blueberry is a showpiece in blue and pink and lace. Its highlight is a bath/sitting room with white sofa and a Victorian clawfoot tub and hand-held shower. A plentiful supply of bubble bath is included. Raspberry, one of the downstairs rooms, has French wallpaper handprinted with tiny berries. There are built-in shelves of books, a fireplace, and a private, elm-shaded deck fragrant with jasmine vines.

Complimentary afternoon tea, cider, and snacks are served in the living room. It's a fine time to peruse the Bayberry's restaurant guide.

Blue Quail Inn

1908 Bath Street
Santa Barbara, CA 93101
805-687-2300

A romantic B&B in central Santa Barbara

Innkeeper: Jeanise Suding Eaton. **Accommodations:** 9 rooms (all with private baths). **Rates:** $82–$165 single or double, $20 additional person; weekday discounts November to mid-May. **Included:** Full breakfast. **Minimum stay:** 2 nights on weekends. **Payment:** Major credit cards. **Children:** Welcome. **Pets:** Not allowed. **Smoking:** Not allowed indoors.

All of the rooms and cottages at the Blue Quail Inn have a pleasant country charm and offer comfortable lodging close to the center of Santa Barbara. Especially appealing and romantic is Wood Thrush Cottage, a quaint and private little brown home just behind the main house. Wood Thrush has two sitting rooms and a bedroom furnished in a French country style with warm colors. It has a refrigerator, a small bath with an old-fashioned clawfoot tub and shower, and a daybed that allows the cottage to hold a third person. Outside, oleander grows by the front porch and around the lawn where lounges await sunbathers.

Jeanise places morning newspapers on the dining room window seat (guarded by Quincy, the quilted bear), offers wine or hot spiced cider and hors d'oeuvres in the afternoon, and will put champagne and balloons in honeymooners' rooms and for birthday celebrations. She has bicycles to lend and will pack a picnic lunch for your Santa Barbara excursion if you request it.

The main house, a one-story family home with big oak and fragrant pittosporum trees in front, has two cheery rooms, Meadowlark and Bobwhite. The other guest rooms are in three more cottages in back. Cardinal, a pretty suite with a deck overlooking the garden, is soft and cushy in forest green and cream, with paisley fabrics and a white Berber carpet. Mockingbird, in Wedgwood blue, has an English country atmosphere. Nightingale has a fireplace and canopy bed and shares a bath with Oriole.

Whippoorwill and Hummingbird are in a cottage tucked away in back under eugenia and orange trees. Still farther back, off-street parking is provided.

The innkeeper, who discovered bed-and-breakfast inns in England, serves breakfast specialties of popovers and muffins in the dining room of the main house or outdoors under the avocado tree. Breakfast includes an egg entrée, baked breads such as kuchen or coffee cake, and fruit.

El Encanto

1900 Lasuen Road
Santa Barbara, CA 93103
805-687-5000
800-346-7039 in California
Fax 805-687-3903

A hilltop resort with an ocean view

General manager: Tom Narozonick. **Accommodations:** 84 rooms. **Rates:** $140–$320 single or double. **Payment:** Major credit cards. **Children:** Welcome. **Pets:** Not allowed. **Smoking:** Nonsmoking rooms available.

Perched on a hill above a beautiful city and harbor, half a mile from the queen of the California missions, El Encanto lives up to its name of enchantment.

On the grounds, palm and banana trees sway over a lawn surrounded by brick walkways and columns. Golden carp swim among the waterlilies in a reflecting pond. Vines twine over arbors and olive and pepper trees shade white, Mediterranean-style villas. Lawn swings and fountains add to the sense of rest and respite.

No two rooms are alike, but they're all furnished tastefully and in warm or neutral colors with a floral motif, befitting the gardens that surround them. Most are two-room suites with louvered shutters, garden views, an honor bar, and TV.

About half the rooms have wood-burning fireplaces, a welcome touch on a cool winter's night, and some have kitchenettes and refrigerators. One has a nursery with a crib and a changing table, and baby-sitting can be arranged. For the most part, however, the resort is not oriented toward very young children.

Some rooms with views are high on the hillside, while others are below, near the main building and swimming pool. A few less desirable rooms look directly out to a parking lot. El Encanto has meeting space for seventy, and business travelers are encouraged, but the hotel does not cater to large tour groups.

The view from the terrace, over eucalyptus trees and rooftops to a blue sea and horizon, is the best in Santa Barbara. This is the place to linger over cocktails while watching the sunset blush the sky.

Once this was the site of student-faculty housing for the University of California; in 1915, the campus was across the road. When the university moved a few miles up the coast to Goleta, El Encanto began operating as a hotel. Later neglected and shabby, it was restored in the late 1970s and redecorated in a French country style.

From the romantic terrace, you might well think you were on the French Riviera, though the sun is setting over Santa Barbara Harbor. Indoors, the lounge and dining room offer the same view. The menu changes daily, though it always features fresh local seafood and produce.

It seems far removed from town, but El Encanto is just a few minutes' drive from Santa Barbara's shops, the beach, and the Santa Ynez Mountains. Mission Santa Barbara is nearby and a must on every visitor's list, while the Natural History Museum and Botanical Gardens are within walking distance.

Four Seasons Biltmore

1260 Channel Drive
Santa Barbara, CA 93108
805-969-2261
800-332-3442
Fax 805-969-5715

A Mediterranean hotel with Pacific views

General manager: Chris Hart. **Accommodations:** 236 rooms, suites, and cottages. **Rates:** $299–$350 double, $30 additional person, suites and cottages $450–$2,420. **Payment:** Major credit cards. **Children:** Under 18 free in room with parents. **Pets:** Allowed with permission. **Smoking:** Nonsmoking rooms available.

Directly facing the Pacific Ocean and backed by the Santa Ynez Mountains, the Four Seasons Biltmore has a magnificent location. The accommodations live up to the setting. Elegance, serenity, and luxury come to mind when touring the 19 acres of landscaped gardens and white buildings with red tile roofs.

The restored hotel dates from 1927, when the Bowman Biltmore chain planned it as the chain's crown jewel. The romantic structure has thick walls, Moorish arches, Portuguese tiles, and little balconies above intimate patios. Recent renovations left the richly designed tile work, carved lamps, and high entry ceiling, but the dark woods were lightened and a more open mood created.

The guest rooms are in two-story buildings and cottages tucked among the shrubs and palm trees of the grounds that keep a crew of gardeners busy. Each room has a view of the ocean, the mountains, the lush gardens, or a pool. Many have balconies or private patios, fireplaces, vaulted ceilings, and oak ceiling fans. Walk-in closets and louvered shutters add to the sense of spaciousness.

In junglelike gardens, the nine cottages vary in size — up to five bedrooms. The larger units have two executive suites. Each cottage has a parlor with fireplace and floral-patterned chairs and soft couches. The most luxurious is the Odell Suite, with four baths, three bedrooms, three fireplaces, and a parlor furnished with antiques.

On the property are an 18-hole putting green, a croquet field, and three lighted tennis courts. A swimming pool shimmers under tall palms and an immense fig tree. The concierge staff can arrange for sportfishing, sailing, horseback riding, polo, scenic tours, and golfing.

The service at the Biltmore, as at all Four Seasons hotels, is far above average. The staff is well trained in the art of pampering guests — even the youngest ones. During the summer and on winter weekends, children can participate in Kids Four All Seasons, a free program of activities.

California style in a Mediterranean resort, with a superb location on the southern edge of Santa Barbara: the Four Seasons Biltmore combines it all with verve and a sense of history. This is a resort for the discriminating traveler who expects fine service in beautiful surroundings.

La Marina is the Biltmore's formal dining room. Its high arched windows look toward the front lawn and across the road to the sea. California cuisine is served in a candlelit setting, with fresh flowers and Wedgwood china.

You may also dine under the stars in the Patio, where the roof rolls back to reveal the sky. The café has an informal garden atmosphere, complete with tropical blooms, rattan furniture, and pink linens. In La Sala Lounge, high tea is served, followed by cocktails and a jazz ensemble.

Several meeting and banquet rooms make the hotel popular with groups, but even large numbers of people don't disturb the serene ambience.

Across the road, on the beach side, is the Coral Casino Beach and Cabana Club, which is open to hotel guests. It has a private beach, cabanas, and a 53-meter pool so close to the sea wall that, at high tide, swimmers may be splashed with sea spray.

The Old Yacht Club Inn

431 Corona Del Mar Drive
Santa Barbara, CA 93103
805-962-1277

A B&B inn close to the beach

Innkeepers: Lucille Caruso, Nancy Donaldson, and Sandy Hunt. **Accommodations:** 9 rooms (all with private bath). **Rates:** \$85–\$145 single or double, \$30 additional person. **Included:** Full breakfast. **Minimum stay:** 2 nights on weekends. **Payment:** Major credit cards. **Children:** Welcome. **Pets:** Not allowed. **Smoking:** Not allowed indoors.

Once upon a time this really was a yacht club. It was built as a private home in 1912, but served as the boaters' headquarters when the first clubhouse was swept out to sea. Then it was moved inland a few yards and in 1980 opened as an inn.

The capable owners are friends who were school administrators in Los Angeles, eager to try something different. They restored the old clubhouse and filled it with turn-of-the-century furnishings. It opened as Santa Barbara's first bed-and-breakfast and is still the only one close to the beach.

The casual, friendly warmth of the inn is evident from the moment you walk in the door and are welcomed by one of the partners — and perhaps by the tiny poodle with the big name, Bella Mia Barboni. The front room of the stucco Craftsman home feels lived-in and homey. Dozens of guidebooks and travel books fill the bookshelves, fresh flowers grace the tables, and a ceramic cat rests on the hearth of the white brick fireplace. Notes from grateful visitors spill from an album on the piano.

On the other side of the room, tables are set for breakfast or for Nancy's famous Saturday night dinners. Coffee is on the sideboard by 6:30 A.M., followed by breakfast served course by course. Orange juice, fruit with flavored yogurt, muffins, a Spanish omelette, and sour cream coffeecake are part of a typical meal.

After one of Nancy's superb dinners you may wish to visit on into the night with other guests — this is a get-acquainted sort of place — or stroll to the beach to see the waves in the moonlight.

Presented three Saturdays a month, dinners are usually booked far in advance. They start with champagne by the fire and move on to a fixed menu that might include a spicy vegetable crêpe, cream of fennel soup, green salad with poppyseed dressing, and an entrée of tender salmon with mustard and tarragon cream sauce. Dessert and coffee follow. Several wines are available. Popular demand brought about a collection of Nancy's favorite recipes called *The Old Yacht Club Inn Cookbook.*

Captain's Corner, the only main floor room, has a king-size bed and a private deck. Upstairs, where the walls hold pictures of yachts and sailing vessels, are four rooms. Castellammare is light, done in lace and shades of rose. It has a two-person whirlpool tub and French doors that open to a balcony. Portofino is cool in blue and has a built-in window seat and dresser and a bath with shower.

The other part of the inn is next door: Hitchcock House, stucco with a red tile roof and a broad deck (made by the talented Nancy) in back. Grapevines climb over the lattice fence and a lemon tree lends bright color to the deck, a pleasant place for lounging.

Hitchcock's four rooms are all on the ground floor and have separate entrances. They bear names of the innkeepers' families (including Gay Swenson, one of the original partners). The most expensive is the Belle Caruso Suite, decorated by Lucille to reflect her Italian ancestry. Julia Metelmann, the largest room, is furnished in an eclectic assortment of antiques. A black and gold dresser and a red and black Chinese dragon carpet are a few of the interesting collectibles.

Every guest room has a phone, but there's no radio or television (though one will be provided in Hitchcock House upon request). This is a place to sip sherry by the fire, relax on the flowery front porch, or chat with the innkeepers, who know a great deal about Santa Barbara and are happy to lend a beach chair or a bicycle and send you in the right direction.

Simpson House Inn

121 East Arrellaga Street
Santa Barbara, CA 93101
805-963-7067
800-676-1280
Fax 805-564-4811

A historic mansion near the heart of Santa Barbara

Innkeepers: Glyn and Linda Davies and Gillean Wilson. **Accommodations:** 13 rooms (all with private bath). **Rates:** $105–$275 single or double; 20% less on weekdays, October–May. **Included:** Full breakfast. **Minimum stay:** 2 nights on weekends, 3 nights on holidays. **Payment:** Major credit cards. **Children:** Welcome. **Pets:** Not allowed. **Smoking:** Not allowed indoors.

This extraordinary inn is one of the loveliest places to stay in Santa Barbara. Though it's very close to the downtown area, it stands secluded behind wrought-iron gates and high hedges on nearly an acre of lawn under majestic oak, pittosporum, and magnolia trees.

The grand Eastlake-style Victorian, built in 1874, came perilously close to demolition to make way for condominiums or office units, but it was saved by Glyn and Linda Davies. Their extensive renovation brought the home back to its original splendor, with some updated comforts, and earned it a Structure of Merit award for its architecture and period setting. Now a historic landmark, the house was built for Mary and Margaret Simpson, the daughters of Scottish immigrants Robert and Julia Simpson, and it remained in the family until 1921. By then, Santa Barbara had been a winter resort favored by the wealthy for decades.

The innkeepers suggest visiting Santa Barbara in fall or winter, when the skies are usually clear and sunny, restaurants and shops are uncrowded, and the calendar is full of cultural events.

The guest rooms, several named in honor of the Simpson family, have down comforters under lace coverlets, antique furniture, and fresh flowers from the garden. In recent years the Davieses have expanded the inn's accommodations beyond the six rooms in the main house. Now there are the Old Barn Suites and three cottages. The restored barn has four attractive suites — Weathervane, Hayloft, Tack Room, and Carriage Room — with antique pine floors, king-size beds, fireplaces, and private decks.

The most expensive rooms are the cottages, furnished with understated elegance. They have fireplaces, Jacuzzi tubs, and private gates that open to an intimate courtyard. In the main house, the largest room is the Robert and Julia Simpson Room, which has a king-size brass bed, clawfoot tub, and French doors to a deck above the rose garden. The Parlor Room has an ornamental fireplace, shelves full of books, and a bay window. Smaller and cozier are the Sun Room, light with white wicker and a private deck, and Katherine McCormick, in deep red and blue, with a queen-size spool bed.

Breakfast, served on the veranda near the garden, includes fresh fruit and juices, an array of cereals, yogurt, homemade muffins, and a main dish such as apple-baked French toast, huevos Santa Barbara, or scones with eggs. Complimentary tea, wine, and hors d'oeuvres are served in the afternoons.

Although this distinguished inn has a stately quality, it offers a warm welcome from the affable owners, who know how to make you feel at home. They've put vast amounts of time and energy into restoring the old place, but managed to do so without losing their sense of humor. And your comfort always comes first. If you want to chat, one of the Davieses or their charming assistant, Gillean Wilson, is available; if you prefer to be left alone with the complimentary morning and evening newspapers, you will be. They know Santa Barbara, too, and will tell you about restaurants, shopping, scenic drives, and attractions not to be missed.

The Upham Hotel

1404 De la Vina Street
Santa Barbara, CA 93101
805-962-0058
800-727-0876
Fax 805-963-2825

A historic hotel with gardens and cottages

General manager: Jan Winn. **Accommodations:** 49 rooms and cottages. **Rates:** $100–$325 single or double, $10 additional person. **Included:** Continental breakfast. **Minimum stay:** 2 nights on some weekends and holidays. **Payment:** Major credit cards. **Children:** Age 12 and under free in room with parents. **Pets:** Not allowed. **Smoking:** Allowed.

The Upham offers a sense of history and charm. The angular, beige, frame building with a long veranda holds comfortable, well-kept rooms, a warm and welcoming lobby, and a restaurant called Louie's. In back of the old hotel are surprises not seen from the street: annexes, cottages, gardens, and a deck with a gazebo sprawl over the property. At the far end is a parking lot.

Louie's Restaurant, in the Upham but under separate ownership, is well known for fine food. The menu is not lengthy, but it offers a good variety and changes several times a year. Pasta and pizza are available, along with beef, lamb, duck, and chicken dishes, a fresh fish of the day, and a good Caesar salad.

The hotel was built in 1871 by a banker, Amasa Lincoln, who sailed to California from Boston to build a New England inn. Using redwood timbers and square-head nails, he crowned his hostelry with a cupola. Cyrus Upham bought the place a few years later, and it has carried his name since.

The lobby is small, with two sitting areas. One is a sunny corner with rattan furniture and potted plants; the other, a quiet retreat by a fireplace flanked with built-in bookshelves. Evening wine, cheese, and fruit are served here. In the mornings, guests help themselves from a breakfast buffet of pastries, juice, tea, and coffee and then repair to the lobby tables or drift to the little terrace, the gazebo, or their own porches.

The cottages are the nicest accommodations, though all the rooms are clean and decorated tastefully. A typical duplex suite has a small porch and, inside, dark gray walls and dim lighting to soothe the eyes after Santa Barbara's white buildings and bright sun. A couch faces a gas fireplace; a large armoire holds a television set. The four-poster bed is covered with a down comforter. You might hear the outside ice maker during the night; otherwise a cottage is a quiet hideaway at the edge of the pretty gardens where roses, lantana, and fuchsias bloom along winding paths.

The most expensive cottage is the very private Master Suite. Tucked in a corner behind a hibiscus-covered fence, it has a patio with an umbrella table. An inviting hammock sways gently under a palm tree. The suite features a brick fireplace, a brass bed, a walk-in closet bigger than some bathrooms, and a two-person whirlpool tub.

The rooms in the main hotel have antique touches such as clawfoot tubs in some baths, but most have queen- and king-size beds. Other rooms are scattered among three additional buildings behind the hotel and gardens. The Carriage House contains five guest rooms and two meeting rooms.

Villa Rosa

15 Chapala Street
Santa Barbara, CA 93101
805-966-0851
Fax 805-962-7159

A small, cozy inn within walking distance of the beach

General manager: Annie Puetz. **Accommodations:** 18 rooms. **Rates:** $90–$190 single or double; winter weekday discounts. **Included:** Continental breakfast. **Minimum stay:** 2 nights on weekends. **Payment:** Major credit cards. **Children:** Over age 14 welcome. **Pets:** Not allowed. **Smoking:** Not allowed.

Built in 1931, this two-story hotel was renovated in 1981 and designed to offer the amenities of a resort with the intimacy of a small inn. A few of those amenities are breakfast in the lounge or in your room, the *Los Angeles Times* delivered to your door, complimentary wine and hors d'oeuvres in the afternoon and port and sherry in the evening, same-day dry cleaning, and a turndown service with roses on your pillow. The staff pays careful attention to guests' needs. If you request an iron, an aspirin, or a Band-Aid, the desk clerk will get it for you and ask if you need anything more.

In the heart of beautiful Santa Barbara, just 84 steps from the sea (somebody counted), Villa Rosa welcomes guests to a Spanish Colonial Revival inn of style and warmth.

The inn is decorated in Southwestern style, with earth and clay colors and rough-hewn beams in the lobby. A fire crackles on cool evenings on the tile hearth. Double doors lead from the lobby and lounge to a pretty courtyard with a pool under pepper, banana, and palm trees.

The guest rooms are done in colors of muted putty, blues,

and rose; accessories are minimal, but their texture and tone are warm. Heavy, weathered pine from New Mexico and rawhide chairs continue the desert-country theme, as do the beehive fireplaces in four rooms. Some of the rooms have partially equipped kitchens. The views vary, from glimpses of the ocean to mountains or the courtyard and gardens. Room 18 offers views of both ocean and pool, a sitting area, a kitchen, and a fireplace.

The inn's courtyard conference room is available to groups (up to twenty people) and there is a full range of audiovisual equipment.

SANTA CRUZ

The Babbling Brook Inn

1025 Laurel Street
Santa Cruz, CA 95060
408-427-2437

A romantic inn set in a garden

Innkeeper: Helen King. **Accommodations:** 12 rooms (all with private bath). **Rates:** $85–$150 single or double, $15 additional person. **Included:** Full breakfast. **Minimum stay:** 2 nights on weekends. **Payment:** Major credit cards. **Children:** Over age 12 welcome. **Pets:** Not allowed. **Smoking:** Not allowed in rooms.

This garden retreat sits on an acre of flowers, pines, redwoods, and waterfalls in the shadow of a cliff by Laurel Creek. The creek, which runs from spring-fed lakes on a hill by the university, meanders through the garden, under bridges, and past guest room windows.

> **Below the deck, brick paths wind through the garden. Water cascades down the rocky cliff, and calla lilies bloom by the edge of the stream. Benches and a gazebo provide resting spots to contemplate this beautifully kept refuge, which is often used for weddings.**

Helen King brings a wealth of experience in the travel industry to her inn in the city. Although its logs and shingles give it a rustic appearance, the accommodations are pure luxury. The original inn was built in 1909 on the foundation of an 1870s tannery and 1790s grist mill. It became a restaurant in 1942 and, in 1981, the first bed-and-breakfast in Santa Cruz. Now it offers lodging in rooms with a French country theme, most named for impressionist painters and decorated in the colors they used. All have phones and most have a fireplace, private deck, and outside entrance; two feature deep soaking jet bathtubs. There's a small television in each closet.

Toulouse Lautrec, with one of the whirlpool tubs, is flooded with light from the curved alcove windows. Monet, in a remote corner of the property and shielded from view, is in Delft blue and white, with a beamed ceiling and private deck across from the waterfall and footbridge.

Degas is decorated with blue and white Laura Ashley wallpaper as a backdrop for prints of the artist's favorite subject, dancers. Secluded Cézanne is one of the largest rooms and is wheelchair-accessible. It has a corner fireplace and a private deck above the brook.

The smallest is Jonquil, a sunny yellow and white bedroom in the original house. It has a gas fireplace and a bed canopied with white eyelet lace. It's the only interior room, just off the reception area and kitchen.

From the kitchen come wondrous smells and tastes. Helen, the mother of six, is a superb cook who prepares an elaborate buffet breakfast with dishes that change daily. Fresh fruit, granola, yogurt, muffins, croissants, and a hot entrée are always served. You may have breakfast in your room, in the garden, or in the dining area at round tables under a glass roof. Tea, coffee, and cookies are available all day, and wine and sherry are offered in the evenings. Guests enjoy sipping their wine on the wide deck, listening to the trickling fountains and rushing brook. Redwood trees grow through the deck, and pots of impatiens and cyclamen stand in nooks and corners.

Helen has menus of nearby restaurants and can provide recommendations. A few favorites are the Salmon Poacher, Theo's, Casablanca, and Shadowbrook.

Chaminade

One Chaminade Lane
Santa Cruz, CA 95065
408-475-5600
800-283-6569
Fax 408-476-4942

A country resort in the hills above Santa Cruz

General manager: Tom O'Shea. **Accommodations:** 152 rooms. **Rates:** $125 Sunday–Thursday, $135–$145 weekends, $25 additional person. **Payment:** Major credit cards. **Children:** Under 14 free in room with parents. **Pets:** Not allowed. **Smoking:** Nonsmoking rooms available.

Chaminade, once a religious retreat, is now a retreat of a different nature. The two-story buildings, roofed with red

Spanish tile, sprawl across 80 acres of landscaped grounds in the wooded foothills of the Santa Cruz Mountains. The resort, a quiet getaway favored as a conference site, is on a hilltop overlooking the city of Santa Cruz and the Pacific Ocean.

A row of windows curves around the front of the main building, and a translucent roof arches over the entry hall and up the stairs to a meeting area. Modern works by California artists adorn the walls. The entire atmosphere is one of open space and light.

The Library, one of the best restaurants in the area, offers six-course à la carte dinners on Friday and Saturday. Examples of the California-style Continental cuisine are medallions of free-range veal in a tangerine demi-glaze, grilled sea scallops with squid ink pasta and saffron cream, and roasted pheasant breast with honey chestnut glaze.

On the lower level are two restaurants. The Library offers formal dining, and casual meals are served in the Sunset Dining Room, which has views of the sea over the treetops. Meals for children under age five are free. Light buffet lunches are available in the Bayview Lounge.

The guest rooms are in smaller outlying buildings, most of them around the landscaped pool area. A typical room has a redwood balcony with a view of the eucalyptus and pine forest. There are two queen-size beds, two private phone lines, a TV, a love seat, and a table and chairs.

Because 85 percent of the hotel's midweek business consists of conference groups, the facilities are geared to the businessperson — private phones, writing tables, convenient extender reading lamps, one-day valet service, a large parking lot. Leisure travelers are more evident on weekends, enjoying the swimming pool and whirlpool spas, four tennis courts, miles of jogging trails that wind through the forest, and the 14,000-square-foot Fitness Center.

The spacious center has a weight training system, sauna and steam rooms, yoga and aerobics classes, basketball, and locker rooms. Upstairs is the Game Room Lounge, with big-screen TV over the bar. It's open evenings for table tennis, pool, and backgammon. Windows on one side overlook the

Santa Cruz Mountains, and on the other allow spectators to watch games in the short basketball court below.

Chaminade takes its name from a French priest and educator, Father William Joseph Chaminade. Father Chaminade founded the Society of Mary (Marianists) in the late 1700s. In 1929, the Marianist Brothers constructed the Chaminade Boys' School in Santa Cruz and opened it in 1930. That building, renovated, now forms the core of the conference center's meeting rooms.

Later the school was turned into a site for religious retreats and then, in the 1970s, remodeled as the present resort and executive conference center.

SHELL BEACH

The Cliffs at Shell Beach

2757 Shell Beach Road
Shell Beach, CA 93449
805-773-5000
800-826-7827 in California
800-826-5838 in U.S.
Fax 805-773-0764

A light, breezy, oceanside resort

General manager: Al Hunter. **Accommodations:** 166 rooms and 27 suites. **Rates:** $115–$160 single or double, $10 additional person; suites $170–$300. **Payment:** Major credit cards. **Children:** Under age 12 free ($10 for roll-away bed). **Pets:** Not allowed. **Smoking:** Nonsmoking rooms available.

Shell Beach is just north of Pismo Beach, the only shore's edge town on Highway 101 between Santa Barbara and San Francisco. The view from the Cliffs, a white and blue, five-story resort on a bluff, is of the wide beach and rolling surf.

The Cliffs mixes luxury and the informality of a beach resort with ease. You're greeted at the door by a bellman in a gray and burgundy uniform and then enter a light, open lobby with white walls and high windows. Across the way is a terrace with white umbrella tables next to a dramatic restaurant with a tropical theme. Birds of paradise are etched on glass partitions; tall palms grow beside anthuriums and other exotic plants. There's also a cocktail lounge with music for dancing nightly. On the other side of the terrace are the pool and spa, on an island surrounded by a waterfall. Beyond is a lawn and paths at the edge of the bluff.

The list of things to see and do in this area is a long one. You can rent horses, fish from the Pismo Beach pier or ask the concierge about a charter boat, tour Hearst Castle (55 miles north), go skin diving, watch the sea otters at play, dig clams, and taste regional wines.

The guest rooms are furnished in traditional style, some with English reproductions and others in French provincial. The suites have white marble baths, Jacuzzi tubs, and balconies with views of the sea.

The Cliffs has complimentary valet parking, a fitness center, gift shop, beauty salon, conference rooms, catering, room service — all the features of a modern resort, plus a stunning location and a helpful staff.

SOLVANG

The Alisal Guest Ranch

1054 Alisal Road
Solvang, CA 93463
805-688-6411
Fax 805-688-2510

A country retreat in the Santa Ynez Valley

General manager: David Lautensack. **Accommodations:** 73 rooms. **Rates:** $285–$305 double, $65 additional person, suites $325–$365. **Included:** Breakfast and dinner. **Minimum stay:** 2 nights. **Payment:** Major credit cards. **Children:** Under age 2 free, age 2 to 4 $40. **Pets:** Not allowed. **Smoking:** Not allowed in public spaces.

Some visitors come to this extraordinary, 10,000-acre retreat just for the horses. Experienced wranglers take guests out on daily trail rides, winding through the meadows, loping along ridgetops, and ambling beside a 96-acre manmade lake where fish leap and deer graze on the shore. It's far from the urban world most guests have left behind.

If you wish to explore, you have many options in this valley of majestic oaks, vineyards, horse ranches, grassy meadows, and little towns. Visit quaint Solvang, tour and taste at nearby wineries, browse the art galleries of Los Olivos, or step into the Old West in Santa Ynez. Guided tours of the area are available.

The Alisal, a three-hour drive from Los Angeles, is in the hills of the Santa Ynez Valley, near the imitation Danish village of Solvang. The resort has been open to guests since 1946, after a long history of cattle ranching. In addition to horseback riding, it offers golf on an eighteen-hole course, seven tennis courts and a pro shop, swimming in a freeform heated pool, boating, fishing, and sailing. Recreational activities are included in room rates on weekdays. There's an additional charge on weekends for golf, tennis, and horseback riding.

Meals (lunch is available at extra cost) are served in a restaurant with a ranch atmosphere. Dinner choices include three entrées plus appetizers, hot bread, salad or soup, dessert, and coffee. Imported and domestic wines, some with Santa Ynez labels, are available. Musicians perform in the Oak Room Lounge, where a fire crackles on cool evenings. Leathery furnishings and western accessories add to the casual, welcoming ambience.

The guest rooms are in single-story cottages under the sycamore trees (alisal means sycamore in Spanish). They're furnished in Old West ranch style, with rough-paneled walls, oak beds and tables, working fireplaces, and paintings of horses. There are no phones, TVs, or radios. Executive suites sleep up to four people and have a patio with an outside fireplace.

The real interest at Alisal lies in the outdoor activities and beautiful surroundings. Horseshoes, croquet, shuffleboard, badminton, and volleyball are a few sports to enjoy on the wide green lawns. The golf course, lush and secluded, is reserved for ranch guests. The resident tennis pro will provide lessons. You may go for a breakfast haywagon ride, jog a half-mile course, play pool or table tennis in the recreation room, soak in a bubbling hot water spa, or relax poolside in a lounge chair. In summer, counselors direct activities for children.

SOQUEL

Blue Spruce Inn

2815 South Main Street
Soquel, CA 95073
408-464-1137
800-559-1137 (in California)

A homey B&B south of Santa Cruz

Innkeepers: Patricia and Tom O'Brien. **Accommodations:** 6 rooms (all with private bath). **Rates:** $75–$120 single, $80–$125 double, $20 additional person. **Included:** Full breakfast. **Minimum stay:** 2 nights on weekends. **Payment:** Major credit cards. **Children:** Not appropriate. **Pets:** Not allowed. **Smoking:** Not allowed indoors.

Each room in this pleasant bed-and-breakfast is named for its own work of art, painted by a local artist. The theme is an indication of the owners' love of art and the care that has gone into the selection of colors, fabrics, and furnishings at the Blue Spruce Inn.

The 120-year-old home stands behind a white picket fence and a lemon tree (no blue spruces, unfortunately — they didn't survive) in a community just south of Santa Cruz. It's a short distance from the beaches of Capitola and Santa Cruz. The O'Briens purchased the home in 1990 and renovated it in addition to working at their regular jobs — Pat as a school principal, Tom in the mental health profession.

Fifteen restaurants are within walking distance of the inn. Theo's is known for its fine French cuisine, the Salmon Poacher for well-prepared seafood, and the casual Star of Siam for flavorful Thai meals and swift service.

If you're new to B&B lodgings, the Blue Spruce is a good choice because of the options available. You may prefer to have breakfast with other guests in the dining area, eat at a table for two by the fireplace, or take breakfast to your own room or patio. If you wish to sit in silence behind the morning newspaper, that's all right too. Breakfast always includes juice, fruit, and an entrée such as baked ham strata or enchiladas.

There are three guest rooms in the main house. The least expensive room is Two Hearts, romantic with its red and white heart motif and furnished with a queen-size canopy bed. Seascape has a gas fireplace, wicker furniture, a small deck and a whirlpool tub. That Bloomin' Farm also boasts a whirlpool.

In back of the main house, by the little pond and flower garden, is the Carriage House, which has a carved oak bed and armoire and a shower with a stained glass mural. Around the corner, somewhat removed from the others, Summer Afternoon offers the most privacy in an airy pastel nest. A small room, Gazebo, is unique, with a picket fence headboard behind the feather bed. Lavish Waverly fabrics, boudoir chairs, a gas fireplace, a television hidden behind shutters, and a phone and small writing desk furnish this room.

Just outside the door, on the deck by the garden, is a hot tub which all guests may use, a relaxing end to a day of exploring the beach or the many local antiques shops and sampling the area's notable restaurants.

Desert Country

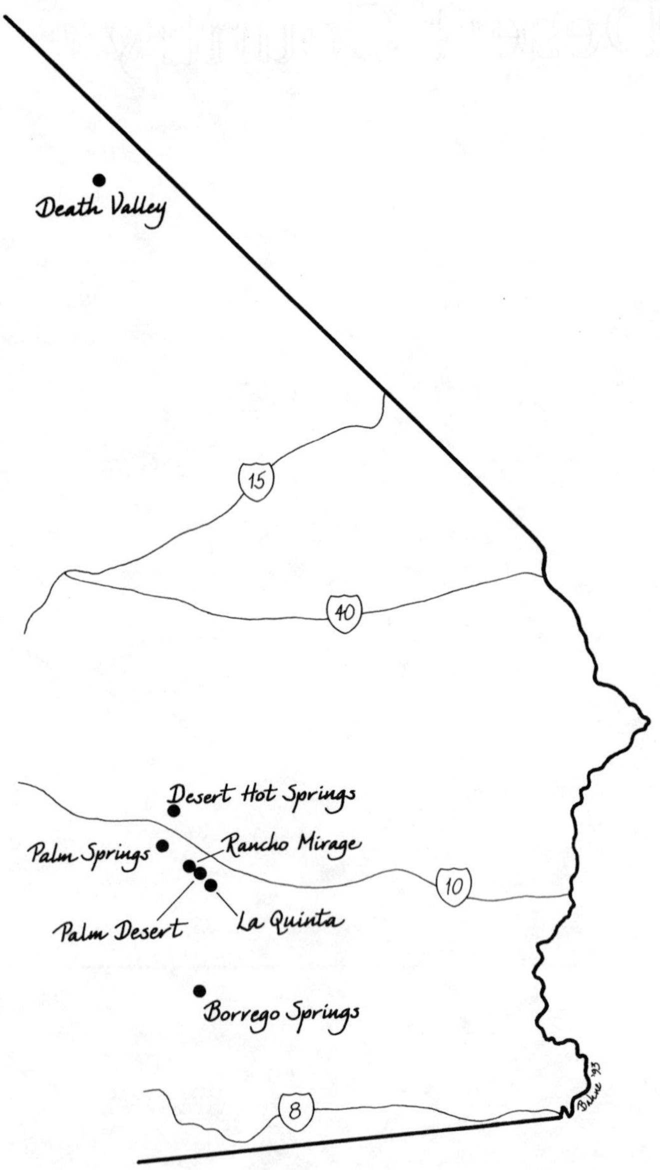
Death Valley
15
40
Desert Hot Springs
Palm Springs
Rancho Mirage
10
Palm Desert
La Quinta
Borrego Springs
8

Borrego Springs
La Casa del Zorro Resort Hotel, 297
Death Valley
Furnace Creek Inn, 298
Desert Hot Springs
Travelers Repose, 300
La Quinta
La Quinta Hotel Golf & Tennis Resort, 301
Palm Desert
Villa Royale, 303
Palm Springs
The Autry Resort Hotel, 305
Korakia Pensione, 306
La Mancha, 307
L'Horizon, 309
Le Petit Château, 310
Oasis Water Resort Villa Hotel, 312
Orchid Tree Inn, 313
The Palms at Palm Springs, 314
Rancho Mirage
The Ritz-Carlton Rancho Mirage, 316

Best Country Inns and B&Bs

Palm Springs
Korakia Pensione
L'Horizon

Best Family Favorites

Palm Springs
Oasis Water Resort Villa Hotel

Best On a Budget

Desert Hot Springs
Travelers Repose

Best Resorts

Borrego Springs
La Casa del Zorro Resort Hotel
Death Valley
Furnace Creek Inn
La Quinta
La Quinta Hotel Golf & Tennis Resort
Palm Springs
The Autry Resort Hotel
Rancho Mirage
The Ritz-Carlton Rancho Mirage

Best Romantic Hideaways

Palm Desert
Villa Royale
Palm Springs
La Mancha
Orchid Tree Inn

Best Spas

Palm Springs
The Palms at Palm Springs

The deserts of California range from the dry expanses of Death Valley National Monument to the rugged mountains and green golf courses of the Palm Springs area.

Death Valley lies in the northeastern Mojave Desert, where great canyons, salt flats, ancient lake beds, and cliffs washed in a multitude of colors draw thousands of tourists yearly. This seemingly desolate land shelters a surprising amount of life — snakes and desert animals, bighorn sheep, a few burros, and, in protected pools, the desert pupfish.

The valley has resorts, campgrounds, swimming pools, a ghost town, a borax museum that records the old mining days, and a grand mansion. Scotty's Castle is a Mediterranean-style structure with three towers and 25 rooms filled with artworks and fine furniture, including a grand piano and pipe organ. Once the home of a sometime miner and teller of tall tales, it's now open for tours.

Far to the south of the great desert lies the Coachella Valley, where Mount San Jacinto rises a steep 10,000 feet from the sandy sea-level floor, a backdrop to Palm Springs. The valley sits atop a huge underground lake, and so the popular resort oasis uses water lavishly. There are more than 10,000 swimming pools and 85 golf courses in the region — there's even a pool with waves big enough for surfing.

Lodgings in the valley, from simple motels to opulent and expensive resorts, are spread through seven adjoining cities; among them are Palm Springs, Desert Hot Springs, La Quinta, and Rancho Mirage. They're famous for their lush golf courses, boutiques, and celebrity homes, but the region has many lesser-known attractions. In the Palm Springs Desert Museum you can view outstanding art and natural science collections; at the Living Desert you'll see animals and plants of the desert. The 1,200-acre park has hundreds of cactus varieties as well as gila monsters, foxes, and gazelles.

Beyond the fountains and green lawns of Palm Springs, the desert has its own haunting, quiet beauty, with rocky outcroppings and cliffs in a multitude of hues and cacti that blossom bright with color in the spring. In nearby Joshua Tree National Monument, you can see cacti, underground springs, palm trees, yucca plants, wildlife and the spring-blooming

Joshua tree among the granite monoliths. One of the best ways to see it is by touring with Desert Adventures. The company's knowledgeable guides will tell you about the botany, wildlife, geology, and history of the fascinating park.

In contrast to the rocky gorges and open desert in much of the valley are the Indian Canyons, a series of canyons with palm trees and streams. Some of the canyons are listed on the National Register of Historic Places, as the Agua Caliente Cahuilla Indians had complex communities here.

For a panoramic view of the valley, ride the Palm Springs Aerial Tramway up San Jacinto Mountain. The cable cars climb through five climatic zones, from the desert floor to the cool mountaintop, in 15 minutes.

California's largest state park is another desert landscape and geological wonder, Anza-Borrego Desert State Park. Known for its diversity, with rocky canyons, dry lake beds, palm groves, and year-round springs, it's a favorite in the spring when the wildflowers turn the desert to fields of color. The park is close to the quiet, pleasant town of Borrego Springs.

BORREGO SPRINGS

La Casa del Zorro Resort Hotel

3845 Yaqui Pass Road
Borrego Springs, CA 92004
619-767-5323
800-824-1884 in California
800-325-8274 in U.S.
Fax 619-767-5963

A luxury hideaway in the Anza-Borrego desert

General manager: Dori Holladay. **Accommodations:** 77 rooms. **Rates:** $60–$250 in summer, $80–$495 in winter single or double, $10 additional person. **Payment:** Major credit cards. **Children:** Welcome. **Pets:** Not allowed. **Smoking:** Nonsmoking rooms available.

Clear air and the silence of the desert surround this unusual resort, spread over 32 acres of landscaped grounds. The first structure, built in 1937, was an adobe ranch house that expanded over the decades into La Casa del Zorro. Some of the original walls and beams remain as part of the lobby and lounge.

The resort is close to Anza-Borrego Desert State Park, California's largest state park, with 600,000 acres of canyons, palm groves, wildflowers, and rugged backcountry.

On the grounds, landscaped with lawns, palm trees, and a fountain, are three night-lit swimming pools and spas, tennis courts, and a putting green. The rose garden and gazebo provide a pretty setting for parties and weddings. Guests can attend aerobics classes, rent bicycles, dine in two restaurants, dance to live music in the Fox Den, rent movies, shop in a boutique, hike nearby trails, and play volleyball and table tennis. Child care can be arranged.

Despite all this activity, the atmosphere is serene at La Casa del Zorro, with casitas spread over the property. Some lodgings are separate cottages with fireplaces and up to four bedrooms. Others have several units in two-story stucco buildings with red tile roofs. All rooms are supplied with coffee and coffeemakers, and a morning paper is delivered to your door. A deluxe suite features a fireplace edged with colorful tiles, artwork and books in lighted niches, a wet bar, and a private patio. An unusual and delightful feature at La Casa del Zorro is its evening treat: instead of a mint on your pillow, you're given a booklet of short stories just right for bedtime reading.

DEATH VALLEY

Furnace Creek Inn

P.O. Box 1
Death Valley, CA 92328
619-786-2345

A resort oasis in the desert

Manager: Jim Heptner. **Accommodations:** 68 rooms. **Rates:** $155–$325 single or double, $14 additional person. **Payment:** Major credit cards. **Children:** Under age 18 free. **Pets:** Not allowed. **Smoking:** Nonsmoking rooms available. **Open:** Mid-October to Mother's Day.

Death Valley is the hottest, driest place in the world. Ground temperatures higher than 200 degrees Fahrenheit have been recorded here in summer. The landscape is stark, almost surreal in its contorted shapes, stretches of salty floor, brilliantly colored rocks, and high mountains. In the midst of this desert on the Nevada border, 300 miles northeast of Los Angeles, Furnace Creek shimmers like a green mirage.

Underground springs feed a garden of tropical flowers and palm trees, a swimming pool, and an 18-hole golf course. The rambling stone inn looks like a Spanish villa among the palms, with its red tile roof and Moorish arches.

Furnace Creek Inn was built in the late 1920s in response to public interest in Death Valley. Visitors were eager to see the strange and desolate beauty of a desert 200 feet below sea level. It had long been known for its rich mineral deposits, especially borax, which was brought out by the famous 20-mule team wagons. The Pacific Coast Borax Company built the resort and promoted it as a train destination in connection with the company's own railroads.

Most visitors take excursions to Death Valley landmarks. You can go on your own or with a guide who will explain the geology and history of Artist's Palette, Zabriskie Point, Dante's View, the jagged salt crystals of Devil's Golf Course, and Badwater, the lowest spot in the United States. Along the way you'll see wild burros, dunes, dry lake beds, and wide craters.

Today the inn's guest rooms are air conditioned and have television, ceiling fans, and whirlpool tubs. All three room categories — Deluxe, Desert, and Garden View — are furnished in a contemporary style in desert tones of sand, salmon, and aqua, and have views of the desert or gardens. In the evening, from your room or patio, you can hear the coyotes howl.

There are two restaurants, one the more formal dining room, serving steaks, chops, and fresh seafood, and the other the casual L'Ottomo's. On the lower level is the Oasis Room Supper Club, where the walls sparkle with borax. The Spanish-style, adobe lounge is popular for cocktails and dancing.

In addition to the golf course and swimming pool, the resort offers four tennis courts, shuffleboard, croquet, and horseback riding. There's no charge for tennis; a round of golf costs $28.

Manmade attractions are as unique as the landscape. Marta Becket's Amargosa Opera House, up a remote canyon, is a remarkable one-woman show. The artist and dancer from New York has been performing for twenty years in the theater she restored in a former ghost town. Scotty's Castle is a Mediterranean-style structure with three towers and 25 rooms filled with artwork and fine furniture and china. Once the home of a sometime miner and teller of tall tales, it's now open to the public and well worth a tour.

DESERT HOT SPRINGS

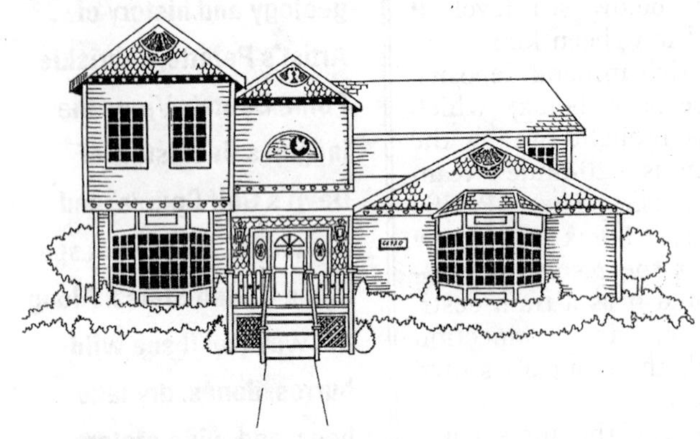

Travelers Repose

P.O. Box 655
66920 First Street
Desert Hot Springs, CA 92240
619-329-9584

A budget-conscious Victorian home in the desert

Innkeepers: Marian and Sam Relkoff. **Accommodations:** 3 rooms (1 with private bath). **Rates:** $55–$75 double, 10% less for single. **Included:** Expanded Continental breakfast. **Payment:** American Express. **Children:** Over age 12 welcome. **Pets:** Not allowed. **Smoking:** Not allowed indoors. **Open:** September to July.

Twelve miles from Palm Springs, Desert Hot Springs is a small, quiet community. On a slope above town, Travelers Repose has a number of pluses for the budget-minded.

It's unusual to find a Victorian home in the desert. This one, blue with dark blue and white trim, was built in the late 1980s by the Relkoffs as their dream home. Sam, formerly a contractor in Los Angeles, made much of the wood furniture.

For unusual views of the desert, take a covered wagon tour or a jeep ride with a Desert Adventures naturalist into the canyons or Joshua Tree National Monument.

In front, by the white picket fence and vine-covered trellis, masses of flowers grow. There's a garden in back, too, by the swimming pool and spa. Breakfast — usually fruit, homemade granola, and muffins — is sometimes served on the patio by the pool. The Relkoffs also provide afternoon refreshments.

The clean, attractive guest rooms are furnished in a country style. Buttons & Bows, on the main floor, is in rose and lace and has an iron and brass bed. Pine Room has a cannonball bed and a dresser and armoire in honey pine, and shares a bath with Heart Room, which has a heart motif. Each room has a view of the mountains that rise 9,000 feet from the desert floor.

For $55 (plus tax), two people can enjoy pleasant accommodations plus breakfast, afternoon tea, the use of a pool, and the hospitality of kindly innkeepers — a bargain in the often-expensive Palm Springs area.

LA QUINTA

La Quinta Hotel Golf & Tennis Resort

P.O. Box 69
494-499 Eisenhower Drive
La Quinta, CA 92253
619-564-4111
800-472-4316 in California
800-854-1271 in U.S.

A village-style resort known for privacy and recreation

Manager: Judy Vossler Woodard. **Accommodations:** 572 rooms and 68 suites. **Rates:** $75–$225 in summer, $165–$350 in winter and spring; suites $180–$1,400 in summer, $350–$2,100 in winter and spring. **Payment:** Major credit cards. **Children:** Under 18 free in room with parents. **Pets:** Small pets allowed with permission. **Smoking:** Allowed.

In 1926, a six-cottage hotel was built in the California desert, 20 miles from the sleepy village of Palm Springs. From that day to this, La Quinta has been known for its hospitality and distinctive style. During the '30s, it was a haven for Hollywood stars such as Greta Garbo, Charlie Chaplin, Bette Davis, Errol Flynn, and Clark Gable. Frank Capra's first visit to La Quinta inspired the creation of *It Happened One Night*. He returned to the hotel to write eight additional scripts.

Water cascades in tiers to a fountain near the hotel entrance and the air carries the sweet scent of grapefruit blossoms.

Since then, the resort has expanded into a 90-acre compound of rooms and suites, 25 swimming pools, and 35 spas. Yet, because of its careful design, there's no sense of overcrowding. Rather, you feel as though it's fiesta time in a village where shops, meeting rooms, and restaurants surround a colorful tile plaza.

You reach the hotel by a cypress-lined drive and enter a small lobby with tile floors, white walls, and Spanish wrought-iron accents. In the Santa Rosa Lounge, Mexican art objects — bright papier mâché fruits, Guerrero coconut masks, a tin-framed mirror — add to the Old California atmosphere. Afternoon tea is available.

A champagne brunch is offered on the hotel's original patio from October to May. Other places to eat include La Cantina, a rustic café and bar; Montaña's for specialty buffets and fine dining and dancing; Morgans, a casual 1920s American café, and the Adobe Grill, where southwestern and Mexican dishes are served.

One- and two-story bungalows, called casitas, are scattered over the property, many behind whitewashed walls espaliered with red-blooming bougainvillea. Each casita has from three to eight units. For the best views of the Santa Rosa Mountains, request a second-floor room.

A typical Double Deluxe room has two beds and a simple decor. The mood is cool, with white walls and white louvered shutters at the windows. The room has a television, a writing table, and a refrigerator. The large baths have double sinks and assorted toiletries that include sewing kits, loofahs, and sachets stamped with a bronze oak tree — the logo of Oak Tree Hotels, La Quinta's managing company.

The suites are larger, with more amenities. Many have private wraparound patios with whirlpools. Wet bars are stocked with liquors and snacks, soft drinks and complimentary boxes of dates. In one suite, louvered double doors divide the sitting room from a white and blue bedroom with a two-poster bed. A second TV is tucked into a niche beside a fireplace that passes through the wall to the bathroom. Wood is provided in another niche.

Twice-daily maid service and same-day laundry and dry cleaning are provided. The resort has nightly entertainment, several gift shops on the central plaza, and all kinds of meeting and conference space (including a 17,000-square-foot ballroom), but its main focus is tennis and golf. There are 30 tennis courts; guests play without charge. Clinics are offered regularly and include video analysis, programmable ball machines, and unlimited open play. Packages are available for both tennis players and golfers.

Championship golf courses are available to La Quinta guests. The 18-hole Dunes course, adjacent to the resort, is especially demanding, with water on eight holes, rolling hills, and scrubby desert to skirt.

PALM DESERT

Villa Royale

1620 Indian Trail
Palm Springs, CA 92264
619-327-2314
800-245-2314
Fax 619-322-3794

A friendly inn with an international theme

Innkeeper: Bob Lee. **Accommodations:** 33 rooms. **Rates:** \$75–\$300 in winter, \$59–\$200 in summer, single or double. **Included:** Continental breakfast.

Payment: Major credit cards. **Children:** Not appropriate. **Pets:** Not allowed. **Smoking:** Nonsmoking rooms available.

This European-style country inn is a gem hidden among the flashier baubles around it. Behind its stucco walls and iron gates, Villa Royale holds many surprises.

> **You may borrow bicycles, purchase a picnic lunch from the inn's restaurant, or join a tour of the boutiques and shopping centers on Palm Canyon Drive.**

First is the series of interior tree-shaded courtyards, each bright with cascading bougainvillea and pots of flowers. There are two swimming pools, one in the main courtyard where a light breakfast is served. You reach the other, smaller pool by following brick pathways that amble past fountains and vine-covered trellises to another courtyard. This Mediterranean-like compound covers 3½ acres. Each guest room has a different country theme: Morocco, France, Portugal, Germany, Italy, England, and Greece are a few. The Spain Room has Spanish ceramic tile edging the curved brick hearth of the fireplace. Decorative plates hang over an arch to the full kitchen, and double doors open to a courtyard with a fountain. The Monte Carlo Suite has red tile floors, a bleached-beam ceiling, and a fireplace. Its private patio faces a garden of roses and palm trees and, at night, the soft glow of filigreed Moroccan lamps hanging in the rubber trees.

Even the smallest room, which has a Dutch theme, is appealing, and it's a bargain to boot (too small for comfort if you're planning a lengthy stay, though).

Compared to recent developments in luxury hotels, amenities are basic: simple soaps, no hair dryers, few writing tables, no stationery. Television sets are hidden under tablecloths. But the charm of the place more than outweighs any such flaws; indeed, many guests view them as attributes.

The atmosphere at Villa Royale is low-key and friendly. Most guests spend at least part of the time relaxing and reading by the pools.

In keeping with the international theme, the Europa restaurant features cuisine from a different country every night, as well as the regular menu. Known as one of the best dining spots in Palm Springs, it offers lunch, dinner, and Sunday brunch. Examples of the excellent entrées are grilled sturgeon with cassis-lime purée, roast duckling in jalapeño orange sauce, and salmon in peach-brandy sauce. California and European wines are available.

PALM SPRINGS

The Autry Resort Hotel

4200 East Palm Canyon Drive
Palm Springs, CA 92264-5294
619-328-1171
800-443-6328
Fax 619-324-6104

A casual resort, centrally located

Director: Rose Narva. **Accommodations:** 185 rooms and suites. **Rates:** $95–$105 in summer, $135–$150 in winter, $25 additional person; suites $225–$300 in summer, $325–$500 in winter. **Payment:** Major credit cards. **Pets:** Not allowed. **Smoking:** Nonsmoking rooms available.

This 13-acre Palm Springs resort is owned by Gene Autry, the famous singing cowboy who starred in numerous Western movies. Favored by groups for its facilities, it's a good choice for individual travelers as well. It's centrally located, has lots of recreation options, the rooms are spacious and comfortable, and the service is exemplary. The reliable, friendly staff is always available yet never obtrusive.

Most of the rooms are off long halls in a modern, two-story building. They're furnished in standard hotel style and have air conditioning and TV with HBO. Some have a refrigerator and coffeemaker. Families with children usually lodge here.

The preferred accommodations, geared to adults, are the roomy, open bungalow suites that have walled patio gardens. The dark decor of the past has been lightened. There's a wet bar, plenty of drawer space, a living room big enough for entertaining, a bedroom that closes off with a pocket door, and a marble bath with double sinks. Around the corner is a pool surrounded by lawns and tall palms. This is the adult pool, closed to those under age 17. There are two other pools as well.

The dining room, overlooking the main pool and courtyard area, is open all day and features American and Mexican foods. Next to it is Legends, a dimly lighted bar that jumps with activity on weekends. Memorabilia from Gene Autry's days as a movie actor decorate the walls and tables.

The experience offered by Desert Adventures is unforgettable. With one of their 32 guides you can tour Indian Canyon, the world's largest natural desert oasis, and learn about the Cahuilla Indians' culture and the geology and botany of the area.

There is no golf course, but guests of the hotel have playing privileges at nearby courses. The resort has six tennis courts. You can take tennis lessons, go hot air ballooning, horseback riding, and bicycling. Several desert tours are available; one of the best is run by Desert Adventures (call 619-778-1733 or 619-324-3378).

Korakia Pensione

257 S. Patencio Road
Palm Springs, CA 92262
619-320-0708

A Mediterranean villa built in the 1920s

Proprietor: Douglas Smith. **Accommodations:** 15 rooms. **Rates:** \$89–\$155 double, \$30 additional person. **Included:** Expanded Continental breakfast. **Payment:** No credit cards. **Children:** Not appropriate. **Pets:** Welcome by arrangement. **Smoking:** Allowed.

In 1924 the Scottish artist Gordon Coutts constructed a villa in the then-remote desert area adjacent to the village of Palm Springs. The architecture was reminiscent of Morocco, where the artist had spent some time, and a radical departure from the Spanish Colonial style favored in southern California.

Over the years, cultural leaders and dignitaries visited the castlelike home (Sir Winston Churchill painted in the upstairs studio), but after Coutts's death the villa deteriorated. In 1989, the Smiths purchased the building and began its restoration; Douglas is an architectural preservationist. The atmosphere and furnishings reflect the five years that Doug spent living in Greece.

Korakia stands behind an oleander hedge and a small courtyard and is entered through a quaint wooden door. Beyond the central room used as a lobby, you can see another courtyard with a small pool. Each guest room is different, but all have kitchens or refrigerators, fresh flowers, crisply ironed sheets, and individual charm. The Art Studio, where Churchill stayed, is a big, open rectangle with a telescope so you can better admire the view of Mt. San Jacinto. The Library, where literary discussions and chamber music concerts were held in decades past, has a beamed ceiling, French doors leading to a shaded patio, a queen-size handmade poster bed, and, of course, shelves full of books. The rooms do not have phones or TVs, though those are available upon request.

The white, uncluttered rooms feature antiques, Oriental rugs, period lamps, leather-bound books, and artifacts from Mediterranean countries.

The Adobe Room, once the villa's master bedroom, is the smallest and is different from the rest, with ochre adobe walls. It's adjacent to the patio fountain and swimming pool. More grand and spacious is the upstairs suite, with a living room, dining room, kitchen, bedroom, and private balcony.

Breakfast is served in your room or on the flagstone terrace beside the antique Moorish fountain, where doves coo in antique bird cages under the fruit trees. A communal kitchen is available for preparing light fare.

La Mancha

P.O. Box 340
444 Avenida Caballeros
Palm Springs, CA 92262
619-323-1773
800-255-1773
Fax 619-323-5928

A cluster of luxurious villas in central Palm Springs

Owners: Ken and Suzy Irwin. **Accommodations:** 54 villas. **Rates:** \$135–\$950 single or double in winter, \$95–\$690 in summer, $25 additional person, reduced rates for longer stays. **Minimum stay:** 2 nights. **Payment:** Major credit cards. **Children:** Welcome; under age 10 not appropriate in pool villas. **Pets:** Not allowed. **Smoking:** Allowed.

One of the most extravagant, secluded, charming getaways in California is right in the middle of Palm Springs. Tucked behind walls and electronic security gates, La Mancha stands on 20 lushly landscaped acres, a Mediterranean-style village of stucco buildings with red tile roofs.

> **Bicycles and white Chrysler LeBaron convertibles are available for jaunting about town. Or you may ride in a limousine, compliments of La Mancha, when you're in the mood for a Palm Springs shopping foray. Airport pickup is complimentary.**

The private villas range in size from one bedroom and one bath to three bedrooms and three baths. Some are one-story casitas, others loft villas with two levels. Every imaginable luxury is provided, depending upon the lodging you choose. Mini-suites, or sections of the three-bedroom villas, are also available.

The most expensive are the four private tennis villas. Each boasts a tennis court, a walled courtyard patio, a private swimming pool, a therapy pool and bath, an outdoor wet bar with icemaker, a split-level living and dining room with a fireplace, an equipped kitchen, laundry facilities, and a state-of-the-art video and sound system.

The luxury estate villas have the same features without the tennis courts. They all resemble fine private homes in a well-to-do neighborhood, but even when the complex is full there's no sense of crowding. Some have their own security entrances and garages — favorites with celebrities who wish anonymity.

In addition to the private pools or spas (or both) in 47 villas, La Mancha has a freeform pool with a waterfall and stream. On a raised deck beside it are yellow tent cabanas and a thatch-roofed bar. There are four tennis courts, two tournament croquet courts, a golf green for chipping and putting, and facilities for small meetings.

You may dine on a terrace near the pool or in La Mancha's

tiny restaurant (just seven tables, though a wall of mirrors makes the room appear twice as large), which serves Continental and Mexican cuisine. One specialty for both dessert and breakfast is a beignet soufflé, an eclairlike puff served with fresh fruits and sauces.

Four stained glass windows depicting scenes from Don Quixote hang in the dining room, clues to the owner's interest in Cervantes's hero. Ken Irwin has long been fascinated with Don Quixote; his own "impossible dream" is the resort he and his wife have made a reality. They specialize in superb service that goes beyond daily maid service and cheese and fruit baskets.

Choose from the international take-out menu, and a driver will pick up and deliver your selections. Request a private dinner in your villa, and the chef will prepare it in your kitchen. If you want a violin serenade of your favorite song, you have only to ask. With the Romantic Interlude package, you'll be served champagne, dinner by candlelight, and breakfast in bed.

This extraordinary hideaway is the place to go when you tire of those incessant autograph hunters — or when you simply want total privacy in a romantic dream.

L'Horizon

1050 East Palm Canyon Drive
Palm Springs, CA 92264
619-323-1858

A tranquil inn for sunshine and relaxation

Manager: Zetta Castle. **Accommodations:** 20 rooms. **Rates:** \$85–\$125 single or double (rates vary according to season). **Included:** Continental breakfast. **Payment:** Major credit cards. **Children:** Not appropriate. **Pets:** Not allowed. **Smoking:** Allowed. **Open:** October–July.

This secluded, quiet enclave is in the desert city of Palm Springs, an oasis within an oasis. Behind walls covered with scarlet bougainvillea, 2½ acres of lawns, tall palm trees, and spicy-scented pepper trees provide the setting for seven low-lying buildings.

Groups will sometimes rent an entire building for \$325; each has three bedrooms and a kitchen. The rooms, decorated in light white and pastels, are tastefully furnished in a contemporary style and have tall, shuttered windows and private patios. In the bathroom, a glass door leads to an atrium fragrant with the scent of orange blossoms. A basket of fruit and chocolates is in each room, and breakfast is brought to your door with a morning newspaper. The staff will bring lunch from the Village Bake Shop, and several restaurants are within walking distance.

Built in the 1950s and remodeled in the late 1980s, the rooms surround a swimming pool, Jacuzzi, and barbecue area with lounge chairs and umbrella tables. There's a fine view of Mount San Jacinto.

L'Horizon lends bicycles and will make reservations for golf, tennis, and horseback riding. The inn also has a library and facilities for croquet, horseshoes, and bocce ball. Desert Adventures offers noteworthy, highly recommended tours to Indian Canyon and Joshua Tree National Monument.

Le Petit Château

1491 Via Soledad
Palm Springs, CA 92264
619-325-2686

A casual, quiet, clothing-optional inn for adults

Innkeepers: Don and Mary Robidoux. **Accommodations:** 10 rooms. **Rates:** $90–$130 single or double; midweek discounts. **Included:** Expanded Continental breakfast. **Minimum stay:** 2 nights on weekends. **Payment:** Major credit cards. **Children:** Not appropriate. **Pets:** Not allowed. **Smoking:** Discouraged.

On the French Riviera, nudity or seminudity on public beaches is accepted. That's not the custom in the U.S., so those who like to swim or sunbathe au naturel turn to places like Le Petit Château. Clothing is optional here, but this comfortable, low-key inn is definitely not a nudist camp. Rather, the guests are people who enjoy swimming, lounging poolside, or soaking in the outdoor whirlpool without a cover-up.

Rooms are in low-lying buildings that form a U around the pool and lounging area. Half the rooms have kitchens. These are not luxury accommodations, but they've been spruced up recently and have attractive furnishings and a light, airy atmosphere. White wicker, flowered comforters, and greenery make them inviting. Your room will also have a clock radio, a television with a movie channel, and a bath with a shower. Pool towels are provided. Room keys open the door to the walled courtyard, which is kept locked.

The breakfast buffet is always laden with juices, cereals, bagels, yogurt, fruit, and pastries. Coffee, tea, and chocolate are available all day, and in the late afternoon wine and cheese are set out by the pool. The inn also has a putting green.

Don, a former salesman, and Mary, a teacher, came to Palm Springs from Los Angeles in 1983, determined to escape a hectic lifestyle. In opening an inn they combined several things they enjoyed: the outdoor life of the desert, nude sunbathing (discovered on a trip to St. Tropez), and meeting like-minded people. Their little inn, located on a quiet side street, is close to the resort town's fine shops and restaurants.

They're happy to share their knowledge of the area and will recommend eating places and attractions. Don is a hiker who welcomes company on the trails of the mountains that rise abruptly from the desert on the edge of town.

Le Petit Château is one of the most relaxing places to stay in southern California; there's no pretense here, and you'll see all adult ages and shapes tanning by the pool. And what could be more pleasant than resting in a bubbling whirlpool under a moonlit sky, with the scent of lemon blossoms permeating the air?

Oasis Water Resort Villa Hotel

4190 East Palm Canyon Drive
Palm Springs, CA 92264
619-328-1499
800-247-4664

A resort community featuring water fun

Resident Manager: Dan Evans.
Accommodations: 110 villas. **Rates:** $159–$289 2–8 people (rates vary with season; weekly and monthly discounts available). **Included:** Expanded Continental breakfast. **Payment:** Major credit cards. **Children:** Welcome. **Pets:** Not allowed. **Smoking:** Allowed.

The entrance to the Oasis is from a circular driveway where figures of dolphins spout in a tiered fountain. Crossing over ponds fed by a waterfall, you enter a small and usually busy lobby. On one side is the coffee shop where guests get breakfast; it's hectic in the morning, and noisy if the big TV is on. You can avoid this by coming in early or late and taking your tray to the terrace.

Oasis Waterpark has seven waterslides, a wave-action pool for surfing (boards may be rented), a 600-foot inner tube ride, and kiddy slides. Also on the property are restaurants, locker rooms, a sportswear shop, and a well-equipped health club.

The 27-acre resort resembles a suburban development, with clusters of two-condominium villas lining curving streets that end in culs de sac. There are separate areas for adults and for families with children. The condos have two bedrooms and two baths, and some are sizable homes.

Typical of the well-furnished deluxe units is one with a white tile foyer, grasscloth walls, and a queen-size sofa bed. The kitchen has a gas stove, dishwasher, microwave, refrigerator/freezer, toaster, and coffeemaker. There's a table for four in the angled breakfast nook and a pass-through counter to the living room. From the balcony, which has a barbecue, there's a view of the Santa Rosa mountains. The bedrooms are clean, spacious, and for the most part well maintained, though you may see a few chips and scratches on the walls and furniture. Daily maid service is provided.

Facilities on the hotel property include eight swimming pools, nine spas and sunning decks, and five lighted tennis courts. The area's biggest attraction is the nearby Oasis Waterpark, a 21-acre playground open daily from March to Labor Day and on weekends in September and October. A fee is charged for admission to the park, but hotel guests receive complimentary passes.

Orchid Tree Inn

261 South Belardo Road
Palm Springs, CA 92262
619-325-2791
Fax 619-325-3855
800-733-3435

A garden retreat with the tranquility of old Palm Springs

Proprietors: Bob Weithorn and Karen Prince. **Accommodations:** 40 rooms, suites, and cottages. **Rates:** $45–$210 in summer, $70–$250 in winter and spring, single or double, $15 additional person; discounts for longer stays. **Included:** Continental breakfast, November 1–May 31. **Minimum stay:** 2 nights on weekends. **Payment:** Major credit cards. **Children:** Not appropriate. **Pets:** Not allowed. **Smoking:** Nonsmoking rooms available.

When old-timers wax nostalgic about the Palm Springs of the past, this is the kind of place they remember with fondness. At the Orchid Tree, the charm of Palm Springs in the 1920s and 1930s still exists. The Spanish bungalows, built in 1934, have been carefully restored and updated. They (and the suites and studios) have ceramic tiles, hand-painted flower stencils, and a variety of furnishings, including Spanish Colonial, Queen Anne, lodgepole pine, wicker, and Old West style leather and saddle blankets. Most rooms have kitchens with gas stoves and dishware in pre-war patterns. There are private balconies, patios, beautifully landscaped gardens, two large pools, a spa area, and mountain views.

Trellised walkways around the complex are bordered with citrus and other trees, flowers, birdbaths, and birdhouses.

Next to the spa is the Aqua Caliente building, a gathering place where breakfast is served. Its '30s theme is enhanced by wall sconces with wrought-iron cutouts, stained glass windows, and the saddle blanket cushions and cacti evocative of old California. Seminars and classes that focus on the arts and self-realization are planned for this site.

No room service or meals (other than the winter breakfast) are offered at the Orchid Tree, but there are 35 restaurants within walking distance. The picturesque, serene inn is just a block from central Palm Springs.

The Palms at Palm Springs

572 North Indian Avenue
Palm Springs, CA 92262
619-325-1111

A spa resort in a desert oasis

General manager: Mark Joseph Kandarian. **Accommodations:** 43 rooms. **Rates:** $125–$220 per person. **Included:** All meals. **Minimum stay:** 2 nights. **Payment:** Major credit cards. **Children:** Not appropriate. **Pets:** Not allowed. **Smoking:** Nonsmoking rooms available.

A week's stay at this attractive, well-managed spa is likely to send you home relaxed, refreshed, and pounds lighter. It's both invigorating and tranquilizing.

The Palms, a compound of low stucco buildings, is shielded

from busy Indian Avenue by its landscaped grounds and main building, which houses the beauty salon, gift shop, and office. On the second floor is a library where evening programs are held, massage rooms, and a lounge called the Winners Circle. There's a kitchen with iced tea and coffee, and a sun room in one corner.

While you're losing weight and gaining health, you're encouraged to see the desert sights, enjoy the shops (Desert Fashion Plaza is within walking distance), and participate in outdoor activities.

The guest rooms radiate off the central courtyard and pool. Some visitors may be lounging in the sun under the palms and grapefruit trees while others are joining in a spirited session of water exercises.

Unlike most spas, the minimum stay is two nights, so you can spend just a couple of days being pampered and exercised — though you won't see the same benefits that a week or more will provide. You pick the activities you prefer from those available each day. It's recommended that you take at least one aerobic, one stretch, and one strength-training class daily. Private fitness consultations are available at additional cost.

The spa offers a wide range of classes and programs for health and beauty. Aerobics in and out of the 90-degree swimming pool, dancing, walking, weight training, and yoga are led by qualified, enthusiastic instructors. The Palms focuses on fitness, but a number of beauty treatments are available: facials, waxing, manicures, pedicures, and hairstyling.

Since weight loss is the goal of most guests, food is of great interest. Expert nutritionists plan delicious meals that amount to 1,000 calories a day. It's not a strict regimen, however, and if you wish to add other items, more choices are available. A typical lunch is pasta salad, crab quiche, fresh broccoli spears, an onion roll, and a fruit flan — plenty for most waist-watchers. Meals are served in the dining room near the central courtyard. There are two juice and broth breaks during the day.

The clientele is about 75 percent female at The Palms. There are usually about 65 guests in the winter and fewer in the summer, the season for special packages and discounts. The rooms are spacious; typically they have pale peach walls, rattan chairs, and pastel quilts. Telephones, televisions, closets with luggage racks, and baths with tub and shower are in all rooms. Those in the building away from the pool have private patios or balconies. Daily maid service is provided.

The private rooms are the most expensive. The others have two beds and are shared with another guest.

The Palms at Palm Springs is owned by Sheila Cluff, who also runs other fitness enterprises. She brought a background of experience in figure skating, physical education, fashion, and television to her present position as a leader in the field of fitness and beauty. In The Palms, she has created a spa that is also a resort.

Because the spa is affiliated with the Palm Springs Plaza Resort and Racquet Club, guests may use the club's courts for a fee. Public courts are nearby.

Other Palm Springs attractions include the many golf courses, aerial tramway rides, hot air ballooning, bicycle riding, and celebrity homes tours.

RANCHO MIRAGE

The Ritz-Carlton Rancho Mirage

68-900 Frank Sinatra Drive
Rancho Mirage, CA 92270
619-321-8282
800-241-3333
Fax 619-321-6928

A traditional luxury hotel above the desert

General manager: Scott Nassar. **Accommodations:** 219 rooms and 21 suites. **Rates:** $95–$250 in summer, $200–$350 in winter for 1 to 4 people; suites $400–$900 in summer, $500–$1,000 in winter. **Payment:** Major credit cards. **Children:** Under 17 free in room with parents. **Pets:** Not allowed. **Smoking:** Nonsmoking rooms are available.

Above the desert valley and village of Rancho Mirage, on a 650-foot-high plateau south of Palm Springs, the adobe-colored buildings of the Ritz-Carlton stand like great boulders in a rocky landscape. It's a stark setting, here in the rugged foothills of the Santa Rosa Mountains, but inside the contrast is astounding. You enter a world of European antiques, marble floors, crystal chandeliers, heavy drapes, and museum-quality oil paintings on paneled walls. At the far end of the long lobby is a scene that appears surreal but is in fact a picture window framing a view of the desert and mountains beyond a terrace with white canvas umbrellas.

Some of the sky views are glorious. Ask for a west-facing room and you may see both color-streaked skies at sunset and pastel reflections against Mount San Jacinto at sunrise.

All hotels with the Ritz-Carlton name specialize in a strong classical tradition of luxury, along with an emphasis on personal service. Rancho Mirage is no exception. Ignoring the desert surrounding it, the resort is all damask drapes, dark woods, and formal furniture.

The accommodations feature custom crown moldings, writing tables, balconies or patios, and marble baths with telephones. Plush terrycloth robes and Scottish Fine shampoos are among the amenities. The decor, in muted tan and gold, reflects the hills outside while setting a tone of understated luxury. Television sets are tucked into antique reproduction highboys; stocked honor bars hide behind false drawers.

The resort has a fitness center with workout equipment, steam and sauna rooms, and massage. The center is near the outdoor pool, which is in a grassy plateau above the Coachella Valley. Across the road are ten tennis courts, a pro shop, and a Tennis Club restaurant. Several nearby golf courses are open to guests. The closest is Rancho Mirage Country Club.

The hotel restaurants vary. For fine cuisine, diners reserve a table at the Club Grill, which has relaxed its previous stringent formality. In the 75-seat dining room, Continental and American dishes are beautifully presented. If you can't decide on dessert after an elegant meal, order the Black Plate — you'll be served tastes of lemon tart, cheesecake, and chocolate mousse, among other delectable items. There are two more casual cafés, one with outdoor tables, and afternoon tea is served in the lobby lounge. Poolside snacks are served all day.

The friendly service in this atmosphere of refined gentility is pure West Coast. The bellman who carries your luggage may linger to lean on the balcony railing and chat about the desert sunset and life in Palm Springs. The desk clerk may grab your arm and point out an unusual sight he thinks you shouldn't miss: the bighorn sheep that wander in every day from the mountains to graze on the lawn. This may be the Ritz, but it's still California.

North Coast/
Mount Shasta

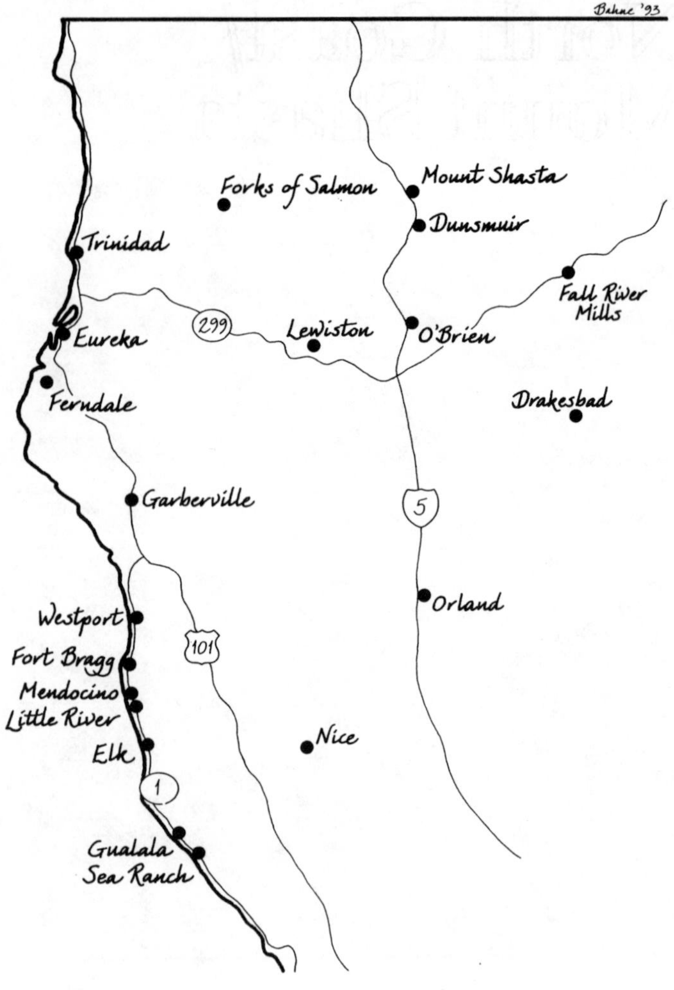
Bahne '93
Mount Shasta
Forks of Salmon
Dunsmuir
Trinidad
Fall River
Mills
299
Lewiston
O'Brien
Eureka
Drakesbad
Ferndale
Garberville
5
Orland
Westport
101
Fort Bragg
Mendocino
Little River
Nice
Elk
1
Gualala
Sea Ranch

Drakesbad
Drakesbad Guest Ranch, 325
Dunsmuir
Caboose Motel, 327
Elk
Elk Cove Inn, 329
Greenwood Pier Inn, 331
Harbor House, 332
Eureka
An Elegant Victorian Mansion, 334
Carter House, 336
Fall River Mills
Rick's Lodge, 338
Ferndale
The Gingerbread Mansion, 339
Forks of Salmon
Otter Bar Lodge, 341
Fort Bragg
Sandcastle, 343
Garberville
Benbow Inn, 344
Gualala
The Old Milano Hotel, 346
St. Orres, 348
Lewiston
Trinity Alps Resort, 349
Little River
Glendeven, 351
Heritage House, 353
Little River Inn, 355
Sea Arch, 357
Mendocino
The Headlands Inn, 358
Hill House of Mendocino, 360
Hranrad House, 361
Joshua Grindle Inn, 362
MacCallum House, 364
Reed Manor, 366
Sea Haus, 367
The Stanford Inn by the Sea, 368
Mount Shasta
Ward's Big Foot Ranch, 370
Nice
Featherbed Railroad Company, 371
O'Brien
Holiday Harbor, 373
Orland
The Inn at Shallow Creek Farm, 375
Sea Ranch
The Sea Ranch, 376
Trinidad
The Lost Whale Inn, 378
Trinidad Bed & Breakfast, 380
Westport
Howard Creek Ranch, 382

Best Intimate City Stops

Eureka
An Elegant Victorian Mansion
Carter House

Best Country Inns and B&Bs

Dunsmuir
Caboose Motel
Garberville
Benbow Inn
Little River
Glendeven
Mount Shasta
Ward's Big Foot Ranch
Nice
Featherbed Railroad Company
Orland
The Inn at Shallow Creek Farm
Westport
Howard Creek Ranch

Best Family Favorites

Lewiston
Trinity Alps Resort
Mendocino
Sea Haus
O'Brien
Holiday Harbor
Trinidad
The Lost Whale Inn

Best Inns by the Sea

Elk
Elk Cove Inn
Greenwood Pier Inn

Harbor House

Fort Bragg

Sandcastle

Gualala

The Old Milano Hotel

St. Orres

Little River

Heritage House

Little River Inn

Mendocino

The Headlands Inn

Hill House of Mendocino

Joshua Grindle Inn

MacCallum House

The Stanford Inn by the Sea

Trinidad

Trinidad Bed & Breakfast

Best Resorts

Sea Ranch

The Sea Ranch

Best Romantic Hideaways

Ferndale

The Gingerbread Mansion

Little River

Sea Arch

Mendocino

Hranrad House

Reed Manor

Best Wilderness Retreats

Drakesbad

Drakesbad Guest Ranch

Fall River Mills

Rick's Lodge

Forks of Salmon

Otter Bar Lodge

For unspoiled, uncrowded wilderness, head for California's far north. The Klamath, Shasta, and Trinity regions are vast stretches of thick forestland, rugged mountains, alpine meadows, rushing rivers, and deep canyons. Towns are few and cities nonexistent.

Mount Shasta, rising 14,162 feet from the valley floor, dominates much of the landscape. South of the dormant volcano is Shasta Lake, fed by rivers and dammed to form an immense reservoir where every sort of freshwater recreation is available.

East of Shasta and I-5 are trout-filled rivers, dark lava beds, and sanctuaries for birds and wildlife. In Lassen Volcanic National Park, deep craters and steaming sulfur vents are reminders of Mount Lassen's explosive past. The southernmost volcano in the Cascade chain, 10,000-foot Lassen last erupted in 1917.

West of I-5 lie the Trinity Alps, where angular peaks reach 8,000 feet above evergreen forests and steep ravines. This is prime fishing and backpacking country.

Still farther west is, finally, the edge of the continent — the end of the American frontier. Here the redwoods grow, the tallest trees in the world. Most of the primeval forests are gone now, cut for lumber, but in Redwood National Park and the state parks along Highway 101, cathedral-like groves are preserved. The largest park is near the little town of Trinidad.

Continuing south past Eureka, a bay city known for its Victorian architecture, Highway 101 turns inland toward Garberville and then hugs the coastline again, offering spectacular scenes of rugged beauty. Ceaseless waves, their spindrift pluming, crash against craggy cliffs and sea arches; white surf curls against smooth sand. Coves and inlets, lagoons and tidepools wait to be explored. From any bluff along the way you may see gray whales spouting as they migrate between Alaska and the sheltered waters off Baja California.

Small communities such as Mendocino, Little River, and Elk, separated by high cliffs and empty beaches, punctuate the winding ribbon of coastal road from Oregon to San Francisco Bay.

DRAKESBAD

Drakesbad Guest Ranch

Chester, CA 96020
916-Drakesbad 2 via Susanville operator
Off-season:
California Guest Services
2150 North Main Street, #5
Red Bluff, CA 96080
916-529-1512

A woodsy lodge near Mount Lassen

Owners: John and Pam Koeberer. **Accommodations:** 19 rooms. **Rates:** $110–$125 single, $85–$98 per person double, $70–$75 additional person, $56 child age 2-11, weekly rates available. **Included:** All meals. **Payment:** MasterCard, Visa. **Children:** Under 2 free in room with parents. **Pets:** Discouraged. **Smoking:** Allowed. **Open:** June to October.

The only lodge in Lassen Volcanic National Park, in northern California, Drakesbad offers an extraordinary summer wilderness experience, combining basic comforts with outdoor leisure and backcountry exploration. Meadows, lakes and trout streams surround the property. Hiking trails wind through 150 miles of verdant forest, glaciated canyons, and volcanic terrain. Horseback rides to scenic spots in the park are scheduled daily. And on the sprawling ranch there's a naturally heated swimming pool, open 24 hours a day.

The ranch, nestled in a scenic valley 2½ miles from the park's southeastern entrance, was founded by E.R. Drake a century ago. In 1900 he sold it to the Sifford family, who named it Drakesbad for the hot springs and pools on the property. For fifty years the Siffords operated the ranch much as it is today. The present owners have made improvements but have retained its rough texture.

All accommodations are modest but clean and well kept. Some share shower facilities, and most use kerosene lamps rather than electricity. The six rooms on the second floor of the main lodge have half baths; tubs and showers are in a modern outdoor bathhouse. Housekeeping is provided daily.

The main floor of the lodge is where guests stop by to sit in the rocking chair by the stone fireplace, read, work on a jigsaw puzzle, or buy candy and film. In this big, knotty pine room with scuffed wooden floors, braided rugs, and rusted old farm tools hanging on the walls, there's a sense of timelessness. You know that although changes have been made, this is just how it must have looked years ago. Typical of the ranch's informality, if you are the last person to leave the lodge at night, you're asked to turn out the lanterns that hang from ceiling beams.

Hiking trails cross areas of devastation with steaming fumaroles and boiling mud pots caused by past volcanic outbursts. Bumpass Hell Trail shows dramatic examples of geothermal activity. The hike with the most panoramic views is Lassen Peak Trail, which leads to the summit.

Outside, a long veranda faces a lawn with picnic tables, a volleyball net, a campfire pit, barbecues, and a path that leads through the adjacent field to the pool.

Across the way, under pine and fir trees, are three bungalows, each with two adjoining units with knotty pine walls and rustic furnishings. They have a propane heater and a private bath and can connect to the next room to make two bedrooms and two baths. Similar rooms are in an annex, a duplex, and four cabins among the trees on the other side of the property, not far from the stables. There are no locks on the doors, so it's wise to lock valuables in your car.

Meals are served in the dining room, a separate building with pine walls, a potbellied woodstove, and wooden tables and chairs. Hearty ranch breakfasts and dinners are served at your table; lunch is buffet style. Beer and wine are available.

You can take guided horseback trips to lovely spots in the 106,000-acre park, such as Devil's Kitchen, Boiling Springs Lake, Terminal Geyser, Kings Creek Falls, and Willow Lakes. Along the way you may see bears, marmots, deer, and golden mantled squirrels, as well as wildflowers and birds.

DUNSMUIR

Caboose Motel

Railroad Park Resort
100 Railroad Park Road
Dunsmuir, CA 96025
916-235-4440

A group of railroad cars, restored as lodgings

Proprietors: Bill and Delberta Murphy. **Accommodations:** 22 cabooses, 1 boxcar, 4 cabins. **Rates:** $60 single, $55–$85 double, $5 additional person. **Payment:** Major credit cards. **Children:** Welcome. **Pets:** Welcome with approval. **Smoking:** Nonsmoking rooms available.

In the 19th century, the last car on a train was used for storage space and living quarters, and it became the personal domain of the conductor. To live the life of such a railroader, visit Caboose Motel. It takes a leap of imagination, for these cabooses go nowhere — each is anchored firmly to its own brief stretch of track just off I-5, south of the little town of Dunsmuir in the mountains of northern California.

The cabooses bear fresh coats of paint — green, blue, yellow, and, mostly, a familiar railroad red. Each has a different interior decor; some are painted, others paneled in knotty cedar. A typical rectangular room has a brass bed, a table and chairs, a dresser, a coffeemaker, and a TV with satellite reception. Blue fluffy curtains hang at small windows. The effect is not unlike a mobile home except for the metal braces and pipes, the iron ladders and lofts that are evidence of the car's railroading days. The only other mementos are the photographs on the walls.

A loose circle of cabooses surrounds a free-form swimming pool, wooden deck, and spa. A stream runs by, winding through the property to a pond. Off to the side are four attached housekeeping cabins, which hold four people each.

The resort's office and gift shop are in a faded yellow building that resembles an old-fashioned train depot with a high boardwalk entrance. Near it is the showpiece of the resort, its restaurant. Made from antique dining cars, it's steeped in railroad history. Above the bar is a hand-built scale model of the Cascade, which ran from San Francisco to Portland in the

1930s. Antique hand tools, lamps, and steam gauges make this a railroad buff's delight.

Bill and Delberta Murphy are proud of their region and of their resort in the Sacramento River Canyon. They lend mountain bikes and will direct you to hiking trails and the trout pond. Their unusual resort also has sixty campsites and RV sites.

Dinners are served in an equally nostalgic atmosphere, with a view of relics of the steam era. Among them are an 1893 Wells Fargo car, a gear-driven logging engine, and a restored water tower. The menu offers quite plain American fare — steak, chicken, iceberg lettuce, and black pepper from the 24-inch grinder dominate the dining scene. The restaurant is only open for dinner.

For other meals, drive a mile north into Dunsmuir, where there are several good cafés (try Rosie's Ice Cream Parlor for homemade soups and sandwiches).

Outside the Patio Car, there's a deck for relaxing with a cocktail and enjoying the fine view of the gray spires of Castle Crags State Park. In the shadow of these steep granite outcroppings, the last Indian battle fought with bows and arrows occurred in 1885.

ELK

Elk Cove Inn

P.O. Box 367
6300 South Highway 1
Elk Cove, CA 95432
707-877-3321

An ocean-view inn and cottages

Innkeeper: Hildrun-Uta Triebess. **Accommodations:** 8 units (all with private bath). **Rates:** $98–$138 weekdays, $108–$148 weekends. **Included:** Full breakfast. **Minimum stay:** 2 or 3 nights on weekends and holidays. **Payment:** No credit cards. **Children:** Not appropriate. **Pets:** Not allowed. **Smoking:** Not allowed indoors.

The main house of this clifftop inn was built in 1883 by the L. E. White Lumber Company as an executive guest house. Hildrun-Uta discovered the secluded Victorian home and fell in love with it and the village of Elk in 1967. With visions of an inn offering lodging and fine meals in the European tradition, she bought the place and opened it to guests in 1968.

The rooms are in the main house, two cabins, and a two-unit building at the edge of the cliff. They have fine views of the seaweed-strewn sandy beach and offshore rocks. The furnishings are simple but comfortable. Fresh flowers, potted greenery, and hand-embroidered linens add a personal touch, accented by the fragrance of sun-dried sheets and towels.

Every room has a tray with a complimentary bottle of sherry.

The rooms in the duplex addition feature large bay windows, high beamed ceilings, skylights, and fireplaces. The windows in the Greenwood Room overlook Greenwood Creek and the beach below. Even the shower stall, its tiles bright with handpainted folk art, has a long window with a view.

Climbing roses, boxes of pink geraniums, and flower beds under the cypress trees give this gabled white inn and its guest cottages a country atmosphere. The inn stands on 1½ acres on a cliff above the ocean.

The large, bright rooms upstairs in the main house have paneled wainscoting, window seats, and skylights. They share a sitting area and a redwood deck. The newest addition is the Swallow's Nest, a small corner room on the main floor which has access to the deck.

The energetic innkeeper is usually at work on a new project, but whatever the current state of construction, she'll greet you with a dazzling smile and a hearty welcome and treat you like an honored friend. Breakfast at Elk Cove is served in the dining room of the main house. Hildrun-Uta is likely to prepare a huge, fluffy omelet, fresh fruit, juice, and muffins with jam. The sugarless muffins, sweetened with dates and almonds, are a delicious specialty, to be enjoyed while you gaze at the cove and the sea. Or you can take them with you to the gazebo or down the path that leads to the beach. On the way you may see the great blue herons or snowy egrets that often visit, or the two ravens that are virtually pets.

The inn is close to several Anderson Valley wineries and 15 miles south of the shops and art galleries of Mendocino.

Greenwood Pier Inn

Box 36
5928 Highway 1
Elk, CA 95432
707-877-9997

An artistic inn overlooking the sea

Innkeepers: Isabel and Kendrick Petty. **Accommodations:** 11 rooms (all with private bath). **Rates:** \$80–\$195 single or double, \$10 additional person. **Included:** Continental breakfast. **Minimum stay:** 2 nights on weekends in most rooms. **Payment:** Major credit cards. **Children:** Welcome. **Pets:** Allowed with prior arrangement. **Smoking:** Allowed.

A bower of flowers, an art gallery, a charming café, clifftop views of the Pacific surf — all this and comfortable rooms make up the unique Greenwood Pier Inn. The energetic and talented innkeepers started their venture in 1980 with two cottages. Now they have a complex of lodgings, all connected by paths that wind through extravagant gardens, high above the sea.

It's a ten-minute walk to the beach from the inn. You can walk in the state park south of Elk, go sea kayaking or horseback riding, and see the giant redwoods in Hendy Woods State Park, 19 miles inland.

The rooms have hand-painted tiles, stained glass by regional artists, leaded glass windows, skylights, and pieces collected by the Pettys on their world travels. In one corner you might see a huge vase filled with calla lilies four feet high; in another, a pink dressing table painted with flowers.

In Sea Castle North and Sea Castle South, Kendrick's seascapes hang on the walls and sliding glass doors open to a deck at the edge of a cliff, overlooking the ocean. A staircase spirals up to a tub for two next to a wide window. Books fill the shelves, and tapes are provided for the tape deck.

This is a place of exuberance, color, and quirky character. You'll see curtains askew, rough walls next to Oriental artifacts, and an eclectic mix of art and furniture. Isabel's artistic sense and enthusiasm make it all work. She sews the quilts, designs clothing and jewelry, paints portraits, bakes the breads and desserts served in the café — and if you need marriage counseling she can provide that, too.

The restaurant is open with a limited dinner menu on Friday and Saturday. On other nights, a reasonably priced meal will be brought on a tray to your door, if you wish. Breakfast is also brought to your room.

Don't miss a trip to Greenwood Pier's intriguing country store and garden shop.

Harbor House

P.O. Box 369
5600 South Highway 1
Elk, CA 95432
707-877-3203

A seaside home in the grand style

Innkeepers: Dean and Helen Turner. **Accommodations:** 10 rooms (all with private bath). **Rates:** $125–$205 single, $165–$245 double, $50 additional person; winter discounts available. **Included:** Breakfast and dinner. **Minimum stay:** 2 nights on weekends. **Payment:** No credit cards. **Children:** Under age 12 not appropriate. **Pets:** Not allowed. **Smoking:** Not allowed indoors.

On a bluff facing a spectacular seascape is Harbor House, one of the finest examples of luxury lodging on the coast. The all-redwood inn stands above Greenwood Landing, once a busy port for lumber schooners.

The beamed ceiling and paneled walls in the living room glow with the rich patina of polish and age. A century-old Persian rug lies under deep cushioned couches grouped around the big fireplace. In one corner is a Steinway console piano; concerts are occasionally held in this room. A niche near the fire holds a phone and shelves of books and games for guests to use.

Beyond is the dining room, where a wall of windows faces the irresistible view. Breakfast here is different every day: fruit juice, homemade pastries and breads, and coffee are always available to accompany main dishes such as eggs Benedict, huevos rancheros, pancakes, and quiche. Eggs come from the inn's own chickens. Dinners feature home-grown produce, meats and cheeses from nearby farms, and fresh seafood. California wines are served.

The guest rooms, six of them in the main house, have antique furnishings and fireplaces. Harbor Room, one of the largest, has room for two beds, a sofa and chair, and an English library table. The views of the sea from this attractive, rose-colored room are stunning. Lookout is the smallest and most popular room in the house. It has a deck that is ideal for watching the sun set over the Pacific.

The inn was built in 1916 by the Goodyear Redwood Lumber Company as a residence and guest house for VIPs — it's a larger version of the Home of Redwood building at the Panama-Pacific International Exposition, held in San Francisco in 1915.

The other rooms are in four red and white cottages on the south side of the inn, under tall cypress trees. Rooms 1 and 2 share a deck that juts dramatically over a ravine that descends to a cove. For privacy, the deck is divided by a lattice with an ivy vine. Rooms 3 and 4 have partial ocean views from their decks; 4 is closest to the highway and therefore least desirable (however, the busy road quiets at night).

Harbor House offers comfortable accommodations, beauteous surroundings, fine food, and, most important, superb service. Dean and Helen Turner, former school administrators in Los Angeles, took over the inn in 1985 and have added their personal style of friendly warmth to the well-appointed sanctuary. They'll point out the path that leads from the lawns and garden down to the cove, introduce you to the attractions of Elk and Mendocino, and join you by the fire for evening conversation and music. Winter is a good time to visit, they say. The weather is often clear, and the coastal storms are thrilling to watch.

EUREKA

An Elegant Victorian Mansion

1406 "C" Street
Eureka, CA 95501
707-444-3144 or 707-442-5594

> *A historic home with warm hospitality*

Innkeepers: Doug and Lily Vieyra. **Accommodations:** 4 rooms (1 with private bath, 3 share 3 baths). **Rates:** $75–$115 single or double (corporate and midweek rates available). **Included:** Full breakfast. **Payment:** MasterCard, Visa. **Children:** "Precocious, well-behaved, older children welcome by prior arrangement." **Pets:** Not allowed. **Smoking:** Not allowed.

When you're greeted at the door by a smiling "butler" in formal dress who escorts you to an elegant parlor and then to a finely furnished guest room, you know you're in an unusual bed-and-breakfast. Doug Vieyra is the well-dressed greeter. Full of enthusiasm, he and Lily will show you around the parlors, the library, the sitting room, and the garden, suggesting a game of croquet or a ride in an antique automobile. One parlor has painted ceiling medallions and a fainting couch;

another has a pink and green tiled fireplace with intricate fretwork. All the rooms contain period furnishings, and the walls are adorned with old family portraits.

The house was built in 1888 for William Clark, a businessman and Eureka's mayor. Now it's on the National Register of Historic Places and is a California State Historic Site. It's a prime example of Queen Anne–influenced Eastlake Victorian architecture.

One of the most ornate and well preserved of Eureka's numerous Victorian homes, the inn is owned by people who delight in sharing its history and beauty with their guests.

Of the three shared bathrooms, one is upstairs and two are on the main floor. Robes are provided for the trip down the hall and for visiting the Finnish sauna. Each room has a queen-size bed, a desk, and a sitting area. Some have views of Humboldt Bay and the Samoa Peninsula. The least expensive is the Senator's Room, which contains a marble-topped bedroom set that belonged to Lily's grandmother. The Van Gogh Room, a small suite, honors the artist with reproductions of his works. Lily Langtry, a celebrated 19th-century actress, once performed in Eureka, so one room is named for her. It is highlighted by an oak four-poster bed and a Palladian window that overlooks Humboldt Bay. French country furnishings create a warm, bright atmosphere in The Governor's Room. It has a fine view and a small connecting room for a third person.

The day begins with breakfast at a single table set with red and white china on a lace cloth. It includes orange juice, fresh fruits, homemade breads, and a main course that varies daily. Ask the Vieyras what there is to see and do in the area and you'll be given a list that could keep you busy for days. Stroll through the shops, galleries, and restaurants of Old Town, see Eureka's architectural treasures, cruise on the bay, or take a deep sea fishing charter. Don't miss the astonishing Carson Mansion, probably the most-photographed Victorian creation in California.

Doug and Lily have an array of books and magazines, lend tandem bicycles, and hold occasional musical events. In the afternoon they serve pie or ice cream sodas. These sociable hosts claim to provide "the lavish hospitality of a bygone era." With good cheer and charm, that's exactly what they do.

Carter House

1033 3rd Street
Eureka, CA 95501
707-445-1390

> *A Victorian replica with contemporary flair*

Innkeepers: Mark and Christi Carter. **Accommodations:** 5 rooms (all with private bath). **Rates:** $125–$185 single or double. **Included:** Full breakfast. **Payment:** Major credit cards. **Children:** Not appropriate. **Pets:** Not allowed. **Smoking:** Not allowed in guest rooms.

The port city of Eureka boasts a wide variety of Victorian architecture, including what is probably the finest example in the country, the ornate Carson Mansion.

Another Victorian-style home is the Carter House — but this one was built in the 1980s, not the 1890s. Mark Carter, a long-time admirer of 19th century design, had restored several houses before he found a book of drawings by Samuel and Joseph C. Newsom, architects of the Carson Mansion and other Eureka buildings. One drawing showed a house that had been built in San Francisco in 1884 and destroyed in the 1906 earthquake. Mark decided to recreate that house in Eureka. He and a crew of three hand-crafted the spacious four-story structure, following the Newsom plans in almost every intricate detail.

High, curtainless windows, polished oak floors, white walls, and a collection of abstract art make a pleasing contrast to the rich, dark wainscoting and woodwork. Orchids add delicate color. A basket of apples stands on the sideboard in the front parlor; in the evenings, you'll find cookies and decanters of after-dinner drinks. Wine and hors d'oeuvres are served in the afternoons.

This handsome redwood inn draws travelers who admire the quality of workmanship and Victorian structure, yet appreciate the light, uncluttered interior.

Mark and Christi have furnished the guest rooms with a few well-chosen antiques, fresh flowers, clock radios, robes, and special soaps. The two 2-bedroom suites are good choices for families or couples traveling together. The suite on the second floor is particularly spacious and has a fireplace, numerous windows, and a tiled bathroom with a whirlpool tub and a double-headed shower.

Three more rooms, plus kitchen facilities, are offered in the Cottage, a remodeled historic home near the inn.

There are fine restaurants in Eureka, but the best by far is in the Hotel Carter, across the street from the Carter House. Mark and Christi Carter's second hotel has 23 tastefully furnished rooms and romantic suites, but its claim to fame is the superb restaurant that has earned a nationwide reputation. Here you'll find dishes based on fresh ingredients, a relaxed atmosphere, an exceptional wine list, and a talented chef. Dinner entrées might include sautéed marinated duck with apple-raspberry-ginger sauce, grilled Idaho rainbow trout with a basil and bay shrimp beurre blanc, and rosemary-braised lamb. A lighter café menu is available.

Carter House guests go to the restaurant for breakfast — one of the best breakfasts you'll ever have at an inn. The emphasis on quality is evident in the breads, pears poached in wine sauce, eggs Florentine, pasta, and strawberry cake (and that's just one flower-garnished meal).

The well-tended gardens that supply much of the produce and herbs for the restaurant intrigue guests almost as much as the food. The Carters offer garden tours and lectures.

FALL RIVER MILLS

Rick's Lodge

Glenburn Star Route
Fall River Mills, CA 96028
916-336-5300 (April–November)
916-336-6618 (November–April)

A fishing lodge in the wilderness

Proprietors: Rick and Linda Piscitello. **Accommodations:** 12 rooms. **Rates:** $60 single, $80 double, $100 for three. **Minimum stay:** 2 nights. **Payment:** MasterCard, Visa. **Children:** Welcome. **Pets:** Allowed. **Smoking:** Allowed. **Open:** April–November.

Fall River flows through the Burney Basin, 300 square miles of wilderness in northeastern California. In the clear, spring-fed river, five- to eight-pound trout feast on an abundance of insects and challenge the skills of fly-fishers.

Fall River has been called the best dry fly-fishing water in America, but the fish here are crafty. Patience and expertise are essential.

Rick's Lodge provides one of the few points of access to the river, as most of the frontage is privately owned. Built as a private retreat more than forty years ago, it's been owned by Rick Piscitello since 1971. He has rebuilt the shiplap mahogany main lodge, dining room, bar, and the cabins facing the riverbank. On five acres of lawns and trees, they all have the same wonderland view of mountains and limpid water.

The paneled cabins are rustic on the outside but have modern interiors. Linens are replaced daily. Of utmost importance to virtually every guest is the fly-tying bench, equipped for two people, in each cabin.

The restaurant, serving three meals a day, has a steakhouse menu with dinner prices in the $8 to $24 range. Every Sunday night there's a barbecue on the deck, an all-you-can-eat affair featuring steak, chicken, or ribs.

The lodge has a fly shop and offers 3-day fly-fishing schools. Guides and boat rentals are available, or you may bring your own boat. A boat with motor rents for $35 for a half-day, $50 for a full day.

This is not a wading or shore-fishing stream. Fishing is from small, electric-powered boats on several miles of the upper Fall River. It's all catch-and-release, a test of skill and cunning. If you want to try for the wild trout in a wading stream as productive as Fall River, Hat Creek is a 15-minute drive. Forty minutes north is the famous McCloud River, breeding ground of the native McCloud rainbows. And there are nine lakes in the area.

For a break from fishing, an eighteen-hole golf course is ten miles from the lodge. You can also pitch horseshoes at Rick's, and there's a satellite TV in the lounge.

FERNDALE

The Gingerbread Mansion

400 Berding Street
Ferndale, CA 95536
707-786-4000

A historic home in a Victorian village

Innkeeper: Ken Torbert. **Accommodations:** 9 rooms (all with private bath). **Rates:** $90–$185 double, singles $15 less, $20 additional person; rates vary by season and day of the week. **Included:** Full breakfast. **Minimum stay:** 2 nights on summer weekends and holidays. **Payment:** MasterCard, Visa. **Children:** Welcome. **Pets:** Not allowed. **Smoking:** Not allowed indoors.

In the far northwestern corner of California, the little town of Ferndale lies steeped in the past. The entire village of restored Victorian buildings is a State Historical Landmark. Its Main Street is probably the brightest in the West, with facades painted in a rainbow palette of hues that lend welcome color to the often-foggy area.

Bicycles, painted peach and yellow to match the inn, are available for exploring the village and countryside. The quiet roads run past acres of green fields and dairy farms that once formed the economic base of the region (which is why the Victorian mansions are called butterfat palaces).

The most striking home in this quiet backwater is the Gingerbread Mansion. The ornate bed-and-breakfast inn is surrounded by English gardens with boxwood-edged paths that wind through archways and tulip beds, past fountains and statuary. In the center is a silver reflecting ball on a pedestal.

The mansion, built in 1899, is a showcase of turn-of-the-century elegance. Four parlors are filled with antiques and settees where visitors may browse through travel books and magazines, play games, and enjoy an elaborate tea with petits fours and chocolate-dipped strawberries in the afternoons. A 1,000-piece jigsaw puzzle depicting the mansion lies partially completed on a separate table.

Several guest rooms have clawfoot tubs. In fact, the Fountain and Gingerbread suites each have two such tubs for his-and-hers bubble baths. The twin tubs in the luxurious Fountain Suite are side by side, facing a mirrored wall. The bed has a canopy, and a bay window looks out on the village and garden. In the Gingerbread Suite, the tubs are in the bedroom on a raised platform surrounded by a Victorian railing.

Each room offers something special. The Rose Suite has two fireplaces and a tub in a flowery bower, with mirrors on the walls and ceiling. Strawberry Hill, in peach and green, has a fireplace and lots of windows and light; Garden overlooks a multitude of flowers; and Lilac has a lovely stained glass window. Hideaway, one of the newer rooms at the back of the inn, has a country garden atmosphere but is consistent with the mansion's style in its molding detail and carved wood.

One of the outstanding features here is the innkeeper's attention to detail. Nothing a guest could need has been overlooked. There's no radio or TV, but you'll find bathrobes in your dresser drawer, hand-dipped chocolates by the bed, and a tray of coffee or tea on the hall sideboard in the morning.

Breakfast, served at two tables in the formal dining room, includes fresh juice, a hot entrée, and various pastries. Parking space is not provided, but there's plenty of curbside parking in Ferndale, where rush hour consists of three cars and a truck on the same street at the same time.

Ferndale has shops, art galleries, a repertory theater, and a museum. Yearly events fit the small-town image: an ice cream social in September, a county fair and horse races in August, an Easter egg hunt. There's also the Beef Bar-B-Que, the Firemen's Annual Main Street Games, and for something out of the ordinary, the Portuguese Holy Ghost Festival (many of the early settlers were Portuguese).

In late May the Great Arcata-to-Ferndale Cross-Country Kinetic Sculpture Race takes place. In wild and crazy contraptions, racers from around the country compete for three days and two nights, ending in a grand finale on Main Street.

FORKS OF SALMON

Otter Bar Lodge

14026 Salmon River Road
Forks of Salmon, CA 96031
916-462-4772

A wilderness lodge offering rest and recreation

Proprietors: Peter and Kristy Sturges. **Accommodations:** 5 rooms (with 4 shared baths). **Rates:** $100 per person per day in fall, $1,050–$1,090 per week in spring and summer. **Included:** All meals. **Payment:** No credit cards. **Children:** Welcome with prior arrangement. **Pets:** Not allowed. **Smoking:** Not allowed. **Open:** April 17–November 15.

If you want to get away completely, into remote, rugged wilderness where steelhead swim in emerald green waters, consider Otter Bar. It's a mountain refuge of comfort and style where you can fish, kayak, ride a mountain bike, and feast on excellent food.

> **These vacations are for people looking for a place far off the beaten path with exceptional quality and beautiful scenery. There are no bars or restaurants anywhere in the area, so bring your own beverages and plan on good food and company, fine fishing, expert instruction, and adventurous thrills.**

The lodge takes only 12 guests at one time. "We want to keep it small, personal, and private," says Peter Sturges, who built the low, rambling ranch house to blend with the forested environment. A water wheel generates power and a woodstove and immense stone fireplace provide heat. Antiques and handmade furniture fill the rooms.

Outside are a redwood hot tub and a wood-fired sauna, and each guest room has a private deck. The beds all have down comforters. In the living room, guests enjoy the stereo, VCR, and books. Meals always receive heartfelt praise. You'll be served five-course dinners (roast lamb, salads and vegetables from the garden, velvety cheesecake), buffet lunches, and full breakfasts (omelettes, fresh fruit, hot currant scones, coffee).

The original intention was to create a wilderness retreat and fishing lodge, but along the way Otter Bar Lodge also grew into one of the nation's foremost kayaking schools and mountain bicycling destinations.

Getting to Otter Bar is an adventure in itself. The lodge is a two-hour drive west from Yreka, or 2½ hours east of Eureka, along the Salmon River that cuts through the Salmon Mountains, bounded on the north by the Marble Mountain Wilderness. The last few miles are on a tortuous, narrow road high above the river. Two miles beyond the village of Forks of Salmon you reach the lodge, a welcome sight under the maple, oak, and madrone trees.

The activities are divided by season. Kayaking and bicycling are offered in summer and early fall. Later, fishing takes over. The Salmon is known for its runs of classic fly water, riffles, and deep, slow pools. You can fish from the bank, wade, or go out in a drift boat with Peter as a guide.

Skilled instructors teach visitors to kayak, from beginning skills to advanced techniques in rough whitewater. All equipment is provided. The trails and fire roads that snake through the forests are ideal for mountain biking. At Otter Bar Lodge, you can enjoy a mountain bike holiday that includes instruction and plenty of riding over terrain as easy or as challenging as you choose. Summer afternoons are usually too hot for serious riding, so those are the hours for swimming in the river, lounging on white sandy beaches, and rafting.

FORT BRAGG

Sandcastle

Fort Bragg, CA
Mailing Address:
Mendocino Coast Reservations
P.O. Box 1143
1000 Main Street
Mendocino, CA 95460
707-937-5033

A modern home by the shore

Contact: Ahn Bradley. **Accommodations:** 4-bedroom house, sleeps 12. **Rates:** $125–$250 plus $50 cleaning fee, plus $100 security deposit. **Minimum stay:** 2 nights. **Payment:** MasterCard, Visa. **Children:** Welcome. **Pets:** Allowed with permission. **Smoking:** Allowed.

This large, contemporary home, its glass wall jutting toward the sand dunes and sea, faces the coast north of Mendocino, just beyond a residential area of Fort Bragg. From the big living room you can see the blue Pacific sparkling in the sun or watch the fog roll in while you toast cozily by the fire (firewood is supplied).

There are books, magazines, games and puzzles, a stereo,

and a television with VCR. The cooks can join in the conversation from the open kitchen, well equipped with a microwave oven, a dishwasher, and a coffeemaker.

Beyond the kitchen is a large deck with a hot tub and barbecue. Electric blankets cover queen and twin beds. The four bedrooms share two baths.

Stables are close by, and you can go horseback riding on the bridle and walking path that runs parallel to the low, grassy dunes across the street from Sandcastle.

Sandcastle is within walking distance of MacKerricher State Park, which has ten miles of beach and a lake stocked with fish. Fort Bragg is the home of the famous Skunk Train excursions that travel through scenic redwood forests. The town's calendar is full of activities that appeal to visitors: a whale festival and rhododendron show in spring, the World's Largest Salmon BBQ in July, a rodeo in August, and a Paul Bunyan Days celebration in September.

With accommodations for twelve and numerous amenities, this home by the sea is a good choice for a family reunion or other group gathering.

GARBERVILLE

Benbow Inn

445 Lake Benbow Drive
Garberville, CA 95440
707-923-2124

Old-fashioned atmosphere with contemporary touches

Proprietors: Charles and Patsy Watts. **Accommodations:** 55 rooms. **Rates:** $88–$260 single or double, $15 additional person. **Minimum stay:** 2 nights on weekends. **Payment:** MasterCard, Visa. **Children:** Welcome. **Pets:** Allowed by prior arrangement. **Smoking:** Not allowed. **Open:** Mid-April–December.

This unusual inn in the north coast redwood country is a National Historic Landmark. The three-story, half-timbered hotel was built in 1926 and welcomed many famous people, including Herbert Hoover and Eleanor Roosevelt, before it gradually fell into disrepair. Charles and Patsy Watts, fifth in the line of owners, have spent several years restoring the inn to its original elegance. The Benbow stands just west of (and unfortunately close to) Highway 101, south of Garberville.

The inn overlooks little Benbow Lake, which is filled only in summer, when the Eel River is dammed. You may swim in the lake, and canoes and paddleboats are available from the Park Service.

Inside the hotel are a lobby and lounge, paneled in dark woods, with an immense stone fireplace at one end. Alcoves hold partially completed jigsaw puzzles, and every afternoon guests may be found pondering them as they enjoy their tea and scones or mulled wine. Off the lobby is a bar with an antique fireplace and a dining room that offers Continental cuisine. The menu emphasizes seafood and poultry, featuring such dishes as baked sole and salmon with wild rice, roasted duck with lingonberries and apples in a Grand Marnier sauce, and quail with grapes and wild rice.

In back of the hotel is a large, partially shaded terrace with several guest rooms beyond it, each with its own patio overlooking the lawn and river. The separate Garden Cottage boasts a four-poster canopy bed on a carpeted platform. Books on the mantel, a grandfather clock, and an Oriental rug fit the mood of rock-solid stability in a room that's big enough to dance in. It also has a whirlpool tub and separate shower in the bath.

The older guest accommodations in the main hotel are on the small side, but are tastefully furnished with antiques, reading lamps, and a basket of well-worn paperback mysteries. They're just right for an evening of reading by the crackling fire in the parlor — when you're not working on a puzzle or sipping sherry.

GUALALA

The Old Milano Hotel

38300 Highway 1
Gualala, CA 95445
707-884-3256

A landmark inn with lush gardens and a panoramic view

Innkeeper: Leslie Linscheid. **Accommodations:** 7 rooms (all with private bath), 1 cottage, 1 caboose. **Rates:** $80–$165 single or double. **Included:** Full breakfast. **Minimum stay:** 2 nights on weekends. **Payment:** Major credit cards. **Children:** Not appropriate. **Pets:** Not allowed. **Smoking:** Not allowed indoors.

The setting for this historic landmark hotel could not be more splendid — three acres of lawns and gardens bordered by tall cedar trees on the edge of a cliff. In the cove below, waves crash against boulders and slide over smoothly worn pebbles, with the sea stretching beyond to a misty horizon.

On this prime property a mile north of Gualala and 100 miles north of San Francisco, the hotel opened in 1905 as the Milano, noted for its Italian food and hospitality. Since 1984 it has been owned by Leslie Linscheid, who continues to offer excellent meals and comfortable accommodations to north coast travelers.

The house is furnished with rich Victorian pieces set against floral wallpapers and red carpeting. Two guest rooms, a parlor, and a dining room occupy the main floor. The dining room is a full restaurant, open to the public Tuesday through Sunday, with a menu that changes seasonally. A prix fixe dinner might be quail stuffed with rice and plums, grilled pork tenderloin, or filet mignon in a cabernet demi-glaze. Seafood is fresh and local, as are most vegetables and herbs. There's an extensive wine list.

The small restaurant has a stone fireplace and the original back bar from the hotel's early days. Fringed lampshades, a candelabra, a gilt-framed mirror, and an old-fashioned cash register add to the period mood.

On the other side of the house is the Master Suite, the largest and most expensive room. It has a sitting room with a separate outside entrance, a bed of carved wood, and, best of all, a superb ocean view. Of the five upstairs rooms, Room 3 is the smallest. It has a double bed, a little desk graced with fresh flowers, and a large closet where you'll find towels and a flashlight for night visits to the outdoor spa. This room overlooks the garden, with its huge dahlias and rose-covered trellis.

The other rooms all have sea views and individual furnishings, such as a comfortable armchair by a window, a high armoire, built-in bookshelves, framed musical scores, and a high brass bed. Most rooms have double beds (some are soft, so if you prefer a firm mattress, be sure to request it).

When you're ready for the ultimate in relaxation, sign up for a private sunset session in the spa, pick up your towel and flashlight, and amble down the path to the secluded hot tub. As you soak in bliss, you're gazing out at craggy Cathedral Rock and a blue-green sea.

Outside, behind the circular herb garden and immense fuchsias, and under salmon-colored passion flowers, is Passion Vine Cottage. This cozy spot has a Jotul woodstove, a double bed, a full kitchen, and a reading loft. There's a shower stall in the tiny bathroom.

The Caboose, or Engine 9, is a railroader's dream, tucked among the cedars for privacy. A warm and rustic nest, it has a woodstove, a small bath, and a refrigerator. There's a deck at one end of the authentic car and an observation cupola on top.

Breakfast is served in the dining room, in your own room, or on the patio. Leslie oversees the preparation of such morning delectables as fresh fruit turnovers, quiche, French toast, and baked eggs. After breakfast you might stroll through the gardens and down to a rocky beach at the foot of the cliff, where you're likely to see seals, sea lions, numerous birds, and possibly whales on their annual migrations. Other activities include badminton and croquet. Nearby are tennis, golf, horseback riding, bicycling, hiking, and fishing.

St. Orres

P.O. Box 523
Gualala, CA 95445
707-884-3303

A seaside hotel and cottages with unusual architecture

Reservations manager: Jan Harris. **Owners:** Rosemary Campiformio and Eric and Ted Black. **Accommodations:** 8 rooms (share 3 baths), 11 cottages. **Rates:** $60–$75 single or double in hotel, $85–$270 in cottages. **Included:** Full breakfast. **Minimum stay:** 2 nights on weekends. **Payment:** MasterCard, Visa. **Children:** Welcome (roll-aways available). **Pets:** Not allowed. **Smoking:** Allowed except in dining room.

You've probably heard that there was a Russian settlement on the coast in the late 1800s, so when you first see the St. Orres' onion-domed towers and weathered cedar exterior, you might think it's a remnant of the past. But it's not even a restoration. The inn was built in the mid-1970s by California master carpenters Richard Wasserman and Eric Black. Their love of fine wood is evident throughout their handsome creation. The doors are of California oak, the redwood walls are paneled in intricate geometric patterns. The work of local craftspeople furnish the inn, from the stained glass windows to the colorful velvet quilts on the beds. The colors and styles look a bit dated now, but the overall effect is impressive.

Across the road from the inn, at the bottom of grassy cliffs, are coves to explore and the inn's private beach, a bit of sheltered sand where St. Orres Creek joins the Pacific surf.

One tower holds a spiral staircase that winds up to the guest rooms on the second floor. In the other is a restaurant of renown, where meals are served in an octagonal room with three levels of windows rising to the dome. Diners can look across the highway to rugged bluffs above the sea.

The guest rooms in this building share three baths: "his," "hers," and "ours," which boasts an oversize dual shower. The rooms aren't large, but they're designed with care to avoid a cramped feeling.

The cottages are more spacious and modern. Three are off paths that wind up the hillside to the edge of a redwood forest where wild orchids grow. Tree House has an elevated sleeping area, a Franklin stove, and French doors that open onto a sun deck with a wide ocean view. Rose Cottage also has an elevated bed, and Wildflower is a rustic cabin with a sleeping loft.

In the newest area, Creekside, are seven more cottages with polished woods, skylights, and ocean or forest views. They have the use of a hot tub under multitiered glass domes, a sauna, and an expansive sun deck edged with flower boxes.

The most dramatic cottage is Pine Haven, which accommodates four. The two-bedroom, two-bath home has three copper domes, a beach stone fireplace, a breakfast nook with an ocean view, a wet bar, and a patio by the old apple tree.

All the cottages have refrigerators and coffeemakers. Breakfast will be delivered in a basket, or you may go to the dining room if you prefer.

St. Orres stands above the highway, outside the village of Gualala, 3 hours north of San Francisco.

LEWISTON

Trinity Alps Resort

Trinity Alps Road,
Star Route Box 490
Lewiston, CA 96052
916-286-2205

A family favorite in the wilderness

Owners: Morgan and Margo Langan. Hosts: Morgan and Nadine Langan. **Accommodations:** 40 cabins and 3 apartments. **Rates:** $395–$715 week, 2-10 people; $50 week additional person; off-season and group rates available. **Minimum stay:** 1 week in June, July, and August; 3 nights in May and September. **Payment:** No credit cards. **Children:** Welcome. **Pets:** Allowed with prior arrangement. **Smoking:** Discouraged. **Open:** May 15 through September.

This family resort has changed very little since it was built in the 1920s. Its rustic cabins stand on 90 acres of forest surrounded by 500,000 acres of magnificent Trinity Alps Wilderness, west of Clair Engle (Trinity) Lake in northern California. High mountain peaks rise above tree-clad slopes, while the wild Stuart Fork flows through the property carrying rainbow and native brown trout.

In the evenings there are talent shows, square dancing, movies, and bingo. Singalongs around the campfire, rafting, backpacking, and doing nothing but relaxing are big favorites.

Trinity Alps Resort is off a steep, winding road north of Weaverville, a village with an eventful logging and railroad history. The Langan family bought the resort in 1986 and quickly learned that their guests wanted nothing changed or "improved." Many had been coming here for years and considered it their place, perfect in all its quaint and woodsy charm. So the cabin doors are creaky, the furniture is worn, and the iceboxes are originals. Ice picks are provided, and ice can be purchased at the store — an opportunity to give the kids a taste of life in the old days.

The large, rambling general store is the community gathering place, where you're bound to meet everyone if you sit on the porch a while. In the store you can buy groceries (except for fresh produce and meat), fishing supplies, and locally hand-crafted gifts. There's a soda fountain and, toward the back, a recreation room with a pool table and video games.

A daily schedule of activities is posted on a bulletin board, along with the dinner entrée (in September only). During the summer, guests choose from a full menu. In September, the main course might be barbecued beef ribs or steak marinated in Margo's special vinaigrette. Children's portions are available. Most visitors prepare their own meals, planning to eat once or twice in the restaurant above the river.

Simple cabins are tucked among the wild lilacs and maple and alder trees along a mile of the Stuart Fork. Each has a sleeping veranda, one or two bedrooms, a bath with a shower, an outdoor barbecue, and an equipped kitchen.

Entering one of these cabins is like stepping back in time sixty years. The screen door slams and you're in a kitchen with uneven painted floors, a gas stove, a linoleum-covered table, and a wooden counter at the sink. In the bedroom are a double and two single metal beds. A few steps farther is the veranda overlooking the trees and river. Strung around it is a clothesline, where those seeking privacy hang sheets. You sleep well on the veranda, for you're surrounded by the world's most peaceful sounds: leaves rustling in the breeze and a rushing, gurgling river below.

The larger one-bedroom cabins sleep six. Some two-bedroom units have two bathrooms and can accommodate ten people. Bring your own linens and blankets or rent them from the office at $15 per bed. No towels are available, so be sure to bring them. A crib will be supplied for $15.

The range of activities includes fishing, swimming, tennis, badminton, volleyball, horseshoes, gold panning, inner tubing, and basketball. The stable has dependable trail horses. Children under age eight may ride ponies on paths around the resort. Hiking trails along the river lead to limpid pools and waterfalls, and wilderness trailheads are just two miles away.

LITTLE RIVER

Glendeven

Little River, CA 95456
707-937-0083

A stylish, artistic country inn

Innkeepers: Jan and Janet deVries. **Accommodations:** 10 rooms (all with private bath) plus Barn Suite. **Rates:** $70–$120 single, $90–$140 double, $20 additional person; Barn Suite $185–$275 for 2-6 people. **Included:** Expanded Continental breakfast. **Minimum stay:** 2 nights on weekends, 3 nights on some holidays. **Payment:** Major credit cards. **Children:** Welcome. **Pets:** Not allowed. **Smoking:** Not allowed indoors.

Little River is a quiet village that scarcely causes a ripple in the twisting coastal road south of Mendocino. But the scenery around it is spectacular: giant redwoods, open fields dotted with wildflowers, rocky beaches, and high cliffs above the Pacific. Jan and Janet deVries own a sturdy clapboard farmhouse overlooking Van Damme Bay, built in 1867 by one of the area's first settlers. The deVries' artistic skills are evident in the old home. They have created a gracious, comfortable inn on a slope of Monterey cypress and eucalyptus trees, with brick walks, camellias, and pampas grass in the front garden.

> **The Kelley House Museum in nearby Mendocino has a map for walking tours, and the Mendocino Art Center shows some of the area's talented artistry. There are several good restaurants.**

Guests are housed in three buildings: the Main Farmhouse, Stevenscroft, and Barn Suite. The Eastlin Suite, on the ground floor of the main house, has a sitting room, French rosewood bed, fireplace, and French doors that open to a brick terrace and a view of the bay. Other farmhouse rooms are smaller but equally charming, furnished with antiques and decorated with color and verve. A perennial favorite is The Garret, an extravagantly floral attic room with dormer windows framing meadow and ocean views.

Stevenscroft contains four rooms, all with fireplaces. Bayloft, accented with redwood, has a cozy bed alcove with skylight above and a wide view from a bay window. On the second floor, Briar Rose has high vaulted ceilings, a French country decor, and a private balcony. Pinewood and East Farmington are warm, sunny rooms, both with private decks.

The original barn, extensively remodeled, has two bedrooms and one and a half baths. The suite tastefully combines hand-crafted country furniture and contemporary and antique pieces. A fireplace warms the redwood-detailed walls and sunlight filters through shuttered windows. The suite's deck faces east toward the gardens and hills. Pink roses climb the barn trellis, and window boxes are bright with pink geraniums. Gallery Glendeven, on the ground floor, displays contemporary crafts, including chairs made by Jan deVries.

Breakfast is served in the dining area of the main house or brought to your room in a basket. Fresh fruit, coffee, juice, muffins, and apples baked with brown sugar and currants are some of the savory morning treats. Sherry is decanted in the evenings next to the fireplace in the parlor, where the company is convivial. Notify the innkeepers in advance and they will have a tidbit platter of French bread, cheese, fruits, and chocolates waiting when you arrive, at a cost of $35.

Glendeven is a quarter of a mile north of 1,800-acre Van Damme State Park, which extends from deep forest to the coast. Two miles north of the inn is the pretty town of Mendocino, founded by New Englanders who brought their distinctive architecture to the California coast.

Heritage House

Little River, CA 95456
707-937-5885

A romantic inn on a seaside cliff

Proprietor: Gay Dennen Jones. **Accommodations:** 72 rooms. **Rates:** $130–$315 single, $150–$335 double, $65 additional person. **Included:** Breakfast and dinner. **Payment:** MasterCard, Visa. **Children:** Welcome. **Pets:** Not allowed. **Smoking:** Allowed. **Open:** Mid-February to November.

This romantic inn on the Mendocino coast began with a farmhouse built in 1877 in the Maine style popular in the area at the time — probably because so many settlers came from Maine. The yellow farmhouse is still here, covered with ivy.

The main activity here is walking the paths and brick steps that wind between cottages and around the cliff, while admiring the moody Pacific.

Loren and Hazel Dennen bought the place in 1949, run-down and abandoned, and transformed it into a top-quality inn. Opening with three rooms in the farmhouse, they expanded over the years until today most of the lodgings are in cottages with two to eight rooms. The Dennens' daughter, Gay, now runs the inn.

The cottages, tucked unobtrusively into the landscape on a cliff above the sea, were given names associated with early buildings in the area, such as Country Store, Bonnet Shop, Barber Pole, and Ice Cream Parlor. Two cottages have a more recent history: Same Time and Next Year were a single cottage in 1978 and were used in the film *Same Time Next Year*. The cabin was split in two after the movie, with each half taking half of the movie title.

Furnishings vary from contemporary pieces to four-posters and antiques bought from local families. Many pieces were hand-crafted in the community and many more came around the Horn and up the coast by schooner a hundred years ago. The newer luxury units include whirlpool tubs, wet bars, and wood-burning fireplaces.

The farmhouse is now used as the reception area, restaurant, and lounge, with three guest rooms upstairs. Meals are served in the dining room (jackets and ties encouraged), where cane chairs stand at tables set with pale linens, candles, and flowers, all reflected in a wall of mirrors. Beyond the main room is a smaller dining area; next to that is a deck with a stunning view of the cypress trees, a rocky headland, and the ocean.

Breakfast is a major event. First is the buffet with fruit, cereal, and juice. Then you order one of five hot dishes, such as eggs Benedict, French toast, pancakes, eggs, and bacon or sausage. The restaurant is open to the public for dinner if it's not filled with guests. There's a choice of three entrées:

poached yellowfin tuna, grilled chicken breast with pesto, and roast pork loin are examples. Saturday is prime rib night.

The lounge in the farmhouse is an addition made from an apple storage house that was dismantled and moved. Apple House is a comfortable place to relax by the huge brick walk-in fireplace, read, play cards, or, if the musical urge strikes, play the grand piano. With prism chandeliers and roughhewn walls, the atmosphere in the lounge successfully combines rusticity with elegance. And the view is breathtaking.

If you're looking for more active pursuits, Mendocino is five miles up the coast. The art-oriented community has shops, galleries, and restaurants.

Little River Inn

Little River, CA 95456
707-937-5942

> *An ocean view homestead expanded into a resort*

Innkeepers: Dan Hervilla and Susan McKinney. **Accommodations:** 55 rooms and cottages. **Rates:** $65–$115 single, $75–$125 double, $10 additional person; 20% less on weekdays, November-March; cottages $190–$155. **Minimum stay:** 2 nights on weekends. **Payment:** No credit cards. **Children:** Under 12 free in room with parents. **Pets:** Not allowed. **Smoking:** Nonsmoking rooms available.

In the mid-19th century, pioneers came to Little River from Maine to log the region's redwood forests that built the row-houses and mansions of San Francisco. One of those pioneers was Silas Coombs who, in 1853, built his family a home that also served as a haven for stagecoach and lumber schooner travelers. Two generations later, Cora Coombs and Ole Hervilla were married, and the homestead was turned into the Little River Inn. The parlors became lobbies and dining rooms, and the conservatory was converted into a bar. Cattle pastures and apple orchards were later cleared to make way for a new golf course. The inn is still in the same family — Dan Hervilla and Susan McKinney are brother and sister.

The most private and luxurious lodgings are the cottages, in their own wooded enclave by the sea. They all have private decks with lounge chairs and good views of the crashing waves. Each unit has a brick fireplace and tiled bath with tub and shower. Two have Jacuzzis.

The main house, white with gables and window boxes and an old-fashioned veranda, is situated on a slope above the busy (and often noisy) highway. Its rooms are furnished in early California style, with antiques and double beds.

The other rooms are in a newer two-story motel annex, duplex units higher on the hillside near the golf course, and cottages across the road on low bluffs above the sea. More than half the rooms have fireplaces. The rooms in the annex are furnished with oak tables and chairs and sliding glass doors that open to a long, shared balcony. From the cottages here you can see the cove and beach across the highway and watch the skin divers bob in the sparkling surf. For sweeping, unrestricted views, request Hilltop Annex, near the nine-hole golf course.

Breakfast, dinner, and Sunday brunch are served in the dining room in the main house. The breads, soups, and desserts are all made on the premises; the restaurant specializes in seafood and steaks.

Two lighted tennis courts and the golf course are open to the public as well as to guests, so the inn bustles with activity, especially in the summer.

Sea Arch

Little River, CA
Mailing Address:
Mendocino Coast Reservations
P.O. Box 1143
1001 Main Street
Mendocino, CA 95460
707-937-5033

A private home on an oceanside cliff

Contact: Ahn Bradley. **Accommodations:** 2-bedroom private home. **Rates:** $125–$150 single or double plus $50 cleaning fee, plus $100 security deposit. **Minimum stay:** 2 nights. **Payment:** MasterCard, Visa. **Children:** Over age 12 welcome. **Pets:** Not allowed. **Smoking:** Allowed.

The agency that handles this home on the coast has a list of sixty-odd accommodations; Sea Arch is one of the best. Built in the early 1960s, the two-story, gray-shingled home stands at the edge of a cliff high above the ocean, surveying a panorama of sea and sky.

Kelp gardens float on the waves near the cove at the foot of the rocky cliff, and sea lions bark from their rocky perches in the surf. The blue Pacific shimmers as far as the eye can see.

Sea Arch's many windows are designed to take advantage of the view, both upstairs and down. There's a massive stone chimney on one side, for the living room fireplace. Wood fills a basket by the hearth, and more cut wood is stacked outside. Cushions are piled on a bench along a glass wall, where guests can play games, work on puzzles, listen to the large collection of classical records, or just admire the mesmerizing vista.

The well-stocked kitchen has every utensil a cook needs, a couple of cookbooks, a phone, a small TV, and battery lanterns and candles for emergency use. Doors from the small dining area lead to a patio under the pine trees.

The house has a three-quarter bath on the main floor and a full bath upstairs with the two bedrooms. One carpeted room contains a twin bed with trundle that can be pulled out to make a king-size bed. It has a desk and closet and an eastern view that looks into the trees rather than toward the ocean.

The main bedroom is larger and has a telephone and shelves of books. Paneled and decorated in earth tones, it provides a comfortable hideaway.

Sea Arch is for those who want to do nothing but watch the ever-changing ocean. You can follow the antics of the squirrels as they scamper among the pine trees, stroll to the pond in back, or thumb through the owners' numerous books about the Mendocino area. You can fire up the barbecue and grill some fresh seafood for supper, or drive a few miles north to the shops, restaurants, and beaches of Mendocino. But most guests prefer to settle by the fire for a quiet, romantic evening, with soft music accompanying the thunder of the distant surf.

MENDOCINO

The Headlands Inn

P.O. Box 132
Mendocino, CA 95460
707-937-4431

> *A historic home with views of a coastal town*

Innkeepers: Sharon and David Hyman. **Accommodations:** 5 rooms (all with private bath). **Rates:** $103–$172 single or double. **Included:** Full breakfast. **Minimum stay:** 2 nights on weekends, 3–4 nights on holidays.

Payment: No credit cards. **Children:** Over age 12 welcome. **Pets:** Not allowed. **Smoking:** Not allowed.

This attractive Victorian home was built in 1868 as a small barbershop on Main Street; a second story was added in 1873 to serve as living quarters for the barber and his family. Later it became a restaurant. In 1893 it was moved to its present location, on the corner of Howard and Albion streets, by horses pulling the house over log rollers. The Headlands has been a popular bed-and-breakfast inn for several years. The Hymans, who have owned it since late 1992, made few changes when they took over.

Guests are welcome to relax by the fireplace in the little parlor or enjoy afternoon tea and cookies in the sitting area on the upstairs landing.

The guest rooms, named for former owners of the historic home, have fireplaces and antique furnishings. Bessie Strauss is a spacious room with a Victorian settee, pots of greenery, an oversize armoire, and, the most oustanding feature, an ocean view from the bay window. The bed in W.J. Wilson is a four-poster. There's a private deck, pleasant for an alfresco breakfast. George Switzer, on the third floor, is a many-angled hideaway with window seats at alcove windows. A green velvet chair stands by the fireplace where a fire is laid and extra wood is at the ready in a brass holder.

John Barry, also on the third floor, is named for the home's original owner. It has a view across the nasturtium beds and lawn to open fields, part of the town, and the sea. The fifth room is in a separate building, Casper Cottage, just right if you want complete privacy. It has a cannonball four-poster, a sitting area with a small refrigerator, and a large bath complete with bubbles and tub toys.

Breakfast is brought to your room on a tray, along with a San Francisco Chronicle. The artistically arranged meal may include baked pears in ginger sauce, Mexican artichoke soufflé, muffins, and a pitcher of hot coffee, tea, or cocoa.

The Hymans keep an array of menus, brochures, and maps on hand, and they're glad to help you with sightseeing plans. You'll want to browse in the shops and art galleries, many in historic buildings, and try Mendocino's excellent restaurants, such as Café Beaujolais and Chocolate Moose.

Hill House of Mendocino

P.O. Box 625
10701 Palette Drive
Mendocino, CA 95460
707-937-0554
800-422-0554 in northern California
Fax 707-937-1123

A New England–style inn overlooking the Pacific

Proprietor: Robert Short. **Accommodations:** 44 rooms. **Rates:** $110–$175 single or double, $10 additional person. **Minimum stay:** 2 nights on weekends. **Payment:** Major credit cards. **Children:** Welcome. **Pets:** Not allowed. **Smoking:** Allowed.

If you watch *Murder, She Wrote,* this hotel may look familiar. The popular television program, which supposedly takes place in New England, has been filmed here, with Hill House as the backdrop. It fits well with Mendocino, a north coast town built mostly by settlers from Maine.

The gray-green inn trimmed in white stands on a hill behind a white picket fence among neat gardens. With a jaunty whale weathervane on the pitched roof, it has the look of a classic hotel on the New England coast. Built in 1978 with that architecture in mind, it has been expanded since to include a two-story wing with guest rooms off two courtyards.

In the main house are two sitting areas, a lounge, a restaurant, and a chapel for meetings and weddings. In the spacious front parlor and lobby, chess is set up for the next group of players. With antiques, lace curtains, and a quiet atmosphere, the mood is of another time and another place. On the walls are photographs of the actors and crew of *Murder, She Wrote,* along with pictures of Mendocino in an earlier day.

Upstairs, diners enjoy sweeping coastal views while lingering over Continental cuisine. The atmosphere is romantic, with deep rose walls, crystal, and candlelight. Fresh fish, steak, chicken, and pasta dominate the menu. A number of wines have Mendocino County labels.

The theme is modern and casual in Spencer's Lounge, which has a large-screen TV and a sunken fireplace area — just the spot to relax with a warm brandy on a brisk fall evening.

About half the guest rooms have views of the ocean. They all have television, direct-dial phones, and baths with tubs and showers and assorted toiletries. A typical room with a view features brass beds with comforters, lace curtains, burgundy carpeting, and antique reproductions. An armoire holds hanging clothes. Through the windows you see the dark green of cypress trees on grassy bluffs and the Pacific beyond them. The second-story rooms have the best views. The fireplace suites are the most expensive and spacious.

Hranrad House

Mendocino, CA
Mailing address:
Mendocino Coast Reservations
P.O. Box 1143
1001 Main Street
Mendocino, CA 95460
707-937-5033

A private guest house in a dramatic, secluded setting

Contact: Ahn Bradley. **Accommodations:** 2-bedroom private home. **Rates:** $150–$175 single or double, $25 additional person, plus $50 cleaning fee and $100 deposit. **Minimum stay:** 2 nights. **Payment:** MasterCard, Visa. **Children:** Over age 12 welcome. **Pets:** Not allowed. **Smoking:** Not allowed.

North of Mendocino, in a private community, Hranrad House is reached by a narrow, winding access road. An immense, beveled, copper roof covers the house, which was built in 1980. Inside, the floors and a 12-foot front door are of polished redwood. In one big room, with spaces divided by the central fireplace, are a living area with a wall of windows, a screened four-poster metal bed, and a kitchen with a walnut counter, Jenn-Air range, microwave, refrigerator, freezer, and all the tools a cook might need. There's a stereo with CDs, a TV in the kitchen, and shelves of books. Local phone calls are free. On the desk is a booklet of information on the house and nearby restaurants and attractions.

Seclusion and privacy in a stunning, contemporary home overlooking the Pacific are what you find at Hranrad House (the Anglo-Saxon name means Whales' Road House).

In the glass-walled bathroom you may feel that you're showering in a goldfish bowl, but your privacy is assured, protected by cypress trees, streams, stretches of grass, and rocky headlands above the water. There are no near neighbors.

French doors open to a deck on the west. Beyond it are the rugged headlands, with chasms and caves to explore, and a panorama of sea and sky.

Joshua Grindle Inn

P.O. Box 647
44800 Little Lake Road
Mendocino, CA 95460
707-937-4143

A farmhouse with 19th-century charm

Innkeepers: Arlene and Jim Moorehead. **Accommodations:** 10 rooms (all with private bath). **Rates:** \$90–\$135 single or double. **Included:** Full breakfast. **Minimum stay:** 2 nights on weekends. **Payment:** Major credit cards. **Children:** Not appropriate. **Pets:** Not allowed. **Smoking:** Not allowed.

This quiet New England–style home sits on a knoll overlooking Mendocino. The two-story white farmhouse was built in 1879 by an early settler who came from Maine to make his fortune in redwood lumber. Joshua Grindle prospered, becoming the town banker and primary owner of the Bank of Commerce, forerunner of the Bank of America. The home he built remained in the Grindle family until 1967.

You are welcome to play the antique pump organ, enjoy a game of backgammon or chess, read by the fire, or chat with the innkeepers about the exceptional attractions of the Mendocino area.

In 1978, the house opened as the first bed-and-breakfast in Mendocino. The inn and its two-acre property were purchased in 1989 by the Mooreheads, who came from San Francisco seeking a change. They have kept the furnishings and style established by the previous owners virtually intact.

There are five guest rooms in the main house, some with an ocean view and others with a wood-burning fireplace. Early American antiques in cherrywood and pine fill the rooms. The Grindle is the room Joshua built for himself, above the kitchen for warmth. It's a big, hearty room with a sitting area overlooking the town's distinctive water towers and the bay.

The Library room has a four-poster bed, country pine furniture, a floor-to-ceiling bookcase, and a fireplace set with hand-painted tiles. Treeview is the inn's least expensive room. It's a light, airy space with such old-fashioned touches as a cut-paper lampshade and a sled now used to hold magazines. From the window you can see 100-year-old cypress trees.

Behind the main house stands the redwood Water Tower, of recent vintage but architecturally designed to blend with the old water towers of Mendocino. It has three guest rooms on two floors furnished in antique country pine. An interesting detail is the absence of art on the walls of the second-story room; pictures will not hang flat because the walls slant inward as the tower rises.

Two rooms are in the saltbox cottage. North Cypress contains Early American antiques and a Franklin fireplace; South Cypress has Shaker furniture. The Salem rocker and wing chair are inviting places to read by the fire as the coastal fog creeps in. There's no sea view from the cottage, but it has a pretty little garden.

Breakfast is taken in the main house at a long, narrow harvest table which dates from the 1830s. The Mooreheads serve fresh fruit, a choice of cereals, homemade muffins, and a hot dish such as tomato-basil frittata. In the evening they place California cream sherry and fruit in the parlor.

MacCallum House

P.O. Box 206
45020 Albion Street
Mendocino, CA 95460
707-937-0289

A historic Victorian home in a picturesque town

Proprietors: Joe and Melanie Reding. **Accommodations:** 20 rooms (some with private bath). **Rates:** \$75–\$180 single or double, \$15 additional person; midweek winter discounts available. **Included:** Continental breakfast. **Minimum stay:** 2 nights on weekends, May through December. **Payment:** MasterCard, Visa; personal check preferred. **Children:** Welcome. **Pets:** Not allowed. **Smoking:** Not allowed.

When Daisy MacCallum was married in 1882 her parents, William and Eliza Kelley, gave her a house across the street from their own home as a wedding present. The Kelley house is now a museum of Mendocino and coastal history, and Daisy's home, where she lived until her death in 1953, is a busy and popular inn.

The Redings have put considerable effort into preserving the atmosphere Daisy created in her gracious Victorian home. Active socially and in civic affairs, Daisy entertained often, seeking to promote refinement in this frontier lumber town. She would have approved of the restored garden and the furnishings that were resurrected from the attic. She might have been less approving of the bar — she was a staunch temperance advocate — but today's visitors appreciate the friendly, casual Grey Whale Bar.

There's a wide range of accommodations. Those in the main house, which share baths, have double beds, country antiques, and windows that get morning sun or have an ocean view. Some mattresses are soft, so request a firm one if you need it. The attic rooms, off a hall papered with the San Francisco Chronicle from the 1920s, look over the gardens or Mendocino's rooftops. You must go down a short flight of stairs to the bathroom.

MacCallum House is noted for its restaurant. Its walls lined with Daisy MacCallum's books, the restaurant serves Continental cuisine based on fresh regional ingredients.

The other rooms are in the former barn and cottages. Two rooms on the barn's ground floor share a bath; the suites have their own. One suite with a private entrance has hefty beams from the original barn and redwood slabs for the kitchen and bath counters. There's no view — in fact, the bed is set against a window facing the street — and the room is somewhat dark, but it's roomy and comfortable. From the bed you can watch the fire in the stone fireplace. In the kitchen are a small refrigerator, stove, and beaten copper sink. The bath has a Roman tub, a tile shower, and a small and impractical copper basin.

Other barn accommodations are equally individual. An upstairs suite features a stone fireplace, a burl coffee table, and a similar rough-beamed style but with country antiques and a lighter atmosphere. In the bath are a shower with a skylight and the same pretty but small copper sink.

The units in the Carriage House are furnished with wicker and vintage pieces and have Franklin stoves and private baths. The Greenhouse has two platform beds, a rustic Franklin fireplace, and a private patio. The three-story Water Tower offers the best ocean view. The Gazebo, once a child's playhouse, has a double bed with a wicker headboard. There are two tiny windows, each barely a foot square. The outside bathhouse, a few steps away, has a stained glass window in the shower.

MacCallum House is not a hideaway. Crowds come and go,

and tourists are forever wandering through the gardens and taking photos of the picturesque home and its weathered picket fence. Also, the inn is done in a curious mixture of new and old that works well only part of the time. Yet, steeped in Mendocino history and reflecting the personality of the strong woman who lived here for most of her adult life, it has an ambience that draws guests back again and again.

Reed Manor

P.O. Box 127
Mendocino, CA 95460
707-937-5446

A luxurious mansion on a hilltop

Innkeepers: Monte and Barbara Reed. **Accommodations:** 5 suites. **Rates:** $175–$350 per room, 1–4 people. **Included:** Continental breakfast. **Minimum stay:** 2 nights on weekends. **Payment:** MasterCard, Visa. **Children:** Welcome. **Pets:** Not allowed. **Smoking:** Not allowed.

Reed Manor, which opened in 1990, sits on the highest hill in Mendocino. Here the former owners of Hill House, a hotel across the road, have created a haven of luxury and intimacy. Behind a brick entrance and courtyard is an imposing house with slate floors, sofas covered with tapestry fabrics, crystal chandeliers, and lighted display cases showing the owners' numerous collections. There are celebrity dolls, wildlife sculptures and plates, paintings, and a remarkable array of model cars. There's even a stained glass window showing a 1955 Chevrolet convertible. The suites each have a whirlpool tub, a fireplace, TV with VCR, a refrigerator (where a light breakfast is stored), a phone with an answering machine, and a private deck or patio. Two rooms have wet bars. In the Napoleon Room, the Reeds' Napoleon collection is on display, including books, plates, wineglasses, and a chess set. This room has a four-poster bed and a grand view of Mendocino.

The Morning Glory room, on the main floor, also faces the village and the sea. From this room's open-sided tub, you can see the TV and fireplace. Ma Maison, in country French style, has no view; it faces the gardens and has its own sunny, fenced deck. Imperial Gardens is decorated with an Oriental motif. This suite's wallpaper has poppies touched with gilt; it also has a bamboo mat ceiling, and Chinese and Japanese plates and figures.

Nut bread, fruit, juice, and coffee are provided in the rooms. The Reeds have a library of several classic movies, such as *Gone with the Wind,* to lend, along with the episodes of *Murder, She Wrote* that were filmed in Mendocino. They keep an album of restaurant menus and will make recommendations and reservations.

The inn is next to a hillside cemetery ("We have quiet neighbors," Bob jokes) that is an interesting place to stroll, reading headstones that date from 1852.

Sea Haus

P.O. Box 1143
Mendocino Coast Reservations
Mendocino, CA 95460
707-937-5033

A cozy family home in a residential area

Contact: Ahn Bradley. **Accommodations:** 3 bedrooms (1 bath). **Rates:** \$100–\$135, plus \$50 cleaning fee, plus \$100 security deposit. **Minimum stay:** 2 nights. **Payment:** MasterCard, Visa. **Children:** Welcome. **Pets:** Not allowed. **Smoking:** Allowed.

This comfortable two-story family home is on a quiet residential street in the heart of Mendocino. It's within walking distance of the town's myriad shops and Mendocino Headlands State Park. Roomy and private, it's an excellent choice for a family visiting the north coast, as it offers conveniences such as a washer and dryer and an ironing board. The dining area has seating for four at a round oak table.

The immaculate kitchen is stocked with dishes, pans, and utensils, as well as a few spices and a cookbook from a renowned Mendocino restaurant, Café Beaujolais. From the window you catch glimpses of the bay beyond the trees.

A woodstove stands on a hearth in the living room; firewood is stacked beside it. Shelves filled with books and a soft leather couch are invitations to relax and read by the fire.

Down the hall are a laundry room, a bath with a shower, and the master bedroom. Scenes of Mendocino hang on the walls of this pastel room, furnished with a queen-size bed, a couch, a phone, and a clock radio. A door opens to a deck and a fenced backyard where rosemary and fuchsia grow.

Youngsters enjoy riding the Skunk Railroad, which runs for 40 miles through scenic redwood country, and clambering among the tidepools of MacKerricher State Park in Fort Bragg.

The other bedrooms are up steep stairs on the second floor. They're separated by an open arch. One contains a four-poster double bed and the other two twins, all with white chenille spreads. From the south room's long window there's a view of the sea (cobwebbed by a maze of telephone wires). The north room views rocky headlands, cliffs, and blue water in the distance. This pleasant little room has a rocker and a small writing table. Throughout the house you'll see such personal touches as family photos and exquisite needlepoint. The owners clearly take pride in their seaside haven and expect you to make yourself at home and take care of the place as they would.

Weekly and monthly rates are available. The cleaning fee is nonrefundable (and not taxed), but if the house is left in order, the security deposit will be returned to you.

Points of interest when you're bringing children to the Mendocino area include the beach and clifftop trails; Jughandle State Reserve, where five terraces, created by erosion and ocean waves, show 500,000 years of geological change; and Pygmy Forest, with its dwarf pines and cypress trees.

The Stanford Inn by the Sea

P.O. Box 487
Coast Highway 1 and
Comptche-Ukiah Road
Mendocino, CA 95460
707-937-5025

A country inn with ocean views

Innkeepers: Joan and Jeff Stanford. **Accommodations:** 24 rooms and suites and 1 cottage. **Rates:** $165–$185 single or double, suites $195–$245, $15 additional person. **Included:** Expanded Continental breakfast. **Minimum stay:** 2 nights on weekends, 3 nights on holiday weekends. **Payment:** Major credit cards. **Children:** Welcome. **Pets:** Allowed with permission. **Smoking:** Not allowed indoors.

Where Big River meets Mendocino Bay, Stanford Inn faces the sea from a green hillside. Once this area grew produce for villagers and loggers during the redwood lumber boom. Today, llamas and horses graze under the old apple trees. The stagecoach road is now a hiking trail, and canoeists paddle the river where logs once floated to the mill.

Big River flows gently through a narrow canyon, winding between redwoods and firs, passing the habitat of ospreys and great blue herons.

Joan and Jeff Stanford took over a standard two-story motel and turned it into an outstanding hostelry in 1981. They now offer charming accommodations and a wide range of services. The long, dark-shingled ranch house, set above pastures and ponds, has rooms off a loggia with ivy-covered columns. In the lobby are menus from area restaurants and a gift shop corner. A generous buffet breakfast, served in the adjoining parlor, includes champagne as well as fruit, yogurt, granola, muffins, and coffee.

The guest rooms are individually decorated and furnished with country antiques, plants, a decanter of wine, a coffeemaker, and a television and VCR (the inn has some 200 movies to rent). Most have a refrigerator and a fireplace.

The second-floor rooms are the best because of their balcony views. They overlook gardens, a pond with swans and geese, and the bay, ocean, and a corner of Mendocino. To the south, the view is of a sheltered, wooded headland that juts into the sea.

There are two suites in a cottage by the river; one sleeps five people and the other two. Don't miss a tour of the inn's bountiful organic gardens. The raised beds supply produce to area restaurants.

The Stanfords have canoes to rent, providing an opportunity to explore the estuary filled with wildlife.

Big River is tidal for eight miles, so you can float up on the incoming tide and back as it recedes.

Other activities include swimming in the indoor pool, bicycling, hiking, fishing, beachcombing, and whale-watching. The best sites for spotting whales are the coastal headlands, Mendocino village headland, or the beach at Fort Bragg, six miles north.

MOUNT SHASTA

Ward's Big Foot Ranch

1530 Hill Road
Mt. Shasta, CA 96067
916-926-5170

A country bed-and-breakfast with a view of Mt. Shasta

Innkeepers: Barbara and Phil Ward. **Accommodations:** 2 rooms (with private baths). **Rates:** $55–$65 single, $60–$70 double. **Included:** Full breakfast. **Payment:** No credit cards. **Children:** Welcome. **Pets:** Not allowed. **Smoking:** Not allowed indoors.

You may not see Big Foot, the elusive and possibly fictional hairy giant of the woods, but there's plenty to keep you occupied here in the Mount Shasta foothills. Near the Wards' ranch there are two lakes for swimming, boating, and fishing; three golf courses; downhill and cross-country ski areas; and dozens of wilderness hiking trails.

If you just want to relax on the deck and enjoy the quiet and the stunning view of Mount Shasta, Ward's is the perfect place for it. Phil and Barbara, both former educators, bought the ten-acre property in 1980 and opened their bed-and-breakfast three years later. Avid gardeners, they have created a little paradise on a hill above a trout stream, with flower baskets hanging from oak trees, broad lawns, and vegetables and blooms in profusion.

When you arrive, you're welcomed not only by the Wards and their two golden retrievers — Jasper the donkey and Bobbin the lovable llama will press their noses against the fence, hoping for a pat and a treat.

The single-story red house with white trim, built in the mid-1960s, is roomy and comfortable, with a living room for conversation and a family room with a piano, television, and stereo. On sunny days, breakfast is served on the big redwood deck, where barrels of pansies and petunias lend bright spots of color, and a tall tree provides shade. From here you have glimpses of strutting peacocks and of the cherry, apple, and peach orchard near the driveway.

A mile away, on Old Stage Road, there's a hatchery that produces 13.5 million trout yearly. When it was built a century ago, this was the largest hatchery in the world. Next door, a museum displays pioneer artifacts and a Model T Ford fire engine.

One of the guest rooms has a king-size bed with a flowered comforter, a big closet, and a view of the deck and green, lacy cedar branches. A cabinet full of toys and shelves of books are reminders of the family atmosphere the Wards share. The other room, with a bath across the hall, features a queen-size bed and a soothing pastoral view.

When Phil rings the triangle in the morning, it's time for a "bodacious Big Foot breakfast" that includes ebleskivers and Dutch babies or sourdough pancakes. Horseshoes, volleyball, table tennis, and croquet are among the ranch's activities, and because the indefatigable Barbara and Phil love kids, they've hung rope swings in the trees.

NICE

Featherbed Railroad Company, A Bed & Breakfast Resort

P.O. Box 4016
2870 Lake Shore Boulevard
Nice, CA 95464
707-274-4434

A lakeside resort of railroad cars

Innkeepers: Lorraine and Len Bassignani. **Accommodations:** 8 cabooses. **Rates:** $75–$108 in winter, $83–$116 in summer. **Included:** Expanded Continental breakfast. **Payment:** Major credit cards. **Children:** Welcome. **Pets:** Not allowed. **Smoking:** Not allowed.

Railroad buffs and aficionados of the unusual are bound to fall in love with this assemblage of vintage cabooses. They're permanently stationed on five tree-shaded acres in Nice, close to the north shore of Clear Lake. The lakefront property is enhanced by such touches as turn-of-the-century street lamps, park benches, and an authentic old English phone booth.

The stationary railroad cars are a few yards from Clear Lake, which is popular with watersports enthusiasts. The Bassignanis rent boats and jet skis. The fishing is good; Clear Lake is noted for its largemouth bass and crappie.

Effervescent Lorraine and affable Len Bassignani have impeccably restored the cabooses, a labor of love. Before opening in 1989, the couple and their partner-son removed thick layers of grime, soot, and rust that had accumulated on the 25- to 50-year-old cars.

Why cabooses? "We were looking for something different to put our hearts into," explains Lorraine, "and both Len and I have always loved trains. It took several years to locate the cabooses to carry out our dream. This is a family endeavor."

Would-be conductors never had it so good. The interior of each caboose has been decorated around a theme. The romantic Lovers Caboose has a hand-hewn four-poster featherbed draped with a lace canopy, and a whirlpool tub for two. The Rosebud, painted in ashes of roses, is abloom with roses on the floral bedspread, matching balloon valance curtains, and hand-painted flowers (all done by Lorraine) on the walls. It has a Jacuzzi for two.

Mint Julep, as refreshing as its name, has mint-green walls and white wicker furniture. A cushioned cupola provides a retreat for sipping a cool drink, reading, or conversing.

Casey Jones, the only car with a railroad theme, features a red, cream, and navy blue decor, with a gleaming brass bed, authentic switchman's lanterns, and vintage railroad prints. Unlike the other cars, this caboose was left largely intact, which you can see in the original brass fittings, exposed pipes, and two padded conductor's chairs in the cupola. Other cars include Wine Country, Mardi Gras, Chocolate Moose, and the Loose Caboose.

Each caboose has a coffee pot, a television, books and games, fresh flowers, and potpourri. Special touches include sewing kits, candies on the pillows, and newspapers delivered to the door. Breakfast is served in the Bassignanis' 100-year-old ranch house. You may choose to eat on the flagstone veranda or by the swimming pool. Breakfast includes juices, fresh fruit, assorted breads and quiches, and coffee and tea.

Lake County is an emerging wine-producing region, and tours of nearby wineries are available. Other attractions include Clear Lake State Park and Anderson Marsh State Park, a Native American archaeological site and excellent bird-watching area. The Harbor Bar & Grill in Nice is recommended for its good food and interesting decor.

O'BRIEN

Holiday Harbor

P.O. Box 112
O'Brien, CA 96070
916-238-2383
800-776-2628

A cruising houseboat on Lake Shasta

Owners: Stephen and Ann Barry. **Accommodations:** 70 houseboats. **Rates:** $1,085–$2,085 per week in summer, 6–12 people; $125–$250 per day off-season. **Minimum stay:** 3 nights in summer, 2 nights in winter. **Payment:** MasterCard, Visa. **Children:** Welcome. **Pets:** Allowed with permission. **Smoking:** Allowed.

Three rivers and a major creek are the main water sources of Shasta Lake, at the northern end of the Sacramento Valley. The Sacramento flows in from the northwest, the McCloud from the northeast, and Squaw Creek and Pit River join on the east side. A huge dam, with the highest center overflow spillway in the world, forms the sprawling blue lake. It has 370 miles of shoreline, bounded by steep wooded hills. Snow-capped Mount Shasta looms on the north. A favorite type of freshwater recreation on this immense body of water, especially with families and groups, is houseboating.

Running a houseboat is easy. If you can drive a car, you can handle one of these floating RVs. Moving slowly on pontoons, they never exceed a speed of six or seven knots. At night they tie up along the shore, usually in a protected cove.

Holiday Harbor, tucked against Bailey Cove on the McCloud, is an easily accessible resort, 15 minutes from Redding and a mile off I-5. The Barrys take pride in keeping their houseboats in peak condition. Theirs is one of the few companies offering smaller size houseboats suitable for six or eight people. They also have 54-foot boats that can sleep 12.

The boats each have one or two sleeping areas, one or two bathrooms with a tub or shower, an equipped kitchen, and an eating space. All have roof decks. Furnishings are simple — molded plastic chairs, some bunk beds, and benches that pull out to become double beds. Pillows, soap, dishes, and pots and pans are supplied. You bring your own groceries and blankets, linens or sleeping bags.

"This is glorified camping," cautions Steve Barry, "and most people love it. They come in uptight and stressed out, and by the time they leave they're so relaxed they're practically comatose." The Barrys have owned Holiday Harbor since 1980, when they left a business life in San Francisco.

Some houseboaters like simply to cruise on the lake and inlets, enjoying the slow pace and taking a dip now and then. Others fish, swim, visit Lake Shasta Caverns, and hike the numerous trails. Steve recommends the walk to an old iron mine on Bully Hill. For more fun on the water, you can rent anything that floats from Holiday Harbor's "Toy Box": canoes, kayaks, jet skis, sailboards, paddleboats, rowing sculls, ski boats (with water skis), sailboats, and more.

Bring your fishing rod, or get one at one of the many sporting goods stores around the lake, and you can fish for rainbow and brown trout, salmon, smallmouth bass, largemouth bass, crappie, and catfish. To catch the big trophies, fish the lake in cooler months. It gets hot in summer — 90 to 100 degrees and more. But temperatures can plummet 30 degrees at night.

ORLAND

The Inn at Shallow Creek Farm

Box 3176
County Road DD, Route 3
Orland, CA 95963
916-865-4093

A relaxing retreat in the country

Proprietors: Kurt and Mary Glaeseman. **Accommodations:** 4 rooms (2 with private bath). **Rates:** \$55–\$75 single or double, \$15 for roll-away. **Included:** Full breakfast. **Payment:** MasterCard, Visa. **Children:** Not appropriate. **Pets:** Not allowed. **Smoking:** Not allowed.

Behind a white picket fence, shaded by big walnut trees, this turn-of-the-century ranch house offers comfortable lodging and an atmosphere of serenity. On the three-acre farm, west of I-5 and 20 miles from Chico, there are citrus orchards, plums, persimmons, figs, and pomegranates. Squirrels scamper in the trees and chickens and geese scratch near the barn.

Kurt and Mary Glaeseman opened their place to guests in early 1987, after visiting many B&Bs. "We modeled ours after things we liked," Mary says. They have furnished the inn with soft easy chairs, country antiques, books (they're both teachers), and such conveniences as air conditioning and electric baseboard heat.

The common room, with TV, stereo, and a stone fireplace, is for guests' exclusive use; the Glaesemans occupy separate, attached quarters. Next to the common room is the dining room, its windows overlooking the front lawn. Breakfast is served here at one table — fresh muffins, juice and fruit from the farm's trees, egg dishes, and homemade breads. There's a sun porch too, where breakfast is occasionally served.

The suite off the parlor is the former master bedroom. It has white walls and louvered shutters, and its own phone. The upstairs rooms have the use of a phone on the landing, and they share a bath with a tub and shower. Heritage Room has an old-fashioned flavor, with its morning glory wallpaper, priscilla curtains, and framed valentines. The Brookdale Room, which has room for a roll-away bed, has a big window overlooking the trees.

The four-room caretaker's cottage, across the yard from the

ranch house, has a kitchen, a wood-burning stove, and an enclosed porch.

At this casual, friendly place you can feed the chickens, go for walks, or relax with a book under a fragrant orange tree. You might also explore the little-known northern Sacramento Valley, where the fields turn gold and purple with poppies and lupine. In spring the undulating hills are a brilliant green and dotted with oak trees. You can pick kiwis and boysenberries, visit a pioneer cemetery, go boating and fishing on Black Butte Reservoir, bird-watch at the wildlife refuge, and attend the rodeo at Paskenta. Orland has a few coffee shops, and Chico a number of good ethnic restaurants.

The Glaesemans raise unusual birds such as Polish crested chickens, buff orpingtons, and voiceless Muscovy ducks. One of the farm's most endearing creatures is Rutherford B. Squeak, the pet goose who considers Kurt his best friend.

SEA RANCH

The Sea Ranch

Lodge: P.O. Box 44
The Sea Ranch, CA 95497
707-785-2371
Rental Homes:
Sea Ranch Escape
P.O. Box 238
The Sea Ranch, CA 95497
707-785-2426
800-SEARANCH (for information on all accommodations)

A resort colony and coastal retreat

Lodge manager: Chris Cochran. **Accommodations:** 20 lodge rooms, 55 rental homes. **Rates:** Lodge $125–$180 single or double, $15 additional person; rental homes $200–$620 for 2 nights, plus refundable deposit. **Payment:** Major credit cards.

Minimum stay: 2 nights on weekends in lodge, 2 nights in rental homes. **Children:** Under age 6 free in lodge rooms. **Pets:** Allowed in some rental homes. **Smoking:** Nonsmoking units available.

The Sea Ranch, 29 miles north of Jenner on a wild and lovely stretch of the Sonoma County coast, is a second-home colony and resort on one of the last great Mexican land grants. The location, on 5,000 acres of bluffs and wooded slopes overlooking the Pacific, is outstanding.

Sea Ranch has two swimming pools, tennis courts, and sauna, as well as private beaches and miles of trails through forest and meadows. As you walk the headlands, you may see blacktail deer, great blue heron, or even a bobcat or gray fox.

The architecture blends unobtrusively into its surroundings. The vertical gray siding and fences are brightened by barrels of flowers, but most of the color here comes from wildflowers and natural vegetation, not from planted gardens.

The lodge is the center of social life for the 1,130 homes on the property. Its inviting lounge has a stone fireplace, grand piano, rough-hewn walls, and wide windows overlooking the bluffs and sea. The dining room, open for three meals a day, serves American cuisine with an emphasis on fresh ingredients and seafood. Breads and desserts are baked on the premises, and the coffee is the ranch's special blend. The view from the picture windows is spectacular.

The guest rooms are in an L-shaped building north of the lodge. Two are family units with two bedrooms. Several have fireplaces with wood provided, and almost every room has an ocean view. There are no phones or television sets, though there's a TV in the bar and pay phones in the lodge. Carpeted and furnished in the style of a good-quality motel room, the accommodations are comfortable, but not outstanding.

Sea Ranch's privately owned rental homes, which sleep from two to eight people, offer the best variety of accommodations. Several agencies handle the rentals; Sea Ranch Escape carries many of the finest in the choicest locations. Among them are two of the original award-winning condominium units.

Set on bluffs directly above the ocean, in grassy meadows, or under the pines and redwoods east of the highway, the homes are, for the most part, furnished in a tasteful, contemporary style. Your rental might contain a dishwasher, washer and dryer, stereo, video player, pool or Ping-Pong table, or any combination of the above.

You can bring your own bed linens, towels, and kindling for the fireplace, or the rental agency will provide them at extra cost. Sea Ranch Escape has three levels of service: you can bring supplies and do your own cleaning, have the agency make up the beds and clean, or choose to have everything, including the catering of meals, taken care of.

The most expensive rentals are the newest. One is a four-bedroom, three-bath home with a Jacuzzi in the master bath. It has an ocean view from the edge of the bluff and is a five-minute walk from the recreation center and the beach.

On the property is a challenging, top-rated, nine-hole golf course. Nearby are a clubhouse, snack bar, and pro shop.

TRINIDAD

The Lost Whale

3452 Patrick's Point Drive
Trinidad, CA 95570
707-677-3425

An oceanfront inn ideal for families

Innkeepers: Susanne Lakin and Lee Miller. **Accommodations:** 6 rooms (all with private bath). **Rates:** November–April $90–

$120, May–October and major holidays $100–$130; $15 additional adult, $10 additional child age 3-16. **Included:** Full breakfast. **Payment:** MasterCard, Visa. **Children:** Under 3 free. **Pets:** Not allowed. **Smoking:** Not allowed.

Adults and children alike are enchanted by this warm, spacious, Cape Cod–style inn with plank floors and a modern country decor. High on a grassy bluff, it faces the Pacific and the sea lions that bask and bark on Turtle Rock.

The blue frame house, which stands behind a white picket fence covered with roses, was built in 1989 as a bed-and-breakfast. Susanne and Lee and their two daughters came to Trinidad from Los Angeles, ready to try a different way of life. They purchased four acres of land, built their B&B, and started welcoming visitors.

For dinner, try the nearby Larrupin' Café, which is famous for its barbecue sauce and excellent cooking. With advance notice, the innkeepers will arrange for childcare while you dine.

One large room with a wall of windows serves as a common area where guests have breakfast and afternoon tea and cookies and relax by the woodstove fire. Children are served breakfast first, in the kitchen, and then are entertained with television and toys while the adults enjoy a leisurely meal of fruit and a main dish such as corn fritatta or bread pudding with carmelized rum sauce.

The guest rooms can sleep four. All are soundproofed and practical, but a light decor, fresh flowers, greenery, and books and magazines lend sparkle as well. Two rooms have balconies and skylights, and four have stunning ocean views.

Visitors can play croquet on the wide lawn. Youngsters enjoy feeding the cats, ducks, goats, and rabbits, and they love the charming playhouse. You can walk a path to a private beach, relax in the hot tub, go deep-sea fishing, explore tidepools, windsurf in freshwater lagoons, and walk in Redwood National Park, the largest redwood forest in the world. It's a 15-minute drive from the inn.

Trinidad Bed & Breakfast

P.O. Box 849
560 Edwards
Trinidad, CA 95570-0849
707-677-0840

A casual home with panoramic ocean views

Innkeepers: Carol and Paul Kirk. **Accommodations:** 4 rooms (all with private bath). **Rates:** $90–$130 single, $105–$145 double, $30 additional person; midweek discounts November-March. **Included:** Full breakfast. **Minimum stay:** 2 nights on weekends and holidays. **Payment:** MasterCard, Visa. **Children:** Welcome (rooms accommodate 2 people). **Pets:** Not allowed. **Smoking:** Not allowed.

The most populous state in the union has a number of great vacation spots waiting to be discovered; Trinidad is one of them. This is not palm tree country — Trinidad Bay is on the far north coast, 22 miles above Eureka, just off Highway 101. Fog often drifts in, and the winter storms are wild. Nightlife consists of stargazing on clear nights or curling up with a good book and hot cider by a fire.

If that prospect appeals, and you like gorgeous scenery, pristine beaches, good fishing, and intriguing history, you may enjoy Trinidad. You're close to wilderness here, with forests of redwood giants lining the highway. Redwood National Park is 20 miles to the north. Between it and I-5 on the east are many mountains and very few roads.

Overlooking Trinidad Bay, with broad views of the coastline and harbor, is a 1949 Cape Cod-style home with accommodations for travelers. When you arrive, Carol and Paul greet you with warmth and show you where to find the cider mix and cookies and the refrigerator for chilling wine. It's clear that they want you to feel welcome in their pleasant home. Hot and cold beverages are available all day.

In ancient times, Trinidad was Tsurai, a village of the Yurok Indians, active until the early 1900s. Direct descendants of the tribe continue to live and work in the area. One Yurok builds dugout canoes for museums and gives seminars on the art of canoe construction.

The guest rooms have a comfortable, casual atmosphere, traditional furnishings, and ocean views. The first floor suite has a fireplace and king-size bed. There's a telescope in the upstairs suite so you can watch the boats and whales go by. Both suites have microwave ovens, and popcorn is provided. If you are in one of the two rooms in the main house, you'll be served a family-style breakfast in the dining area; if you're staying in a suite with an outside entrance, breakfast will be brought to your room.

The house sits on a cliff directly above Indian Beach and the bay, facing south down the coast; you can see all the way to Mendocino Cape. Across the street is a little lighthouse, a memorial to those lost at sea. It's a replica of the working lighthouse around the corner.

Trinidad was named by a Spanish explorer, Don Bruno de Hezeta, in 1775. Landing on Trinity Sunday, he erected a wooden cross, christened the point of land Trinidad, and held the first mass in California's history. The Spanish cross remained until 1913 when a granite cross replaced it.

The town became a port supplying gold-rush miners, a lumber town, and, in the 1920s, a whaling station. Lying in the path of the great gray whales' annual migration, it's an excellent place for viewing them. From the headlands, and even from the Kirks' front yard, you can see mother whales with their new youngsters heading north from Baja California.

Other activities are beachcombing for agates, walking the trails of Trinidad Head, and watching sea lions cavort on the rocks. You can charter a boat at the pier if you want to fish for salmon or cod or go crabbing. An excursion boat offers harbor cruises. At Telonicher Marine Lab you can see aquariums, touch intertidal animals, tour the research lab, and watch slide presentations on marine life.

WESTPORT

Howard Creek Ranch

P.O. Box 121
40501 North Highway 1
Westport, CA 95488
707-964-6725

An old-fashioned farmhouse near the sea

Innkeepers: Sally and Charles (Sonny) Grigg. **Accommodations:** 4 rooms in farmhouse, 3 cabins, separate suite. **Rates:** $55–$125 single or double. **Included:** Full breakfast. **Minimum stay:** 2 nights on summer weekends and holidays. **Payment:** Major credit cards. **Pets:** Allowed by prior arrangement. **Smoking:** Allowed in designated areas.

On the northern coast, where mists swirl around jagged headlands, coves protect sandy beaches, and every curve in the road presents another sweeping ocean view, there's a rural valley with a creek running through. On this idyllic site a farmstead was built in 1871 by Alfred Howard, an early settler. The house, made entirely of heart redwood, still stands

— the oldest home in the Westport area. Even today you can see the name of Lucy Howard, one of Alf's daughters, scratched in the wavy glass of an upstairs window pane.

Sally and Sonny Grigg are the third owners of the 40-acre ranch, a small portion of the land grant that once extended over 2,000 acres of grassy slopes and wooded hills. Their restoration efforts have turned the historic home into a bed-and-breakfast for travelers looking for seclusion in the country near (not directly facing) the sea.

A 75-foot swinging footbridge spans Howard Creek, which flows past the big barn to the beach 200 yards away. Deer and elk roam the area, along with a resident porcupine.

The house stands in a colorful garden, which is the source of the fresh flowers in the rooms. On the hillside are a hot tub, a sauna, showers, and an ornamental pool fed by a creek. Horses and cows graze the pastures.

In the main house, the spicy scent of potpourri fills the air, while the original fireplace warms the parlor. The antiques-furnished parlor draws guests to Sally's extensive book collection, the chess set, and the Griggs' musical instruments. At a single table in the dining room Sally serves a substantial breakfast of bacon or sausage, eggs, fresh fruit, and orange muffins.

There's one guest room on the main floor, opening to a patch of colorful flowers. Country antiques furnish the suite, which has a star quilt on the bed and scatter rugs on polished wood floors. In the sitting area is a small kitchen with a refrigerator and microwave oven. Upstairs, two more rooms offer comfortable accommodations; one has a cozy loft under a leaded glass skylight.

Other lodgings include a redwood cabin at the edge of the woods and quaint Meadow Cabin, covered with passion vine and nasturtiums. Meadow Cabin has a woodstove and a shower. Most unusual is the Boat House, which was constructed around the hull and galley of a boat. Sheltered by eucalyptus trees on the bank of Howard Creek, it holds a woodstove, microwave oven, and a refrigerator, as well as its own bath.

The spacious Barn Suite, in the partially restored barn, has a hand-crafted redwood interior, a king-size bed, a fireplace, a kitchenette, and an ocean view. The Griggs also have a beach cabin with a king-size bed and an ocean view.

Activities in the area are plentiful. You can stroll and beachcomb on miles of sand, explore tidepools, or go bird-watching. Sally and Sonny know all the nearby Nature Conservancy trails and panoramic viewpoints. Farther afield, you may drive to Fort Bragg and Mendocino (about 25 miles south) for shopping and dining.

Sierra Country

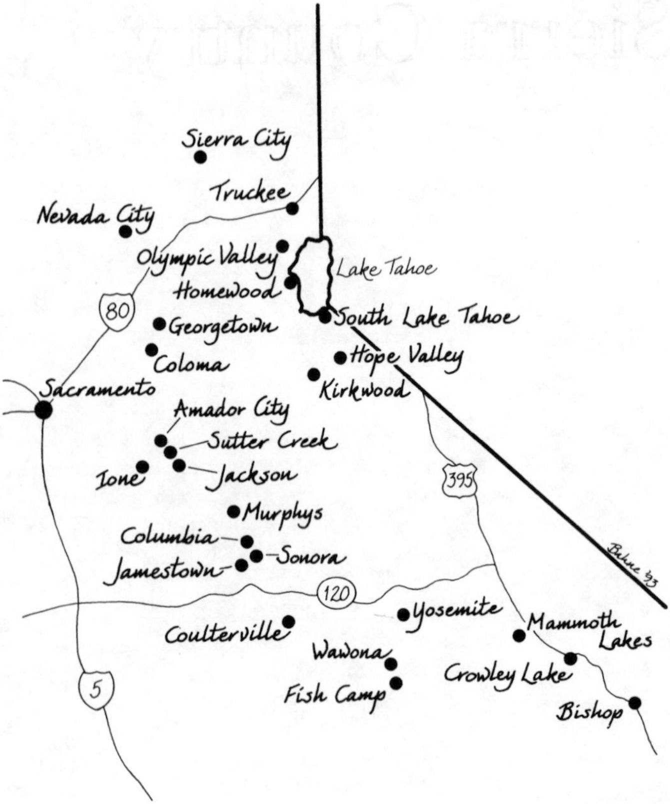

Sierra City
Truckee
Nevada City
Olympic Valley
Lake Tahoe
Homewood
80
South Lake Tahoe
Georgetown
Hope Valley
Coloma
Kirkwood
Sacramento
Amador City
Sutter Creek
Ione
Jackson
395
Murphys
Columbia
Sonora
Jamestown
Bahne '93
120
Yosemite
Coulterville
Mammoth Lakes
Wawona
Crowley Lake
Fish Camp
5
Bishop

Amador City
Imperial Hotel, 391
Bishop
Chalfant House, 393
Coloma
The Coloma Country Inn, 394
Columbia
City Hotel, 396
Fallon Hotel, 398
Coulterville
The Hotel Jeffery, 400
Crowley Lake
Rainbow Tarns Bed & Breakfast, 402
Fish Camp
Tenaya Lodge, 403
Georgetown
American River Inn, 405
Homewood
Rockwood Lodge, 407
Hope Valley
Sorensen's, 409
Ione
The Heirloom, 411
Jackson
Gate House Inn, 413
The Wedgewood Inn, 415
Jamestown
The National Hotel, 416
Kirkwood
Caples Lake Resort, 418
Mammoth Lakes
Alpers' Owens River Ranch, 420
Edelweiss Lodge, 422
Mammoth Mountain Inn, 424
Tamarack Lodge Resort, 426
Murphys
Dunbar House, 1880, 428
Nevada City
Grandmere's Bed & Breakfast Inn, 430
Red Castle Inn, 432
Olympic Valley
Resort at Squaw Creek, 434
Squaw Valley Lodge, 435
Sacramento
Abigail's, 437
Amber House Bed & Breakfast Inn, 439
The Delta King Hotel, 440
Hartley House, 442
Radisson Hotel Sacramento, 443
The Sterling Hotel, 444
Vizcaya, 446
Sierra City
Busch & Heringlake Country Inn, 448
Sonora
Llamahall Guest Ranch, 450
South Lake Tahoe
Lakeland Village Beach & Ski Resort, 452
The Christiania Inn, 453
Sutter Creek
Sutter Creek Inn, 455
The Foxes Bed and Breakfast Inn, 457
Truckee
Northstar at Tahoe, 459
Wawona
Wawona Hotel, 461
Yosemite
The Ahwahnee, 463

Best Intimate City Stops

Sacramento
- Abigail's
- Amber House
- Delta King Hotel
- Hartley House
- The Sterling Hotel
- Vizcaya

Best Country Inns and B&Bs

Amador City
- Imperial Hotel

Bishop
- Chalfant House

Coloma
- The Coloma Country Inn

Columbia
- City Hotel
- Fallon Hotel

Coulterville
- The Hotel Jeffery

Georgetown
- American River Inn

Homewood
- Rockwood Lodge

Ione
- The Heirloom

Jackson
- Gate House Inn
- The Wedgewood Inn

Mammoth Lakes
- Edelweiss Lodge

Murphys
- Dunbar House, 1880

Nevada City
- Grandmere's Bed & Breakfast Inn
- Red Castle Inn

Sierra City
Busch & Heringlake Country Inn
South Lake Tahoe
The Christiania Inn
Sutter Creek
Sutter Creek Inn

Best Family Favorites

Fish Camp
Tenaya Lodge
Hope Valley
Sorensen's
Sacramento
Radisson Hotel
Sonora
Llamahall Guest Ranch

Best Resorts

Mammoth Lakes
Mammoth Mountain Inn
Olympic Valley
Resort at Squaw Creek
Squaw Valley Lodge
South Lake Tahoe
Lakeland Village Beach & Ski Resort
Truckee
Northstar at Tahoe

Best Romantic Hideaways

Sutter Creek
The Foxes Bed and Breakfast Inn

Best Wilderness Retreats

Crowley Lake
Rainbow Tarns Bed & Breakfast

Kirkwood
Caples Lake Resort
Mammoth Lakes
Alpers' Owens River Ranch
Tamarack Lodge Resort
Wawona
Wawona Hotel
Yosemite
The Ahwahnee

The broad Sacramento River delta holds the capital city of Sacramento, with its peaceful tree-shaded streets, lovely capitol grounds, art museums, and restored Old Town. Sutter's Fort, a state historic park, replicates the fort built in 1839 by John Sutter on the American and Sacramento Rivers.

Not to be missed in Old Sacramento is the California State Railroad Museum, which exhibits restored locomotives, a luxurious private railroad car, and hundreds of items from train history. It's near the waterfront, where old-fashioned paddlewheelers cruise the river. Sacramento is the gateway to the gold country in the foothills of the Sierra Nevada. Ghosts of the forty-niners still linger in former mining communities like Sutter Creek, Jackson, and Jamestown. Nevada City has carefully nurtured its old frontier heritage by restoring a 19th-century atmosphere. Columbia, a state park, is an authentic recreation of a mid-1800s mining town. Reach deeper into the High Sierra and you find a lake-dotted wilderness with cliffs, waterfalls, and immense sequoia trees. The granite mountains, John Muir's "range of light," extend from the Cascades on the north to the desert Tehachapis.

South of dazzlingly blue and clear Lake Tahoe, the largest alpine lake in North America, is California's crown jewel: Yosemite National Park. At its heart lies Yosemite Valley. Sculpted by glaciers eons ago, it's an awe-inspiring wonderland of vertical cliffs, massive granite domes, streaming waterfalls, and lush meadows. With three million visitors annually, Yosemite can seem as crowded as a San Francisco suburb. But a few steps away from the campgrounds, 750 miles of trails traverse pristine country where the only sounds you hear belong to the wild.

Tioga Pass Road leads through Yosemite's northern peaks and subalpine meadows and descends sharply to desert on the east side. The road south then heads toward Mammoth Lakes and some of California's best skiing and High Sierra scenery.

In Owens Valley, between the Sierra Nevada and Inyo/

White Mountain range, you can go hiking, fishing, horseback riding, and boating. South of Bishop, in the Inyo National Forest, you can walk among the earth's oldest living trees, bristlecone pines. The oldest in this awe-inspiring forest of twisted trunks and weathered branches is 4,700 years.

Still farther south are Mount Whitney, at 14,494 feet the highest peak in the continental United States, and Badwater in Death Valley, 282 feet below sea level.

AMADOR CITY

Imperial Hotel

A historic hotel in gold country

P.O. Box 195
Amador City, CA 95601
209-267-9172

Proprietors: Bruce Sherrill and Dale Martin. **Accommodations:** 6 rooms (all with private bath). **Rates:** $60–$70 weekdays, $75–$90 weekends and holidays, $5 less for single. **Included:** Continental breakfast. **Payment:** Major credit cards. **Children:** Welcome. **Pets:** Not allowed. **Smoking:** Not allowed in guest rooms.

This brick hotel, which faces busy Highway 49, was first built as a mercantile store and then redone and opened as a hotel in 1879, when Amador was a bustling town. It was made to last — the walls at its base are twelve bricks thick, and four bricks thick at the roof.

The Imperial closed in 1927; the present owners restored it in 1988, adding bathrooms and air conditioning and other modern niceties. Their restaurant, open for dinners and Sunday breakfast, has achieved distinction for its fine cuisine. Breakfast is served here, on a patio, or in your room. The original hotel bar is opposite the restaurant.

In the heart of the gold country, and once a major mining center, Amador City is known today for its numerous antiques shops and for the excellent restaurant in the Imperial Hotel.

Upstairs, the guest rooms have such old-fashioned features as high ceilings, antique beds, and paddle fans on the ceiling. They have a delightfully whimsical decor, with designs by the talented John Johansen. One, for example, has a corner armoire with ties, socks, and a gown painted as if they're hung over the door. The baths are contemporary, in white and brass, and have hair dryers.

A deck with flowerpots and chairs is at one end of the second floor hall. Across the front of the hotel there's a balcony accessible to guests. Inside, on the landing, are a desk and phone, shelves of books and games, and a basket of fruit.

Since the Imperial is close to the highway, it's best to request a room at the back if you're a light sleeper.

BISHOP

Chalfant House

213 Academy Street
Bishop, CA 93514
619-872-1790

A cozy B&B on the east side of the Sierra Nevada range

Innkeepers: Fred and Sally Manecke. **Accommodations:** 7 rooms (all with private bath). **Rates:** $50–$80 single, $60–$90 double, $15 additional person. **Included:** Full breakfast. **Payment:** Major credit cards. **Children:** Over age 8 welcome. **Pets:** Not allowed. **Smoking:** Not allowed.

Chalfant House offers comfortable lodging while you explore the Owens Valley area. The turn-of-the-century inn, built for the publisher of the first newspaper in the valley, is a block from Main Street and within walking distance of shops, restaurants, and a pleasant park. Each guest room is named after a member of the Chalfant family and is furnished with antiques and handmade quilts. The rooms are also all air conditioned. The suite, above the antiques store behind the house, has a queen-size bed, a sofa bed, and a kitchen.

Bishop is a small, peaceful town in the Owens Valley of the Eastern Sierra, halfway between Reno and Los Angeles. It provides easy access to mountain trails, lakes, the Mammoth Mountain ski area, and the ancient bristlecone pine forest.

The Maneckes have restored the B&B with care. They put equal effort into creating a welcoming atmosphere for their guests. They'll greet you with a mug of hot cider in the cool months and a frosty drink in summer, take you to and from the Bishop airport at no charge, provide a sink for cleaning the fish you catch and a freezer to store it in, and invite you to join them for homemade ice cream sundaes in the evening. Sometime before you leave their inn they'll take your picture, and they'll send it to you later, accompanied by the newsletter they publish.

Breakfast, which includes fruit, homemade breads and jams, and a hot dish such as banana French toast, is served on fine china in the dining room; you can take your coffee to the little side terrace under the grape arbor. There's a piano and TV in the parlor, where guests gather to visit with each other and their hospitable hosts.

COLOMA

The Coloma Country Inn

P.O. Box 502
2 High Street
Coloma, CA 95613
916-622-6919

> *A quiet country home in a historic park*

Innkeepers: Cindi and Alan Ehrgott. **Accommodations:** 5 rooms (3 with private bath) plus 2 suites in Carriage House. **Rates:** Rooms $89–$99; Carriage House $120–$145. **Included:** Full breakfast. **Payment:** No credit cards. **Children:** Welcome. **Pets:** Not allowed. **Smoking:** Not allowed indoors.

In 1848 gold was discovered in the American River, in the foothills of the Sierra Nevada. That event changed the face of the nation, helped the Union win the Civil War, and brought both fortune and disaster to thousands. By 1865, at least $750 million in gold had been mined in California.

It all started here, in the little town of Coloma, when James Marshall pulled a nugget from the tailrace of John Sutter's lumber mill. Richer diggings were soon found elsewhere, and Coloma became the commercial center for nearby mining camps.

Alan Ehrgott is a veteran pilot and offers hot air balloon flights over the American River valley. First thing in the morning, balloonists are given a light snack and then a ride over the pine trees, the oak-studded hills, and the American River. The flight is followed by champagne and a full breakfast.

Saloonkeepers prospered mightily from the newfound gold. Hugh Miller, who ran a saloon in Coloma, built himself a fine home in 1852. This home, after several renovations, is now a delightful inn at Marshall Gold Discovery State Historic Park.

Coloma Country Inn has been open as a bed-and-breakfast since 1983. The Ehrgotts offer warm hospitality and a touch of New England in the furnishings and decor — you'll find plaid wingback chairs, patchwork quilts, hand-dipped candles, and charming wall stencils. Breakfast is served on an heirloom Duncan Phyfe table. The house stands behind a white picket fence on two and a half acres of beautifully landscaped grounds, with fruit trees, flowers, a gazebo, and a pond where bullfrogs croak among the cattails.

In the main house, the Rose Room is bright with roses and has a private courtyard. Lavender Room is a light, cheerful space in lavender and white, with an apple tree out the window and a view of the pond. The Blue Room has long, narrow windows hung with lace and framed with flowers. It shares a bathroom with the Garden Room, which is furnished in white wicker and pine. Each room has a small sitting area.

A few yards away, behind a lavish country garden and brick courtyard, is the Carriage House, with two enchanting suites. Cottage Suite is a good choice for families, since it has two bedrooms and a kitchenette (not for cooking full meals, but quite adequate for storing snacks). Geranium Suite lives up to its name, with a garden motif and geranium-patterned quilt. It also has a kitchen.

You may have breakfast in your room, on the patio, or in the dining room, where French doors open to the grassy slope above the pond. You'll be served juice, fresh fruit, homemade baked goods, and a hot entrée such as scrambled eggs with salsa. Cookies, lemonade, and iced tea are in the kitchen, where guests are welcome.

The innkeepers have bicycles to lend and will arrange for whitewater rafting trips. When you tour the state park, you'll see a replica of Sutter's sawmill, James Marshall's cabin, tinsmith and blacksmith shops, and other historic structures.

For dining out in Coloma, the Ehrgotts recommend Vineyard House, which has a Continental menu and 19th century atmosphere. They also urge guests to get into the spirit of the period at the Olde Coloma Theater, where melodramas are presented on weekends.

COLUMBIA

City Hotel

P.O. Box 1870
Main Street
Columbia, CA 95310
209-532-1479

A frontier hotel in an Old West town

Manager: Tom Bender. **Accommodations:** 10 rooms. **Rates:** $65–$85 single, $70–$90 double, $15 additional person. **Included:** Expanded Continental breakfast. **Payment:** Major credit cards. **Children:** Age 2 and under free in room with parents. **Pets:** Not allowed. **Smoking:** Not allowed in guest rooms or parlor.

Horses clop down the street in Columbia, pulling stagecoaches to the Wells Fargo office. The blacksmith is in his shop repairing wagons. Melodramas are performed regularly at the theater. The barber cuts hair in an 1856 barber shop, and old-fashioned candies are sold in the sweet shop. And the same hotel that housed successful miners is open for business.

City Hotel is a two-story brick edifice that opened in 1856, fell into disrepair when the boom faded, and reopened in 1975 as a museum and hotel under state ownership. Now, just as in earlier days, lace curtains hang at glass-paneled doors and a ticking clock and heavy safe stand behind a wood registration counter. The crowd in the What Cheer Saloon isn't quite as boisterous as in decades past, but the atmosphere is convivial around the cherrywood bar, which was shipped around the Horn from New England.

Columbia is the best-preserved gold-rush town in the Mother Lode. Faithfully restored, it's now a state park where you can experience life as it was in the 1850s, when this was a boomtown of 15,000 people and 40 saloons. When you walk into town (no cars are allowed) you enter the mid-19th century.

The frontier inn is well kept and comfortable, and the service attentive. The highly reputed restaurant serves a light French cuisine and has a wine list that includes labels from Amador County, an area noted for its zinfandels. The restaurant and hotel are also a training ground for students in hospitality management at nearby Columbia College. Eager and enthusiastic, they assist a professional staff.

Guest rooms are upstairs, two in front (Balcony Rooms), four down the hall, and four off the large parlor (Parlor Rooms). In the Victorian parlor are games, playing cards, and a revolving bookcase of books and magazines. A breakfast of fresh juice, granola, fruits, and breads from the hotel kitchen is set out in the parlor and may be taken to your room.

The rooms are on display when unoccupied. When you stay here, the chain across the door is unhooked and you're left to spend the night as a traveler of a century ago, in the finest accommodations the gold country had to offer. The rooms are larger than they were when the hotel was strictly for gentlemen; ladies were allowed only in the parlor and dining areas. The addition of running water is another modern nicety. There's a half-bath in each room; showers are down the hall. You're supplied with robes and slippers. Oriental rugs, 12-foot ceilings, lace curtains at high windows, and carved furniture bring back another era. The two Balcony Rooms have private balconies facing the trees above Main Street.

Room 1, a perennial favorite, is the haunted room. It seems that a wealthy man from the Midwest bought a massive carved bedroom set for his bride and had it shipped to San Francisco. But the newlyweds never slept in the bed, for the bride died of a fever. The grieving husband shut the furniture in a warehouse. Later, after a stint in a museum, it ended up in a Balcony Room here, and occasionally visitors insist that they feel peculiar vibrations.

In Columbia State Historic Park, you can have your name stamped on a horseshoe or printed in headlines in a period newspaper, ride in a stagecoach, and pan for gold. Buy leather goods and wines, stop by the ice cream parlor, tour the museum, and have lunch or dinner at the best restaurant in town, the City Hotel.

Fallon Hotel

P.O. Box 1870
Columbia, CA 95310
209-532-1470

> *A Victorian hotel in a gold-rush setting*

Manager: Tom Bender. **Accommodations:** 14 rooms. **Rates:** $40–$85 single, $45–$90 double, $10 additional person; suite

$115. **Included:** Continental breakfast. **Payment:** Major credit cards. **Children:** Age 2 and under free in room with parents. **Pets:** Not allowed. **Smoking:** Not allowed in rooms or parlor.

In Columbia State Historic Park, where gold rush days have been brought to life, the Fallon Hotel offers lodging just as it did when Columbia was a rip-roaring mining town in 1857. Owned by the state, the hotel was authentically restored in 1986 using many of the antiques and furnishings discovered in the neglected, dilapidated building.

Next to the hotel is a tree-shaded garden with a brick terrace. In the nearby Fallon Theater, the Columbia Actors' Repertory performs year-round.

Now, when you enter the lobby, you're engulfed in the atmosphere of a fine Victorian hotel in the countryside. A green plush love seat and burgundy velvet couch are set off by an Oriental carpet and dark, carved moldings. When the restoration began, bits of the original wallpaper were found still clinging to the walls, so the noted firm of Bradbury and Bradbury was called in to recreate them. Elaborate, colorful designs cover the 15-foot walls and ceiling.

Upstairs guest rooms contain double or twin beds and half baths. Spacious and modern shared showers with skylights are down the hall. Baskets with soaps, towels, robes, and slippers are provided. At the end of the hall, French doors open to a balcony overlooking the traffic-free street — no cars are permitted in Columbia — and some rooms have private balconies.

The best and largest rooms are toward the front of the hotel, but all are homey and comfortable, with carved or iron bedsteads, rocking chairs, and throw rugs on pine floors. Every morning, juice, coffee, assorted muffins and rolls, and jam are served in the ice cream parlor.

COULTERVILLE

The Hotel Jeffery

P.O. Box 440B
1 Main Street
Coulterville, CA 95311
209-878-3471
800-464-3471 in U.S.

A former stage-coach stop in the Sierra foothills

Proprietors: Karin Fielding and Louis Bickford. **Accommodations:** 21 rooms (5 with private bath), 1 suite. **Rates:** $59–$74 single or double, $10 additional person; suite $99 for up to 4 people. **Included:** Continental breakfast. **Minimum stay:** 2 nights on holiday weekends. **Payment:** MasterCard, Visa. **Children:** Under 12 free in room with parents. **Pets:** Not allowed. **Smoking:** Allowed.

Travelers looking for the Old West love the Jeffery — it's the real thing, here in the foothills of the Sierras, 31 miles west of Yosemite National Park.

The three-story rock and adobe hotel was first built in 1850 as a store and fandango hall for the Mexican community. It burned and was rebuilt three times over the years, but has been owned by the same family since 1851. Karin Fielding, one of the present owners, is a descendant.

There is little luxury at the Jeffery, but plenty of character and charm. In 1903 Theodore Roosevelt stayed in Room 1, one of two rooms with bay windows above the main street of this sleepy little village. Some windows overlook the county park across the street, which has a playground, swimming pool, and tennis courts.

The rooms are of different sizes, and there are a few cracks in the walls from the settling of the building. Pegs or rails with hangers take the place of closets. Big windows, transoms above the doors, and ceiling paddle fans provide air circulation. Each floor has four bathrooms for the rooms that share baths.

The former stagecoach stop has a classic saloon with sawdust and peanut shells on the floor, lace at the windows, and a second-story balcony with flags at the railing.

The hotel was redone in 1988 and now has nicely decorated rooms large enough for families. The two most spacious rooms, done in blue and peach, are on the third floor. Like most old hotels, the Jeffery claims a ghost room that a spirit visits on occasion. You wouldn't know it to see the place; on the third floor, it's cheerful in bright red and has twin beds.

There is a meeting/banquet room with 1,600 square feet of space, and a nice courtyard in back. The plain and simple restaurant serves breakfast and dinner (barbecued ribs and fried chicken are popular items). Magnolia Saloon, with authentic frontier flavor, has pool tables and one of the oldest bars in the West. On display are military memorabilia and a whimsical, life-size scene of old-time poker players.

Coulterville has antiques shops to browse and a historical museum that is well worth visiting.

CROWLEY LAKE

Rainbow Tarns Bed & Breakfast

Route 1, Box 1097
Crowley Lake, CA 93546
619-935-4556

An Old West farm home in the country

Innkeeper: Lois Miles. **Accommodations:** 3 rooms (all with private bath). **Rates:** $95–$125. **Included:** Full breakfast. **Minimum stay:** 2 nights, 3 nights on holidays. **Payment:** No credit cards. **Children:** Over age 12 welcome. **Pets:** Not allowed (except horses). **Smoking:** Not allowed indoors.

On the east side of the Sierra range, 18 miles south of Mammoth Lakes, is a tiny community called Tom's Place. You can find it on your road map, but in reality it's little more than a restaurant and bar. About a mile farther, on a dirt road, is Rainbow Tarns, a secluded, quiet, country home.

The log and white block inn, built in the 1920s against granite boulders, has a rustic quality that is right out of the Old West. A battered wagon wheel leans against the veranda's log posts. In the living room there's a stone fireplace and a fixture made from a wagon wheel and horseshoes. Family antiques, such as Lois's grandfather's cradle, decorate the room.

The guest rooms are furnished in country style, with lace

curtains and down duvets to warm you on chilly mountain evenings (the elevation is 7,000 feet). Rainbow Room has a queen-size bed, an oversize bath with a double Jacuzzi, and a deck. Gemini, with a view of the boulders and hillside, also has a whirlpool and a queen-size bed.

The restaurant at nearby Convict Lake is the place for dining by candlelight. Tom's Place, down-home and friendly, is where local residents go for good hamburgers and conviviality.

This is a homey, casual spot where guests are welcome to use the kitchen and the innkeeper may join you for a family-style breakfast. She serves a hearty meal — fruit, eggs from the farm's chickens, pork chops, browned potatoes, along with a basket of muffins and zucchini bread are typical. A plate of cookies, a bowl of fruit, and beverages are always available.

From the veranda or chairs on the grass you can watch the trout leap and ducks swim in the ponds. Bodie, Lois's lovable dog, will keep you company. Also on the farm are chickens, a cat, and Jamal, a white horse. Guests may bring their own horses, too, at no charge.

From Rainbow Tarns you can go bicycling or horseback riding, hiking on the John Muir Trail, cross-country skiing in open meadows, bathing in hot mineral springs, bird-watching, and stargazing.

FISH CAMP

Tenaya Lodge

P.O. Box 159
1122 Highway 41
Fish Camp, CA 93623
209-683-6555
800-635-5807
Fax 209-683-8684

A mountain lodge near Yosemite's border

Manager: David Norbut. **Accommodations:** 242 rooms and 17 suites. **Rates:** Summer $175–$190, winter $129–$165, $10 additional person; suites $250–$350. **Payment:** Major credit cards. **Children:** Under age 17 free in parent's room. **Pets:** Not allowed. **Smoking:** Nonsmoking rooms available.

Marriott's Tenaya Lodge opened in 1990, the only major resort built in the area in more than 50 years. Set on 35 hilly, wooded acres just two miles south of the entrance to Yosemite National Park, it's different from most Marriott hotels.

The Tenaya has two restaurants: the Sierra, featuring northern Italian dishes, and the Parkside Deli, an all-day coffee shop that will pack a picnic lunch upon request. The rustic Lobby Bar, with a three-story stone fireplace, is a lively saloon that serves drinks and light fare.

The three-story resort is like a mountain lodge with an American Indian and Southwest theme. In the spacious lobby are stucco walls, chairs fashioned from twigs and branches, and earthtone fabrics. All the amenities of a modern hotel are here, and the staff is enthusiastic and helpful.

There's an institutional tinge to the hotel, which you'll notice in the crowds, the bland music in the restaurant, and the convention groups. However, it does not detract from the cheerful ambience, and for family travel it can be a plus: you know what to expect. And the big parking lot and minimal landscaping have a purpose — all that concrete is a required firebreak.

The comfortable, well-furnished rooms are soundproof and have mini-bars, TV, direct-dial phones, and individual climate control. Some suites have dining rooms and balconies. Cribs and babysitters are available.

Tenaya Lodge welcomes families with a variety of activities and services. There are both indoor and outdoor swimming pools, sauna and steam rooms, mountain bikes, horseback riding, croquet, nature walks, and a summer day camp for youngsters ages 5 to 12. The camp offers arts and crafts, nature hikes, meals, and movies. The morning forest walks, led by a knowledgeable nature guide, are worthwhile for all ages.

The main attraction, though, is Yosemite. You can admire the magnificent park from the valley floor, but to fully appreciate its wonders, hike away from the hordes of visitors, perhaps to Nevada Falls or Yosemite Falls. Or come in the winter, when the meadows and great granite domes are blanketed in snow and the park is not crowded.

GEORGETOWN

American River Inn

P.O. Box 43
Main at Orleans
Georgetown, CA 95634
916-333-4499
800-245-6566 in California
Fax 914-333-9253

A casual, quiet inn near a former mining camp

Innkeepers: Will and Maria Collin.
Accommodations: 20 rooms (11 with private bath), 6 suites. **Rates:** \$85–\$115. **Included:** Full breakfast. **Payment:** Major credit cards. **Children:** Welcome. **Pets:** Not allowed. **Smoking:** Allowed.

Georgetown is a quiet backwater between the middle and south forks of the American River, about an hour's drive east of Sacramento. There are few tourist attractions here — just scenic surroundings of mountains, lakes, and streams.

The original American Hotel, built in 1853, was lost in flames forty-six years later. Fire was commonplace in those days, often destroying entire towns. One Georgetown blaze raced up Main Street to a cache of miners' dynamite, which exploded and tossed debris for two miles.

The promise of gold drew prospectors to Georgetown, in the foothills of the Sierra Nevada, in the mid-1800s. The mining camp, then called Growlersburg, was a rich source of the precious stuff. By 1853, an estimated $2 million in gold had been found; one famous nugget weighed in at 126 ounces.

Today the American River Inn is a complex covering a square block on the same site as its forebear. Three buildings are set among lovely gardens, with a pheasant aviary and a swimming pool. The main building, with a veranda and a long balcony, houses fifteen guest rooms.

The comfortable accommodations have a flowery charm and furnishings that include unusual brass beds, antique lamps and armoires, and clawfoot tubs. At the end of the upstairs hall, lighted by red glass lamps, a door opens to the front balcony overlooking the quiet road.

Each room has a different decor, ranging from country calico to Victorian grandeur. There are two suites on the third level, one with a canopy bed and fireplace. The main house also has a gift shop and a parlor with a potbellied woodstove, wingback chairs, and a bar in the corner. Classical music plays in the afternoon while guests enjoy wine and appetizers and thumb through the album of local history. On the walls are historic prints of naval heroes and, of course, a "God Bless America" sampler.

A substantial breakfast is served at small tables in the dining room. Belgian waffles with bananas, spinach quiche, sausages, and ham are some of the dishes prepared, always with muffins, fruit cup, coffee, and tea.

In back of the hotel, down brick steps and past a big magnolia tree, are the fig-shaded pool and the aviary. Next to the patio, the Queen Anne House has five guest rooms, two with private baths. The big living room has a brick fireplace, Oriental carpets, and double doors to the deck. The most romantic of the light and airy rooms is the upstairs suite, with a partially canopied bed, white brick fireplace, and a balcony with a wrought-iron railing.

A third building holds the five Woodside Mine Suites, which have living rooms, wet bars, and one or two bedrooms. Attractively furnished in wicker and brass and decorated with stenciled designs, they have private entrances from the garden and the parking area.

The innkeepers can help you plan sightseeing tours of the gold country and will arrange for whitewater rafting trips or hot air balloon rides over the American River. They'll lend bicycles for biking the back roads that wind through masses of purple iris and brilliant yellow daffodils and Scotch broom.

Hiking, fishing, and golf are nearby. The hotel has a putting green and driving range, and facilities for horseshoes, badminton, table tennis, and croquet. The kitchen will prepare a luxury picnic basket for a day of exploring, at $95 for two. It includes a bottle of wine, and you may keep the basket and all its accessories for future picnics.

HOMEWOOD

Rockwood Lodge

P.O. Box 226
5295 West Lake Boulevard
Homewood, CA 96146
916-525-5273
800-LETAHOE

A comfortable bed-and-breakfast near the lake

Innkeepers: Constance Stevens and Louis Reinkens. **Accommodations:** 4 rooms (2 with private bath). **Rates:** $100–$175. **Included:** Full breakfast. **Minimum stay:** 2 nights on weekends, 3 nights on holidays. **Payment:** No credit cards. **Children:** Under 18 not appropriate. **Pets:** Not allowed. **Smoking:** Not allowed.

"Skiing down Homewood Run feels as if you're flying right into the lake." Connie Stevens is enthusiastic when she's talking about skiing and Lake Tahoe, two of her favorite subjects. She and her husband, Louis Reinkens, live in an ideal area to enjoy them both. Their bed-and-breakfast is just across the road from the lake and within walking distance of downhill ski slopes.

Homewood is a quiet community on the northwestern shore. Rockwood Lodge was built in 1939, in old Tahoe style of stone and knotty pine, as a vacation home for a dairyman from Vallejo. Forty-five years later, Connie and Louis left their Bay Area home, bought Rockwood, renovated it, and opened it to guests. Longtime travelers themselves, they know the comforts travelers look for.

There are several excellent restaurants along Tahoe's shores. In the summer, you may rent or charter a boat for fishing. Brown and Mackinaw trout inhabit the clear waters of the lake.

There are walk-in closets, thick velour bathrobes, wines and appetizers by the fire or on the patio, cordials in the evenings, sweets by the bed, and books to read. The innkeepers can lend beach towels and chairs in the summer and gloves and scarves in the winter. There are ski and bicycle storage areas, backpacks and walking sticks to borrow, and flashlights for evening walks.

Once inside the lodge — even on August weekends when Tahoe traffic and crowds reach temper-fraying levels — the atmosphere is one of peace, soft music, and good taste. Wingback chairs and fender benches provide seating comfort in the living room, where a fire on the stone hearth takes away the chill of winter evenings. On the mantel is a miniature of the Tahoe steam train that once ran to the lake.

French doors open to the dining room and breakfast table. Connie and Louis prepare fresh juice, croissants, and preserves, quantities of fruit, Dutch babies with blueberries, Belgian waffles, and other delectable items which they serve here or on the patio.

The guest rooms are named for places around the lake: Zephyr Cove, Emerald Bay, Secret Harbor, and Carnelian Bay. Zephyr Cove, the only room on the third floor, contains an extra-long double bed and pedestal sink. From its windows you look into the green branches of a 100-year-old pine tree. This room shares a bath and a half with Emerald Bay, on the second floor. Secret Harbor, overlooking the lake, is the largest room and has extra appeal: a four-poster bed, an 18th-century cobbler's bench, and a bath with double shower. All the rooms feature feather beds, down comforters, and sitting areas.

HOPE VALLEY

Sorensen's

14255 Highway 88
Hope Valley, CA 96120
916-694-2203

A group of wilderness cabins near Carson Pass

Proprietors: John and Patty Brissenden. **Accommodations:** 29 cabins (all with private bath). **Rates:** $55–$175 summer, $70–$225 winter. **Minimum stay:** 2 nights on weekends, 3 nights on some holidays. **Payment:** Major credit cards. **Children:** Welcome (crib charge $10). **Pets:** Allowed (in 2 cabins) with prior arrangement. **Smoking:** Not allowed.

South of Lake Tahoe and north of Yosemite, the rugged, mountainous country of the High Sierra has a scenic grandeur that rivals the Alps. In fact, it's called Alpine County and most of it is public land — a colossal park of nearly 800 square miles of lakes, meadows, rivers, mighty forests, and high peaks.

Just east of Carson Pass, where Kit Carson explored and

mapped the territory, are the green meadows of Hope Valley and this homey resort.

Owned by the Brissenden family since 1981, Sorensen's offers a full range of sports and other outdoor activities that appeal to guests of all ages. Favorites are fishing, fly-tying and rod building courses, hiking, river rafting, kayaking, bicycling, soaking at the hot springs, and llama trekking. In winter, the resort is a cross-country ski center, with 60 miles of trails in the peaceful valley and Toiyabe National Forest. Ski lessons, equipment rentals, and classes in winter survival skills are available.

The Sorensen family homesteaded here a century ago; in 1902 they built a cluster of cabins, the start of a resort that is still expanding. It now covers 165 acres at an elevation of 7,000 feet.

All but three of the cabins are clustered in the woods around a central building, which houses a country café (serving three hearty meals daily) and a gift shop. Each little building and its steeply pitched roof is outlined with tiny lights, creating a charming village effect at night.

Most of the cabins, which are named for local trees and flowers, have woodstoves (wood is supplied) and kitchens. Breakfast is provided for the three with no cooking facilities.

Piñon, next to the sauna cabin, is one of the coziest, with pecky cedar walls and an old-fashioned tub. Aspen, in 1930s knotty pine, has a homespun style with calico bedspreads. Waterfir is beloved by romantics looking for a quiet spot. Nestled among the aspen trees, with a creek running by, it has a brass double bed, a kitchen in the same room, and a woodstove with a rock hearth.

The most unusual cabin is Norway House, a replica of a 13th-century, sod-roofed Scandinavian home. The cabin sleeps eight, using a carpeted loft, and has a kitchen with a stovetop range and microwave oven. In back there's a deck with benches under the aspen trees. One of the off-site cabins which sleep up to six people is across the river; the others are near the hot springs.

This is a great place for children. John Brissenden, a former preschool teacher, has built a cunning log playhouse and stocked a pond with fish for kids under 12. There are puzzles, games, a playground, and horseshoes, as well as special programs like the October Star Watch and the Husky Express dogsled tours.

If you're interested in both hiking and history, sign up for the Historical Emigrant Trail Walking Tour. The tour crosses parts of the Mormon-Emigrant Trail and the early Pony Express Route.

For an enchanting winter holiday, come to Sorensen's in December and cut a fragrant Christmas tree. After a day on the snowy mountain, return to the café for hot cinnamon cocoa, mulled wine, or spiced cider, and shop for gifts of books, jams and jellies, watercolors, and Native American wall hangings.

IONE

The Heirloom

P.O. Box 322
214 Shakeley Lane
Ione, CA 95640
209-274-4468

A quaint B&B in a gold-country town

Innkeepers: Patricia Cross and Melisande Hubbs. **Accommodations:** 6 rooms (4 with private bath). **Rates:** $59–$91. **Included:** Full breakfast. **Minimum stay:** 2 nights on weekends. **Pay-**

ment: No credit cards. **Children:** Over age 10 welcome. **Pets:** Not allowed. **Smoking:** Not allowed indoors.

The Ione Valley, southeast of Sacramento, was a supply center for miners during the gold rush, with the village of Ione (called Bedbug or Freezeout in those days) its center. The more genteel name was chosen from a popular 19th-century book, *The Last Days of Pompeii.* Later, Ione served the farmers and ranchers of the fertile valley which is now one of Amador County's zinfandel grape-growing areas.

Set back from the road, the inn is reached by a lane bordered with black walnut trees. A brick path leads to the front door and a white-paneled living room filled with furnishings from the owners' collections.

An early settler in the valley built a home in Ione like those he'd left in Virginia. Today it's The Heirloom, a classic brick Greek Revival mansion with columned porticoes and balconies entwined with wisteria.

The large room holds a white fireplace, soft couches and chairs, tall windows, numerous books, and a rosewood piano that once belonged to the famed entertainer Lola Montez. An Oriental chess set, antique dolls, fans, and glassware reflect the innkeepers' many interests.

The guest rooms in the main house are named for the seasons and decorated accordingly. Autumn, in rust tones, has a basket of crisp apples and a wreath of dried weeds. French doors open to a semiprivate balcony above the garden. Summer is light and colorful in seafoam green and dusty rose. This room has an Eastlake walnut bed and a twin daybed and overlooks a 150-year-old English walnut tree.

Winter, the most popular room, has a private entrance from the balcony and a view of the garden and pine trees. Spring is in jonquil yellow, white, and green. It shares a bath with Autumn and has a private balcony.

A few yards from the main house is a separate cottage called Rooms for All Seasons. Made of adobe with a sod roof, it contains two rooms, both with private baths. One has an Early American theme; the other is Early California style. They're done in hand-hewn cedar, redwood, and pine, and hold intriguing collections of furniture and artifacts.

Patricia and Melisande receive rave reviews for their gracious hospitality; the comfort of guests is their foremost concern. Without undue fanfare they make you feel welcome and at ease. They lend bicycles, place candies and fruit and fresh flowers in your room, and guide you to the hammock and croquet set. Their breakfast menu changes regularly. An example of one morning's meal is fresh orange juice, baked pears, orange and cheese pastry, pumpkin muffins, cheese soufflé, and excellent coffee and teas.

No other meals are served, but the innkeepers will refer you to area restaurants.

JACKSON

Gate House Inn

1330 Jackson Gate Road
Jackson, CA 95642
209-223-3500

A Victorian in gold country

Proprietors: Bev and Stan Smith. **Accommodations:** 4 rooms (all with private bath) and Summerhouse. **Rates:** \$80–\$115 single, \$85–\$120 double, \$20 additional person. **Included:** Full breakfast. **Minimum stay:** 2 nights on weekends. **Payment:** Major credit cards. **Children:** Over age 12 welcome. **Pets:** Not allowed. **Smoking:** Not allowed indoors.

On an acre of sloping land that blooms with a thousand daffodils in spring, this turn-of-the-century Victorian home stands in quiet seclusion in the heart of the gold country. It was built by the son of one of Jackson's earliest settlers, A. Chichizola, a merchant and rancher, and today looks much as it did when it was new.

Parquet flooring, Oriental carpets, antique furnishings, and a leaded and stained glass window retain the home's period atmosphere. Blue velvet settees and a French rosewood table grace the parlor.

The single guest room on the main floor has a brass bed, a marble-topped sideboard, and, in the bathroom, the home's original lion-foot tub. Upstairs, the Brass Room features

Louis XVI walnut furniture, while the Master Suite boasts an Italian tile fireplace. It's the only room with a hall bath, just a couple of steps away.

Woodhaven, at the top of the stairs and under the eaves, has a country atmosphere with pine furnishings, a braided rug, and a brass bed. There's a half bath on one side of the room and a clawfoot tub on the other. Windows with lace curtains overlook the lushly flowered garden. Woodhaven has a sitting room and can accommodate an extra adult; the inn has no cribs for young children.

Jackson is close to all the diversions Amador County offers: wineries, golf courses, historic gold-mining towns, and the Indian Grinding Rocks State Historic Park. Gate House is within walking distance of several restaurants. Teresa's, with good Tuscan food and a lively atmosphere, is popular with residents and visitors alike.

Next to the garden is a screened area with table tennis and a barbecue. Brick-walled flowerbeds and rosebushes edge a path leading to a secluded swimming pool.

A favorite among returning guests is Summerhouse, a cottage by the back gate and arbor. Built as the caretaker's residence, it has an antique wooden headboard, air conditioning, and a woodstove on a brick hearth. There's a whirlpool tub for two in the bathroom.

Guests can choose whether to have breakfast in their rooms or in the dining room at a single table set with fresh flowers and English china. The menu varies; among the Gate House specialties are baked omelettes and apple-nut muffins. Guests have the use of the kitchen refrigerator and complimentary soft drinks.

The Wedgewood Inn

11941 Narcissus Road
Jackson, CA 95642
209-296-4300
800-933-4393

A gracious country home

Innkeepers: Jeannine and Vic Beltz.
Accommodations: 6 rooms (all with private bath). **Rates:** $85–$130 double, $10 less for single. **Included:** Full breakfast. **Payment:** MasterCard, Visa. **Children:** Welcome. **Pets:** Not allowed. **Smoking:** Not allowed indoors.

If you had saved all those toys that are now collector's items, along with your parents' and grandparents' heirlooms, you too could furnish a home like the Wedgewood. Items the Beltzes have saved and antiques they've collected fill the rooms of their gracious Victorian replica, a blue frame house in the country, six miles east of Jackson, off Highway 88. Both Vic and Jeannine have an artistic flair that is evident in the stained glass, needlework, and lace lampshades on display throughout the inn.

They're gardeners, too, and have landscaped the grounds in an English country style, with flowerbeds, a rose arbor, a gazebo, and fountains.

Pendulum clocks tick in the quiet parlor, where there's a woodstove and a baby grand piano. In the dining room beyond, guests gather for breakfast — a memorable meal of several courses. Baked apples, spiced pears, quiche, and blueberry-sour cream coffee cake are a few of the dishes served. Afternoon refreshments and early morning coffee are also provided.

With the Wedgewood as your headquarters, you can explore the gold country, shop for antiques, and tour museums. Back at the inn, you can play croquet or horseshoes or relax in the hammock under the oak trees.

The Wedgewood is a comfortable home operated by kindly people with traditional values. They set out Christian books and say grace at breakfast. If this is not to your liking, you may not feel at ease, though the innkeepers handle the issue with tact and do not push their beliefs.

The upstairs guest rooms are spacious and have views of the garden and oak grove or the wooded hills. Victorian Rose is the most popular, with its wood-burning stove, carved English bedroom set, walnut table, and tapestry chairs. It has a balcony (shared with Wedgewood Cameo) overlooking the rose arbor. Heritage Oak holds a four-poster and tapestry rocker, and Country Pine, in green and peach, features an iron scroll bed and carved armoire. On the third floor is Granny's Attic, a light, airy room with a four-poster bed and a skylight.

The Carriage House, a separate cottage, is a two-room suite with a private patio and a canopy bed.

JAMESTOWN

The National Hotel

P.O. Box 502
Main Street
Jamestown, CA 95327
209-984-3446

A historic hotel in a picturesque gold-mining town

Proprietor: Steven Willey. **Accommodations:** 11 rooms (5 with private bath). **Rates:** $65–$80 double; midweek discounts available. **Included:** Continental breakfast. **Payment:** Major credit cards. **Children:** Welcome, except on weekends. **Pets:** Allowed by prior arrangement. **Smoking:** Discouraged.

Fortunately for those who love the past, progress has bypassed Jamestown. Because it looks much as it did in the 1870s, the well-preserved gold-mining town has been used as a background for such movies as *High Noon* and *Butch Cassidy and the Sundance Kid,* and for the television series *Little House on the Prairie.*

If you've caught gold fever and hanker for a real nugget, you may find one in August during Gold Nugget Days. Clues, sold for a dollar each, lead modern argonauts to nuggets hidden around town.

Some two and a half hours east of San Francisco and just south of Sonora, Jamestown is considered the gateway to the Mother Lode. Tourists love its antiques shops and the classic brick and gingerbread Emporium. One of the most historically significant buildings in Jamestown is the National Hotel, which has been open continuously since 1859. Today, as in the past, it offers comfortable accommodations, good food, and a convivial atmosphere.

Many a bag of gold dust has changed hands over the redwood bar in the saloon, where guests register. It's a casual, friendly spot, with a bartender who serves concoctions with such labels as Lynchburg Lemonade and Snakebite as well as more usual drinks. The guest rooms, up carpeted stairs, are furnished in country antiques with handmade patchwork quilts and lace curtains. "They're simple because that's the way they were in the 1800s in the gold country," says the congenial innkeeper.

Steve Willey and his brother have owned the hotel since 1974 and have been instrumental in helping Jamestown turn from slow decay to a revitalized community. They were careful in restoring the National to keep it authentic — except for the plumbing. Now all the rooms contain washbasins and five have spotlessly clean private baths. The others share two baths down the hall.

The doors to rooms that are not occupied are open, so you can peek in and select your favorite. A typical example has a brass bed with a handmade quilt, lace curtains, pegs to hold hanging items, and fresh flowers. Some rooms overlook the courtyard and masses of vines; you can reach out the window and pluck a handful of grapes.

In the downstairs dining room a buffet breakfast is set out for guests: fruit, coffee, juice, boiled eggs, and fresh breads. Victorian relics — white kid boots, a doll, long gowns — are on display here. The restaurant's meals are excellent, with a different special daily and more than 80 wines from regional wineries available. Champagne brunch, lunch, and dinner are served. In the summer, you can eat outside under the grape arbor, at white tables shaded by lattices covered with the green vines of Virginia creeper.

Television does not fit the hotel's motif (though it will be provided upon request). Jigsaw puzzles, chess, checkers, and bragging at the bar are activities more in tune with the times. Jamestown also offers other forms of entertainment. You can shop for antiques, see stagecoach robberies enacted, pan for gold, ride a steam train, and, in June, attend the widely acclaimed Dixieland Jazz Festival.

KIRKWOOD

Caples Lake Resort

P.O. Box 8
Kirkwood, CA 95646
209-258-8888

A lodge and cabins at the edge of a lake

Proprietors: John Voss and sons JT, Bob, Joe, and Mike. **Accommodations:** 7 lodge rooms (with shared baths), 7 cabins. **Rates:** \$35–\$75 for 1–3 people in lodge, \$75–\$120 for 1–6 people in cabins. **Minimum stay:** 5 nights in cabins, 2 nights in lodge in July and August (policy is flexible). **Payment:** MasterCard, Visa. **Children:** Welcome. **Pets:** Not allowed. **Smoking:** Not allowed.

On the shore of a small, peaceful lake 30 miles south of Lake Tahoe, this rustic resort offers comfortable accommodations, good food, and friendly hospitality in the High Sierra. Caples

Lake is just west of Carson Pass, at a 7,800-foot elevation against a rugged range of mountains that soar to 10,000 feet.

Although it's been painted and given new curtains and colors, the lodge doesn't look like much from the road — a simple building behind a parking lot. The most modern thing about it is the phone booth on the broad, uneven front deck. But inside you'll find an admirable restaurant and guest rooms with new, queen-size beds. The windows overlook the one-square-mile lake, and forested slopes and snow-tipped peaks beyond.

Hiking in the High Sierra is an incomparable wilderness experience. Trails wind through canyons and meadows, around towering peaks, and across cold rushing streams. If you follow the clearly marked Emigrant Trail, you will walk in the footsteps of early pioneers.

Caples Lake Resort was built in the late 1940s and bought by the Voss family in 1982. The Vosses have been gradually remodeling since then. In the small, rough-hewn dining room, fresh flowers stand on tables made of log rounds. Classical music plays while diners feast on fresh seafood and pastas, steaks, and chicken. Labels of empty wine bottles lining the window sills indicate the range of wines former guests have enjoyed. Top off your dinner with homemade cheesecake, and you'll wonder if you really are in the wilderness.

Also on the main floor of the lodge is a lounge where, in the winter, guests like to warm their toes by a crackling blaze in the stone fireplace. The guest rooms upstairs are small but adequate. Room R5 is a good choice for picturesque lake and mountain views. All the lodge rooms share two remodeled bathrooms with showers.

Weathered cabins with pitched roofs stand on granite slopes a few yards from the lodge. All the cabins have kitchens, bedding, wall heaters, and barbecues. Number 2 is the largest and has a private deck under the trees. Number 5 features paneled walls, an old-fashioned kitchen with a gas stove, and a fine lake view. Number 3 has a sheltered wooden porch, knotty pine wainscoting, and a corner nook in the kitchen.

All the lodgings are clean and well-maintained, if a bit

worn at the edges, as you'd expect in the mountains. Rates vary according to the season, the length of stay, and the number of people in a room.

Behind the lodge is a sauna at water's edge and a small marina and launch facility. Here you may rent motorboats and canoes. You can fish in the stocked lake and in other small lakes and snow-fed streams in the back country, within hiking distance.

Horseback riding is offered by a nearby stable. Pack trips can be arranged for treks into the backcountry. Grover State Park hot springs are 28 miles away, and whitewater rafting is available on the Carson River. In winter, at the nearby Kirkwood ski area, you can glide over 75 kilometers of groomed cross-country tracks, through open bowls and pine forests. For downhill skiers there are 11 lifts and more than 55 runs, starting at a base of 7,800 feet. The mountains of the Sierra Nevada rise above Kirkwood to Thimble Peak's height of 9,876 feet.

MAMMOTH LAKES

Alpers' Owens River Ranch

Route 1, Box 232
Mammoth Lakes, CA 93546
619-648-7334
or 648-7243 (summer)
619-873-3466 or 647-6652 (winter)

A rustic, historic ranch in the Sierras

Innkeeper: Alice Alpers. **Accommodations:** 9 cottages (all with private bath). **Rates:** $35 per person. **Minimum stay:** 2 nights. **Payment:** No credit cards. **Children:** Under age 5 free; under age 14 half-price. **Pets:** Not allowed. **Smoking:** Allowed. **Open:** Late April through October.

The spring-fed waters of the upper Owens River, in the eastern Sierra Nevada range near Mammoth Lakes, create an ideal spawning ground for trout. Along a two-mile stretch of the river, the Alpers family offers an opportunity to fly-fish for the rainbows and German browns. There's also a trout pond for fishing in float tubes.

Their ranch has been in the family since 1905, when Alice's father-in-law, Fred Alpers, bought the property from the original homesteader. The original cabin, dating from the 1860s, still stands.

When you want a break from fishing, you can hike the trails that offer breathtaking views of the Sierra Nevada and White Mountain ranges, tour the fish hatchery, go on a photography expedition, or simply relax in the peace and quiet. If you tire of cooking meals, Mammoth Lakes, a resort town 12 miles away, has several good restaurants.

The riverside ranch occupies 225 acres of lush, irrigated meadowland in one of the largest Jeffrey pine forests in North America. It was used as a cattle ranch until 1920, when guest accommodations were added. Alice first visited the area in that year, and has lived on the ranch since 1935. Ask her for a story and she'll share her prodigious knowledge of local history. You're likely to find her in the picturesque log lodge.

The pine log cabins are rustic but comfortable. Electricity, generated by water wheel, is used only for electric lights. There is no television, and you do your own cooking. Each cabin has a woodstove, a deck, and a screened porch.

Three cabins are suitable for two or three people, five will accommodate four to six, and one is large enough for a bigger group. It has a good-size kitchen and two baths. The ranch welcomes clubs and groups.

Word of mouth brings guests to Alpers' Owens River Ranch, and it has become a tradition for many families to return year after year. Children enjoy the Huck Finn angling in Alpers Creek, which is stocked with trout from the ranch's hatchery. There are also swings and a tetherball to keep the youngsters happy.

When they're old enough, they join the adults in the resort's main attraction: fly-fishing. Beyond the two-fish limit, all fishing is catch-and-release. A fishing guide service is available.

Edelweiss Lodge

P.O. Box 658
Mammoth Lakes, CA 93546
619-934-2445

A chalet-style inn with a quiet atmosphere

Innkeepers: Duffy and Diane Wright. **Accommodations:** 9 units (all with private bath). **Rates:** $90–$140 in winter, $60–$110 in summer (2 to 6 people), $10 additional person. **Minimum stay:** 2 nights on weekends. **Payment:** Major credit cards. **Children:** Under age 5 free. **Pets:** Not allowed. **Smoking:** Nonsmoking rooms available.

Mammoth Lakes, on the slopes of Mammoth Mountain in the High Sierras, is a resort town that draws vacationers all year. In summer its environs offer great hiking, sailing, fishing, and canoeing. But ski season, from November to June, is really special. And Edelweiss is one of the places where skiers like to stay.

Forest green shutters with heart cut-outs and carved porch railings decorate the alpine chalets, which cover three-quarters of an acre south of town. The personable owners, who came from the Bay Area and took over the lodge in 1987, offer clean, roomy, one- and two-bedroom accommodations with equipped kitchens. A typical unit in a two-story building has honey-colored walls of knotty pine, a vaulted ceiling with hand-hewn beams, and a twin bed tucked into an alcove in the living room. Café curtains hang at the kitchen window, and there's a television set (complete with HBO) on the counter. A few rooms have stone fireplaces, others feature woodstoves, both have ample quantities of wood supplied. Area artists painted the landscapes on the walls.

After a day of skiing in crystal air, under an intense blue sky, you can luxuriate in the cedar and tile whirlpool spa at Edelweiss. Sign up to reserve a time and you'll have it all to yourself.

At Edelweiss you can go cross-country skiing from your door. For downhill skiers, a short drive or shuttle bus ride takes you to Mammoth's 39 chairlifts and groomed slopes of powdery snow.

The lodge offers quiet relaxation under the pine trees. It's not the place to stay if you're looking for the lights, music, and action some mountain resorts provide. Duffy Wright says, "What I like best about running this place is seeing guests who arrive tired and tense leave a few days later relaxed and happy. Some people never leave their cabin. They just sit and read or look out the window and rest."

Mammoth Mountain Inn

P.O. Box 353
Mammoth Lakes, CA 93546
619-934-2581
800-228-4947 in California
Fax 619-934-0700

A mountainside resort for all seasons

General manager: Tom Smith. **Accommodations:** 214 rooms. **Rates:** $69–$145 2-13 people in summer, $80–$265 winter weekdays, $95–$325 winter weekends and holidays. **Payment:** Major credit cards. **Children:** Welcome. **Pets:** Not allowed. **Smoking:** Allowed.

Mammoth Mountain, in the eastern High Sierra south of Yosemite National Park, is one of the major ski areas in the country, drawing thousands yearly to its 3,000 acres of skiable terrain. On its broad slope, a short drive from the resort village of Mammoth Lakes, stands Mammoth Mountain Inn, the only full-service hotel in the eastern Sierra.

The redwood inn's exterior, with its steeply pitched roof and balconies with flags snapping in the wind, resembles a large mountain chalet. Inside, a stone fireplace rises to the loft lounge, where another fireplace offers warmth on winter evenings.

Guest rooms in the main lodge have two double or queen-size beds. Portable cribs are available. The furnishings are comfortable and modern, with television, phones, plenty of closet space, and a balcony filled with flowers in summer. Some rooms view the 11,035-foot mountain; others, the parking lot.

In the motel annex, rooms and suites range from a studio that accommodates two to a two-bedroom unit with a loft that sleeps thirteen. Several have kitchenettes, dining tables, and sitting areas. Preferred for mountain views are the corner rooms (515, 516, 617, or 717) and the executive suite, number 600. The best buy is a studio with a kitchenette. The resort has undercover parking, laundry facilities, and whirlpools.

Drive up to Minaret Vista to see sensational views of the 13,000-foot Ritter Range and the Ansel Adams Wilderness. Devil's Postpile National Monument, east of Mammoth, is well worth a visit. This 60-foot wall of symmetrical basalt columns is a geological wonder.

At the Mountainside Grill, the main restaurant, try the homemade soups, the teriyaki chicken, and the chef's special prawn dish. There's nothing rustic in this mountain retreat — you may choose to sip a good California wine while listening to Chopin. The other restaurant, Yodler, is casual and resembles a Swiss chalet.

You may rent skis and buy lift tickets at the lodge across the road from the inn or at the lobby desk if you've purchased a room-and-ski package. The slopes are just out the door. Mammoth has 31 lifts, 150 trails, and 30,000 vertical feet of ski runs. You can also cross-country ski, go wind-skiing on the open meadows, and skate on Convict Lake.

Skiers flock to Mammoth Lakes in winter, but the area is a fine summer destination as well. It has cool mountain air, dozens of clear alpine lakes, miles of backcountry trails, and good fishing. To encourage summer visitors, Mammoth Mountain Inn offers mountain biking, fly-fishing, horseback riding, and hiking packages, among others. Mammoth is only 35 miles south of the Tioga Pass entrance to Yosemite National Park, so Yosemite tours are popular.

The inn also offers gondola rides to the summit, outdoor barbecues, a play area for children, and child care.

Tamarack Lodge Resort

P.O. Box 69
Mammoth Lakes, CA 93546
619-934-2442
800-237-6879 in southern California

A lakeside wilderness resort in the High Sierra

Proprietors: Carol and David Watson. **Accommodations:** 12 rooms (5 with private bath), 1 suite, 25 cabins. **Rates:** $60–$160 in rooms, $85–$300 for 1–11 persons in cabins; rates vary according to number of people and season. **Minimum stay:** 2 nights on weekends, 4 or 5 nights summer and holidays. **Payment:** Major credit cards. **Children:** Infants free. **Pets:** Not allowed. **Smoking:** Not allowed indoors.

You know you're in wild country when the sign on your cottage wall reads, "Bears dwell here. Do not leave food on your porch or near windows." On the other hand, the restaurant a few steps from your door serves beef Wellington, rack of lamb, eggplant parmigiana, and the latest in colorful pasta dishes.

Tamarack Lodge is located on the shore of the Twin Lakes, the last and lowest of the Mammoth Lakes group, which lie in an immense glacial basin scooped out of the eastern High Sierra. Here in the woods, three miles from the resort town of Mammoth Lakes, the lodge was built in 1924 by the Foy family of Los Angeles. (The family later gained fame from the Bob Hope movie, *The Seven Little Foys.*) It had expanded into a full cross-country ski resort by the time the Watsons took over in 1986. They retained the rustic quality but have been making improvements over time.

The lakes teem with native brown trout, brooks, and native and stocked rainbows, offering some of the best fishing in the eastern Sierra. At the lodge they'll give you maps and information on obtaining day packs, rowboats, and canoes. They will also pack you a lunch to take along.

Entering the lodge, you find a pine parlor where kerosene lamps stand on the mantel of the stone fireplace. A log table holds coffee and snacks available for purchase. It's a cozy scene in winter, when skiers come in to a hot lunch and mulled wine and cider by the fire.

The guest rooms on one side of the hall upstairs view the forest and cabins, and those on the other overlook the lakes and mountain peaks. The decor is simple but comfortable, with white curtains and baskets of dried flowers. Top of the Lodge, a two-bedroom suite, has great views of the lakes and mountain ridges. It has a living room, a dining area, and a small kitchen.

The housekeeping cabins are clustered under pines and aspens on six wooded acres. They all have carpeting, linens, and kitchens, and a few have fireplaces. There is no daily maid service in the cabins but you can pick up fresh towels at the lodge; weekly cleaning is provided for extended stays.

After a day of skiing or hiking, you may not want to cook. Lakefront Restaurant, at the south end of the lodge, is the only other choice; fortunately, it's excellent. It serves California cuisine and California wines. Breakfast is also available.

The resort rents ski equipment, offers private and group lessons, and grooms 25 miles of cross-country trails. You can ski right from your door. The variety of terrain and beautiful forest and mountain views provide plenty of winter interest. In summer, boating, hiking, fishing, and mountain biking are favorite activities. Miles of trails lead to Mammoth Mountain and its pass and crest, Coldwater Canyon, and spectacular Cascade Canyon. A day's hike to the west takes you to Red's Meadow and Devil's Postpile National Monument.

MURPHYS

Dunbar House, 1880

P.O. Box 1375
271 Jones Street
Murphys, CA 95247
209-728-2897

An inviting B&B in a historic gold-mining town

Innkeepers: Barbara and Bob Costa. **Accommodations:** 4 rooms (all with private bath). **Rates:** $105–$145. **Included:** Full breakfast. **Minimum stay:** 2 nights on weekends. **Payment:** MasterCard, Visa. **Children:** Not appropriate. **Pets:** Not allowed. **Smoking:** Not allowed.

Murphys is a quiet little town now, drowsing in the Sierra sun, but in 1850 it bustled with action as prospectors and miners rushed in, lured by gold. Over a ten-year period, Wells Fargo shipped more than $15 million in gold dust from the Murphys office. Meanwhile, settlers looking for more than quick riches moved in.

In 1880, Willis Dunbar built an Italianate home for his bride, Ellen Roberts of Douglas Flat. A citizen of substance, he was the superintendent of the local water company, a member of the state assembly, and the head of a ranch and a lumber company. Willis and Ellen raised five sons in their big country home.

A century later, the Dunbar home became Calaveras County's first bed-and-breakfast, and in 1987 Barbara and Bob Costa took it over. They welcome guests looking for pleasant, homey accommodations with character and history. This is the sort of place where you sit in wicker chairs on the porch and sip lemonade on summer afternoons, while bees hum in the old-fashioned flower garden.

The roomy parlor is decorated in English chintz. Lace and flowers and turn-of-the-century photographs fill the house, but it's not overly fussy and the furnishings aren't all antiques. "This is our home," says Barbara. "We enjoy sharing it and we treat guests as new friends."

The innkeeper likes to serve breakfast by candlelight in the dining room or outside at white wrought-iron tables. You can also have breakfast in your room. Some of Barbara's best dishes are crab and cheese delight, peach or cherry turnovers, fresh fruit with Grand Marnier sauce, and a sweet fruit spritzer. She provides appetizers in the afternoon and homemade chocolates in the evening. Each guest receives a complimentary bottle of locally produced wine.

> **Crowds come to Murphys and the surrounding area in fall to see the brilliant foliage against dark green pine trees. Murphys boasts six wineries, tennis courts, a community swimming pool, and three nearby golf courses. It's a short drive from the village to Mercer Caverns, Moaning Caves, and Calaveras Big Trees State Park, where ancient sequoias grow.**

All the guest rooms have woodstoves, refrigerators, and TVs with VCRs. In the Sequoia Room on the ground floor you can watch the birds bathe while you do the same; the clawfoot tub, screened from the bed, stands by a window overlooking the back lawn and birdbath. The bed has a lushly flowered comforter and ruffled pillows; bouquets of dried flowers hang on the wall above. By the door, a pair of high laced boots look as if they've just been left by their owner. Space for hanging clothes is limited. A basket of lemon drops, a painted globe lamp, delicate doilies, and windows overlooking the wraparound porch and white picket fence are touches that give the inn distinction and charm.

The Cedar Room, off the dining area, is a suite with a sitting area, a two-person Jacuzzi, and a sun room overlooking the back lawn and flowers. Champagne is served to guests who stay in the suite. Ponderosa, at the front of the house, is light and sunny in yellow. Sugar Pine faces the side yard. In addition to a clawfoot tub painted with flowers, it has a separate shower and sizable dressing area.

The Costas' love of gardening shows in their landscaped half acre. Lilac and crape myrtle bloom in the front yard, elm trees line the fence, and baskets of blooms provide color on the veranda.

NEVADA CITY

Grandmere's Bed & Breakfast Inn

449 Broad Street
Nevada City, CA 95959
916-265-4660

A stylish B&B in a restored historic town

Innkeepers: Geri and Douglas Boka. **Accommodations:** 7 rooms (all with private baths). **Rates:** \$100–\$150 single or double, \$20 additional person. **Included:** Full breakfast. **Payment:** MasterCard, Visa. **Children:** Welcome. **Pets:** Not allowed. **Smoking:** Not allowed.

It was in Nevada City in 1859 that a bit of blue clay brought in to the assayer's office set off the silver mining rush to the Comstock Lode. Ott's Assay Office still stands, along with other historic structures, in a town that carefully preserves its past.

The A.A. Sargent residence, built in 1856 by the owner of the first newspaper in Nevada County, is one of these historic buildings. Sargent was also a miner, lawyer, and U.S. senator. His wife, Ellen Clark, was an influential suffragist. In 1985 the Sargent home became Grandmere's.

Behind a black wrought-iron fence, the white house with

dark trim has an open veranda with inviting wicker chairs. The interior is equally welcoming, with a clean and stylishly simple decor.

The guest rooms all have queen-size beds and pine chests painted with flower designs by the home's former owner. The Master Suite boasts a private sun porch with a sofa sleeper overlooking the back garden. Danny's Room has a country atmosphere, with a bed of peeled pole pine, louvered shutters, and wicker chairs. Maggie's Room contains a four-poster bed with a patchwork quilt. The roomy bath has a shower stall, and there's plenty of space in the armoire for hanging up clothes. Mama & Papa's Room is in the corner, where the balcony wraps around the house. Spacious and dignified, it has a dark four-poster with puffy pillows on its floral quilt, a sofa bed, wingback chairs, and a little writing table in an alcove.

Nevada City offers a cleaned-up view of a past era. When a freeway sliced the town in two, the citizens decided to turn their backs on it and bring history to life on either side. No trucks, no neon, no overhead wiring — nothing intrudes on the quaint mood. Gaslights cast an old-fashioned glow on twisting streets of cobblestone, and almost every shopfront has a romantic story.

If you're traveling with a child, your best choice is Gertie's Room, which has a private garden entrance. Once the billiards room, it's now a light, bright suite with white wicker furnishings. The suite accommodates four and has a small kitchen with a sink, refrigerator, and microwave oven. All other rooms have air conditioning, but this one stays cool naturally.

Outside the door, fragrant wisteria climbs above the umbrella tables on the patio. Early in the morning, guests like to choose a mug in the dining room, help themselves to coffee, and wander out to the patio and garden. Here they stroll among the lilacs, redwoods, and spruce trees along daisy-edged paths until breakfast is ready.

Fruit, juice, spinach quiche, potatoes with cheese, croissants, and bread pudding are a few of Grandmere's morning options. Coffee and tea are available during the day, and the cookie jar is always full.

Nevada City has several excellent restaurants, among them is The Creekside, which offers patio dining along Deer Creek.

Red Castle Inn

109 Prospect Street
Nevada City, CA 95959
916-265-5135

> *An elaborate hillside mansion overlooking a gold-country town*

Innkeepers: Mary Louise and Conley Weaver. **Accommodations:** 7 rooms (all with private bath). **Rates:** $70–$140 double, $20 additional person. **Included:** Full breakfast. **Payment:** Mastercard, Visa. **Children:** Young children not appropriate. **Pets:** Not allowed. **Smoking:** Not allowed indoors.

This mansion was built in 1860 for Judge John Williams, his wife, Abigail, and eleven children — four of their own and the rest taken in as orphans. Some say their nanny, a woman in gray, can still be glimpsed occasionally in the former children's quarters.

Even without a ghost the Red Castle is full of reminders of the past. It became an inn in 1963, after a major restoration effort. The current owners continue to put careful attention into creating a world far from the late 20th century. Mary

Louise has done extensive research and insists on authenticity in the period furnishings. "This is a mixture of 'what might have been' and whimsy," she says.

The Weavers collect Renaissance Revival furniture. In the parlor, an Oriental carpet covers the floor and a prism chandelier flickers light on gold walls. Wingback chairs, a pump organ with candle sconces, and a vase of peacock feathers set the Victorian tone. Afternoon tea is served, with spiced tea and cakes and pastries.

This red brick Gothic Revival mansion, dripping with gingerbread, has been a landmark in Nevada City for more than a century. Set high against Prospect Hill, it overlooks the little town that is a living museum of the gold rush era.

Breakfast is a buffet in the main foyer. You may help yourself to orange juice or berry flips, homemade breads, poached apples with cinnamon, quiche, granola, and coffee or tea. You can take your tray to the parlor, your room, or to the garden.

Each guest room has its own character. Forest View, a honeymoon favorite, is the only room on the lower floor, one flight down from the entrance. It has a small chandelier (complete with dimmer switch) inside the lacy folds of the bed's canopy, and a private entrance under old, gnarled grapevines. It also has private access to the balcony and garden.

The Rose Room has a pineapple four-poster, a prism chandelier above the bed, red velvet curtains, and tall French doors to the wraparound porch. It's a pretty room; however, the bathroom is small and the washbasin awkward to use. The Garden Room, also on the main level, is big and bright and has a canopy bed and a sitting area. One of its striking features is an antique hall tree of carved walnut.

It's a steep climb to the upstairs rooms, but some guests prefer these for their charm and decor. There are two suites on the third floor, and the entire fourth floor, formerly the judge's study, is now a two-bedroom suite with a sitting room. In this private enclave, nooks under the eaves have quaint arched windows at knee level.

Gravel paths wind down the hill, under a grove of trees, from the house to the road below. From there it's a few yards to the freeway overpass and the main historic part of town.

Here you'll find quaint shops, fine restaurants, and gold rush memorabilia in a preserved remnant of the Old West.

OLYMPIC VALLEY

Resort at Squaw Creek

P.O. Box 3333
400 Squaw Creek Road
Olympic Valley, CA 96146
916-583-6300
800-327-3353
Fax 916-581-5407

An all-purpose resort in a dramatic mountain setting

General manager: Robert Mc-Eleney. **Accommodations:** 405 rooms and suites. **Rates:** $165–$855 single or double, $25 additional person, rates vary seasonally. **Payment:** Major credit cards. **Children:** Under age 16 free in room with parents. **Pets:** Not allowed. **Smoking:** Nonsmoking rooms available.

In late 1990, this $100 million resort opened on 626 acres near Lake Tahoe. Year-round outdoor recreation is the main draw of the complex, which has a dramatic setting at the base of Squaw Valley's surrounding peaks.

In winter, skiers come for some of the nation's most challenging slopes. A triple lift links the resort with the Squaw Valley network of 32 lifts covering 8,300 acres of ski slopes. Groomed trails on the meadows and hillsides attract the cross-country skier. There's an ice skating pavilion, and you can take bell-jingling sleigh rides over the snow.

Golfers and tennis players take over in the summer. Squaw Creek has an eighteen-hole championship golf course designed by Robert Trent Jones, Jr. Its scenic, mountainous terrain includes wetlands, ponds, and a meandering creek. There are also putting greens, a practice range, and a pro shop.

Seven miles of walking and biking paths surround the golf course, while five miles of horseback riding trails continue through the meadows and into the hills. The resort has three swimming pools and spas in an aquatic center with a waterfall, and a fitness center featuring weight training equipment, an aerobics studio, massage rooms, and a beauty salon.

The casual Cascades restaurant, serving regional American foods and elaborate buffets, showcases a stone hearth as an open cooking area. You can eat on the balcony here, overlooking Squaw Peak. There's also a bistro with a deck that skiers appreciate for its easy access; a pub with video entertainment; and a French restaurant, Glissandi, for a more elegant mood.

Although it's surrounded by forest and mountains, the atmosphere here is more suburban country club than wilderness. In addition to a nine-story, glass-faced building with guest rooms, there are the main Plaza Building and a promenade of retail shops. The Plaza holds the fitness center, a 36,000-square-foot conference center, and three restaurants.

All the guest rooms, most of them suites, have views of the valley. They contain fine-quality cherrywood furniture and have such amenities as dimmer lights, two TVs (with movies available), coffeemakers, robes, and wet bars. The housekeeping department can fill almost any need. Express video checkout is another convenience.The lodge is popular with business groups for its 33,000 square feet of meeting space and up-to-date audiovisual equipment.

Squaw Valley Lodge

P.O. Box 2364
Olympic Valley, CA 96146
916-583-5500
800-922-9970
Fax 916-583-0326

A contemporary hotel in a skier's paradise

General manager: Art Takaki. **Accommodations:** 154 rooms. **Rates:** \$100–\$305 (rates vary by season and number of people). **Minimum stay:** 2 nights on weekends in ski season. **Payment:** Major credit cards. **Children:** Free in room with parents. **Pets:** Not allowed. **Smoking:** Nonsmoking rooms available.

In 1960 the eighth Winter Olympics was held in Squaw Valley, a wide bowl at the foot of Squaw Peak, west of Lake Tahoe. Today you can step out the door of the lodge and ski the expert runs where Olympians raced. The 32 lifts lead to slopes with challenges for every level of skill. Six mountain peaks, all overlooking Lake Tahoe, hold 8,300 acres of slopes. The highest is Squaw Peak, at 8,900 feet. The lodge is at an elevation of 6,200 feet.

The Squaw Valley beginners' area may be unrivaled in the world because of its location — on top of the mountain instead of the bottom. It's accessible by cable car or gondola, so you don't have to ski down. If you're more adventurous and prefer a wilderness experience on undeveloped slopes, you'll find vast areas have been left untouched.

The modern lodge is surrounded by pine trees and in summer by lawns and flowers. The rooms and condominiums overlook a protected terrace and free-form outdoor pool and whirlpool tub. Just off the terra cotta tile terrace is the fitness center, with a well-equipped weight room and three tile whirlpools. Potted palms and windows that view the snowy peaks make this one of the lodge's most attractive features.

The open lobby area has a touch of the Southwest in its decor, with desert colors, rough rocks as lamp bases, leather couches, framed weavings, and Indian paintings.

The rooms are in three buildings. Those in Buildings A and B are furnished in Scandinavian style; those in C have a southwestern decor. They all have pegs with copper troughs below for hanging wet clothing. A typical room has a waist-high partition dividing the bed from the sitting area, generous cupboard and drawer space, and a compact kitchenette with a microwave oven, stove, dishwasher, and refrigerator. Skis may be kept in your room or stored near the rental shop. You can have minor tune-ups done at the shop as well.

The Squaw Valley resort area has the facilities you would expect in a major resort. There are restaurants and delis and malls, a beer garden, a doctor's office, and a ski school.

More than 150 instructors staff the ski school, offering a wide variety of programs for all ages and abilities and several specialty clinics. Daycare for children is available. Squaw Valley makes an unusual guarantee: register (for a nominal fee) as a beginner, intermediate, or expert, and if the wait for lifts at your skill level is longer than ten minutes, you receive a full refund and ski free the rest of the day.

When the snows melt and wildflowers spring up in the meadows, the valley offers summer pleasures, such as hiking, bicycling, horseback riding, and fishing in mountain streams. You can swim and play tennis at the lodge.

Between mid-June and October, you can take the cable car to the 8,200 feet level for a stunning panorama of the High Sierra, and have lunch or Sunday brunch at Alexander's Bar & Grill on the mountaintop. Also at the top are a swimming lagoon and spa, mountain bike rentals, and ice skating.

SACRAMENTO

Abigail's

2120 G Street
Sacramento, CA 95816
916-441-5007

A city B&B with homey comforts

Innkeeper: Susanne Ventura. **Accommodations:** 5 rooms (all with private bath). **Rates:** $95–$135 single or double, $35 additional person. **Included:** Full breakfast. **Minimum stay:** 2 nights on some holidays. **Payment:** Major credit cards. **Chil-**

dren: By arrangement. **Pets:** Not allowed. **Smoking:** Not allowed indoors.

Homey hospitality is the special attraction of this Colonial Revival mansion near downtown Sacramento. Built in 1912, the big white house with teal trim has large rooms and is furnished with antiques, but it's Susanne Ventura's friendly personal service that makes the inn truly distinctive.

One of Susanne's thoughtful touches is the bulletin board near the front door where she posts notices of art gallery shows and other events in Sacramento. She and her husband, Ken, will recommend restaurants and make reservations for you. One highly recommended spot is Biba's, where classic northern Italian food is served in a cheerful, urban atmosphere.

Baskets of nuts and apples are set out for snacking, and a thermos of hot water and tins of cocoa and tea are on the antique English sideboard upstairs. Robes hang in the armoires. Every room has a phone and each bathroom contains a cabinet filled with toiletries. Susanne seems to have thought of everything a pampered bed-and-breakfast guest could want, including cats (Sabrina and Abigail).

Four of the guest rooms are on the second floor, and one is off the landing. The morning sun floods through eleven windows in the Solarium Room, which has its own balcony. Because its bathroom is across the hall, it is the least expensive.

The Uncle Albert Room looks as if it belongs to someone's kindly uncle, with books piled on the armoire, a wingback chair, and a secretary desk. The guest book in this room is full of interesting comments, most of them directed to Uncle Albert. In the dining room, Susanne serves a two-course breakfast that includes entrées such as stuffed French toast, pancakes, quiche, and fruit cobbler. She'll bring a Continental breakfast to your room if you prefer, but she encourages guests to get acquainted over the long table. Outside, there's a fenced patio and hot tub.

Amber House

1315 22nd Street
Sacramento, CA 95816
916-444-8085
800-755-6526
Fax 916-447-1548

A stately home in a central location

Owners: Michael Richardson and Jane Ramey. **Accommodations:** 9 rooms in 2 houses (all with private bath). **Rates:** \$80–\$195. **Included:** Full breakfast. **Payment:** Major credit cards. **Children:** Well-behaved children welcome. **Pets:** Not allowed. **Smoking:** Not allowed.

Only eight blocks from midtown Sacramento, the Capitol Building, and the Convention Center, Amber House is popular with business travelers, offering both easy access to the city and a relaxing retreat. It's in a residential neighborhood where elm trees line streets of turn-of-the-century homes.

If you're eating out, some good choices are Biba's for Italian food; Celestin's, with a Caribbean menu; and Harlow's, serving innovative California cuisine in a lively, art deco atmosphere.

The inn is actually two houses, side by side, with very different styles. The main house is a 1905 Craftsman home in rich brown, with the original woodwork intact. It has stained glass windows, antique furnishings, a fireplace in the living room, and a cozy den with books, games, and puzzles. Guests are welcome to plunk the banjo that rests in the corner, curl up on the window seat with a book, peruse restaurant menus, and sip sherry in the evenings.

This house is called the Poet's Refuge, with each room named for a poet and containing examples of the poet's work. Lord Byron, on the first floor, has a brass and white iron queen-size bed and a Jacuzzi for two in the bath.

Chaucer, in deep yellow and gold, is the smallest room. Emily Dickinson, though it has the most charm, is the least expensive — it has a double bed and the bath is detached (robes are provided). The room is light in white and blue, with many windows and wicker and iron furniture.

Next door is Artist's Retreat, a well-restored 1913 white stucco home with a Mediterranean look. The Monet room, with a garden atmosphere, lies behind beveled glass curtained in pastel fabric. Degas features ballet prints, a queen-size canopy bed, and a double-size Jacuzzi tub. Renoir, a semi-suite, also has a Jacuzzi for two. Van Gogh, the most expensive room, is a favorite for its sun-filled solarium bath that has a wicker chaise and a tub for two.

The innkeepers understand that visitors' hours vary — business travelers are early risers while vacationers like to sleep in — so breakfast is served at the hour you request it, any time from 7 A.M. to checkout. That's an example of their determination to meet guests' needs. "We'll accommodate in any way we can to make our guests' experience perfect," say the owners. That includes supplying silver and china if you wish to have dinner delivered to your room by a restaurant. Or you can dine on the veranda or in the dining room.

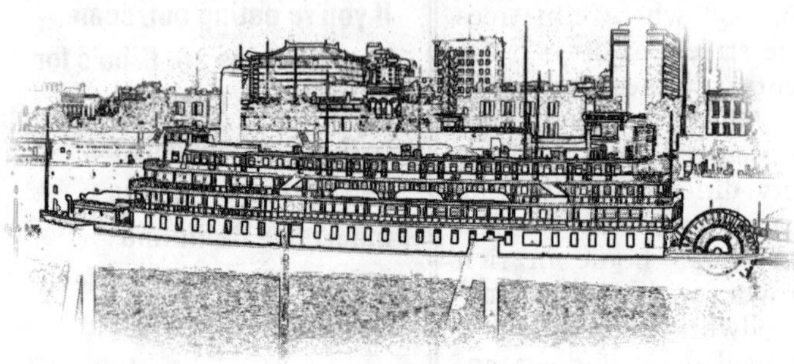

The Delta King Hotel

1000 Front Street
Sacramento, CA 95814
916-444-5464
800-825-5464
Fax 916-444-5314

An old-fashioned stern-wheeler on the Sacramento River

General manager: Charlie Coyne. **Accommodations:** 44 staterooms and suites. **Rates:** Staterooms $85–$125 single or double, suites $350–$400. **Included:** Expanded Continental breakfast.

Payment: Major credit cards. **Children:** Welcome. **Pets:** Not allowed. **Smoking:** Allowed.

If you yearn to return to the days when river travel reigned supreme, step aboard the historic *Delta King,* an authentic 1926 stern-wheel paddle steamer permanently moored along the waterfront of Old Sacramento.

The five-story, 285-foot-long paddle wheeler was built during the peak of the steam navigation period in the Sacramento Delta. Like its twin, the *Delta Queen* (now on the Mississippi River), the *Delta King* once plied the Sacramento from the capital to San Francisco. Although the riverboat was originally built for a then-staggering sum of $1 million, the restoration has cost more than $8 million.

Preserved as a 28-acre historic district, Old Sacramento includes the Sacramento History Center, a State Railroad Museum (the largest of its kind), an 1860s railroad station, and shops and restaurants. All are within easy walking distance of the gleaming white *Delta King.*

Now restored to its original condition, the King gleams with polished brass fittings and the patina of wooden paneling, window trim, doors, and benches. A carpeted grand staircase sweeping up from the main deck to the saloon level is back in place. At the top of the stairs is the mahogany-paneled Delta Lounge, featuring an oyster bar and decorated with stained glass scenes of the Sacramento River of yesteryear. The lower deck lounge, the Paddlewheel Saloon, offers dancing on weekends. The gigantic revolving paddle wheel can be seen through the glass-walled stern.

Even more luxurious and spacious than the originals, the staterooms and suites are furnished in period antiques and some of the baths have clawfoot tubs and pull-chain toilets. Other features such as air conditioning and tile showers have been added. The Captain's Quarters is a posh suite with a king-size bed, a wet bar, and a wheelhouse loft.

Morning fruit, juice, granola, yogurt, and pastries are served to overnight guests in the Pilothouse Restaurant. It also serves lunch, dinner, and a highly reputed Sunday brunch.

The 43,745-square-foot vessel contains a theater showing musical revues and other productions. Weddings can be performed on board, and an outdoor plank landing is next to the boat for receptions. Valet parking is available.

The last of California's original steam paddle wheelers, the *Delta King* is on the National Register of Historic Ships.

Hartley House

700 22nd Street
Sacramento, CA 95816
916-447-7829
800-831-5806

A bed-and-breakfast in a gracious Victorian home

Innkeepers: Margarita Banda and Michele Bowers. **Accommodations:** 5 rooms (all with private bath). **Rates:** $79–$125 single or double. **Included:** Full breakfast. **Payment:** Major credit cards. **Children:** Not appropriate. **Pets:** Not allowed. **Smoking:** Not allowed indoors.

This turn-of-the-century home is in a residential area but is close to downtown, the capitol, and the Convention Center. Built in 1906, the house was known for decades as Mrs. Murphy's Boarding House. Its character has been preserved in the original hardwood floors, dark woodwork, leaded and stained glass windows, and brass light fixtures converted from gas. Antique furniture and artworks were carefully selected to match the period decor, with modern comforts added to suit today's tastes.

Hartley House offers a Romance Package for $180. It includes candlelight, fresh flowers, and champagne or sparkling cider — you can keep the vase and wineglasses — chocolates, fruit, bath salts, and a massage.

The rooms have English place names. Brighton, once a sun porch, has a light and sunny aspect with twelve windows in three walls. Dover, the largest room, has a curved brass bed. The others are Canterbury, Southampton, and Stratford. Downstairs, the large living room has a four-window bay with a window seat and a fireplace. Couches provide comfortable seating for a game of chess or for lounging by the fire.

During the week, most guests are business and professional travelers who appreciate rooms with private phones, TV, and air conditioning, as well as fax capabilities. All the guests also like the lavish breakfasts. Michele, who loves to cook, says that "if you leave hungry it's your own fault." She prepares dishes such as strawberry French toast, Swiss eggs, and blueberry pancakes, served with fruit, muffins, juice, and coffee. Cookies are baked daily, lemonade is always available in the refrigerator, and brandy is set out at night.

The atmosphere here is a nice combination of casual fun and professional service. Robes are provided in the rooms, and after a day or so, many guests wear them to breakfast. At Christmas, visitors share cookies and eggnog while they help to decorate the house.

Radisson Hotel Sacramento

500 Leisure Lane
Sacramento, CA 95815
916-922-2020
800-333-3333

A comfortable family hotel on a lake

Manager: Richard Williams. **Accommodations:** 314 rooms and suites. **Rates:** \$84–\$104; suites \$184–\$368. **Payment:** Major credit cards. **Children:** Under age 18 free. **Pets:** Allowed. **Smoking:** Nonsmoking rooms available.

Close by the American River as it skirts the heart of Sacramento is this pleasant, pink stucco hotel with a red tile roof. Several features make the hotel exceptional, especially if you're traveling with children. It centers around a small lake, edged by a lawn and weeping willow trees; paddle boats are available for fun on the water. Bicycles can be rented for riding the comparatively flat roads, there's an outdoor swimming pool, and child care can be arranged. A well-designed, air-conditioned fitness room is open to adults only.

The three-tiered Palm Court Restaurant, overlooking the lake, serves three meals a day and a Sunday brunch. Next to it is the Lakeside lounge for cocktails, dancing, and live music.

The Fanfare Terrace offers live entertainment Thursday, Friday, and Saturday nights, featuring jazz, country, blues, and rock music. At one end of the lake is a gazebo, a popular place for weddings.

If you're in Sacramento in late summer, don't miss the state fair, a popular event for more than 100 years, with a midway, horse shows, and exhibits.

The guest rooms, all with patios or balconies, are in several two-story buildings. They have similar up-to-date furnishings and comforts, but some are rather motel-like and face the parking lot. Preferred rooms are on the second floor by the lake.

The Sterling Hotel

1300 H Street
Sacramento, CA 95814
916-448-1300

A sophisticated, historic hotel

Proprietors: Richard and Sandi Kann. **Accommodations:** 12 rooms. **Rates:** $95–$225 single or double, $15 additional person. **Payment:** Major credit cards. **Children:** Welcome. **Pets:** Not allowed. **Smoking:** Not allowed.

The Sterling is a small luxury hotel in central Sacramento. Its amenities and convenient downtown location — near the capitol, convention center, and county courthouse — make it a favorite of business and government travelers, while its elegance and style draw discriminating vacationers.

Among Sacramento's attractions are the lovely tree-shaded capitol grounds and the oldest public art museum in the west, Crocker Art Museum. Old Sacramento has a railroad museum, a reconstruction of Sutter's Fort, and more than 250 shops and restaurants.

The three-story, century-old Victorian structure was renovated in 1987, removing all vestiges of the apartment building it had been for fifty years. Now it has a gracious facade with a generous porch entry, a lobby with a marble floor, and a lounge where guests enjoy morning coffee. Oriental simplicity is emphasized by Japanese paintings and Chinese rugs. More ornate are the lobby mirror framed in painted birds and flowers and the filigreed brass chandelier hanging from the open loft.

There are no ruffles or fringes in this contemporary hotel, but touches of its origins may be seen in the molding detail, lace curtains, and paintings by old masters. The spacious guest rooms, on all three floors, have four-poster or canopy beds and Queen Anne furniture. The pink marble baths contain pedestal sinks with gleaming brass taps and oversize whirlpool tubs and showers enclosed by brass and glass.

On the hotel's lower level is an exquisite little restaurant, Chanterelle. It seats only forty people in three glass-partitioned rooms of restrained decor. The Continental cuisine is expensive but is considered some of the best in Sacramento. Fresh regional ingredients are used with traditional French techniques and California creativity. A specialty is veal with chanterelle mushrooms.

Next door is the Glass Garden, a conservatory imported from England. The 40-foot-long structure, with a glass roof in three graceful tiers, is used for receptions, parties, dances, and weddings.

Vizcaya

2019 21st Street
Sacramento, CA 95818
916-455-5243

An elegant home with both antiques and contemporary comforts

Innkeepers: Sandi and Richard Kann. **Accommodations:** 9 rooms (all with private bath). **Rates:** $95–$225 single or double. **Included:** Full breakfast. **Payment:** Major credit cards. **Children:** Welcome. **Pets:** Not allowed. **Smoking:** Not allowed indoors.

Formerly called the Driver Mansion Inn, Vizcaya is one of the classiest bed-and-breakfasts you'll encounter. Calico and teddy bears would definitely be out of place here. Stately antiques, thick carpeting, and fine art set the theme.

Pink, white, and red roses flank the pillared porch of the big house, which is set on a slope above a busy street. (You may park on the street, and there are a few parking spaces in back.) Traditional furniture faces a white brick fireplace in the parlor, where beverages are available, by request, in the afternoons.

Breakfast is served at glass-topped tables in the dining room (or in your room, for a $15 fee). Fresh fruit, juice, and excellent coffee are prepared along with Belgian waffles, French toast, quiche, or other main dishes.

The six guest rooms in the main house are all furnished with antiques or reproductions, desks, private phones, TV, and shirred white curtains at wide leaded glass windows. The baths are in modern white tile with glass and brass showers. The third floor penthouse includes a Jacuzzi. The three-room Carriage House is furnished with antiques and set in a garden of brick walks edged with impatiens and shaded by oak, crape myrtle, and persimmon trees. Each room has a Jacuzzi tub.

This bed-and-breakfast inn was once a private mansion owned by Philip Driver, a prominent attorney in the late 1800s. The mansion remained in the Driver family until 1977 and now is owned by the Kanns, who are also part-owners of the luxurious Sterling Hotel.

The *Sacramento Bee* is supplied, and Sandi will recommend restaurants and suggest sightseeing attractions if requested. With intuitive tact, she knows when to leave people alone. "I try to be available, but not hover," she says. "We offer hotel-type accommodations, but with a warmer, more personal atmosphere."

Vizcaya now offers space in an adjacent building for banquets and receptions for up to 450 people.

SIERRA CITY

Busch & Heringlake Country Inn

P.O. Box 68
Sierra City, CA 96125
916-862-1501

A mountain hide-away in a former mining town

Innkeeper: Carlo Giuffre. **Accommodations:** 4 rooms (all with private bath). **Rates:** $85–$110 single or double. **Included:** Full breakfast. **Payment:** MasterCard, Visa. **Children:** Welcome. **Pets:** Not allowed. **Smoking:** Not allowed.

Tucked away in the northern Sierra Nevada range, on the North Fork of the Yuba River, about an hour's drive north of Lake Tahoe, lies Sierra City, a little town of charm and historic interest. The area was opened to mining in the 1850s; saloons and churches and the Wells Fargo office inevitably followed.

Wells Fargo was housed in the Busch building, a three-story structure made of clay from a nearby brickyard in 1871. Western Union, a general store, and a third-floor dance hall were also in the building constructed by miner and entrepreneur A.C. Busch. Mr. Heringlake became his partner.

In 1986 Carlo Giuffre bought the red brick building, which had been deteriorating for years, and began the long restoration process. He spent two and a half years meticulously returning the place to its original status, creating a beautifully crafted inn that combines the old and the new.

On the ground floor is an Italian restaurant and a cozy conversation corner where hikers and skiers gather by the massive woodstove in the evenings. The stove, artfully made from an old boiler, railroad ties, and miners' picks, is a conversation piece in its own right.

In the summer the Kentucky Mine Museum is open for tours and there's a concert series in July and August. Winter offers Nordic skiing, ice-fishing, and relaxing by the flickering fire.

The guest rooms upstairs, named after historic mines, have wide plank floors and pine and cedar wainscoting and furniture. The Phoenix Room is a large, sunny space in a corner, with a fireplace in blue ceramic tile, a pineapple four-poster bed, a wet bar, and a whirlpool tub. In the Young America Room there is a brass bed and a whirlpool for two in the bath. Marguerite is a comfortable corner room with a double shower, while Lusk Meadow has a queen-size bed, armoire, and views of the mountains. A hearty American breakfast — including eggs, bacon, potatoes — is served in the restaurant.

The hotel is on Sierra City's main street, where the stagecoach used to stop. Across the road are private homes and shops. Ask the innkeeper about access to the river below and about hiking and mountain biking trails in the Lakes Basin area, a series of crystal clear mountain lakes. You can try gold-panning or fishing in the river, and there are good picnic spots along its banks.

SONORA

Llamahall Guest Ranch

18170 Wards Ferry Road
Sonora, CA 95370
209-532-7264

A modern home in a woodland setting

Innkeeper: Cindy Hall. **Accommodations:** 2 rooms (both with private bath). **Rates:** $95 double, $15 additional person. **Included:** Full breakfast. **Minimum stay:** 2 nights on holiday weekends. **Payment:** No credit cards. **Children:** Welcome. **Pets:** Not allowed. **Smoking:** Not allowed indoors.

At Llamahall Guest Ranch, visitors are welcome to feed the llamas and take them for walks on trails that wind through the woods down to Curtis Creek. Cindy is training the animals to pull carts and takes them to hospitals and convalescent homes to cheer patients.

But there's more to the ranch than llamas. You can hike to the Indian Grinding Rocks, swim in a nearby lake, fish at a local trout farm, pan for gold in the creek (Cindy lends placer pans), and romp with the dogs. Ride the Jamestown steam train, which runs on summer weekends, or, in winter, ski on the slopes at Ski Dodge Ridge, 40 minutes away. The ranch has an outdoor hot tub and sauna.

Indoors there are games and toys, a piano, drums, an autoharp, and a guitar that you may borrow for music fests. Cindy will pull out the television set if requested.

Her big, modern, redwood house is set against a hillside above the creek, under tall oak trees. It's quiet in this woodland scene, though it's just outside Sonora, about 120 miles east of San Francisco. The babbling of the creek and the rustle of oak leaves are the only sounds you hear.

"Llamas are lovable," says Cindy Hall, as one of the long-necked, woolly creatures nuzzles her shoulder. Twelve of them (occasionally more, since they're breeding pairs) live on this five-acre ranch in the gold country.

The comfortable, casual living room has a square grand piano, a stone fireplace, and windows that overlook the wooded hillside. A table is set for breakfast here, or you can sit at black wrought-iron tables on the wide deck. A fruit plate, muffins or coffee cake, fresh juice, and cereals are provided, along with eggs cooked however you like them.

The guest rooms, Flora and Fauna, are on the lower level. Each has a private Dutch door entrance. Flora is decorated with Victorian brambleberry wallpaper, and the ceiling border in Fauna is a frieze of deer and other forest creatures. Fauna has plum carpeting, a black iron bed with a trundle, a desk, and windows viewing the deck and trees. Children's books lie on the shelves. In the spacious bath are a clawfoot tub with ring shower, a pedestal sink, and a chain-pull toilet.

The refrigerator downstairs is stocked with soft drinks and iced tea, which you'll enjoy as you relax on the deck under a sky full of stars.

SOUTH LAKE TAHOE

Lakeland Village Beach & Ski Resort

P.O. Box 1356
3535 Highway 50
South Lake Tahoe, CA 96156
916-541-7711
800-822-5969
Fax 916-541-6278

A lakeside resort for year-round recreation

General manager: Patrick Ronana. **Accommodations:** 215 units. **Rates:** \$75–\$130 double in lodge, \$85–\$400 3–10 people in annex. **Minimum stay:** 2–4 nights in some rooms. **Payment:** Major credit cards. **Children:** Welcome. **Pets:** Not allowed. **Smoking:** Allowed.

The resort complex of Lakeland Village is on the southern shore of Lake Tahoe, facing a thousand feet of private sandy beach. Under tall pine trees, its 19 acres contain two swimming pools, two tennis courts, saunas, a spa, a lakeside clubhouse, and a boat dock.

Despite its proximity to Highway 50, location is the resort's major attraction. It borders the sapphire blue lake, Heavenly Valley ski area is a mile and a half away (a free shuttle is available), and the casinos of Nevada are one mile to the northeast.

More than twenty other ski areas surround the lake, many of them offering shuttle service. You can also ferry to the north shore on the Tahoe Queen paddle wheeler. Lakeland Village rents skis and equipment but does not offer ski storage; several rooms have porches that may be used for storage, however.

During the summer, you can rent paddleboats, play golf at five courses in the area, or throw a private party at the clubhouse. Tennis lessons are available and there are two swimming pools. Other recreation includes bicycling, hiking, fishing, windsurfing, rafting, and horseback riding.

The rooms in the three-story lodge range from studios with Murphy beds to one-bedroom suites; there are also privately owned two-story townhouses, which go up to four bedrooms with three baths. All the rooms have cable TV with HBO, equipped kitchens, fireplaces, and phones.

The townhouses, especially those on the waterfront, are recommended over the lodge rooms. Not only do they have enviable views and easy access to the beach, they're larger and better maintained. They are also farther from the highway. The furnishings in the lodge rooms are comfortable and functional, but they fall short of top-resort standards.

With up to 500 inches of snow and 300 days of sunshine annually, Tahoe's slopes are famous for magnificent scenery and challenging skiing. Heavenly Valley has a network of lifts to Tahoe's highest skiing, with a top elevation of 10,100 feet and a vertical drop of 3,600 feet. About half the ski area is devoted to intermediate slopes, with the other half divided between beginner and advanced runs.

The four-bedroom lakefront townhouses have a master bedroom with two beds and a vaulted ceiling that soars above two lofts, one with two bedrooms and the other set higher, with its windows overlooking the lake. Glass doors slide open to a deck right on the beach. Plenty of closet space, an entry where wet clothing can be hung to dry, and personal touches in books and artwork make this a homelike, all-purpose, family choice.

There's a coin-operated laundry on the property, and parking is free.

The Christiania Inn

P.O. Box 18298
3819 Saddle Road
South Lake Tahoe, CA 95706
916-544-7337
800-422-5754

A luxurious small inn near the ski slopes

Owners: Jerry and Maggie Mershon. **Accommodations:** 6 rooms (all with private bath). **Rates:** $85–$175 winter, $60–$125 summer, single or double, $25 additional person. **Included:** Continental breakfast. **Pay-**

ment: MasterCard, Visa. **Children:** Welcome. **Pets:** Not allowed. **Smoking:** Not allowed in dining room.

This trim, white and brown, chalet-style mountain lodge nestles among the pines at the 6,500-foot level south of Lake Tahoe, next to the Nevada border in the Heavenly Valley resort area. Just outside the front door, stretching up the face of a Sierra peak, are the snowy slopes of one of California's major ski centers. The lifts include an aerial tram, a detachable quad chair, six triple chairs, ten double chairs, four pomas, and five "mitey mites."

You can ski back and forth between two states on the broad, well-groomed runs that go as high as 10,100 feet. There are runs suitable for every skill level, from easy novice trails to Mott Canyon, for super experts.

There are hundreds of lodgings in South Lake Tahoe and Heavenly Valley; Christiania is one of the more luxurious, intimate, and convenient to the ski lifts. On the main floor is a dining room with an immense stone fireplace and windows overlooking the ski slopes. Burgundy carpeting and pink linens and candles make the restaurant a romantic setting for Continental cuisine.

Across the hall is a dimly lit après-ski lounge. Here you can perch at the bar and watch the big TV screen or relax on a low-slung couch before a blazing fire.

Each guest room has a highly individual decor. Four are suites with fireplaces. The Master Suite features a high loft containing a bed with mirrors above edged in blue lights. There are books on the shelves, potted palms, puffy pillows on a couch by the tile fireplace (firewood is supplied) and an alcove with windows facing the ski slopes. There is a television, a wet bar, refrigerator, and both a closet and an armoire. It's all a bit overdone, in California florid style, but it is impressive.

Room 5 is totally different. At the back of the inn, it looks out on tall pine trees. It has a fireplace and is furnished in a country fashion, in calico and raw pine. Room 3, also at the back of the building, resembles a residential apartment. It's carpeted in blue and has a fireplace, displays of seashells and butterflies, and many books and plants.

A breakfast of croissants, juice, and coffee or tea is brought to your room on a silver tray.

The inn has ski storage facilities but does not rent or sell equipment. The staff will direct you to nearby rental shops.

SUTTER CREEK

Sutter Creek Inn

P.O. Box 385
75 Main Street
Sutter Creek, CA 95685
209-267-5606

> *A gold-country B&B of character and charm*

Innkeeper: Jane Way. **Accommodations:** 18 rooms (all with private bath). **Rates:** $50–$115 single or double weekdays, $88–$135 weekends, $25 additional person. **Included:** Full breakfast. **Minimum stay:** 2 nights on weekends. **Payment:** No credit cards. **Children:** Under age 15 not appropriate on weekends. **Pets:** Not allowed. **Smoking:** Nonsmoking rooms available.

This historic home with a breezy, friendly atmosphere was one of the first bed-and-breakfasts in California. Jane Way fell in love with the place while touring the gold country with her children in the mid-1960s. Since that time she has continued to expand the inn, and it's now a sizable complex that has nevertheless retained its homey original character.

The Greek Revival structure, built in 1859, stands on Sutter Creek's main street (Highway 49, often heavy with traffic), behind attractive lawns and gardens. Some guest rooms are in the main house; others are tucked away in outbuildings by the grape arbor and terrace.

The Amador County Museum, Chaw Se Indian Grinding Rock State Historic Park, and the Kennedy Tailing Wheels are among the historic sights. You'll find more active recreation at Mace Meadows Golf Course, Kirkwood ski area, and on Mokelumne River and Amador and Camanche lakes.

Visitors are drawn irresistibly to the large living room, for Jane has filled it with comfortable couches and chairs, a spinet piano, games, magazines, a chess table set up for play, and many of her hundreds of books. A corner cabinet holds antique china, and a grandfather clock stands in dignity against one wall, faithfully sounding the Westminster chimes.

All the guest rooms have electric blankets and air conditioners. Many contain fireplaces, and some have swinging beds (which can be stabilized if you don't like the notion of gentle swaying all night long). There are three rooms in the main house. The Library Room has lots of books in addition to three beds and a small deck. The East Room is cheerful in sunny yellow, with a cozy alcove painted in stenciled designs. Traffic noise can be a problem. Fortunately a sound conditioner emits the soothing murmur of rain and surf to help block less welcome sounds.

The West Room has windows under the eaves. Its yellow bath, bright with flowers and stripes, is original. This was the first house in Sutter Creek to have an indoor bathroom. The Garden Cottage, behind the grape arbor, is fronted by a porch with wicker furniture; its interior is dark in natural woods. The Miner's Cabin and Cellar Room each have a fireplace.

The Carriage House is the most expensive accommodation, with a four-poster canopy bed, a brick fireplace, and two baths. One of the most romantic choices is The Loft, reached by climbing outside stairs past clematis vines winding up the branches of a tall Chinese elm. It has a four-poster bed, a vaulted beamed ceiling, and high windows above the gardens.

The menu for the country breakfast varies, but typical of Jane's morning choices are zucchini-walnut bread, Spanish omelettes, fresh fruit, coffee and tea. The personable innkeeper has a wide range of interests, most of them reflected in the book titles and items displayed in her inn. Handwriting analysis, reflexology, therapeutic massage, palm reading, and psychic experiences are often topics of conversation, for Jane also enjoys visiting with guests as time allows.

She and her assistants are happy to give visitors suggestions for day trips and points of interest.

The Foxes Bed and Breakfast Inn

P.O. Box 159
77 Main Street Sutter Creek,
CA 95685
209-267-5882

A luxurious bed-and-breakfast in the gold country

Innkeepers: Pete and Min Fox. **Accommodations:** 6 rooms (all with private bath). **Rates:** $95–$135 single, $100–$140 double. **Included:** Full breakfast. **Minimum stay:** 2 nights on weekends. **Payment:** Major credit cards. **Children:** Not appropriate. **Pets:** Not allowed. **Smoking:** Not allowed indoors.

Since the day the Foxes opened their gold-country bed-and-breakfast in 1980 with a single guest room, the inn has been praised as one of the best in California. Gracious hosts with a sure sense of visitors' needs, the innkeepers go out of their way to provide every comfort — and they make it seem easy, a rare skill in this demanding business. Their 1857 home is in the center of Sutter Creek, a pretty little town surrounded by hills studded with oak and pine trees. The town and the stream that runs through it were named for John Sutter, whose sawmill on the American River caught the sparkle of gold in 1848 and set off the great gold rush.

The innkeepers will direct you on sightseeing expeditions and make restaurant recommendations. Pick up a walking tour map of Sutter Creek and you'll learn some history and discover more of the town's charm as you stroll.

The Foxes, Pete and Min, moved up to Sutter Creek from southern California several years ago. They first became antiques dealers, then opened their home as a B&B and later expanded into the Carriage House in back. Now their inn is so well known for its consistent high quality that early reservations are a must.

Traffic noise from Highway 49 recedes when you enter the house, as the melodic strains of Chopin flood the foyer and parlor. Doors with etched glass panes lead to the parlor furnished with antiques. The windows overlook the front porch, its columns entwined with wisteria, and a yard filled with flowers and ferns.

You can have breakfast in the garden, but it's usually brought to your room on a silver tray, with items you've selected the night before: fresh juice, eggs as you like them or the house specialty of cream-poached eggs on an English muffin, fruit, and muffins and jam.

The guest rooms are air conditioned. The Honeymoon Suite, the only ground floor room in the main house, is the biggest and has a private entrance. Blue velvet wingback chairs face a brick fireplace; the bed has a partial canopy. The Victorian Suite, upstairs, was the Foxes' first bed-and-breakfast room. There's a handsome 9-foot headboard on the bed, a matching dresser, a gold velvet couch in the sitting area, and a small bath with a shower. The Anniversary Room features a carved headboard and a ten-foot mirrored armoire.

All three rooms in the Carriage House have private entrances and cable TV hidden behind armoire doors. The bay window in the Garden Room overlooks the garden, while Fox Den is cozy, with a library and wood-burning fireplace. The Blue Room has an extra-large bath and a carved bedstead with a partial canopy.

Among the amenities the Foxes provide are tape decks and tapes of restful music, the *Sacramento Bee* at your doorstep in the morning, plenty of storage space for clothes, covered parking, and elegant breakfast settings with linen napkins.

There's only one drawback here: Highway 49 runs through the middle of town, its cars and rumbling trucks more than a mild annoyance. The Foxes have installed storm windows, and some residents are hoping for a bypass, which would restore Sutter Creek's serenity.

TRUCKEE

Northstar at Tahoe

P.O. Box 2499
Truckee, CA 95734
916-562-1113
800-533-6787
Fax 916-587-0215

A family resort near Lake Tahoe

Reservations manager: Patrick Petrini. **Accommodations:** 235 units. **Rates:** $129–$585 1-10 people in winter, $99–$303 in summer (rates cover a range of accommodations, from standard hotel rooms to 3-4 bedroom homes). **Minimum stay:** 3 nights in winter, 2 nights in summer. **Payment:** Major credit cards. **Children:** Welcome. **Pets:** Not allowed. **Smoking:** Nonsmoking rooms available in hotel.

Skiing and snow play draw crowds to Northstar in winter, while summer's pleasures on the 2,500-acre resort six miles from Lake Tahoe include hiking, mountain biking, fishing, swimming in the pool, horseback riding, tennis, and golf.

The resort is ideal for family vacations because there's such a wide variety of recreation. Those who are too young for the ski slopes or tennis courts are happily ensconced in the Minors' Camp, a program for children ages two to six. Every day they sing, listen to stories, paint, take walks, and are given snacks and a hot lunch. If they're in the Ski Cubs program (age three and up) they receive a skiing lesson, too. In the summer, an experienced staff gives children ages two to ten tennis and swimming lessons and takes them horseback riding.

While the kids are busy, their parents are skiing on Mount Pluto and Lookout Mountain, which have 2,200 vertical feet of ski slopes. Lifts include a high-speed gondola, three express quad chairs, three triple chairs, and three double chairs.

With the expansion of downhill skiing facilities, Northstar has opened the Summit Deck & Grille at the top of Mount Pluto. The restaurant offers Mexican food and microbrewery beers.

Cross-country and telemark skiing lessons are available. There are 45 kilometers of groomed trails near the lodge.

In summer, golf packages, including two- and five-day tennis camps, are a good value. The eighteen-hole, par 72 course has water hazards on fourteen holes, a driving range, a resident pro, and a pro shop. There are ten courts.

Northstar Village has several restaurants, bars, and shops. Timbercreek is a steakhouse serving dinner in summer and all meals in winter. The first floor of the Village Building holds a sport shop in winter that is a conference room in summer; its second and third floors have hotel rooms and loft suites. The rest of Northstar's lodgings are in five clusters of privately owned condominiums scattered across the wooded hills. Each has a fireplace (firewood is provided), cable television, a covered deck, and a kitchen with microwave oven. A typical two-bedroom, two-bath condo is a split-level unit with a living room, kitchen and bath on the upper level, and two bedrooms and a laundry room downstairs.

The condos in the Indian Hills cluster are farthest from the village, high on a hill, with a view of the surrounding mountains and the valley below. A free shuttle bus takes guests back and forth in winter; in summer, buses come on request.

Winter is busier than summer at Northstar, but that is likely to change as the resort continues to entice visitors with special packages and a wide array of activities and events.

WAWONA

Wawona Hotel

Yosemite National Park, CA 95389
Reservations:
Yosemite Park Reservations
5410 East Home Street
Fresno, CA 93727
209-252-4848

A gracious lodge in south Yosemite

Manager: Judy Durr. **Accommodations:** 103 rooms (48 with private bath). **Rates:** \$63.25–\$86.25 single or double, \$10 additional person, \$5 under age 12. **Payment:** Major credit cards. **Children:** Welcome. **Pets:** Not allowed. **Smoking:** Not allowed in public spaces. **Open:** Weekends year round, closed weekdays November–December.

Wawona, in the southwestern corner of a park that is one of the world's great natural wonders, resembles a fine plantation home in the South. The main hotel has a big veranda with white columns and wicker furniture overlooking an expanse of lawn and a water lily pond. The pace is slower here, compared to the midsummer rush in Yosemite Valley.

Some wilderness lodges feature rough logs and antler trophies, but not this one. Here the lobby is white and pink, with a flowered ceiling border and carpeting in teal and burgundy. Vintage furniture provides seating near the two stone fireplaces.

On one side of the lobby is a restaurant, a large white room with two walls of high windows framing views of the trees. Dinners and buffet lunches feature standard fare, good but not exceptional.

At the opposite end of the lobby is a small lounge with high ceilings, round marble tables, and a grand piano. The tall windows still have the original wavy glass put in more than a century ago, when Henry Washburn and John Bruce opened the hotel. It was owned by the Washburn family until 1932. Now Wawona, like the rest of Yosemite's lodgings, is run by Yosemite Park and Curry Company.

Upstairs are 26 guest rooms, a few with private baths but most sharing four men's and four women's baths. Modern and well-maintained, they are tiled and have showers.

Typical of the small, comfortable accommodations is Room 202, a tidy space with a white iron bed, flowered wallpaper, pegs (but no closet), and a stack of towels on the dresser. The largest rooms are 213 and 220, good choices for a family.

The famed Mariposa Grove is south of Wawona, just inside the southernmost park entrance. Yosemite's largest tree grows here, soaring skyward in a community of giant sequoias. Trams operate daily, and a trail winds through the awesome grove.

Other rooms are in five side buildings with one or two stories. The oldest is the Clark Cottage, which dates from 1876. Cool and green under its cloak of vines, it has eight boxy rooms with windows to the wraparound porch.

The Annex is ideal for golfers. Surrounded by porches, it stands on the edge of a nine-hole golf course, and there's a golf shop on the lower level. The large lounge is appropriately called the Sun Room for the light that floods through glass doors on three sides.

All the rooms at Wawona are reserved early, often as much as a year in advance.

On the property are tennis courts, a pool, a putting green, and riding stables. Near the stables is the Pioneer Yosemite History Center, a collection of historic buildings and horse-drawn wagons. A self-guiding trail and tours led by a ranger describe the people and events that led to the establishment of the park.

You can relive the days of stage travel in Yosemite with a ten-minute stage ride and hear legends and stories at evening campfire talks given regularly by park rangers.

YOSEMITE

The Ahwahnee

Yosemite National Park, CA 95389
Reservations:
Yosemite Reservations
5410 East Home Street
Fresno, CA 93727
209-252-4848

A grand lodge in a glorious natural setting

Manager: Debbie Price. **Accommodations:** 99 lodge rooms, 24 cottages. **Rates:** $208 double, $20 less for single, $20 additional person. **Payment:** Major credit cards. **Children:** Under 4 free in room with parents; $5 age 4–13. **Smoking:** Smoking rooms available; no smoking in common areas.

The Ahwahnee, faced with native granite and concrete stained to resemble redwood, fits comfortably into its magnificent surroundings — the great granite cliffs, roaring waterfalls, and majestic forests of Yosemite Valley. The hotel stands among pine and cedar trees on the valley floor, with the Royal Arches soaring 2,000 feet behind it.

Since it opened in 1927, celebrities and unknowns alike have adored the Ahwahnee. Winston Churchill, John F. Kennedy, Will Rogers, Greta Garbo, Walt Disney, and Lucille Ball slept under its imposing roof, as have hosts of others. Queen Elizabeth and the Duke of Edinburgh stayed here, and two rooms are named for them.

Dinner at the Ahwahnee is an unforgettable experience. Two walls of floor-to-ceiling windows look over the grassy meadows to Glacier Point and the long ribbon of Yosemite Falls. Tables extend the length of the immense room, and each holds a single tall candle. Overhead, dozens of candles are suspended from pine beams in wrought-iron holders. The atmosphere is at once festive and formal, contrasting wilderness and urbanity in a single setting. Jackets and ties are requested, but no longer required. A pianist performs during dinner.

Several special events are offered during the year. The oldest is the Bracebridge Dinner, a celebration based on Washington Irving's story of a Yorkshire Christmas. The feast and theatrical production are now so in demand that five dinners are held, so that 1,800 of the 60,000 applicants can attend. They're chosen by lottery.

A Native American motif enlivens the hotel's heavy beams and the sturdy furniture. Some of the most interesting designs are on the ceiling of the Great Lounge.

Everything in the six-story hotel is on a grand scale. Fireplaces are big enough to stand in, windows are 24 feet high, the restaurant is 130 feet long and has a 34-foot ceiling supported by pillars of sugar pine. Yet despite the size, it's not intimidating — just impressive.

The Indian theme continues in the geometric-patterned fabrics in the guest rooms. The rooms are more elegant than rustic, with pastels of pale green and salmon, weathered copper, and amenities such as telephones, robes, and hair dryers. Many have king-size beds and all have private baths. The royal rooms contain a fireplace and library. The highlight of the Presidential Suite is its open balcony, from which you have a spectacular view up and down the valley.

Other rooms are in cottages in the woods, reached on lighted paths. Each has a slate front porch, chunky furniture, dark woodwork, and deep windows. For a group traveling together, a five-bedroom, five-bath cottage is ideal.

The Ahwahnee has a gift shop with Indian baskets, weavings, Ansel Adams lithographs and paintings, and books on Yosemite.

There are tennis courts and a swimming pool. Stables in the park offer horseback rides. Bicycles can be rented and guided tours arranged. A 26-mile, two-hour tour by bus or tram car across the valley floor will introduce you to the history, geology, and plant and animal life that abounds here.

There are times when the most abundant life appears to be human, as 3 million visitors a year stream through the park. That's when you may want to explore the 750 miles of trails in Yosemite's backcountry. But whether you're alone at the top of a waterfall or basking in the sun in the Ahwahnee's solarium, you're sure to feel the power of this magnificent natural wonder.

Southern California

Anaheim
Disneyland Hotel, 472
Avalon
Garden House Inn, 474
The Inn on Mt. Ada, 476
Zane Grey Hotel, 478
Balboa
Balboa Inn, 480
Beverly Hills
The Peninsula Beverly Hills, 481
The Regent Beverly Wilshire, 483
Big Bear Lake
Knickerbocker Mansion, 484
Carlsbad
La Costa Resort and Spa, 486
Pelican Cove Inn, 488
Coronado
Hotel Del Coronado, 489
Le Meridien San Diego at Coronado, 491
Loews Coronado Bay Resort, 493
The Village Inn, 495
Dana Point
Blue Lantern Inn, 496
Dana Point Resort, 497
Del Mar
L'Auberge Del Mar, 499

Escondido
The Golden Door, 500
Fawnskin
Windy Point Inn, 501
Hollywood
La Maida House, 503
Sunset Marquis Hotel and Villas, 504
Idyllwild
Strawberry Creek Inn, 506
Julian
Julian Hotel, 507
Shadow Mountain Ranch, 509
La Jolla
The Bed & Breakfast Inn at La Jolla, 511
La Jolla Beach & Tennis Club, 512
La Valencia Hotel, 514
Prospect Park Inn, 516
Laguna Beach
Eiler's Inn, 517
Surf & Sand Hotel, 519
The Ritz-Carlton Laguna Niguel, 520
Lake Arrowhead
Château du Lac, 522
Lake Arrowhead Hilton Resort, 524
Long Beach
Hotel Queen Mary, 525
Los Angeles
Beverly Prescott Hotel, 527
The Biltmore Hotel, 528
Checkers, 530
Hotel Bel-Air, 532
Hotel Nikko at Beverly Hills, 534
Ma Maison Sofitel, 535
The New Otani Hotel & Garden, 537
St. James's Club and Hotel, 539
Westwood Marquis Hotel and Gardens, 540
Malibu
Malibu Beach Inn, 543
Marina del Rey
Marina del Rey Hotel, 544
Newport Beach
Doryman's Inn, 546
Pasadena
The Ritz-Carlton Huntington Hotel, 547
Rancho Bernardo
Rancho Bernardo Inn, 549
Rancho Santa Fe
The Inn at Rancho Santa Fe, 550
Rancho Valencia, 552
San Clemente
Casa Tropicana, 554
San Diego
Balboa Park Inn, 555
Catamaran Resort Hotel, 556
Horton Grand Hotel, 558
Pan Pacific Hotel, 559
San Diego Princess, 561
The Cottage, 563
U.S. Grant Hotel, 564
Santa Monica
Hotel Shangri-La, 566
Loews Santa Monica Beach Hotel, 567
Seal Beach
The Seal Beach Inn and Gardens, 569
Temecula
Loma Vista Bed & Breakfast, 571
Vista
Cal-a-Vie, 572

Best Intimate City Stops

Beverly Hills
The Peninsula Beverly Hills
Hollywood
La Maida House
Sunset Marquis Hotel and Villas
Los Angeles
Beverly Prescott Hotel
Checkers Hotel
Hotel Bel-Air
St. James's Club and Hotel
Westwood Marquis Hotel and Gardens
San Diego
Horton Grand Hotel

Best Country Inns and B&Bs

Avalon
Garden House Inn
The Inn on Mt. Ada
Zane Grey Hotel
Idyllwild
Strawberry Creek Inn
Julian
Julian Hotel
Shadow Mountain Ranch
Temecula
Loma Vista Bed & Breakfast

Best Family Favorites

Anaheim
Disneyland Hotel
Lake Arrowhead
Lake Arrowhead Hilton Resort

Best Grand City Hotels

Beverly Hills
The Regent Beverly Wilshire

Los Angeles
The Biltmore Hotel
Hotel Nikko at Beverly Hills
Ma Maison Sofitel
The New Otani Hotel & Garden
San Diego
Pan Pacific Hotel
U.S. Grant Hotel

Best Inns by the Sea

Balboa
Balboa Inn
Carlsbad
Pelican Cove Inn
Coronado
Hotel Del Coronado
Dana Point
Blue Lantern Inn
Dana Point Resort
Del Mar
L'Auberge Del Mar
La Jolla
The Bed & Breakfast Inn at La Jolla
La Jolla Beach & Tennis Club
La Valencia Hotel
Prospect Park Inn
Laguna Beach
Eiler's Inn
Surf & Sand Hotel
Long Beach
Hotel Queen Mary
Malibu
Malibu Beach Inn
Marina del Rey
Marina del Rey Hotel
San Clemente
Casa Tropicana
Santa Monica
Hotel Shangri-La
Loews Santa Monica Beach Hotel
Seal Beach
The Seal Beach Inn and Gardens

Best On A Budget

Coronado
The Village Inn
San Diego
The Cottage

Best Resorts

Carlsbad
La Costa Resort and Spa
Coronado
Le Meridien San Diego at Coronado
Loews Coronado Bay Resort
Laguna Beach
The Ritz-Carlton Laguna Niguel
Pasadena
The Ritz-Carlton Huntington
Rancho Bernardo
Rancho Bernardo Inn
Rancho Santa Fe
The Inn at Rancho Santa Fe
Rancho Valencia
San Diego
San Diego Princess

Best Romantic Hideaways

Lake Arrowhead
Château du Lac
Newport Beach
Doryman's Inn
San Diego
Balboa Park Inn

Best Spas

Escondido
The Golden Door
Vista
Cal-a-Vie

Best Wilderness Retreats

Big Bear Lake
The Knickerbocker Mansion
Fawnskin
Windy Point Inn

Southern California, from Malibu to San Diego, is richly diverse and full of contrast. There are gorgeous white beaches and palatial homes, mountain lakes and simple cottages. In the metropolitan sprawl of greater **Los Angeles,** you'll find movie studios, freeways, smog, great museums, surfers, chic shops, and 9 million people, all spread over 4,083 square miles. L.A., founded by eleven families from Mexico in 1781, was a sleepy village until the railroad arrived in the late 1860s and a land boom began. Lured by images of a subtropical paradise, immigrants sought their fortunes in oranges. By 1889, 13,000 acres were producing oranges for shipment. Then the discovery of oil brought enormous wealth.

But it was the film industry, begun in 1910, that established the town as the glamour capital of the world. The Los Angeles area offers nonstop entertainment and numerous sporting and cultural events. Shopping is important recreation, especially in the designer boutiques of Rodeo Drive in **Beverly Hills** and the dozens of clothing and antiques shops on Melrose Avenue.

Symphony, ballet, and opera companies are active, and the museums are outstanding. The downtown Los Angeles County Museum of Art (LACMA) holds an important collection of pre-Columbian works, American paintings spanning two centuries, Indian and Southeast Asian art, and European and Japanese masterworks. In the Museum of Contemporary Art (MOCA), works of the postwar period are displayed under natural light in open galleries. The Huntington is noted for its British art collection, botanical gardens, and library of rare books and manuscripts. The J. Paul Getty Museum, on a seaside hilltop in Malibu, may be the richest museum in the world. Ancient Greek and Roman sculptures and European masterpieces are displayed in a replica of a Pompeiian villa.

North of Los Angeles loom the San Gabriel and San Bernardino Mountains, high enough to be capped with snow in winter.

Traveling south along the coast, each community has individual character, from arty **Laguna Beach** to a touch of New England in **Dana Point,** from the thoroughbred racing in **Del Mar** to **La Jolla's** exclusive shops and stunning setting. **San Diego,** the seventh largest city in the country, is best known for its ideal climate and extraordinary visitor attractions. The beach at **Coronado** and Balboa Park's marvelous zoo are not to be missed. Young and old alike are thrilled by Sea World; the orca whale show is nothing less than astonishing.

The city has a major waterfront convention center, a restored Old Town with walk-through exhibitions on life in early San Diego, and a Gaslamp District of restored 19th-century buildings. In the heart of downtown is Horton Plaza, an innovative, multilevel shopping center that offers entertainment and restaurants as well as dozens of intriguing shops.

Inland from the beach and the bay, in the hills north of San Diego, are the wealthy communities of **Rancho Santa Fe** and **Rancho Bernardo.** A few miles away, tucked against the hot, dry hills, lie the peaceful enclaves of **Vista,** an avocado and citrus growing center, and **Escondido,** the heart of San Diego County's wine industry. Farther east there's a quaint old gold-mining town, **Julian,** now known for its apple orchards and relaxed atmosphere.

ANAHEIM

Disneyland Hotel

1150 West Cerritos Avenue
Anaheim, CA 92802
714-778-6600

A jolly hotel complex near Disneyland

Manager: Hideo Amemiya. **Accommodations:** 1,131 rooms and suites. **Rates:** $140–$240 January to June, $145–$245 June to December, $15 additional adult; suites $300–$2,000. **Payment:** Major credit cards. **Children:** Under 17 free in room with parents. **Pets:** Not allowed. **Smoking:** Nonsmoking rooms available.

Here's a resort to thrill the young at heart. It not only has all kinds of entertainment, recreation, and restaurants, it's just a short monorail ride from the Magic Kingdom itself, the fantasy playground of every kid. The hotel was built in 1955 by Jack Wrather, a Texas oilman who agreed with Walt Disney that the new theme park would draw enough visitors to merit a new hotel. So he bought 60 acres adjoining Disneyland and built the "official hotel of the Magic Kingdom." Now it's a major attraction in its own right as well as an award-winning convention hotel. Most of the accommodations are in the three towers surrounding Seaports of the Pacific, a marina playland and shopping and dining extravaganza.

The landscaping at Disneyland Hotel is extraordinary. A team of gardeners works continually to keep the floral color blazing, and the property is kept as immaculate as the clean streets of Disneyland.

Despite the impressive size of the hotel, it is easy to find your way around, thanks to the signs and footpaths that cross the villagelike grounds. There are three swimming pools, ten tennis courts, and Papeete Beach, a pseudo-Polynesian stretch of sand complete with shipwreck decor. Around the Seaports of the Pacific lagoon are remote-controlled boats, two-seater pedal boats, and a video game center.

Free entertainment adds to the hotel's considerable vacation value. Regular features are Fantasy Waters, a twice-nightly display of fountains, lights, and music, and the country-and-western singing nightly at the Wharf Bar. The Neon Cactus Saloon features entertainment and dancing.

The restaurants range from Mazie's, a sidewalk café serving garnish-your-own hamburgers and hot dogs, to Granville's Steak House, featuring steak, prime rib, and lobster in a dressy, candlelit setting. The children's favorite is Goofy's Kitchen, with an all-you-can-eat buffet taking second place to the Disney characters who join kids for breakfast. Others include Shipyard Inn, on the marina, and Caffe Villa Verde, where Italian foods are served. Special children's menus are available at all the hotel's restaurants.

Hotel facilities include car rentals, foreign currency exchange, laundry and dry cleaning, a limousine, and interpreter services.

With all this, guest rooms seem almost secondary. On the other hand, they're crucial to the hotel's appeal. A standard room is clean and comfortable and has a small stocked refrigerator, a television with closed-circuit channel and Disney channel, and a narrow balcony overlooking the marina. On a clear day you can see from Bonita Tower to the beach. Each room has a reproduction of Disney artworkon the wall; the originals hang in the public spaces. A few rooms are in Garden Villas and Oriental Gardens, two-story buildings located apart from the center of activity and entered through attractive gardens.

With an operation as carefully orchestrated as the famous theme park, it's not a surprise to learn that as many as four weddings a day have been held in the rose garden gazebo.

AVALON

Garden House Inn

P. O. Box 1881
Third & Claressa
Avalon, CA 90704
310-510-0356

A flowery inn on an island

Innkeepers: Jon and Cathy Olsen.
Accommodations: 9 rooms (all with private bath). **Rates:** \$125–\$250 single or double (weekday and off-season discounts available). **Included:** Expanded Continental breakfast. **Minimum stay:** 2 nights on summer weekends. **Payment:** Major credit cards. **Children:** Not appropriate. **Pets:** Not allowed. **Smoking:** Not allowed indoors.

On lovely Santa Catalina Island, some 26 miles west of the southern California mainland, this three-story inn stands a few blocks from Avalon's protected harbor. Open to travelers since mid-1987, it is one of the most comfortable and attractive places you will find on this island.

The white frame house was built in 1923 to resemble a San Francisco townhouse. It was purchased in 1987 by Jon Olsen; after he renovated the place, his parents and sister joined him to help run it as a bed-and-breakfast lodging.

There's a small foyer at the entrance with games, cards,

and a telephone for guests' use (there are four more in the house). Beyond is the cozy living room where a walnut-paneled fireplace is tucked against the corner, facing two pale rose couches and a table with magazines and photo albums showing the building's restoration. Wine and cheese are served here in the afternoon, sherry and cookies later in the evening.

There's a suite with a private entrance on the main floor; other guest rooms are on the second and third floors. The white tile bathrooms have some of the original fixtures, saved to lend a period tone. There's a TV and VCR in each room, and a library of videos is available.

Creative design techniques were used to keep the rooms from feeling crowded. In the small pink room on the second floor, the bathroom facilities are divided into three sections, each a former closet. There's no clothes closet, so a hall tree is used instead. Yet the corner room, furnished in a '30s style, does not seem cramped. It has a private terrace behind French doors, with a white wicker chaise longue. One flowery second-floor room is flooded with light from seven windows.

"We provide a homey atmosphere, along with all the things travelers look for," says innkeeper Cathy Olsen. "We have a refrigerator stocked with ice and mineral water for guests, we'll recommend restaurants and supply maps. Anything you need for a comfortable stay, we'll try to help."

There are three guest rooms on the third floor. One has a '30s art deco atmosphere, with curved headboards and bone and brass furniture. Another has fabric of green plaid on the high bed, creating a totally different look. An upper-story sun deck, set up with café tables, overlooks Avalon Bay and the carrotwood trees, ferns, and grape ivy in the patio garden below.

Breakfast, a generous buffet of cereals, pastries, and fruit, is served on the protected patio under white umbrellas.

In the summer, Catalina swarms with day-trippers. But the crowds are in a holiday mood and there are no traffic jams since only residents are allowed to have cars. Many visitors putt around in golf carts. Cafés and shops are clustered within easy walking distance, and tours to other attractions are available.

The island, once owned by William Wrigley, Jr., is now mostly owned by the Catalina Conservancy, dedicated to preserving the environment. If you hike in the interior valleys and mountains, you'll see abundant wildlife and flora.

Getting to Santa Catalina is part of the fun. You can reach the island in minutes by helicopter, or go by boat for a more leisurely trip. From San Pedro, near Long Beach, Catalina Express will get you to Avalon in 60 minutes.

The Inn on Mt. Ada

398 Wrigley Road
Mailing address:
P.O. Box 2560
Avalon, CA 90704
310-510-2030

An elegant, historic mansion on a Santa Catalina hilltop

Innkeepers: Susie Griffin and Marlene McAdam. **Accommodations:** 6 rooms (all with private bath). **Rates:** $230–$470 weekdays November–May, $320–$590 weekends and June–October, single or double, $100 additional person. **Included:** All meals. **Minimum stay:** 2 nights on weekends and weekend holidays. **Payment:** Major credit cards. **Children:** Age 14 and older welcome. **Pets:** Not allowed. **Smoking:** Not allowed.

As you approach the Avalon harbor of Santa Catalina Island, you notice on your left, above the bobbing boats and pretty little town, a white Georgian Colonial mansion crowning a hillside. Once the summer estate of William Wrigley, Jr., (of chewing gum fame) and his family, now it is the Inn on Mt. Ada, one of the finest bed-and-breakfast inns in California.

From almost every angle you see a panorama of the harbor, ocean, and mainland coast from Malibu to Oceanside. In the living room, wingback and Chippendale chairs invite you to sit by the fire or admire the view. A baby grand stands in one corner, and bookshelves line the walls beside the fireplace.

The house was built in 1921 for Wrigley, who also held title to the entire island. It remained in the family until the 1970s, when they gave the land to the Santa Catalina Island Conservancy and the mansion to the University of Southern California for use as a conference center.

Later it was leased to a partnership dedicated to preserving the mansion and providing superb hospitality. It was opened as a bed-and-breakfast inn for guests accustomed to, or wanting a taste of, personal luxury.

Listed on the National Register of Historic Places, the mansion is as grand as it was when the Wrigleys were in residence and their visitors were Presidents Wilson and Coolidge and the Prince of Wales. Many original details have been retained, such as paneled walls, French doors, built-in bookcases, and curved ceilings. There are six fireplaces.

The inn sits on five and a half acres on Mt. Ada (named for William Wrigley's wife), overlooking the harbor and town.

The dining room, elegant with teal silk wallcoverings and an Austrian crystal chandelier, has French doors that open to the breeze-washed patio. A hearty breakfast is served here at tables for two or four. Tea and coffee, juice, and muffins are followed by a fruit dish such as apple crisp and then an entrée, perhaps French toast and sausages. If exercise seems a necessity after this meal, a trail at the edge of the property will lead you on a brisk 15-minute walk up the canyon and back, giving you a sense of the island's rugged backcountry.

A light lunch is provided. Dinner, from a set menu, includes a house wine, homemade bread, and a dessert such as chocolate mousse. Trays of cookies, fresh fruit, and other snacks are replenished during the day, as are beverages.

Each guest room is decorated in the colors of the surrounding land and seascape. Most impressive is the Grand Suite, with a four-poster canopy bed, a fireplace, and French doors to a private balcony. Next door is the Second Suite, which has a lighter touch. It also has a fireplace.

Room 3, in a corner, views both the harbor and the ocean. It too is furnished with a high four-poster and fireplace. The smallest is Number 6, a corner room that is decidedly limited in space, but the scaled-down furniture keeps it from feeling too cramped. It does have a walk-in closet and a full bath. Portable TVs and a phone are available. Since visitors do not drive on Catalina, the inn has golf carts for guests at no charge. A courtesy van provides complimentary pick-up and drop-off at the boat dock.

Other amenities include nightly wine and hors d'oeuvres, early morning coffee, and arrangements for island tours. All this is combined with a friendly, casual warmth that makes The Inn on Mt. Ada not just a classic mansion with a view, but a welcoming home of charm.

To get there, take the ferries that make daily trips from the mainland. Catalina Express is recommended for its smooth, fast (60 or 90 minutes) ride.

Zane Grey Hotel

P.O. Box 216
Avalon, CA 90704
310-510-0966

A western adobe inn overlooking Santa Catalina harbor

Owner: Karen Baker. **Manager:** Laurie Carter. **Accommodations:** 18 rooms (all with private bath). **Rates:** $55–$125 single or double, $35 additional person; rates vary seasonally. **Included:** Continental breakfast. **Minimum stay:** 2 or 3 nights on weekends. **Payment:** Major credit cards. **Children:** Welcome. **Pets:** Not allowed. **Smoking:** Discouraged indoors.

Zane Grey, the famous author of westerns and adventure stories, was born in Ohio in 1872 but moved west after his first novel was published. His romantic tales reflected his love of the outdoors and made him the foremost writer on the American West for two generations of readers.

In 1926, he and his family decided that Santa Catalina Island, 26 miles from the coast of southern California, was the ideal location for a home. So they built the Pueblo on a hillside above the village of Avalon, facing east to the harbor, the sea, and the mainland. There Grey lived and worked until his death in 1939. Now the adobe home is a hotel with modern plumbing and queen-size beds, but otherwise much as it was when Zane Grey made it his haven.

By the time you have spent a few days on lovely Catalina, enjoying the dreamlike quiet and casual ambience of the Zane Grey Hotel, you may find yourself in agreement with the author's words about the place: "It is an environment that means enchantment to me. Sea and Mountain! Breeze and roar of Surf! Music of Birds! Solitude and Tranquility! A place for rest, dream, peace, sleep."

A courtesy taxi will pick you up at the boat landing and wind up the hill to the hotel. Before you enter, you'll notice unusual artwork that deceives the eye: John Bailey's realistic wall paintings of cacti and geraniums.

Most of the guest rooms are named for Zane Grey novels. Half overlook the ocean, half view the hills. The rooms are simply but comfortably furnished in a southwestern theme, with Hopi Indian designs in rugs and weavings. Some can accommodate up to four people. None has television or phone.

At the end of the hall is Zane Grey's living room with the original fireplace and log mantel, mosaic art, beamed ceiling, hewn plank door, and oak dining table. Grey himself brought back the teak beams from one of his fishing trips to Tahiti. Guests are welcome to play the grand piano or curl up by the fire with one of Grey's books from the hotel's collection.

Better yet, step from the rustic living room onto the terrace to drink in one of the island's most beautiful views of the yacht-filled harbor, rolling hills, and vast blue sea.

An arrowhead-shaped swimming pool lies beside gardens of jade and pepper trees. Morning coffee and toast are served here, on the outer terrace, or in the living room.

BALBOA

Balboa Inn

105 Main Street
Balboa, CA 92661
714-675-3412

A 1920s villa-style hotel near the ocean

General manager: Lalith James. **Accommodations:** 34 rooms and suites. **Rates:** $90–$160. **Payment:** Major credit cards. **Children:** Welcome. **Pets:** Not allowed. **Smoking:** Allowed.

Balboa is the image of a southern California beach scene. In the heart of the hubbub is the Balboa Inn, a historic landmark that resembles a European villa.

Sun worshippers on the sand, T-shirt shops, boutiques, roller skaters, a ferris wheel, and a carousel — they're all here, creating an atmosphere of fun and perpetual summer.

Built in 1928, the restored hotel has retained hints of the period. The tile lobby is cool and usually quiet. Beyond it is a shady courtyard for outdoor dining next to the Almare restaurant, which serves Italian food. An outdoor staircase leads to the guest rooms on the second and third floors. There are sixteen types of rooms and eight small suites, each with slight differences in decor. Typical is Room 217, with pine furniture and a view of the ocean and pier. If you're tall, Room 220 is ideal. Designed for the basketball player Kareem Abdul Jabbar, who once owned the hotel, it has high doors and an extra-long king-size bed.

There's a large pool surrounded by a sun deck. Room service is available. Activities in the area include concerts at the Balboa Pavilion a few blocks away, ferry rides to Balboa Island, and rides on the Catalina Flyer to Catalina Island, 26 miles away. Balboa and Newport have numerous restaurants, several specializing in fresh seafood.

BEVERLY HILLS

The Peninsula Beverly Hills

9882 Little Santa Monica Blvd.
Beverly Hills, CA 90212
310-551-2888
800-462-7899
Fax 310-858-6663

An elegant, luxurious villa in the city

General manager: Ali Kasikci. **Accommodations:** 200 rooms, including 32 suites. **Rates:** \$265–\$325 single or double, suites \$425–\$2,500. **Payment:** Major credit cards. **Children:** Welcome. **Pets:** Small pets allowed in villas, by arrangement. **Smoking:** Nonsmoking rooms available.

Like a carefully tended residential estate, the Peninsula Beverly Hills is surrounded by lush gardens and foliage. Tiles, planters, trellises, and fountains add to the European character of this outstanding hotel's landscape. In the heart of Beverly Hills, it's an oasis of elegance and beauty, with a quality attained by very few hotels.

Only four stories high, this French Renaissance hotel resembles a grand private villa. The cool, white, narrow lobby opens to the Living Room, a salon with a fireplace and windows overlooking sculpture and greenery. Light lunches and high tea are served here while a harpist plays.

Pale apricot walls, luxurious fabrics, peach marble, and detailed woodwork are some of the design touches that create the atmosphere of a luxurious home. When you arrive in your room, you are greeted with lemonade or Chinese tea and home-made cookies — another gracious, personal touch. There are night-lights by the bedside console, baskets filled with travelers' needs such as a toothbrush and razor, and orchids and deep soaking tubs in the bathrooms. Each room has a stocked bar and refrigerator, three phones, computer and fax hookups, and a safe.

A member of the exclusive Peninsula Group, this hotel opened in 1991 and caters mostly to a moneyed clientele of individual travelers and small groups — you'll never find convention crowds here. It's twelve miles from downtown Los Angeles and the L.A. airport.

The suites feature full sound systems, art objects from around the world, and, as a final reminder that you are staying in out-of-the-ordinary lodgings, personal stationery that states you are in residence at the Peninsula.

Separated from the main hotel, five two-story villas contain 16 lavishly furnished rooms and suites. They range in size from 580 to 2,250 square feet. Some have kitchens, individual security systems, spas, terraces, and fireplaces.

One of the hotel's best features is its rooftop garden with spa and 60-foot heated outdoor pool overlooking Beverly Hills and Century City. White poolside cabanas may be reserved for a fee, which includes a phone, fruit basket, and other amenities. The rooftop café serves light meals and cocktails.

The hotel's main restaurant is the Belvedere, with garden views and a classic Continental cuisine. By contrast, the Club Bar is a handsome lounge in maple and brass, with a collection of museum-quality California landscapes.

The Regent Beverly Wilshire

9500 Wilshire Boulevard
Beverly Hills, CA 90212
310-275-5200
800-421-4354
Fax 310-274-2851

A glamorous landmark hotel

Manager: Alberto Del Hoyo. **Accommodations:** 155 rooms, 150 suites. **Rates:** $255–$395, suites $425–$4,000. **Payment:** Major credit cards. **Children:** Welcome. **Pets:** Allowed. **Smoking:** Allowed.

The rococo facade of the Beverly Wilshire Hotel has been a famous landmark since 1928. It was glamorous then, but after a $100 million renovation, the word has new meaning. As the Regent Beverly Wilshire, it's one of the world's grand hotels.

Guest rooms are in two wings, the Beverly and the Wilshire, which are divided by a domed entrance road. In the lobby, marble columns, inlaid woods, massive bouquets, and tall palms whisper of elegance and good taste.

The Regent Beverly Wilshire takes justifiable pride in all its eating spots, but the Dining Room is in a class by itself. Surrounded by lush French art, Regency furnishings, and parquet floors, you can order poached salmon with cucumbers and grapefruit in red currant sauce, Maine lobster with mango ginger chutney, venison medallions with black currants, and other imaginative dishes. The lengthy wine list offers a wide range of labels and prices. Remarkably, the foods are low in cholesterol, cooked without salt or butter.

The spacious, well-furnished guest rooms are decorated in sunny pastels. They have all the amenities of a modern luxury hotel, including three phones and the inevitable mini-TV in the bathroom. There are hair dryers, scales, robes, Nina Ricci toiletries, wonderfully fluffy pillows, and lots of pink marble. On each floor there's a room attendant who can be summoned with the push of a button. The attendant will mend a hem, pack your bags, produce an iron and ironing board, or bring in a basket of baby needs and a crib.

The five-room, three-bath presidential suite retains the hotel's period flavor; other special suites are the cabana and veranda suites.

On the second floor of the Beverly Wing is a fitness center with weight machines, saunas, hot tubs, a snack bar, and an outdoor pool (a replica of Sophia Loren's pool in Italy) surrounded by jardinières of bougainvillea and creeping fig. Massage, facial, manicure, and pedicure treatments are available.

Socialites, business moguls, celebrities, and tourists mingle on the busy main floor, headed for brunch or a memorable dinner in the Dining Room, tea or cocktails in the Lobby Lounge, drinks in the clublike bar, or hamburgers and milkshakes at the Café.

Business travelers appreciate the secretarial, telex, copying, computer, and delivery services. Shoppers revel in the hotel's location — it's directly across the street from Rodeo Drive, the famous street of expensive designer shops. Other nearby streets have appealing boutiques, cafés, and art galleries, and there are major department stores on Wilshire Boulevard.

BIG BEAR LAKE

The Knickerbocker Mansion

P.O. Box 3661
869 South Knickerbocker
Big Bear Lake, CA 92315
909-866-8221

A roomy log house close to ski trails and a national forest

Innkeeper: Phyllis Knight. **Accommodations:** 10 rooms (5 with private bath; 5 share 2 baths). **Rates:** $95–$165 single or double, $10 additional person. **Included:** Full breakfast. **Minimum stay:** 2 nights on weekends. **Payment:** MasterCard, Visa. **Children:** Welcome. **Pets:** Not allowed. **Smoking:** Not allowed.

In the early 1920s, Bill and Rose Knickerbocker built this big, rambling log house in the woods, near the waterside village of Big Bear Lake. They raised five children here, and Bill gained some measure of local notoriety for his wild poker games — there are still bullets embedded in the walls.

Now it's a place for romantic retreats, ski trips, and active vacations. The inn is a mile and a half from Bear Mountain and close to Snow Forest; it's a three-block walk to shops and the lake. The national forest behind the inn is webbed with hiking and mountain biking trails. The inn also offers table tennis, horseshoes, croquet, and darts.

In the dining room, a homey place with family photos and a loom (Phyllis is a weaver), everyone eats at one table. Fruit, muffins, yogurt, blueberry pancakes, and crêpes filled with chicken, peppers, and cheese are some of the breakfast dishes.

You'll be greeted by Nellie, a friendly border collie, and led into the foyer and parlor, where couches wait by the stone fireplace. The room is filled with entertainment possibilities, including a piano, puzzles, games, and books. From the parlor, the front door opens to a veranda with a hammock for two, a quiet spot to relax under the ponderosa pines.

The stairs that lead up to the guest rooms in the main house are fashioned from split logs. The Blue Room is sunny and bright with a patchwork quilt and flowered wallpaper. Rose's Room has rustic paneling and bunk beds tucked into a closet — suitable when you're traveling with children. These rooms share a bath at the end of the hall. Calico, with a hammock on the balcony and glimpses of the lake, is nice in summer; it adjoins and shares a bath with Treasure Room.

The suite on the third floor holds four people. It has a woodstove, a TV with VCR, a CD player, a microwave, a refrigerator, and a double whirlpool. All the rooms have television, heirloom quilts, and robes and towels you can take to the outdoor Jacuzzi. The other rooms are in the carriage house, reached by a covered walkway, past a redwood deck that is fine for lounging in the sun. The carriage house rooms have fireplaces and Victorian accents and are good choices when you favor seclusion at the edge of the forest.

Special events and seminars are often held at the Knickerbocker. Several weekends a year an astronomer comes in from Griffith Observatory and sets up a telescope so stargazers can scan the heavens.

CARLSBAD

La Costa Resort and Spa

Costa del Mar Road
Carlsbad, CA 92009
619-438-9111
800-854-5000
Fax 619-438-3758

A large luxury resort in the country

Managing director: Darrell Sheaffer. **Accommodations:** 400 rooms, 77 suites, and 6 executive homes. **Rates:** $215–$325 single or double, suites $375 and up, executive homes $1,000 and up. **Payment:** Major credit cards. **Children:** Under age 18 free in room with parents. **Pets:** Not allowed. **Smoking:** Nonsmoking rooms available.

La Costa is the quintessential California resort. It combines a concern for health and fitness with luxury, fine dining, outdoor recreation, and lavish entertainment — all in a complex that sprawls over 400 acres of hills in the southern California sun. It's just off I-5, 90 minutes south of Los Angeles and 30 minutes north of San Diego.

Opened in 1965, La Costa received a $100 million remodeling in 1987 that gave it a softer, more romantic appearance, with rose-colored buildings, red tile roofs, and arched walkways and windows. All the rooms are decorated in a classic mood, in teal, peach, and tan. The best rooms in the main building are those inside, overlooking tall ferns and eucalyptus trees. The outside rooms, which view the road and parking lots, are more susceptible to noise.

The other rooms are near the spa center, golf courses, and tennis courts. Suites are twice the size of standard rooms, but all are spacious and have terrycloth robes, large mirrors, lighted vanity tables, televisions and phones, and baskets of individual toiletries. Most of La Costa's suites have one or two bedrooms; the executive homes have two to five bedrooms and up to three and a half baths. Complimentary valet parking and transportation to your rooms are provided.

Patio lunches are served near the tennis courts and golf courses. The Spa Dining Room is geared to those looking for tasty and satisfying low-sodium, low-fat meals. In the evening, live entertainment is presented in the Tournament of Champions Lounge and the International Saloon.

The extensive spa facilities feature rock steam baths, Swiss showers, facials, massages, herbal wraps, and loofah scrubs. There's a complete fitness program of exercise and nutrition classes. However, La Costa is more worldly resort than sequestered spa. It bustles with activity and caters to groups looking for a variety of pleasures.

The resort's conference center can hold up to a thousand people for a reception. The complex, which includes a grand ballroom and 14 meeting rooms, boasts advanced audiovisual systems and simultaneous translation capability.

Eight restaurants offer a wide range of dining choices. Champagne Room, open for dinner only, has French cuisine. China, silver, and waiters in tuxedoes add luxury to the intimate dining room. Jackets and ties are required. Ristorante Figaro emphasizes Italian cooking, Pisces serves seafood, and in Gaucho Steakhouse you may order well-prepared beef from a waiter in full Argentinian gaucho costume. José Wong's combines Oriental and Mexican menus in a bright, colorful atmosphere in which the flamenco dancers, the mariachi band, and the sushi bar all seem at home.

The resort has racquet courts, swimming pools, and two 18-hole championship golf courses where major golf events take place. Bicycles are available to rent. A special day camp for children aged five to fourteen offers arts and crafts, golf and tennis lessons, and nature walks.

Pelican Cove Inn

320 Walnut Avenue
Carlsbad, CA 92008
619-434-5995

A B&B in a beach-resort town

Innkeepers: Scott and Betsy Buckwald. **Accommodations:** 8 rooms (all with private bath). **Rates:** \$85–\$175 single or double, \$15 additional person. **Included:** Full breakfast. **Minimum stay:** 2 nights on weekends. **Payment:** Major credit cards. **Children:** Age 12 and older welcome. **Pets:** Not allowed. **Smoking:** Not allowed.

Carlsbad, once known for its mineral waters, is a comparatively little-known resort town 30 miles north of San Diego. The Buckwalds are happy to tell guests about its attractions.

All the guest rooms in Scott and Betsy's bed-and-breakfast have private entrances, fireplaces, and ceiling fans. Each has a feather bed and down comforter, antique furnishings, and a television. Thoughtful details include good reading lamps, handmade herbal soaps, and baskets of fruit and candy.

Laguna, with a colorful lavender and floral decor, has white wicker furniture. Newport, which faces the street, features an unusual conical ceiling of green beams beneath the inn's distinctive cupola. Carlsbad has a high bed, an antique reproduction complete with step stool and mirrored headboard. Carlsbad adjoins Balboa, the smallest room. Two of the larger rooms have Jacuzzis.

Breakfast — French toast, artichoke quiche, and waffles are examples of the dishes served — is set on a table in a corner of the front parlor. This small room serves as the lobby, phone room, and visiting area, so it can be cramped. Better to take a tray back to your room, to the gazebo in the garden, or up to the sun deck or rooftop deck.

Pelican Cove is just 200 yards from the beach. Two walkways along the beachfront are popular strolling, bicycling, and jogging paths. The innkeepers will lend you beach chairs, towels, and picnic baskets for jaunts around the area.

The inn is close to tennis, golf, fishing, sailing, and shopping. It's also within walking distance of several restaurants, such as Chin's, where Szechuan fare is served. Try Dini's for its view of the ocean, Neiman's for a Victorian atmosphere, and Henry's for good food and service.

CORONADO

Hotel Del Coronado

1500 Orange Avenue
Coronado, CA 92118
619-435-6611
800-468-3533
Fax 619-522-8262

A historic landmark resort on the beach

General manager: Dean Nelson. **Accommodations:** 691 rooms. **Rates:** $149–$359 single or double, $25 additional person; suites $399–$459. **Minimum stay:** 2 nights on weekends. **Payment:** Major credit cards. **Children:** Under 5 free in room with parents. **Pets:** Not allowed. **Smoking:** Nonsmoking rooms available.

The Del, as it's affectionately called by frequent guests, is a living legend, a significant piece of southern California's history. Modern comforts add to the rich patina of past glories. The Del Coronado opened in 1888, the result of the dreams of Elisha Babcock, a railroad tycoon who wanted to build a resort that would be "the talk of the Western World." The hotel, built on a peninsula in San Diego Bay, was the largest structure outside New York City to have electric lights..

Quickly established as a cultural oasis in the sparsely settled West, the resplendent Del drew celebrities, dignitaries, and royalty. Twelve U.S. presidents stayed at the hotel during its first hundred years; Frank L. Baum wrote part of *The Wizard of Oz* here and based the Emerald City on the towered Victorian structure.

Nowadays, most people arrive at the hotel by driving across a high bridge that connects San Diego to Coronado, a quaint village with winding, tree-lined streets and shops tucked away in courtyards. Coronado also has a municipal golf course, several small hotels, and a Navy presence.

The original five-story, amply curved structure of the Del Coronado is still in use today, along with two newer sections closer to the beach. The guest rooms in the main building are grouped around the Garden Patio. Lawns, palm trees, and a latticed gazebo make this a favorite spot for weddings and relaxation away from the hubbub of the lobby and arcades of shops. Between the courtyard and the lobby is Palm Court, where you may purchase a Continental breakfast in the morning and order coffee all day.

In the lobby an old-fashioned birdcage elevator, still operating, stands in a corner near the door to the Crown Room, the Del's majestic dining room. One of the largest support-free structures in the country, the redwood-paneled room has a 33-foot ceiling made of sugar pine, crafted without a single nail. Banquets and formal state dinners are held here, though the food is less spectacular than the atmosphere.

The more casual Ocean Terrace is open for breakfast on weekends and lunch and cocktails daily. It overlooks the gazebo bar, the Olympic-size swimming pool, tennis courts, and two miles of sandy beach. You can buy snacks in the basement deli, which was carved from the hotel's original stone cistern, and dine in intimate, elegant surroundings in the Prince of Wales restaurant.

Guest rooms retain their period decor while meeting the expectations of today's travelers. The large rooms with private verandas facing the sea are preferred; they have tall windows, king- or queen-size beds, and roomy baths with showers. All the rooms have ceiling fans, TV, phones, safes, and minibars. Movies filmed at the hotel are shown nightly on a movie channel.

Numerous films and television shows have been made on the grounds of the Del Coronado. The most famous and most enduring was *Some Like It Hot*, filmed in 1958 with Marilyn Monroe, Jack Lemmon, and Tony Curtis.

In Ocean Towers, the newer annex, seven floors contain 311 rooms, all redecorated. The guest rooms lack the Victorian ambience that gives the original Del its charm, but they're softer and lighter in decor and provide a retreat from the bustle across the way. The annex has its own swimming pool, and most of the rooms have balconies. All have air conditioning and king-size beds.

The service at the Del Coronado is outstanding. The award-winning staff is enthusiastic and eager to please, from the youngest valets to those who've been loyal to the Del for 40 years and more.

The hotel has meeting and conference rooms and a convention center that accommodates up to 1,500.

Le Meridien San Diego at Coronado

2000 Second Street
Coronado, CA 92118
619-435-3000
800-543-4300
Fax 619-435-3032

An elegant resort on San Diego Bay

Managing director: Sergio Mangini. **Accommodations:** 265 rooms, 7 executive suites, 28 villa suites. **Rates:** \$165–\$225, suites \$375–\$675. **Payment:** Major credit cards. **Children:**

Under age 12 free in parent's room. **Pets:** Not allowed. **Smoking:** Nonsmoking rooms available.

The natural surroundings and the Southern California climate provided inspiration for the design of Le Meridien, an elegant beachfront resort. It sits on 16 acres at the northeast corner of Coronado Island facing San Diego Bay, the bridge, and the city skyline.

In the lobby and public areas, limestone flooring and walls glazed in honey tones provide a backdrop for oversize furnishings that range from big rattan settees to an antique armoire. A large flower arrangement is the centerpiece, and crimson ginger and palms fill corner pots.

At the dock, vessels will stop to take you for a cruise of the harbor or taxi you to Seaport Village, the convention center, and other stops. Bicycling, sailing, water skiing, and windsurfing can be arranged.

In Marius, the softly lit dining room, the cuisine is in the Provençale tradition. For informal meals, L'Escale offers a bright setting with a wall of windows facing the terrace, the pool, and the bay. In the cocktail lounge, La Provence, the San Diegan's passion for sailing is evident. Pictures of old schooners and the sleek, 12-meter *Stars and Stripes* grace the walls.

The guest rooms, which are spread over three floors and outlying villas, have views of the bay, lagoon, or Tidelands Park, a 22-acre community park that borders Le Meridien. The standard rooms, with pale wood furniture and seafoam colors, are comfortable and generously sized. They have minibars, marble-topped vanities, deep tubs, hair dryers, and Lanvin toiletries. The corner executive suites have deeper toned furnishings and Laura Ashley designs.

The villas, named after impressionist artists, are like private homes, each with its own terrace. The villa cluster has its own pool and whirlpool. Celebrities seeking seclusion and visitors on longer stays like these luxury lodgings with one or two bedrooms. They have wet bars, VCRs, built-in cupboards, double-headed showers, and oversize Jacuzzis, along with the more usual amenities. The resort has meeting and banquet space and a business center.

Le Meridien draws raves for the high quality of its service and accommodations, but its most striking feature is the landscaping. Tropical plantings and a pond with pink flamingos set the tone at the entrance. Ducks, swans, and geese swim in a lagoon. As you walk the path that winds through the resort and along the waterfront, you'll see a koi pond, an aviary, fountains, and irises and lilies blooming along the edge of a stream.

The resort has six tennis courts, three pools, and a spa with a wide range of services. The spa packages range from a one-day rejuvenator (massage, facial, herbal wrap, lunch) to three days of body pampering and treatments.

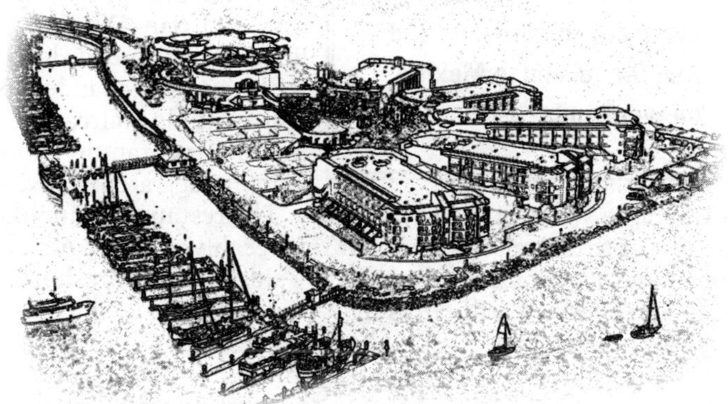

Loews Coronado Bay Resort

4000 Coronado Bay Road
Coronado, CA 92118
619-424-4000
800-23-LOEWS
Fax 619-424-4400

A waterside resort across the bay from San Diego

Manager: John Thacker. **Accommodations:** 436 rooms and suites. **Rates:** $165–$205 single or double, $20 additional adult; Bayside units $280–$1,500, accommodate up to 6 people; Presidential Suite $1,250. **Payment:** Major credit cards. **Children:** 12 and under free in room with parents. **Pets:** Small pets allowed with prior arrangement. **Smoking:** Nonsmoking rooms available.

San Diego's downtown skyline is across the bay from this lovely waterside resort. The city is only a water taxi ride away, while the marina and beach are just out the door — so visitors here get the best of both worlds. Often conventioneers meeting in San Diego stay here for a change of scene. Boaters like the luxurious and fully secured 80-slip anchorage, directly in front of the hotel, which accommodates small cruisers and mega-yachts.

Recreational facilities include five tennis courts, three pools, and easy access to miles of beach. A shuttle service runs every day to Coronado and San Diego, and to Mexico on weekends.

The curving, three-story buildings stand on a 17-acre private peninsula between Crown Isle Marina and San Diego Bay. Inside is a broad lobby with crystal chandeliers and a double staircase rising to a mezzanine. From here, wide, arching windows frame views of the bay and city. The restaurants are like the rest of the hotel: informal but impeccably tasteful. Azzura Point, on the second floor on the bay side, features fresh local seafood. A bar and grill offers light fare by the pool, and an intersting market and deli off the lobby sells box lunches and gifts and sundries. In Cays Lounge, musicians play nightly.

Every guest room has a balcony and a view of the bay, pool, or marina. Big windows, pastel walls, splashy floral fabrics, and touches of rattan emphasize the sunny resort atmosphere. The hotel also appeals to business travelers who need desks, phones, a business center, and lots of meeting space. Loews has one of the largest ballrooms in San Diego, as well as several breakout rooms and audiovisual equipment.

The Village Inn

1017 Park Place
Coronado, CA 92118
619-435-9318

An inexpensive small hotel in an exclusive community

Proprietors: Betsy and Peter Bogh. **Accommodations:** 13 rooms (all with private bath). **Rates:** $50–$80, 2 to 4 people. **Included:** Continental breakfast. **Payment:** Major credit cards. **Children:** Welcome. **Pets:** Not allowed. **Smoking:** Allowed.

Coronado is an exclusive and charming beach community on a peninsula across the bay from San Diego. It has historic mansions, an 18-hole championship golf course, dozens of specialty shops, restaurants, tennis courts, and a yacht marina. While it does not offer much in the way of budget lodgings, the Village Inn is a nice exception.

The Village Inn is popular with Europeans who know the value of a casual, simple, clean hotel that meets travelers' needs without the expense of added frills.

The white stucco hotel, built in the 1920s, is on a quiet residential street, away from the crowds at the famed Hotel del Coronado, yet less than two blocks from a sandy beach with clean water and good swimming.

Two people may book a small room with double bed for $50 in winter. Four people can sleep in a room with two double beds for $80 in summer. If you stay a week in winter, you get the seventh night free.

All the rooms are on the second and third floors, reached by an elevator with grillwork doors. The rooms have rattan and pine furnishings, ceiling fans, and windows that open outward to catch the cool ocean breezes. (Directly on the Pacific, Coronado is usually about 10 degrees cooler than San Diego.) Four rooms have pine beds with canopies, and two have Jacuzzis.

The Boghs provide homey touches not often found in budget hotels — fresh greenery in the rooms, lacy pillows, alarm clocks and an iron to lend. There are ironing boards in some closets. The coffee kitchen, with a stove and microwave oven, is handy for fixing tea, light snacks, and lunches. A breakfast of muffins, fruit, juice, and coffee is served here.

Up the street from the inn is an excellent wine shop and deli, Park Place Deli. It's a good place to fill a picnic cooler. Take your picnic to the beach with the hotel's beach pack (umbrella, chair, and big towel), and you'll enjoy the pleasures of Coronado at a small fraction of the prices most tourists pay.

DANA POINT

Blue Lantern Inn

34343 Street of the Blue Lantern
Dana Point, CA 92629
714-661-1304
Fax 714-496-1483

A stylish clifftop inn overlooking the harbor

Innkeeper: Tom Taylor. **Accommodations:** 29 rooms (all with private bath). **Rates:** $135–$350 single or double, $15 additional person. **Included:** Full breakfast. **Payment:** Major credit cards. **Children:** Under age 5 free. **Pets:** Not allowed. **Smoking:** Not allowed.

High on a bluff above the Dana Point Yacht Harbor, the Blue Lantern presents panoramic views as well as comfortable accommodations and fine service. Its gabled, gray frame trimmed in white reflects the Cape Cod theme of Dana Point.

Near the inn is the Cannon restaurant, where you can enjoy candlelight dining with a stunning view. For a livelier spot with good mesquite-broiled seafood, try the Harbor Grill in Mariner's Village.

The Blue Lantern is similar to the other Four Sisters inns in its commitment to high quality and attention to detail. Everything here is done well. The reception area, sitting room, library, and dining room are peaceful, welcoming places where you can enjoy complimentary wine and hors d'oeuvres in the afternoon, talk to the concierge about Dana Point's attractions, and pick up a cookie on the way to your room.

The guest rooms are done in coastal colors: seafoam green, sand, lavender, and periwinkle blue. They have traditional and antique furniture, television, phones, shuttered windows, and attractive molding detail. Some rooms have a whirlpool tub, gas fireplace, and a balcony that overlooks the harbor, where waves crash against a long stone breakwater.

In the morning, the *Los Angeles Times* is delivered to your door. An ample buffet breakfast of juice, granola, muffins, and a hot dish such as baked French toast is served in the sun room off the lobby.

Dana Point Resort

25135 Park Lantern
Dana Point, CA 92629
714-661-5000
800-545-SITE
Fax 714-661-5358

A stylish, casual resort on a hill above the sea

Manager: Chris Venner. **Accommodations:** 333 rooms, 17 suites. **Rates:** $170–$280 single or double, $20 additional person. **Payment:** Major credit cards. **Children:** Under 16 free in room with parents. **Pets:** Not allowed. **Smoking:** Nonsmoking rooms available.

South of Laguna Beach is a point of land named for Richard Henry Dana, Jr., who wrote *Two Years Before the Mast.* Dana Point has a yacht harbor, a lighthouse filled with nautical lore, a marine institute, and a complex of shops and restaurants designed to recreate the flavor of the port's 19th-century trading days. And it has, on a grassy hill above the harbor, Dana Point Resort.

The gabled, four-story resort, painted gray with white trim, stands on landscaped grounds overlooking the 2,500-slip harbor. All the rooms have sea views; some have balconies, others their own terraces. They occupy four wings: Laguna, Capistrano, San Clemente, and Del Mar.

The rooms are spacious and comfortably furnished, decorated in neutral tones of beige and gray, with abstract pastel art on the walls. It's not the decor that draws the eye in these rooms, it's the gorgeous view, which makes every visitor immediately open the sliding glass doors and admire the panorama of blue sea and sky. Kimonos with a nautical design hang in the closets. Baths in warm gold marble have a tub and shower, hair dryers, and makeup mirrors.

The mood at Dana Point Resort is that of a casual country club, where guests come for outdoor recreation. You can play tennis, golf at the Links course, take a fishing or whale-watching cruise, or exercise in the health center, which has stationary bicycles, weights, and a rowing machine.

On the first floor are two lounges beyond the light and open lobby. In Burton's, chrome chairs stand at marble tables by the dance floor. From here there's an oblique view of the harbor. Stop in on a Thursday, Friday, or Saturday night for live jazz and cocktails. Next door, in the Lantern Bay Lounge, a pianist plays mellow jazz during the day. This is a pleasant spot for lunch, as local businessfolk will attest. It's a bright, high-ceilinged space, with many windows that have a good view of the resort's lawns and flowers.

Watercolors restaurant is on the lower level, near the lawn that slopes to the road and marina. It serves three meals a day and a Sunday brunch buffet.

At the marina, you can rent sailboards and kayaks, go rowing or parasailing, or take the five-mile walk around the harbor's edge. Jet skis and sailboats may be rented.

In the summer months the resort offers a special day program for children called Club Cowabunga. Supervised activities include flying kites in the park, playing games, and visiting the Marine Institute to explore tidepools and see the whale exhibition. In the evenings, movies and videos are shown.

DEL MAR

L'Auberge Del Mar

P.O. Box 2078
1540 Camino Del Mar
Del Mar, CA 92014
619-259-1515
800-553-1336
Fax 619-755-4940

A modern, open resort in a coastal town

General manager: Karen Komo. **Accommodations:** 115 rooms and 8 suites. **Rates:** $165–$250 single or double, suites $300–$950. **Payment:** Major credit cards. **Children:** Welcome (cribs available). **Pets:** Not allowed. **Smoking:** Nonsmoking rooms available.

On a hill overlooking the ocean, 20 minutes north of San Diego, L'Auberge is a stylish resort with a reputation for excellent quality. It's on the site of the old Hotel Del Mar, which was frequented by Hollywood celebrities in the '20s, '30s, and '40s.

If you come to L'Auberge by Amtrak, you'll have a short walk from the historic train station to the hotel. Many guests enjoy continuing the tradition begun when Del Mar was famous for its glamorous visitors.

The atmosphere is light and open, typical of southern California lodgings. In the marble lobby, which has a double-sided fireplace, skylights allow the sun to stream through to the potted palms and lavish bouquets. This is the heart of the resort, where guests gather for afternoon tea and weekend dinner dances. A buffet brunch is set out on Sunday. Beyond is the terrace with a fountain and flowers and, on a level above, a swimming pool.

You can eat on the terrace or inside in the sunny Tourlas restaurant, which features California cuisine. There's also a poolside grill service.

For recreation, L'Auberge offers two tennis courts, two pools, a full-service spa, and the attractions of Del Mar: golf, shopping, bicycling, surfing, strolling to the beach, and attending the horse races at the famous Del Mar Race Track. The inn has facilities for groups up to 250 people, with nine meeting rooms and a spacious terrace.

The guest rooms have a country French decor and private balconies; some have panoramic ocean views while others look out on the garden, village, or pool. There are full-length mirrors, large marble baths, stocked mini-bars, and amenities such as hair dryers and robes. The suites have gas fireplaces and canopy beds.

ESCONDIDO

The Golden Door

P.O. Box 2548
Escondido, CA 92025
619-744-5777

A serene and classic spa in the country

Manager: Rachel Caldwell. **Accommodations:** 39 rooms (all with private bath). **Rates:** $3,950 per week per person in winter, $3,500 in summer. **Included:** All meals and tips. **Minimum stay:** 1 week. **Payment:** No credit cards. **Children:** Not appropriate. **Pets:** Not allowed. **Smoking:** Discouraged.

There's no sign directing you to the Golden Door on the country road outside Escondido, 30 miles from San Diego, but you will have been told about the security gate, the road that leads to the parking lot, and the gleaming "golden" doors. When you walk through them and cross a bridge above Deer Springs Creek, you have entered a very special world, far removed from the din and bustle of modern life.

Low ocher buildings resembling Japan's honjin inns stand beneath California live oaks, shielded by bamboo and camellias. Behind them are 177 acres of gardens and rolling hills. Each building surrounds a garden courtyard. The Bell Courtyard, off the main building, contains a 300-year-old bell from a Buddhist temple; the Azalea Courtyard, reached through sliding shoji doors from the dining hall, has masses of pink azaleas and a koi pond. A sand garden, stone pagodas and paths, fine antiques, and deceptively simple landscaping create a sense of Oriental timelessness.

The guest rooms are off covered wooden walkways that surround the courtyards. Each simply decorated, comfortable room contains a bed, phone, table and chairs, and, like many Japanese homes, a tokonoma — a corner devoted to flowers and a piece of artwork.

There's no television, except in the lobby, to interfere with the meditative atmosphere that's encouraged here. Instead, each room has thoughtful books on attaining inner peace.

You'll arrive on a Sunday afternoon and start with an interview that reveals your particular needs. Monday morning you'll begin the session with a morning hike in the dry, sunny hills. Then it's breakfast in your room followed by a day of warm-ups, exercise classes in and out of the swimming pool, nutrition and fitness instruction, massages, facials, and herbal wraps. Between activities are juice breaks and low-calorie meals made with ingredients that are, for the most part, organically grown in the spa's own acres of gardens.

In keeping with the Japanese theme of the spa are classes in yoga, silent meditation, and guided visualizations and affirmations — a combination of Eastern and Western philosophies called the Inner Door program.

FAWNSKIN

Windy Point Inn

P.O. Box 375
39263 North Shore Drive
Fawnskin, CA 92333
909-866-2746

A secluded, contemporary home on the lake

Innkeepers: Val and Kent Kessler. **Accommodations:** 3 rooms (all with private bath). **Rates:** $105–$225 single or double. **In-**

cluded: Full breakfast. **Minimum stay:** 2 nights on most weekends. **Payment:** Major credit cards. **Children:** Not appropriate. **Pets:** Not allowed. **Smoking:** Not allowed.

On the north shore of Big Bear Lake, in the San Bernardino Mountains east of Los Angeles, this contemporary home stands on a private peninsula bordered by secluded sandy beaches. Through every window you see a different aspect of the lake, forest, and mountains.

At Windy Point you might rent a kayak or other boat and paddle on the lake (the inn has a private dock), or make the 12-minute drive to Big Bear's ski slopes.

Windy Point offers both serenity and stimulation. You can go for quiet walks, watch the sunset, and play the grand piano or snuggle up by the blazing hearth in the sunken living room. Or you can admire artwork from around the world and visit with the interesting guests who come to the inn.

The guest rooms are on three levels. The Cliffs, on the ground floor, has a corner fireplace in the cozy sitting area, a separate entrance, a refrigerator and wet bar, and a skylit bath. Least expensive, but intimate and romantic, is the Sands, which has a wet bar, a private deck, and a sunrise view.

The most spectacular room is the Peaks, with glass on three sides revealing wide views through the tops of the pine trees to the lake and mountains. There's a king-size bed in the big, open suite, and a whirlpool tub in the tiled bathroom.

Amenities abound: thick towels, individually controlled heat, stereos, VCR, a barbecue — but it's style and personality that make the inn outstanding. Its whimsical sculptures, paintings, and exotic artifacts combine with a sophisticated decorating sense to create a memorable retreat.

Breakfast includes out-of-the-ordinary treats such as bananas Foster crêpes and cinnamon French toast with sautéed fruit. The innkeepers offer afternoon appetizers in the living room or on the deck and will give suggestions on restaurants, provide directions, and even drive you where you want to go.

HOLLYWOOD

La Maida House

11159 La Maida Street
North Hollywood, CA 91601
818-769-3857

A peaceful retreat in residential Hollywood

Innkeeper: Megan Timothy. **Accommodations:** 11 rooms (7 in bungalows). **Rates:** $85–$210 single or double, discounts for stays longer than 1 week. **Included:** Expanded Continental breakfast. **Minimum stay:** 2 nights. **Payment:** MasterCard, Visa. **Children:** Not appropriate. **Pets:** Not allowed. **Smoking:** Not allowed.

This Italianate villa, built in 1926 by Antonio La Maida, exudes romance and beauty from every corner. The inn is distinctive, thanks to the talents and personality of Megan Timothy. She has put her skills at decorating, cooking, painting, sewing, gardening, and carpentry — among others — to play in creating an extraordinary retreat that is a few minutes' drive from the shopping, restaurants, and studios of Los Angeles and Hollywood.

Mediterranean in design, with white stucco walls, a red tile roof, and arched doorways and windows, the 25-room villa combines an Old World background with a fresh California outlook and Megan's inimitable style. On the main floor, off the entry hall, is a living room with two groups of chairs invitingly arranged around the gold marble fireplace. A grand piano stands in one corner. Windows look toward the gardens and lily pond. Also on the main floor are two dining areas, a den filled with books and soft cushions, and a solarium.

Walk up the curving mahogany staircase, past a brilliant red and gold peacock of stained glass (made by Megan, as are the other 96 stained glass creations throughout the inn), and you come to four bedrooms off halls displaying photographs from the innkeeper's world travels. The rooms all have phones, closets with luggage racks and robes, fresh flowers, clock radios, down comforters, and big tile bathrooms; some have whirlpool tubs. A thoughtful touch in each bath is the drawer full of toiletries — razors, toothpaste and toothbrush, Alka-Seltzer, and other extras often needed by travelers.

The Cipresso Suite, the largest, is an airy room overlooking the rose garden and tall cypress trees at the side of the house. It has a four-poster canopy bed and wicker chairs piled with pillows. Vigna is dark and peaceful, with vine-green walls. From the window you see the grapevines that wind over the wall. The other two rooms are also pleasant: Fontana, in crisp blue and white with twin beds, and Magnolia, furnished in white-washed pine. Portable TVs and answering machines are available, and there's an executive conference room that accommodates twenty.

Tropical plants grow in the glass-walled solarium, which opens to a back lawn with a fountain and magnolia trees. The small dining room is where private dinners of culinary distinction are held. If you arrange it with Megan, she'll prepare a light supper before the theater or a four-course dinner with complimentary wine.

The other guest rooms are in nearby cottages. The Streletzia Suite is the most luxurious, with a wood-burning fireplace, rattan furniture, stained glass accents, and a front porch that views a Japanese fern garden with a goldfish pond.

Among La Maida's special features are the swimming pool behind one of the cottages, an exercise room, a complimentary morning newspaper, a library of guidebooks, evening wine, cookies, and breakfasts that are artistic feasts.

Sunset Marquis Hotel and Villas

1200 N. Alta Loma Road
West Hollywood, CA 90069
310-657-1333
800-858-9758

A secluded group of villas set in landscaped gardens

General manager: Rod Gruendyke. **Accommodations:** 118 suites, 12 villas. **Rates:** Suites $215–$275, villas $450–$1,200. **Payment:** Major credit cards. **Children:** Welcome. **Pets:** Not allowed. **Smoking:** Allowed.

This lovely retreat is ideal if you're looking for quiet luxury in the heart of Hollywood. Close to production studios, tourist attractions, and businesses, just a half block south of Sunset Boulevard, they seem a world away once you step into the lobby. A few diners may be seated in the romantic little restaurant on your right.

A fountain trickles on a patio, parakeets chirp in the trees, and rabbits hop among the calla lilies and azaleas. White lounge chairs sit by the pool, each with its monogrammed pink towel. There's a spa and sauna, too.

The three-story stucco hotel and its individual villas stand on two acres of cloistered gardens and hills. You may lunch among the tropical plants at the poolside café or, if your villa is near the second pool, have your order delivered there by the butler.

Hotel rooms are grouped around the pool and terrace. Each room has a TV and VCR, two-line phones, a wet bar, and a bathroom with makeup mirror and hair dryer. In addition to the usual shampoos and soaps, sunscreen lotion is provided.

If the rooms are attractive, the villas — with one or two bedrooms and baths — are stunning. All are light and spacious, with hanging plants, kitchens, and well-proportioned furniture. One unit has a baby grand piano; some have private terraces overlooking the gardens and brick walkways. Chocolates and wine await your arrival, and the butler will light your fireplace and bring in kitchen equipment if you need it.

The attentive service at Sunset Marquis equals the setting. Valet parking and shoeshines are available 24 hours a day, you're given a weather report at the evening turndown, and if you place your breakfast order on the door it will be delivered to your room in the morning. Limousine service is available. The concierge will arrange for theater tickets, tours, flowers, and appointments with hairdressers — all with a smile.

The Sunset Marquis is where many well-known names and faces go for privacy and relaxation. But whether famous or unknown, all receive the same courtesy. One British entertainer, a regular guest for years who now lives in Hollywood, still pops in for poolside lunches. "It doesn't matter how you look, the staff treats everyone well," he says, adding, "Me mum loves it. I put her here when she comes to visit."

IDYLLWILD

Strawberry Creek Inn

P.O. Box 1818
Idyllwild, CA 92349
909-659-3202

A traditional home in the mountains

Innkeepers: Diana Dugan and Jim Goff. **Accommodations:** 9 rooms and cottage (all with private bath). **Rates:** $80–$125 single or double, $20 additional person. **Included:** Full breakfast, except in cottage. **Minimum stay:** 2 nights on weekends, longer on holidays. **Payment:** MasterCard, Visa. **Children:** Welcome in cottage. **Pets:** Not allowed. **Smoking:** Not allowed. **Open:** Year-round except Christmas.

In the rustic mountain village of Idyllwild, high above the desert near Palm Springs, stands Strawberry Creek Inn, a rambling, shingled home with a sense of nostalgia. In the big, open living room, guests like to sit by the fire or browse among the ceiling-high shelves of books in the cozy reading nook. Country antiques, an old-fashioned pie chest, and heirloom quilts furnish the room. On one side, next to a wall of windows, is the breakfast area.

Most of the guest rooms are fairly small. In the main house, the Amish Room, on the ground floor, honors its name with a rocker, a lovely quilt, and Amish mementoes such as candles and cornhusk dolls. Upstairs, the rooms are comfortably and individually furnished with patchwork quilts, ruffled cushions, fresh flowers, and good reading lamps.

Behind the main house is a separate building with rooms that face a courtyard. These are cabinlike retreats with fireplaces, refrigerators, and skylights. Santa Fe has a southwestern decor; Helen's Room is Victorian with a carved walnut bed; Autumn has a four-poster and the rich colors of fall. San Jacinto is a favorite for the stone fireplace, rag rugs, and rustic atmosphere.

The savvy innkeepers have combined old-fashioned furnishings with modern comforts in this 1941 house, which lies on wooded grounds above Strawberry Creek. From every window there are views of tall pine and oak trees.

The cedar shake cottage down by the creek is a quaint spot, nice for honeymooners. (It can also hold four people, using the Murphy bed and sofa bed.) The cottage, decorated in blue, has a stone fireplace, two bathrooms, and a glass-enclosed dining porch, as well as a kitchen with a microwave oven, a gas stove, dishes, and staples for cooking. The bedroom is upstairs under the eaves and has a deep whirlpool tub.

Most visitors have high praise for Strawberry Creek. In the guest books they write, "Beautiful memories," "Friendly atmosphere," and "All you need for a romantic weekend."

JULIAN

Julian Hotel

P.O. Box 1856
Julian, CA 92036
619-765-0201

A historic hotel in a former mining town

Innkeepers: Steve and Gig Ballinger. **Accommodations:** 18 rooms (5 with private bath). **Rates:** $38 single, $60–$110 double weeknights, $78–$145 weekends and holidays. **Included:** Full breakfast. **Minimum stay:** 2 nights on weekends. **Payment:** Major credit cards. **Children:** Welcome. **Pets:** Not allowed. **Smoking:** Allowed.

A hundred years ago the mining town of Julian was a two-day stage ride from San Diego and had fifteen hotels lodging prospectors with gold fever. Now the trip takes less than two hours, and only one hotel is left. The town still draws visitors, but these days they're tourists looking for reminders of the Old West.

You're in another century as soon as you step into the large lobby. A woodstove stands in the center of the room, red velvet curtains hang at the tall windows, and a couple of cats may amble through. You'll be invited to join the other guests for tea and cakes at five o'clock.

The Julian Hotel is the oldest continuously operating hotel in southern California. It was built by freed slaves, Albert and Margaret Robinson, who started with a restaurant and bakery and, as their reputation for hospitality grew, put up the two-story wood frame hotel. Albert planted the cedar and locust trees that circle the hotel today.

The Robinsons' venture was a success, and so it remains. It's on the National Register of Historic Places, a landmark with a frontier flavor.

In the large parlor, classical music plays in the evenings while guests read, browse through turn-of-the-century Sears catalogs, or play Parcheesi. An ample breakfast is served here at tables for four.

Upstairs the rooms are small, but each has space for a modern bed, a dresser with a mirror, a closet, and a table and chair. All beds have electric blankets — nights are chilly at Julian's 4,000-foot elevation. In the honeymoon room, you'll have a wood-burning Franklin stove on a brick hearth, a queen-size bed with a satin spread, and a dressing alcove with clawfoot tub.

As in the old days, baths are shared (they're indoors, however — an improvement over the original). Three rooms off the hotel's porch have private baths, and there are two cottages in back. The one-room cottage off the patio is cozy, with white muslin curtains, a white wicker chair, and a black iron bed under a flowered quilt.

The Ballingers, who have owned the Julian Hotel since the late 1970s, have been careful to retain and restore the hotel's original decor. They have put together a walking tour that points out historic landmarks and will direct you to Julian's several antiques stores, gift shops, and a couple of good restaurants. Try Romano's, the Julian Grill, and, for lunch, Mom's Apple Pies. Julian apples are famous in the region; harvest season brings crowds of tourists and apple buyers.

To add to the memories of the time warp you're visiting, take the half-hour horse and carriage ride and then stop at the Bad Blood Studio Saloon and have your photograph taken in frontier costume.

An excellent way to see more of the area is by following one of the Ballingers' detailed itineraries to nearby Cuyamaca Ranch State Park, the Anza-Borrego Desert, and Palomar Mountain.

Shadow Mountain Ranch

P.O. Box 791
2771 Frisius Road
Julian, CA 92036
619-765-0323

A homey bed-and-breakfast in the country

Innkeepers: Jim and Loretta Ketcherside. **Accommodations:** 6 rooms (5 with private bath). **Rates:** $80–$100 single or double, $150 cottage for 4. **Included:** Full breakfast. **Minimum stay:** 2 nights on weekends. **Payment:** No credit cards. **Children:** Not appropriate. **Pets:** Not allowed. **Smoking:** Not allowed indoors.

This peaceful retreat lies in the rolling, wooded hills outside Julian, a historic mining town east of San Diego. Once an eight-acre apple orchard and cattle ranch, it is now a bed-and-breakfast and the Ketchersides' home. Visitors can join in feeding their chickens, ducks, cattle, and horses.

Loretta, a former nurse, and Jim, a retired superintendent of schools, enjoy meeting people and sharing their country hideaway. If you arrive in the afternoon, you'll be in time for tea and snacks, served on the deck under the trees or by the fire in the large, homey living room. There are games, magazines, and books, and the musically inclined Ketchersides have a piano, violin, and guitars for guests to use.

The ever-busy innkeepers have recently added another cottage, this one partially underground. The cozy, one-room Gnome Home has a woodstove, handmade furniture, and a rock shower resembling a waterfall in the forest.

In the dining area, Loretta and Jim serve a ranch-style breakfast of steak, eggs, onions, potatoes, orange juice, muffins, and an endless supply of coffee will prepare you for an active day. On Sundays, the cook adds pancakes to the array of food. After a few laps in the indoor pool, a game of horseshoes or badminton, and a hike in the Pine Hills forest, you may feel like eating again.

Each guest room is different. The Pine and Oak rooms, in the main house, have brick sitting areas, wood-burning stoves, and country antiques. Grandma's Attic, across a wooden bridge from the main deck, is furnished in wicker and decorated in satin and delicate lace. Outside, next to the path by the wall, is an elaborate miniature village, complete with bridges, trees, and churches. It was made by Loretta's father years ago.

The Enchanted Cottage, on a grassy knoll, is as quaint as a fairy tale cottage in the woods. It has a woodstove and cushioned seat by a mullioned window that looks into the pine trees.

If you've always wanted to sleep in a tree or have nostalgic memories of a childhood tree house, reserve the Ketchersides' most unusual accommodation: the Tree House (available only in the summer). In the branches of an ancient oak tree, the rustic room is reached by a stairway from the lower deck that surrounds the tree. The room contains a double bed, a sitting area, and toilet facilities, but no tub or shower. Its windows view treetops and fields. What could be more satisfying than falling asleep to the sighs of mountain breezes, sheltered in the arms of a great oak.

Manzanita is a two-bedroom cottage a few yards from the house, perfect for couples traveling together. A woodstove on a brick hearth warms the living room on chilly mornings.

The kitchen has a toaster oven, refrigerator, and two burners — useful if you'd like to stay put rather than drive into Julian for dinner. The cottage has a protected deck under the pine trees and a pastoral view of the fields and mountains against the sky. Each bedroom has a separate entrance.

LA JOLLA

The Bed & Breakfast Inn at La Jolla

7753 Draper Avenue
La Jolla, CA 92037
619-456-2066

An inn of charm and architectural interest

Innkeeper: Pierrette Timmerman. **Accommodations:** 16 rooms (15 with private bath). **Rates:** $85–$225 single or double, $25 additional person. **Included:** Continental breakfast. **Minimum stay:** 2 nights on weekends. **Payment:** MasterCard, Visa. **Children:** Over age 12 welcome. **Pets:** Not allowed. **Smoking:** Not allowed indoors.

La Jolla is a chic little town on the coast just north of San Diego. It's known for its scenic beaches and exclusive shops; it is also the home of the Stephen Birch Aquarium Museum, the Scripps Institution of Oceanography, and the La Jolla Museum of Contemporary Art.

Across the street from the museum, a few blocks from the sea, is the Bed & Breakfast Inn at La Jolla. Built in 1913, the boxy stucco inn is representative of the stripped-down style of the architect Irving Gill. Other examples of his influential cubist work may be seen elsewhere in La Jolla. Now restored in a style compatible with Gill's simple plan, it is on the San Diego Historical Registry.

The guest rooms are in the two-story main building and the annex behind it, off a courtyard garden. Bird Rock, a tiny room decorated in Laura Ashley blue and white pinstripes and flowered prints, shares a bath during the day with the inn's manager. It's one of five rooms on the ground level.

Upstairs, on a corner, Cove Room is furnished with a wicker table and rocker. A decanter of sherry sits on the table.

A soft breeze blows through windows that open to a view of trumpet vines over the arbor next door. Until late in the evening, every quarter-hour you'll hear the gentle sound of chimes from a nearby church. Across the hall is Ocean Breeze, a small room with a queen-size bed and a view of the courtyard and large podocarpus tree.

Complimentary wine and cheese are served in the afternoon. You may choose where to have breakfast — in the dining room of the main house, in your own room, on the sun deck, or in the garden.

In the guests' sitting room there's a refrigerator, a television, and a 12-minute video explaining the inn's history and restoration. Shelves contain books, magazines, and games that include LaJollaopoly, in which players trade local properties instead of Park Place and Marvin Gardens.

Off the lounge are a rooftop sun deck and two guest rooms: the Shores, which has antique headboards on twin beds, and Peacock Salon, a brightly decorated room with a garden view.

The largest space is the Irving Gill Penthouse, at the top of the annex. It has a sitting room with a TV, and a small deck with a view. The most spectacular ocean view, looking over rooftops two blocks to the cove, is from Pacific View. It's furnished with antiques in a nautical theme.

La Jolla Beach & Tennis Club

2000 Spindrift Drive
La Jolla, CA 92037
619-454-7126
800-624-2582
Fax 619-456-3805

A beach resort for tennis and swimming

General manager: William Kellogg.
Accommodations: 90 rooms and apartments. **Rates:** $70–$250 per person. **Payment:** Major credit cards. **Children:** Welcome. **Pets:** Not allowed. **Smoking:** Nonsmoking rooms available.

The guest apartments at this private tennis club stretch along a quarter-mile of beautiful beach 15 miles north of San Diego.

About a thousand families in the well-heeled La Jolla area belong to the club, which is located in a palm grove in a residential district, but visitors have full membership privileges.

With 12 championship tennis courts (four of them lighted) and a pro instructor and pro shop, the club is a favorite with tennis players. Surrounding the ten-acre property's tropical lagoon is a nine-hole pitch-and-putt golf course that guests may use for a small fee. A heated junior Olympic-size pool is next to the patio where lunch is served daily. You may also eat in the club dining room, facing the esplanade by the private beach.

The Marine Room is a restaurant so close to the water that cresting waves, illuminated at night, sometimes splash against the windows. Live seahorses swim in the aquarium and skylights open to the sun or stars. A small orchestra plays for evening dancing.

The guest rooms and apartments are in low stucco buildings with red tile roofs. Most face the water and some are just a step from the smooth sand. A typical room is decorated in a seaside motif and has two double beds with rattan headboards, comfortable seating, and an equipped kitchenette. All the rooms are supplied with bottled water or piped purified water.

The club's seahorse logo is everywhere: at the bottom of a pool on a seaside terrace, in a tiled fountain in the central courtyard, on the bright yellow boards supplied as wind protection on the beach. The club also provides beach towels, chairs, and blue and white umbrellas for protection from the sun.

You may rent scuba and snorkeling gear, wetsuits, and surfboards from a nearby surf shop. Snorkeling in La Jolla Cove will allow you to see coral and undersea marine life among the wavy strands of kelp.

With apartment sizes up to three bedrooms, this lodging appeals to families. It provides daily maid service, cable television, self-service laundromats, and a hair salon.

La Valencia Hotel

1132 Prospect Street
La Jolla, CA 92037
619-454-0771
800-451-0772
Fax 619-456-3921

A vintage hotel with a Mediterranean atmosphere

Manager: Patrick Halcewicz. **Accommodations:** 105 rooms and suites. **Rates:** $145–$295 single or double, $10 additional person; suites $325. **Payment:** Major credit cards. **Children:** Welcome. **Pets:** Not allowed. **Smoking:** Allowed.

In the heart of La Jolla, ten miles north of San Diego, this pink stucco hotel has been welcoming travelers and holding social events since 1926. The hotel and the town grew up together on the California Riviera, where palms sway in gentle breezes and the sun shines beneficently on sheltered La Jolla Cove.

On the street level (which is also the fourth floor; three more stories descend a hillside toward the water, and several others rise above), you pass through a colonnade beside a palm-shaded patio to the lobby. Beyond the small, usually crowded registration area and down a few tile stairs is a long parlor with colorful Spanish mosaics, a hand-painted ceiling, and, at the far end, a floor-to-ceiling window with a compelling view of the sea.

La Valencia boasts three restaurants. Mediterranean Room, with its pastel colors, fresh flowers, spectacular view, and acclaimed menu, is a popular spot for breakfast, lunch, or dinner. The Tropical Patio, the outdoor section of the Mediterranean Room, is an ideal for choice for a leisurely lunch on a sunny day.

Café La Rue is next to the Whaling Bar, which has a New England nautical decor. The bar is hung with New Bedford harpoons and lanterns, as wall as ivory scrimshaw and pewter candle holders. There's a model of a full-rigged sailing ship behind the leather booths, and a mural depicting the old whaling days.

From the parlor you look down on tall palm trees, a green park flashing with Frisbees, a sandy shore, and the blue Pacific. Double glass doors open to a balcony above a curved swimming pool and terraced gardens that descend to the road.

The romantic tenth-floor Sky Room, an elegant, intimate space, overlooks the ocean. The imaginative menu features such dishes as grilled scallops on tangerine tarragon sauce and magret of duck with sun-dried wild cherries and ginger. Lunch and dinner are available on weekdays, dinner only on Saturdays.

The hotel has one elevator—the original, still with a human operator. It's swift but is likely to be crowded at peak times. The attractively furnished guest rooms have a traditional European flavor that combines stately lines with the softness of floral fabrics and clear colors. Each has its own climate control, television, and queen- or king-size beds.

A deluxe oceanfront room offers a panoramic view beyond double-glazed windows. A brass chandelier in the living room, mint-green carpeting, soft gold walls, potted plants, and a stocked mini-bar are among the room's furnishings. The marble and black granite bathroom has an oval whirlpool tub.

The hotel has a small health spa and sauna. You can play table tennis or shuffleboard, lounge by the pool or on the beach, or join the vacationers shopping along Prospect Street. The La Jolla Museum of Contemporary Art is a few blocks from the hotel.

Prospect Park Inn

1110 Prospect Street
La Jolla, CA 92037
619-454-0133
800-345-8577 in California
800-433-1609 in U.S.
Fax 619-454-2056

A small inn in downtown La Jolla

Innkeeper: Jean Beazley. **Accommodations:** 23 rooms, 2 suites. **Rates:** $79–$109 single, $89–$119 double, $10 additional person; suites $229–$259. **Included:** Continental breakfast. **Payment:** Major credit cards. **Children:** Welcome. **Pets:** Not allowed. **Smoking:** Not allowed.

Like La Jolla ("The Jewel") itself, Prospect Park Inn is a jewel of a place. The small hotel has a perfect resort location between chic, busy Prospect Street and the green parks, palm trees, and sandy beaches of La Jolla Cove.

For bird's-eye views of the coastline from Oceanside to Mexico, take the scenic drive up Mount Soledad to the top. To get a close look at some of California's most exciting surfing action, go to Windansea Beach. Boomer Beach is also a favorite of experienced surfers.

It's easy to overlook the brick hotel, for its entrance is sandwiched between a corner shop and the showy, pink La Valencia Hotel. But behind the gray and pink awnings and small, light lobby are three floors of charming rooms, all of them furnished in Mediterranean pastels, California style.

There's a minuscule library on the ground floor, with just enough room for a couch, two chairs, and a sideboard where you may help yourself to tea, coffee, chocolate, and cookies any time of day. There are a few shelves of books and magazines and a phone for guests' use. Coke and ice machines are down the hall. All the rooms have television. Studios and penthouses have kitchenettes with microwave and toaster ovens; the mini-suite has a full kitchen. Since the front door is locked and there's no desk clerk on duty after 11:00 P.M., your room key also opens a wrought-iron gate to a side entrance. Underground parking is available.

The Cove Suite is a penthouse that opens to a sun deck overlooking the shops and cafés on the corner of Jenner and Prospect and the park and lovely cove to the west. Continental breakfast and afternoon tea are served on the deck.

The suite has a spacious bedroom, a living area with a fold-out queen-size bed, and a self-contained kitchenette. The Village Suite has similar features. The two penthouses share an entry foyer that may be closed off if a family or couples traveling together wish to share the hotel's upper story.

A few steps away are the famed attractions of La Jolla: beaches, art galleries, boutiques, and restaurants. Highly recommended for dinner is George's at the Cove.

LAGUNA BEACH

Eiler's Inn

741 South Coast Highway
Laguna Beach, CA 92651
714-494-3004

A small inn with a courtyard in the heart of Laguna Beach

Innkeepers: Henk and Annette Wirtz. **Accommodations:** 11 rooms, 1 suite. **Rates:** $100–$175 single or double in summer, $35 less on weekdays and October through May (except holidays); $20 additional person. **Included:** Expanded Continental breakfast. **Minimum stay:** 2 nights on weekends. **Payment:** Major credit cards. **Children:** Not appropriate. **Pets:** Not allowed. **Smoking:** Allowed.

Eiler Larsen was a character in Laguna Beach's past, a colorful Dane who regularly walked the streets and greeted people as they came to town. For many residents and visitors he epitomized the friendly, relaxed attitude of the coastal community. Eiler's Inn represents the same hospitable tradition.

The inn, half a block from the sea, stands in the center of Laguna Beach and faces busy Highway 101. Once you enter the front door, however, the outside world seems far removed. Classical music drifts from the living room, where sectional couches face a corner fireplace and a table full of books and magazines. The cinnamon scent of freshly baked coffee cake is likely to waft from the kitchen.

Laguna Beach is an artists' colony as well as a resort town. You'll find more than seventy art galleries, along with quaint shops and several good restaurants.

You are greeted by the welcoming innkeeper, who will take you back through the brick courtyard, with its trailing bougainvillea and bubbling fountain, to your room, where champagne is chilling.

Two floors of guest rooms form a U around the courtyard. Each room has a different decor — though all are furnished with handsome antiques — and is named for a place of significance in the area. The single suite is the only one named for a person: Eiler Larsen. It's also the preferred room, in an upstairs corner next to the sun deck, with a view of the sea.

The Larsen Suite has a woodstove, a queen-size sofa bed in the sitting area, an equipped kitchen, and a bedroom with a king-size bed. The guest book in the suite is full of raves. A sample: "Cozy by the fire, awakened by sounds of the ocean, all tension is gone — what a romantic and peaceful place."

The next best are the upstairs rooms overlooking the courtyard or sun deck. Those on the main floor are boxy and less inviting, with no view. All the bathrooms have good showers but some are very small.

In the evenings, you're invited to join the other guests for wine and appetizers in the flowery courtyard. On Saturdays a classical guitarist plays. Breakfast is served here or, in cool weather, by the fire in the parlor. Orange juice, boiled eggs, fresh fruits, granola, and, probably, that fragrant coffee cake will make up the morning meal.

Eiler's Inn keeps menus from nearby restaurants, and the innkeepers are happy to recommend their favorites. One of the best and most unusual is Five Feet, which specializes in "nouvelle Chinese." Examples of this happy culinary combination are escargots with black bean–red wine sauce and artichokes stuffed with tiger prawns with Cajun pineapple dressing. Also popular, with excellent food, are Kachina Restaurant and Monique's.

Surf & Sand Hotel

1555 South Coast Highway
Laguna Beach, CA 92651
714-497-4477
800-524-8621
Fax 714-494-7653

A sophisticated beachside hotel

General manager: Peter Phillips. **Accommodations:** 157 rooms and suites. **Rates:** $175–$295 single or double, $10 additional person, suites $425–$675; winter discounts available. **Minimum stay:** 2 nights in July, 3 nights in August. **Payment:** Major credit cards. **Children:** Under 12 free in room with parents. **Pets:** Not allowed. **Smoking:** Nonsmoking rooms available.

A $25 million renovation, which took place from 1988 to 1991, turned the Surf & Sand from quaint to elegant. Now it occupies four buildings of varying heights, and all but three guest rooms have ocean views from private balconies. Directly above the sandy beach, south of the shops and restaurants and crowds of Laguna Beach, this hotel has one of southern California's prime locations.

The rooms vary in size but have the same Mediterranean decor and the same amenities: phones, radios, television, cotton and silk fabrics, original art, and hair dryers and robes in bathrooms of beige marble. They were refurbished in a contemporary style by the noted designer, James Northcutt. Guests find a split of champagne when they arrive, and returning guests receive Godiva chocolates as well. The most luxurious rooms are the two-bedroom penthouses, both with stunning panoramic views.

The Towers restaurant, on the ninth floor of Surf and Sand's main building, is one of the most interesting and stylish in southern California. Towers has a sophisticated art deco theme, with curved glass partitions, mirrored walls, and a wall of windows overlooking the Pacific.

In the center of the complex is a terrace with a pool; below it, overlooking the surf, is Splashes restaurant, the hotel's attempt to prove that fine food and a beachfront location can go together. The Mediterranean-influenced menu changes daily. Examples of the provocative dishes are butternut squash bisque with roasted shrimp, sautéed scallops with sun-dried tomatoes and fennel chutney, and roast chicken with almond and thyme crust, caramelized onions, and balsamic sauce.

In the more formal Towers restaurant you can have cocktails by the granite fireplace and glass-topped grand piano in the lounge. Contemporary cuisine is served, and there's brunch on weekends. Surf & Sand has facilities for groups of up to 250 people, but individuals also receive attentive care. Attendants will set up umbrellas on the beach and serve cocktails and lunch by the pool.

The Ritz-Carlton Laguna Niguel

33533 Shoreline Drive
Laguna Niguel, CA 92677
714-240-2000
800-241-3333
Fax 714-240-1061

An opulent resort on the coast

General manager: John Dravinski. **Accommodations:** 362 rooms, 31 suites, and 27 Ritz-Carlton Club rooms. **Rates:**

$199–$450 single or double, suites $485–$2,500, $50 additional person. **Payment:** Major credit cards. **Children:** Under 17 free in room with parents. **Pets:** Not allowed. **Smoking:** Nonsmoking rooms available.

On a 150-foot shoreline bluff, five miles south of the resort and art community of Laguna Beach, the Ritz-Carlton stands like a Mediterranean aristocrat transplanted to southern California. Outside, the beach beckons, and four tennis courts, an 18-hole golf course, and two pools sprawl enticingly over the landscaped grounds. Indoors, Old World tradition takes over.

This hotel, like the others in the Ritz-Carlton collection, is an example of first-class opulence with a formality unusual in casual California. Those who prefer subdued, classic elegance and strict dress codes to more laid-back lifestyles find it a perfect retreat.

With crystal chandeliers, marble fireplaces, beveled mirrors, richly paneled walls, and custom-made furniture, the hotel is the epitome of the Ritz tradition begun in 1898 by the legendary French hotelier, Cesar Ritz. Since 1927, when the first Ritz-Carlton opened in Boston, the hotels have been noted for their high standards.

The guest services include same-day valet service, airport transportation, secretarial and babysitting services, valet parking, golf bag and luggage storage, twice-daily maid service, a shuttle to and from the golf course and beach, and a multilingual staff. In addition to golf, tennis, and swimming, there is a fitness center with exercise and weight equipment, a sauna, and exercise classes. Individual fitness assessment programs and massage are also available.

Many of these facilities are offered by other luxury resorts. What makes this one different is its standard of consistent quality and service, and its art collection. Museum-quality European paintings, prints, and tapestries hang in the hotel, each catalogued and photographed by an art conservator.

The artwork starts at the porte cochere with a fountain full of bronze dolphins sculpted by California artist John Edward Svenson. It continues through the long lobby, with its Italian marble and hand-loomed carpets, to the maritime theme of the library, with portraits of early American naval officers. A model sailing ship encased in glass stands on a mahogany table before a window that frames a magnificent view of the sea. Shelves of leatherbound books beside the black marble fireplace complete the atmosphere of a peaceful refuge.

The seagoing motif continues with paintings of clipper ships and steamers in the bar. Opposite the bar is the formal dining room, where French art complements the pricey Continental cuisine. The Club Grill is livelier, with a menu dominated by à la carte seafood, steak, and pasta. The mode is hunting-club sporty. Music from the up-tempo combo will entice you into a whirl on the dance floor.

Have breakfast or Sunday brunch in the café above the south-side swimming pool and terrace; in warm months, enjoy light lunches and cocktails at the pool bar.

Each guest room has its own balcony overlooking the curving beach or the gardens and courtyards. Rare ferns, sycamore trees, weeping willows, palms, and native plants surround fountains and lawns. When you can tear yourself away from the view, you'll see that your room has a stocked honor bar, TV with complimentary movies, an armoire, and a safe-deposit box. Terrycloth robes hang in the marble bathrooms.

There is enough at the resort to keep any vacationer occupied, but if you wish to explore, Laguna Beach is a short drive away. The charming village, long known for its devotion to the arts, would be idyllic if a highway didn't slice through the center. The shops are delightful, and there are several good restaurants.

LAKE ARROWHEAD

Château Du Lac

911 Hospital Road
Lake Arrowhead, CA 92352
909-337-6488

A gracious modern home above the lake

Innkeepers: Jody and Oscar Wilson. **Accommodations:** 6 rooms (4 with private bath). **Rates:** $90–$215 in winter, $95–$250 in summer. **Included:** Full breakfast. **Mini-**

mum stay: 2 nights on weekends. **Payment:** Major credit cards. **Children:** Over age 14 welcome. **Pets:** Not allowed. **Smoking:** Not allowed.

On a bluff overlooking Lake Arrowhead, in the San Bernardino mountains, the Wilsons welcome guests who want to enjoy the tranquility of the area and their large, attractive home. This is a place to sleep late, enjoy an excellent breakfast, relax during the day, and enjoy afternoon tea and hors d'oeuvres.

In the winter you can cross-country ski near Lake Arrowhead; in summer walk wooded trails or go to the lake. The Wilsons are beach club members, so their guests have access to the beaches.

The cedar house, which Oscar and Jody completed in 1988, has a touch of Queen Anne style. Built around an atrium with oak trees, it has more than 100 windows that flood the rooms with light. You enter to a living room with a brick fireplace and high ceilings. Beyond is the dining area with doors to a deck and a spectacular view of the lake and mountains. The deck curves around to a gazebo and stairs that lead up to a balcony. From every angle there's another panoramic vista to admire.

Jody, who serves breakfast by the dining room windows, is an expert cook who once had a catering company. She prepares eggs Benedict, potato casserole, quiche, pancakes, sausages in cider, and other entrées that are accompanied by fruit, juice, and hot breads.

The two downstairs guest rooms, which share a bath, are in a separate area that can be closed off — a good choice for two couples. Romantics prefer the spacious Lakeview room, a suite with a brick fireplace, mirrored antique armoire, Jacuzzi tub, and private balcony. It's often reserved months in advance. The Loft is a suite with its own entrance, a four-poster bed, a fireplace, dormer windows, and a tiled bath.

The house is full of angles and nooks. Make your way to the upper level to see Jody's gift corner and on up the stairs to the tower room for seclusion, listening to music, and reading.

"This is a do-nothing area," Oscar says. Formerly in the television industry in Los Angeles, he makes birdhouses, helps run the B&B, and plays the role of gracious host to perfection.

Lake Arrowhead Hilton Resort

P.O. Box 1699
Lake Arrowhead, CA 92352
714-336-1511
800-800-6792
Fax 714-336-1378

A family resort on a mountain lake

Managing director: Gary Upton. **Accommodations:** 261 rooms and suites. **Rates:** $100–$399. **Payment:** Major credit cards. **Children:** Free in room with parents ($15 fee for rollaway bed). **Pets:** Not allowed. **Smoking:** Nonsmoking rooms available.

On the shores of Lake Arrowhead, east of Los Angeles in the San Bernardino Mountains, lies a resort hotel that offers almost anything a vacationing family could want. There are two restaurants, a lounge, an extensive fitness center, tennis courts, a private beach, a lakeside pool, and whirlpool tubs.

In addition to the outdoor recreation, the lodge offers a Kids Club, which entertains children with movies and cartoons, miniature golf, crafts, games, sports, visits to Santa's Village, and meals and snacks. Babysitting is available, with 24-hour advance notice.

The guest rooms in the chalet-like lodge are furnished in contemporary style and have televisions and honor bars. Those with views of the pool or lake are the best.

The most outstanding feature of the hotel is its array of activities. The staff is friendly and eager to help, and the guest services desk is set up specifically to assist in arranging the recreation you prefer. Water sports are popular here, with boating and water skiing high on the list. Hiking, bicycling, and fishing are close behind. You can ice skate all year on the Olympic-size rink in nearby Blue Jay, and, in winter, ski at Snow Valley.

Beau Rivage is the lodge's restaurant for Continental dining and has a lake view. In summer it's open for dinner nightly except Monday, and for brunch on Sunday; in winter it is open only on weekends. The Lobby Café offers informal meals off the open, spacious lobby. Within walking distance of the lodge is Lake Arrowhead Village, a waterside complex of shops and restaurants.

Seminars and conventions are often held at the lodge. It can accommodate up to 400 people in 19 banquet and meeting rooms. A full-time staff assists in coordinating groups, and audiovisual equipment is available.

LONG BEACH

Hotel Queen Mary

1126 Queens Highway
Long Beach, CA 90802
310-435-3511
800-437-2934
Fax 310-437-4531

A historic cruise ship docked in Long Beach harbor

President: Joseph F. Prevratil. **Accommodations:** 365 staterooms and suites. **Rates:** $65–$160 single or double, $13 additional person; suites $180–$575. **Payment:** Major credit cards. **Children:** Under 18 free in room with adult. **Pets:** Not allowed. **Smoking:** Nonsmoking rooms available.

The last and most luxurious of the great ocean liners, the *Queen Mary* is now permanently docked at Long Beach. Her first voyage was in 1936, her last in 1967, when first-class passengers paid $1,282 to travel from Southampton around Cape Horn to Long Beach Harbor. Now owned by the City of Long Beach, the ship is open for tours and to overnight guests who want a cruise experience without leaving the wharf. Called "the ship of beautiful woods," its paneling and inlaid decoration of rare woods create a warm and beautiful interior.

Despite knowing that you can walk off anytime, and despite the fact that the portholes (2,000 of them) view the lights of Los Angeles and the oil refineries of Long Beach, there's a distinct sense of being in an enclosed world, far out at sea, that lends a festive atmosphere to the *Queen Mary*.

The *Queen Mary* is immense. Taller than Niagara Falls, longer than the Eiffel Tower is high, weighing 81,000 tons, she's a majestic sight, even anchored next to a parking lot. Thousands of visitors troop aboard all year round, some to spend a night, others to dine in one of the three restaurants or dance in the art deco lounge, and many simply to tour the historic curiosity.

It's like visiting a theme park. There are marching jazz bands, lifeboat demonstrations, weddings (600 a year), and shops selling English imports. Exhibits show the history of the *Queen Mary*. From royal cruises to World War II transport, the story is fascinating.

The staterooms, in what was once the first-class section, are the largest ever built on a ship. They are on three of the vessel's twelve decks and have the authentic decor of a stylish, if somewhat worn, '30s ship — paneled walls, portholes, the original bathtub spigots for fresh or salt water. The most preferred staterooms are the Duke of Edinburgh, King George, and Queen Mary suites, and the Churchill Suite where Sir Winston himself stayed.

Sir Winston's, dimly lit, with a view of Long Beach Harbor,

is the ship's top restaurant, serving California nouvelle cuisine. The Promenade Café, also with a view of the harbor, is more casual. The Chelsea features a buffet breakfast and lunch and a seafood menu for dinner. The Grand Salon serves a Sunday champagne brunch. You can help yourself to fifty-odd entrées — just as you're likely to find on a real cruise.

The Observation Bar is a stunning art deco cocktail lounge. There's live entertainment here Monday through Saturday.

The Hotel Queen Mary is part of the Queen Mary Seaport, a complex that includes the ship, the Dome (former home of Howard Hughes's *Spruce Goose* airplane), the shops at Queen's Marketplace, and a children's playground called the Queen's Playland.

LOS ANGELES

The Beverly Prescott Hotel

P.O. Box 3065
1224 S. Beverwil Drive
Los Angeles, CA 90035
310-277-2800
800-421-3212
Fax 310-203-9537

A romantic hilltop hotel with a central location

Manager: John P. Strozdas. **Accommodations:** 140 rooms and suites. **Rates:** $125–$350. **Payment:** Major credit cards. **Children:** Welcome. **Pets:** Not allowed. **Smoking:** Nonsmoking rooms available.

The former Beverly Hillcrest hotel, an aging West Los Angeles landmark, has joined the impressive collection of Kimco Hotels — this after a name change and a $12.5 million remodeling job. Like the other Kimco properties in San Francisco, Portland, and Seattle, the Beverly Prescott follows Bill Kimpton's successful formula: affordable rooms, individual — sometimes playful — design, and convenient location.

The hotel, overlooking Beverly Hills, Century City, and West Hollywood, has the sophisticated yet casual charm of a private residence, evident as you enter through wrought-iron gates to a gardenlike loggia with a gossamer-draped daybed. Off the lobby is a living room with warm colors, flowered fabrics, fat yellow hassocks, and a fireplace. Complimentary wine is served here every evening, and coffee and tea are served in the morning. Adjoining the lobby is a meeting room that accommodates up to 80; audiovisual equipment is available. On the twelfth floor is a banquet room with a stunning, 360-degree view of the Los Angeles area.

When you want to dine more formally, L'Escoffier is a short cab ride from the Beverly Prescott. The penthouse restaurant in the Beverly Hilton hotel has won numerous awards for its innovative French cuisine. And it's one of the city's few nightspots where you can dine and dance in an elegant setting.

Guest rooms, each with a balcony with a view, are furnished in bold colors and mahogany and cherry woods. There are honor bars, safes, an outdoor swimming pool, a health club, and 24-hour room service — and a newspaper is brought to your door. If you set your shoes out at night, they'll be returned shined in the morning. Shuttle service is provided to shopping districts.

In contrast to the whimsical decor and plush warmth of much of the hotel, Röx restaurant has a neutral background in the tones of the southern California landscape, with splashes of color in the lights and glass chandeliers. The Röx menu is not extensive, but it's interesting, featuring highlights such as sesame crusted tuna with shiitake mushroom sauce, pork tenderloin with coconut-curry rice, and sautéed foie gras on a pear tart with pomegranate glaze.

The Biltmore Hotel

506 South Grand Avenue
Los Angeles, CA 90071
213-624-1011
800-245-8673
Fax 213-612-1545

A grand hotel of traditional grace and elegance

Manager: Randy Villereal. **Accommodations:** 675 rooms, 25 suites. **Rates:** $129–$250 single,

$129–$250 double, $30 additional person, suites $300–$2,000. **Payment:** Major credit cards. **Children:** Under 18 free in room with parents. **Pets:** Not allowed. **Smoking:** Nonsmoking rooms available.

When the Biltmore opened in 1923 it was the largest and most elaborate hotel west of Chicago. Constructed in Spanish-Italian Renaissance style, with lavish interior ceilings and wall paintings by Italian artist Giovanni Smeraldi, the hotel was — and is — splendid. It has hosted presidents, kings, and Hollywood stars, as well as mere travelers, and along the way it has become a historic landmark.

It's worth visiting the Biltmore just to see the wonderfully ornate Rendezvous Court, where you may take afternoon tea, cocktails, or dessert as you listen to the melodic strains of a piano.

It's been refurbished several times, most recently with a $40 million restoration that spruced up all the public spaces and guest rooms. Furnishings and bathrooms now reflect contemporary luxury, but the artistry that made the Biltmore famous in the '20s may still be seen in the hand-oiled paneling, fine moldings and millwork, carvings, vivid frescoes, and stately columns and pilasters.

Next to the beautiful Rendezvous Court lounge is Bernard's, a classic French restaurant where the lighting is subdued and the meals expensive. Each table is set with a single rose, starched blue linens, crystal, and silver. Much of the 1923 silver set, designed exclusively for the Biltmore, had never been used until it was discovered during the restoration. Lighter and less formal is Ristorante Smeraldi's, serving northern Italian and California cuisine. It's open for three meals a day.

The Grand Avenue Bar, off the main lobby, is noted for its weekday lunch buffet, wines, and jazz, while the European-style Gallery Bar and Cognac Room features beer and liquors. Yet another restaurant is Sai Sai, with a menu of Japanese dishes. The hotel has sixteen grand banquet and meeting rooms.

The Biltmore's concierge desk will handle almost any request: theater tickets, reservations, tours, laundry, and clothes pressing are a few. Room service is available all day. Several languages are spoken by the staff; in this global crossroads, they're all needed.

The guest rooms are spacious and comfortable, if somewhat bland in their furnishings. They have modern or traditional French furniture, including writing tables, armoires that house television sets, and extender reading lamps. You can choose a king-size, queen-size, or two double beds. There are twenty-six room configurations, with three pastel color schemes, and Jim Dine's heart engravings hang on the walls. Each room has a mini-bar stocked with pricey snacks and drinks. All guests have the use of a private health club equipped with an indoor swimming pool, steam room, sauna, whirlpool, Nautilus equipment, and massage service.

To attract the business traveler, the Biltmore offers corporate packages that include an array of special services and amenities. The Club Floor features the hotel's most luxurious accommodations, express check-in and departure, daily newspaper, shoeshine, and twice-daily maid service. On the Club Floor you have access to the Club Lounge, where a concierge, copy machines, translators, and a small library are available. Complimentary tea, cocktails, and a Continental breakfast are served in the Lounge. Business travelers who need fewer amenities like the Executive Floor, which has no concierge or lounge but does offer such services as computer hookups.

The Biltmore represents opulence on the grand scale. It's a fine old hotel that has fortunately been revived with style and a genuine sense of tradition.

Checkers Hotel

535 South Grand Avenue
Los Angeles, CA 90071
213-624-0000
800-426-3135
Fax 213-626-9906

A small, classic hotel of urban elegance

General manager: Volker Ulrich.
Accommodations: 171 rooms, 17 suites. **Rates:** \$185–\$205 single or double, \$20 additional person, suites \$400–\$1,000. **Payment:** Major credit cards. **Children:** Welcome. **Pets:** Allowed. **Smoking:** Nonsmoking rooms available.

In the heart of downtown Los Angeles, near Pershing Square, the Museum of Contemporary Art, and the public library, this posh little hotel is a tranquil and elegant retreat. Built as the Mayflower Hotel in 1927, the 14-story building underwent a $50 million restoration, reopening in 1989 as Checkers, with the finest in furnishings, antiques, artworks, accommodations, and service.

Near the rooftop lap pool there's an equipped weight room and Jacuzzi. Some guests like to work out in the mornings, read the paper, and order a light breakfast here. Sweatsuits and robes are provided.

The lobby, divided into three sections, displays beautiful pieces of contemporary and antique art. Among them are two 19th-century mother-of-pearl elephants, rare old Japanese vases, a Chinese red lacquer screen, and a German armoire of ebony and rosewood that dates from 1725. On the mezzanine above are meeting rooms and a library/sitting room in soft gray, with more Oriental antiques. It's a favored gathering place for small groups, ideal when the lobby is too public and a guest room too private. All the guest rooms, furnished alike, are decorated in soothing, soft colors. They have clock radios, TVs with movie and sports channels, Belgian linens, minibars, writing tables, and phones with international signs on the buttons, in deference to the hotel's many foreign visitors. Attention to detail in appointments and service makes Checkers exceptional.

Orchids in the bathrooms, tub thermometers, makeup mirrors, I. Magnin toiletries, closets that light when the door opens, and padded satin hangers are a few of the special touches. The well-trained staff can respond to almost any need: valet assistance, same-day laundry service, secretarial help, and 24-hour room service are routine. Guests receive complimentary limousine service to any downtown business area, as do dinner guests going to and from the Los Angeles Music Center.

Checkers' intimate restaurant is another serene, elegant gem, in the same tradition and style as its sister hotel, the renowned Campton Place in San Francisco. The chef, Bill Valentine, has earned an enviable reputation for his American contemporary cooking.

Hotel Bel-Air

701 Stone Canyon Road
Los Angeles, CA 90077
213-472-1211
800-648-4097

A luxurious inn of charm and style

Managing director: Frank Boling.
Accommodations: 92 rooms and suites. **Rates:** $275–$395 single, $315–$435 double, suites $495–$2,000. **Payment:** Major credit cards. **Children:** Welcome. **Pets:** Not allowed. **Smoking:** Allowed.

In 1922, the oil millionaire Alonzo E. Bell created a subdivision of estates in the foothills and canyons north of Sunset Boulevard, where palatial homes lie off winding, tree-shaded roads. Named Bel-Air, it became one of the most prestigious residential areas in Los Angeles.

Bell's planning and sales offices were in a Mission-style building that was later converted into a hotel and is now the centerpiece of the present Hotel Bel-Air. Now considerably expanded and renowned for its luxury, celebrated guests, and sequestered location, the hotel is also close to city shopping, restaurants, and offices.

The one- and two-story pink buildings are set on 11½ acres of towering ferns, palms, California sycamores, and native live oaks that shade fountained courtyards, a tumbling stream, and a tranquil pond. In the pond, beautiful (but cranky) swans float regally.

In season, the gardens glow with color, jasmine and gardenia scent the balmy air, and red bougainvillea climbs to terra cotta tiled roofs. The lush grounds are tended by a team of ten gardeners. One of the plantings in their expert care is a 50-foot pink-flowering silk floss tree, largest of its kind in California. It was planted by Alonzo Bell.

When you arrive in the parlorlike lobby, you are asked which newspaper you'd like to have delivered to your door in the morning and then are escorted through the gardens to your room. Classical music plays softly on your radio when you arrive, and the lamps are lit.

Most of the rooms and suites are on the ground level, with glimpses of gardens through rose-draped windows. They vary widely in size and decor; most have a patio or fireplace or both. Some are furnished in a French country style that is light, simple, and classic. Others are traditional American or have a California mission theme. The white tile baths have brass fixtures.

The best choices in the old section are the suites. For consistency in size and style, request a room in the newer section. Each is elegant in pastels and floral fabrics and has its own fountain and whirlpool in a private patio. A few have small kitchens. All guests receive tea service upon arrival and nightly turndown service. Amenities include same-day laundry and dry cleaning, 24-hour room service, and a complimentary shoe shine.

To enter the hotel you cross an arched bridge and walk past a waterfall and Swan Lake. The main building is crowned by a tower that is partly obscured by the brilliant red of flowering trumpet vines.

The restaurant, at the end of a graceful arcade, has banquettes and romantic tables for two by the windows, facing tropical plantings and a terrace that is set for outdoor dining. Contemporary California cuisine is served, using fresh regional ingredients with herbs from the hotel's gardens. Breakfasts are outstanding, and the presentation is stylish.

You may have breakfast, lunch, dinner, and afternoon tea in the restaurant or, for a change, eat light in the bar next door. With a pianist and vocalist performing nightly, the cozy bar is a favorite evening gathering place for Bel-Air residents as well as hotel guests.

There is a heated swimming pool but few other recreational facilities, though tennis and golf are easily accessible. The Bel-Air is mostly a place to retreat and relax, and maybe take a stroll through the quiet, sun-dappled gardens before dinner. But don't forget the shopping opportunities. You're close to Beverly Hills and Rodeo Drive, where glamorous boutiques and designer displays draw shoppers who can afford the best.

Hotel Nikko at Beverly Hills

465 S. La Cienega Boulevard
Los Angeles, CA 90048
310-247-0400
800-645-5687
Fax 310-247-0315

A city hotel with understated luxury and a touch of Japan

General manager: Moenick Manfred. **Accommodations:** 304 rooms, 40 suites. **Rates:** \$220–\$440 single, \$245–\$465 double. **Payment:** Major credit cards. **Children:** Welcome. **Pets:** Welcome. **Smoking:** Nonsmoking rooms available.

The Nikko is sleek, modern, quiet, and very comfortable. Business travelers love this hotel for its high-tech amenities, elegant simplicity, and top-quality service.

When you enter the blocky, seven-story hotel, which stands across the street from Cedars Sinai Medical Center, the sense of purpose is apparent. No one rushes, and voices are low, but few of the people in the beautiful lobby are relaxed vacationers. Most guests are here to get things done.

In the center of the lobby, under a skylight, a stream flows over stone and a fountain plays. Black marble floors with soft leather chairs surround the water; it's a serene place, inviting contemplation when the day's work is done. At the far end of the lobby is the Hana Lounge, with music nightly, and beyond it, windows overlooking the swimming pool. There's one restaurant, the Matrixx, which is open all day serving California and Japanese cuisine.

The guest rooms have king-size beds or two doubles and are outfitted with useful items such as hair dryers, complimentary coffee and tea, satin padded hangers, and robes. The black and ivory baths have deep soaking tubs, one of the reminders of Japan. Another is the rice paper screen used as a window shade. The most unusual features are the state-of-the-art communications systems. A computer connected to the phone can, on command, provide the room temperature and world time zones, control room lighting, operate the CD stereo, and order a wake-up call. Every room has an executive desk and two-line speakerphone with voice mail.

Preferred rooms are those with patios. The Executive Suite is largest and has a separate sitting room.

On the ground floor there's a business center with computers and fax and copy machines; secretarial services are available. The Nikko has conference and meeting facilities and an exercise room and sauna.

Ma Maison Sofitel

8555 Beverly Boulevard
Los Angeles, CA 90048
310-278-5444
800-221-4542
Fax 310-657-2816

A contemporary hotel with a convenient location

Manager: Richard Schilling. **Accommodations:** 311 rooms and suites. **Rates:** $180–$200 single, $200–$220 double, suites $250–$400. **Payment:** Major credit cards. **Children:** Under 12 free in room with parent. **Pets:** Allowed by prior arrangement. **Smoking:** Nonsmoking rooms available.

This sleek ten-story hotel occupies a choice spot in West Los Angeles. It's close to the Pacific Design Center and Cedars Sinai Hospital and across the street from the famed shops of Beverly Center. It's also convenient to Beverly Hills, west side offices, and Melrose Avenue boutiques.

The hotel is functional and attractive, with a Mediterranean ambience. The lobby has stone floors, a sweeping staircase, and textured walls and columns. Colors are muted.

The rooms, too, reflect a southern European style. The color schemes include flowered bedspreads and drapes and walls of soft brick or green with matching carpeting. Upper-floor rooms have French doors leading to outside terraces where one can sit and sip a drink or watch the world pass by below.

The hotel was designed primarily to serve business travelers, with conveniences such as 24-hour room service, three phones per room, voice-activated message centers, mini-bars, and morning newspapers. Some rooms are quite small and lack workable desk space.

If you plan to work during your visit, an Executive King room is a good choice. It has separate areas for sitting, sleeping, and dressing, and includes a desk. The partial suite can be used as one large space or the areas can be separated by drapes for privacy. The closets are ample, but drawer space is very limited. The best rooms are on the north side, facing what residents call the Blue Whale (Pacific Design Center) and the Hollywood Hills beyond. The nighttime view, when it's clear, is spectacular.

In the Ma Maison restaurant on the corner, well-prepared California cuisine is presented in a garden setting. Under a skylight, orange and grapefruit trees grow near vine-covered trellises and tables covered with pink linens. More casual is La Cajole, a bistro where you can dine outdoors if you prefer.

The hotel's conference facilities consist of seven rooms that vary in capacity from 12 to 240. There's a health club for guests' use, with Nautilus machines and a sauna, and an outdoor pool surrounded by decking, lounge chairs, and umbrella tables.

Setting Ma Maison Sofitel above many city hotels are its 24-hour room service, babysitting, and same-day valet service. Also worth noting, if you're bored with airline food, is the box lunch prepared for air travelers, available upon request. Rushed travelers appreciate the Three-Minute Breakfast, a selection of beverages, croissants, pastries, and seasonal fruit set up buffet-style in the lobby.

The New Otani Hotel & Garden

120 South Los Angeles Street
Los Angeles, CA 90012
213-629-1200
800-273-2294 in California
800-421-8795 in U.S. and Canada
Fax 213-622-0980

A Western city hotel with Japanese character

General manager: Kenji Yoshimoto. **Accommodations:** 435 rooms. **Rates:** $145–$205 single, $170–$230 double, suites $400 and up. **Payment:** Major credit cards. **Children:** Welcome. **Pets:** Not allowed. **Smoking:** Nonsmoking rooms available.

When the New Otani opened in 1977, the management did not stress its Japanese heritage and connections. "We didn't want Americans to feel we were simply a Japanese hotel where they could not get by in English or find their eggs and bacon," says Kenji Yoshimoto. But it soon became clear that the touch of Japan was one of the hotel's main attractions. Now it's strongly emphasized, though all employees speak English; in fact, front desk personnel collectively speak 19 languages.

When you leave your car with the valet and enter the three-story lobby, you'll see a dramatic glass sculpture, and behind it the Rendezvous Lounge. In this open area a pianist plays on weekdays. To the left is a shopping arcade; on the right a sweeping staircase winds up to a mezzanine and guest rooms.

East meets West in this 21-story hotel, where you may dine on New York steaks or yakitori, sleep on an American bed or a futon, and listen to cocktail piano music or a Koto player.

The Azalea Restaurant and Bar, on the lobby level, offers a contemporary version of classic Continental cuisine. A Thousand Cranes, upstairs, features Japanese meals at standard tables or in private tatami rooms. This is the place to try sushi, uni (fresh sea urchin), awabi (abalone cooked with sake wine), and tempura in a traditional setting. The restaurant overlooks the "garden in the sky," a tranquil half-acre roof garden of pathways, ponds, and waterfalls bordered with azaleas. Also with a view of the garden is the contemporary Garden Grill, open for Teppan Yaki dining.

Each guest room has a television, refrigerator, and desk in a red lacquer or pastel curved cabinet. Bedside tables match the dramatic red and gray or pastel decor. Shoji screens at the windows and a single flower or delicate piece of art complete the Oriental accent. The bathrooms have phones, hand-held showers, and thick white towels with the hotel's name handsomely embroidered in red. Yukatas (kimonos) are available, as well as standard robes.

For the most interesting experience the New Otani offers, reserve one of the Japanese suites. The parlor is Western, with modern couches and soft chairs, while the sleeping area behind sliding shoji screens is a large, elevated tatami room with a futon. The bath has a sunken tub, traditional in Japan.

At the Sanwa Health Spa, you may relax in a sauna or herb-scented Jacuzzi and enjoy a shiatsu massage. Other features are room service, same-day dry cleaning, a beauty salon, and concierge services.

Special events and programs exploring Japanese culture take place throughout the year. You can learn about the tea ceremony, take a calligraphy lesson, or study one of the many forms of ikebana (flower arranging). Traditional celebrations include Setsubun (the end of winter), the Hina Doll Festival, and Temari, a demonstration of a 1,400-year-old folk art in which colorful silk balls are created.

The New Otani, in Little Tokyo, is close to Los Angeles City Hall, the Music Center, city and county courthouses, and the *Los Angeles Times* building. Across the street is St. Vibiana Cathedral, one of L.A.'s oldest.

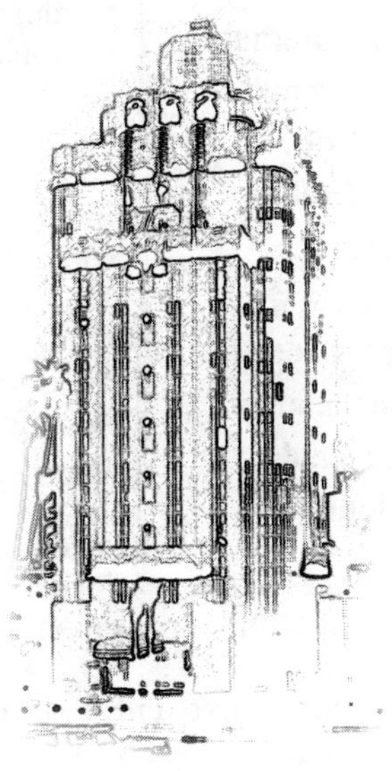

St. James's Club & Hotel

8358 Sunset Boulevard
Los Angeles, CA 90069
213-654-7100
800-225-2637
Fax 213-654-9287

An elegant city hotel with art deco ambience

General manager: Allan Blest. **Accommodations:** 63 rooms and suites. **Rates:** $165–$710. **Payment:** Major credit cards. **Children:** Welcome. **Pets:** Not allowed. **Smoking:** Nonsmoking rooms available.

In the 1930s, this opulent hotel was built as the Sunset Towers, the first all-electric apartment building in California and the tallest (14 stories) building on Sunset Boulevard. Charlie Chaplin, Errol Flynn, Clark Gable, and Jean Harlow were among the screen stars who called it home. Now extensively restored and a member of the international St. James's

Club, it's an art deco landmark, a stunning example of its heyday.

Deco originals and reproductions grace every room, showcasing furniture with walnut burl veneer and replicas of Emile Ruhlmann's classic gondola beds. TVs and mini-bars are hidden in consoles. Marble baths have European fixtures, and some include the modern touch of Jacuzzi tubs.

Other landmark restaurants include Hollywood's oldest, Musso & Frank's Grill, which opened in 1919; Engine Co. No. 28, a restored firehouse; and the oldest eatery in Los Angeles, Philippe, known for its French dip sandwiches and pickled eggs.

The hotel has a well-equipped health club and an outdoor pool. Membership has its privileges in the St. James Club — special functions are often held, parking is free (other guests must pay $15) — but visitors enjoy the same plush surroundings and attentive service.

There's a lounge with live entertainment and a dining room called Terrace City, where you can enjoy fine cuisine and a city view.

Westwood Marquis Hotel and Gardens

930 Hilgard Avenue
Los Angeles, CA 90024
310-208-8765
800-421-2317
Fax 310-824-0355

A gracious hotel of charm near the university

Managing director: Gabriel S. Esquibias. **Accommodations:** 258 suites. **Rates:** $220–$650 single or double. **Payment:** Major credit cards. **Children:** Welcome. **Pets:** Allowed. **Smoking:** Nonsmoking rooms available.

In a typical California blend of urban elegance and unpretentious warmth, the Westwood Marquis strikes a fine balance that is less than grandeur but more than mere good taste.

Behind its ivied walls are excellent restaurants, a plush little lobby, an unflappable concierge, a lounge where tea is served every day but Sunday, and 16 floors of exquisite suites.

In a residential area near the trendy shops of Westwood Village and virtually next to UCLA, the hotel was built in 1969 as a dormitory for university students and later became a retirement home. Since 1979 it has been an exclusive hotel, noted for its polish and personal service.

Hollywood stars stay here when in Los Angeles, as do many top executives in the entertainment, financial, and communications industries. Like other discriminating travelers, they seek integrity, top quality, and an atmosphere pleasing to the senses.

A valet will park your car. Then, from the sidewalk setting of luxuriant greenery, you step into a lobby of Persian rugs, tapestries, and marble. Light from wide windows sparkles on the prisms of glass chandeliers, and fresh flowers add color to every corner. The pastel colors are continued in the suites, which have one, two, or three bedrooms. The baths are in pink or beige marble and have oversize terrycloth robes and towels, hair dryers, two-line telephones, and vanity tables.

In the living room you'll find another phone, a refrigerator, TV, writing table, and Oriental art and impressionist watercolors. All the suites have views of the San Gabriel Mountains or the pool and gardens. If you're in one of the eighteen lavish penthouse suites, you'll have the services of a butler who provides coffee or cocktails, brings in mail, and generally caters to your every whim.

Executive Business Suites are one- or two-bedroom suites that have speakerphones with data ports and voice mail, fax machines, and assorted business publications. Another aspect of the hotel's effort to reach the international business traveler is Business with Breakfast. Portable phones, hand-held computers, and stock market reports are brought to your breakfast table, so you won't waste a moment.

The gardens lend a touch of the country to this city hotel. A lawn rises up a slope from street level to a swimming pool surrounded by flowering plants. The scent of star jasmine fills the air. On one side of the pool are cabanas and changing rooms; on the other a terrace for outdoor dining. Café Perroquet, named for the wild parrots that fly through the gardens, offers light fare grilled over an open fire.

There's another heated pool on the second level, and the hotel has an exercise room, saunas, a Jacuzzi, and steam rooms.

Breakfast, lunch, and a Sunday champagne breakfast are served in the Terrace, under white and green trellises and hanging ferns. Around the corner is the Erté Room for up to twenty-four guests' private dining. It was named after the noted artist and designer whose famous Alphabet lithographs adorn the red walls. The more formal Dynasty Room has a regal setting of porcelain artifacts, exotic plants, softly lit tables, and cushioned booths. Continental cuisine with a California flair is served.

Afternoon tea in the Westwood Lounge is to be savored. To the delicate strains of a harp, you may enjoy sherry or a choice of Twining's teas. A trolley will be brought with sandwiches, golden caviar, scones, petits fours, and pastries that are baked daily on the premises.

You'll find few flaws in this lovely enclave. Traffic noise could be a problem but can be avoided by requesting a suite away from the street. You can hear the steady, annoying hum of a roof generator in some penthouse suites; again, it's avoidable by request. More pleasant are the church bells that ring nightly from across the street, a sound that only adds to the sense of harmony in this fine hotel.

MALIBU

Malibu Beach Inn

22878 Pacific Coast Highway
Malibu, CA 90265
310-456-6444
800-4-MALIBU
Fax 310-456-1499

An oceanside villa with a festive air

Innkeepers: Marty and Vicki Cooper. **Accommodations:** 47 rooms. **Rates:** $150–$245 single or double, $15–$25 additional person; suites $265–$290; rates vary seasonally. **Included:** Continental breakfast. **Minimum stay:** 2 nights on summer weekends. **Payment:** Major credit cards. **Children:** Welcome. **Pets:** Not allowed. **Smoking:** Allowed.

The Malibu Beach Inn, a pink stucco, Spanish-style inn on the beach, will have you smiling the minute you walk in the front entrance. You're bound to love the colorfully painted tiles, Mexican paver tile floors, fountain, and wondrous ocean views.

The three-level inn has a small, open lobby with a fireplace in the sitting area and doors that open to a terrace above the beach. The view extends from Point Dume to Palos Verdes.

The rooms upstairs all have fireplaces, balconies, fabrics in pastels and white, furniture from the Philippines, and bright tiles. Each has a painted tile mural. Television, a stocked refrigerator, and a coffeemaker are provided. There are four rooms on the ground floor that have similar amenities but no fireplaces.

Malibu Beach Inn is ideally located just north of Los Angeles on the famous coastal strip of celebrities' homes and interesting shops. There are all kinds of recreation options: golf, tennis, parasailing, surfing, and scuba diving. The incomparable J. Paul Getty Museum is ten minutes from the inn. Recommended restaurants in the area are La Scala, Beaurivage, Pier View Café, Granita's, Tradinoi, and Monroe's.

MARINA DEL REY

Marina del Rey Hotel

13534 Bali Way
Marina del Rey, CA 90292
310-301-1000
800-8-MARINA in California
800-882-4000 in U.S.
Fax 310-301-8167

A harborside hotel between downtown and the airport

General manager: Ira Kleinrock. **Accommodations:** 154 rooms, 6 suites. **Rates:** $125–$190 single, $145–$210 double, suites $350 and up. **Payment:** Major credit cards. **Children:** Under 18 free in room with parents. **Pets:** Not allowed. **Smoking:** Nonsmoking rooms available.

Sitting on your shaded balcony, watching the sun set over the Pacific and the yachts and sailboats come and and go, you can hardly believe that Los Angeles International Airport is just a ten-minute drive away. But that's the beauty of this hotel. It's convenient to the freeway and the airport, yet it's a sunny retreat where you can fish from the piers, take a harbor cruise, stroll a sandy beach, watch sailboarders dart across the channel, or shop in a New England–style fishing village.

The hotel provides 24-hour complimentary transportation to and from the airport, and cars are available to rent if you need to drive the ten miles to downtown L.A. or elsewhere.

Jaunty in white with blue awnings, the three-story hotel stands at the tip of one of the harbor's peninsulas, allowing for good views from most guest rooms (though some overlook the parking lot). Large windows and open spaces bring the outdoors in. Boats dock at the doorstep, here in the world's largest manmade yacht harbor. The location is this hotel's best feature.

A restaurant and cocktail lounge offer views of the harbor and sea from picture windows. The Seahorse is a formal dining room specializing in seafood such as crab and clams in dill sauce and mussel soup with lime and saffron. Desserts are light, focusing on fresh fruits prepared in tempting ways. If you want to be even closer to the sound of the waves, you may dine outside on the terrace, which has seating for twenty.

Marina del Rey offers all kinds of outdoor recreation. There are four parks where you can jog, ride bicycles, fish from a jetty, barbecue, or listen to free outdoor concerts. Mother's Beach is a favorite spot for swimming and boating, and it has a ramp that accommodates wheelchairs.

The spacious rooms, emphasizing simplicity and comfort, have a Mediterranean atmosphere. A recent renovation considerably brightened the decor of the hotel, which was the first in Marina del Rey when it was built some thirty years ago. Outriggers Lodging Services, which began managing the hotel in mid-1993, has spruced the place up and added more meeting space.

The suites have king-size beds, contemporary couches, console TVs, dining areas, and wet bars, and big closets with full mirrors. For the best view in the hotel, reserve Suite 3139. At times it seems that all the thousands of boats moored at Marina del Rey are sailing just below the suite's balcony, which extends along two sides of the corner room. And the view of the sunset over the main channel is spellbinding.

NEWPORT BEACH

Doryman's Inn

2102 West Ocean Front
Newport Beach, CA 92663
714-675-7300

A small, romantic hotel by the beach

General manager: Kari Yee. **Accommodations:** 10 rooms. **Rates:** $135–$275 single or double, $25 additional person. **Included:** Expanded Continental breakfast. **Payment:** Major credit cards. **Children:** Over age 10 welcome. **Pets:** Not allowed. **Smoking:** Allowed.

This spot on the Pacific shore is unabashedly romantic; the guest rooms have been designed for lovers. Canopy beds piled with ruffled pillows are topped with silk rosettes, lush tropical plants stand in the corners, and fireplaces light at the touch of a switch (these are gas fireplaces, of course, lacking the crackle and character of the real thing, but as a substitute they're not too bad). Most beds are backed by wide mirrors. All the bathrooms have marble sunken tubs.

Other than the beach, points of interest in the area are the 1904 Balboa Pavilion, which has been restored as a restaurant and boat terminal for Catalina Island; the Balboa Island ferry; and Lido Isle, or "Fashion Isle," as it's called for its many shops.

The rooms are lavishly furnished with antiques that recall the 1890s period when the brick hotel was built. The small lobby and rooms are on the second floor, off paneled halls with skylights and hanging ferns. Room 1 is a corner room with a three-door armoire and a down comforter on a brass and white iron bed. Lighter and larger is Room 2, which has an ocean view. Four others also have ocean views. The largest, most expensive, and probably the most romantic is the Master Suite, which has an ocean view, a bed with a draped canopy, and a sunken whirlpool tub.

Coffee is always available in the little breakfast room,

where you can help yourself to morning pastries, boiled eggs, sliced fruits, and yogurt. You may have breakfast here, in your room, or on the rooftop terrace, with its view of Santa Catalina Island.

Parking and a morning paper are provided at Doryman's. The manager is glad to help with any other needs, from an aspirin to a boat reservation to Catalina.

The inn is a seaside retreat for holidays and romance, not a place to do business. The rooms have phones, but as antique reproductions they're not convenient, and the hall telephone is squeezed into a tiny booth.

The only real flaw here is not in the inn itself: since this is a beach resort town, summer brings noisy crowds and traffic.

PASADENA

The Ritz-Carlton Huntington Hotel

1401 South Oak Knoll Avenue
Pasadena, CA 91106
818-568-3900
800-241-3333
Fax: 818-568-3700

A luxurious hotel of classic elegance and style

Manager: William Hall. **Accommodations:** 383 rooms and suites. **Rates:** $145–$240, suites $350–$2,500. **Payment:** Major credit cards. **Children:** Under 18 free with parents. **Pets:** Not allowed. **Smoking:** Nonsmoking rooms available.

Combining resort and hotel amenities, the Ritz-Carlton Huntington offers tennis courts and a tennis pro, a swimming pool, and a fitness center with saunas and steam rooms. The complex is set on 23 acres at the base of the San Gabriel Mountains, a 15-minute drive from downtown Los Angeles.

The hotel opened in 1991, a reconstructed version of the Huntington, a grand and famous hotel built in 1906. The rebuilt version closely follows the original architecture, with its tile roof and imposing design. Two rooms were kept intact: the elegant Viennese Ballroom and the lovely Georgian Room. The genteel ambience was also retained.

Guests at the Ritz-Carlton recognize, appreciate, and can afford the finest.

A typical room has a king or two double beds, yellow damask walls, three phones, and an honor bar. The distinctive black and white marble bathroom has gray walls of shot silk and assorted toiletries. Guests receive twice-daily maid service, robes, evening turndown, and devoted attention from the staff. Those who want even more amenities stay on the concierge floors and enjoy a private lounge and complimentary breakfast, afternoon tea, hors d'oeuvres, and cocktails. The hotel also has six cottages.

Tasteful art objects are displayed and 18th- and 19th-century oil paintings hang on the walls. Overstuffed sofas, fresh flowers, and Oriental carpets add to the atmosphere of comfort and graciousness.

A major draw for business groups is the eight handsomely appointed meeting rooms, large ballroom, and computer and secretarial facilities.

You can dine in style in the Grill and, for casual fare, the Café Restaurant. Lunch and cocktails are available both indoors and out at the Pool Bar, and Continental breakfast, cocktails, and traditional afternoon tea are served in the Lobby Lounge.

The swimming pool is a restoration of California's first Olympic-size pool. A whirlpool has been added, and a pool lounge offering tropical drinks and light fare. To reach the Health Club, you cross the Picture Bridge, a part of the original hotel. Under its peaked roof are carefully restored triangular panels, each painted with a California scene.

Such reminders of its origins give the Ritz-Carlton a timeless atmosphere. Fostering this sense of continuity, the hotel participates in the annual Rose Parade with a float, as it has for 75 years.

RANCHO BERNARDO

Rancho Bernardo Inn

17550 Bernardo Oaks Drive
San Diego, CA 92128
619-487-1611
800-542-6096
Fax 619-673-0311

A Spanish-style resort in the hills

Owner: James Colachis. **Accommodations:** 287 rooms and suites. **Rates:** $125–$205 single or double, $10 additional person; suites $160–$475. **Payment:** Major credit cards. **Children:** Under 12 free in room with parents. **Pets:** Allowed with permission. **Smoking:** Nonsmoking rooms available.

Balmy days and cool nights; tennis, golf, and fine dining; broad loggias and pathways that wind through courtyards with gardens and antique fountains — these are a few of the pleasures at Rancho Bernardo Inn, one of California's outstanding resorts. The setting is lovely, a green valley in the sepia-toned San Pasqual Mountains 30 miles from San Diego.

The original lobby is now the Fireside Room, where you may relax by a fire with board games or cards, and on Friday nights meet the staff over complimentary cocktails at the general manager's reception.

The main building, stucco with a red tile roof, shelters a warm, quiet lobby with low beamed ceilings of limed wood and adobe walls etched with straw. To the left of the entrance is the Music Room, where antique musical instruments are displayed. Piano music begins at four every afternoon, announcing tea time. Complimentary tea, sandwiches, port, and sherry are brought in on silver trays.

The hotel was built in 1962 as part of a development of Spanish-style homes for commuters and retirees.

The guest rooms and suites are in eight low haciendas, each by a courtyard of palm trees and flowers. The rooms are furnished similarly in color schemes of earth tones, gold, and red, and have stocked honor bars, television, and patios overlooking the golf course or a courtyard. In the white tile bathrooms are phones, magnifying makeup mirrors, and hair dryers. Robes hang in the closets, and there are safes for your valuables.

Original artwork graces the guest room walls, while artifacts from Mexico and early California are displayed throughout the inn. The museum-quality works begin at the entrance, near the porte cochere, where a Zuniga bronze statue stands in a grove of sycamore and pine.

The swimming pools have adjoining hydro-spas, and there are three other whirlpools on the property. A sports fitness center offers training equipment, steam rooms, and a juice bar.

The inn's 12 tennis courts are a major recreational draw, as are the special tennis packages. The Tennis College, begun in 1971, has a team of five pros who offer courses in improving your stroke, strategy, and game. Also available are video critiques, tournament arrangements, partner match-ups, tennis movies, and demonstrations.

If you prefer golf, you have several choices. The par-72 West Course unrolls down the valley for 6,400 yards of tricky play. Under the olive and eucalyptus trees are two lakes, a stream, doglegs, and numerous bunkers. Five pros are on hand to help with instruction or arrange tournaments. Two other courses are open to guests: the Temecula Creek Inn course and the 27-hole Oaks North.

RANCHO SANTA FE

The Inn at Rancho Santa Fe

P.O. Box 869
5951 Linea del Cielo
Rancho Santa Fe, CA 92067
619-756-1131
800-654-2928
Fax 619-759-1604

A resort of quiet charm and luxury

General manager: Duncan Hidden. **Accommodations:** 89 rooms, suites, and cottages. **Rates:** $100–$180 rooms and suites, single or double, $10 additional person; cottages $280–$480. **Minimum stay:** 2–3 nights on some holidays. **Payment:** Major credit cards. **Children:** Under 17 free. **Pets:** Allowed in certain cottages at $10 a day. **Smoking:** Allowed.

The scent of money, old and new, is an integral part of Rancho Santa Fe, a quietly wealthy community set in the eucalyptus-covered hills 27 miles north of San Diego.

The Spanish-style village, known for its attractive shops, restaurants, and two golf courses, began in 1923 with a guest house for prospective landowners. The Santa Fe Railroad had imported three million eucalyptus trees from Australia and planted them on 10,000 acres, planning to use them as railroad ties. It didn't work out — the gum trees just weren't suitable — so the railroad turned the land over to residential development.

One of the inn's special features is not in Rancho Santa Fe: it's a beach cottage seven miles away, on the coast at Del Mar. If you want to spend an afternoon by the sea, you'll have a place to shower, dress, and borrow beach equipment.

Eventually the adobe guest house became the Inn at Rancho Santa Fe, and cottages and gardens were added. Steve Royce bought the place in 1958, and it's been a family operation ever since, with daughters and sons, nephews and cousins involved.

The low cottages, containing from two to ten guest rooms, are placed on 20 acres of landscaped grounds and terraced gardens. The main building, the original guest house, has eight rooms and a suite, restaurants, a library, and a lounge. In the Garden Room, breakfast and private banquets are served; beyond it is the Vintage Room, available for cocktails, lunch, and dinner. The Patio Terrace is open for dancing under the stars on summer weekends. Lunches and beverages are served by the long outdoor pool.

Jackets are required for dinner, but the atmosphere at the inn is unpretentious and casual. The service, however, is not at all casual, though it may be unhurried. The staff seems genuinely interested in meeting guests' needs promptly and with a smile.

Croquet, tennis, and golf are major diversions. The Rancho

Santa Fe Croquet Club plays regularly at the inn, while golfers may choose between two private 18-hole courses. The inn has three tennis courts, and lessons may be arranged. For indoor relaxation there are hundreds of books in the library, backgammon, and chess.

Guest rooms are traditionally furnished and have air conditioning, television, and writing desks; most have patios with views of the gardens. Some rooms have fireplaces and kitchens or wet bars. The baths are roomy, with dressing areas and separate showers. There are several private cottages with one, two, and three bedrooms and baths. The largest has its own patio and swimming pool.

Airport limousine service is available for a fee.

The Inn at Rancho Santa Fe has a steady following of fans who return regularly. Evidence that it's a well-loved place is obvious in everything from the attentive service to a rose garden that is cared for by one of the permanent guests.

Rancho Valencia

P.O. Box 9126
5921 Valencia Circle
Rancho Santa Fe, CA 92067
619-756-1123
800-548-3664

A luxurious tennis resort near San Diego

General manager: Michael Ullman.
Accommodations: 43 suites. **Rates:** $295–$750, 2–4 people, $15 additional person. **Payment:** Major credit cards. **Children:** Welcome. **Pets:** Not allowed. **Smoking:** Nonsmoking rooms available.

Like a grand private estate, this John Gardiner tennis resort lies on a hill among terraced gardens and citrus orchards. Twenty miles from the San Diego airport, it's one of the loveliest places in southern California. You don't have to be a tennis player to appreciate all this tranquil resort has to offer.

Rancho Valencia opened in 1989, but it has the atmosphere of a long-established hacienda, with red tile roofs, scuffed Mexican pavers in the lobby, wicker furniture, a tile fireplace, and bleached beams. Fountains splash in the courtyards, and arches over cool walkways are smothered in bougainvillea.

The courtyard by the lobby is open for dining and, on Thursday evenings, for dancing under the stars.

The suites, housed in twenty casitas, are gems of comfort and country luxury. The Rancho Santa Fe suites are the largest. Each has a fireplace, a tile bath, a walk-in closet and dressing room, shuttered windows, hand-painted tiles on the walls, and a garden terrace. Smaller, but with similar amenities and southwestern decor, are the Del Mar Suites. In the morning, fresh orange juice from the trees on the grounds is brought to your door on a tray, with a newspaper and a single red rose.

The resort's widely acclaimed, elegant little restaurant overlooks the hills and serves Continental fare. Next to the restaurant is the Sunrise Room, with brilliant blue and yellow painted tiles, and a patio for outdoor dining. A terrace runs the length of the building, overlooking the tennis courts.

The stone Hacienda Suite is a former private home with three rooms, a private pool, and a deck. Used mainly for VIPs and hospitality events, it rents for $2,000.

The focus of activity here is tennis; about 25% of the resort's guests come for the 18 courts, lessons, clinics, and tennis packages. But many other activities are offered. You can swim in the 25-meter pool, relax in two Jacuzzis, jog on the trails, golf, go deep-sea fishing or hot air ballooning, play polo and croquet, or head for the horse races in nearby Del Mar. Rancho Valencia has a limited number of Turf Club passes available.

The resort provides complimentary transportation to the beach and Del Mar, and shuttle access to the airport and train station.

SAN CLEMENTE

Casa Tropicana

610 Avenida Victoria
San Clemente, CA 92672
714-492-1234

A seaside hotel with a festive, tropical atmosphere

Innkeepers: Rick and Christy Anderson. **Accommodations:** 9 rooms (all with private bath). **Rates:** $120–$350 single or double, $15 additional person; weekday rates available. **Included:** Full breakfast. **Minimum stay:** 2 nights on summer weekends. **Payment:** Major credit cards. **Children:** Welcome. **Pets:** Not allowed. **Smoking:** Not allowed.

An imaginative design allowed this bright and breezy hotel to be built on a 40-foot lot across the road from the beach. It rises five stories against a hillside, a white building with curved arches and a red tile roof. On the ground floor is a restaurant, the Tropicana Bar & Grill, a lively, casual spot with surfboard racks and a beach hut theme. The counter is a surfboard supported by coconut crates, and waterfalls, monkeys, and jungle vines decorate the walls and ceiling. You may order breakfast from the menu in the restaurant or eat in your room or on a tile deck.

Amtrak stops directly across the road, by the San Clemente pier, making the Casa Tropicana an easy destination if you don't want to drive. Exuberantly festive, the hotel is a good choice for romantic surroundings, sun, sand, and surf.

The guest rooms, each with a tropical paradise motif, are off tile walks on the upper floors. They all have television, a refrigerator holding a bottle of champagne, and access to the decks and atrium where coffee is set out early in the morning. All but one have Jacuzzis for two, and several have fireplaces.

Coral Reef, in peach and teal, is furnished in white wicker and bamboo and has a scalloped headboard in tufted green satin. Emerald Forest features coiled vines across the ceiling, Key Largo has Bogart and Bacall posters, and Kokomo is softly romantic in white with purple and blue accents and palm fronds. Out of Africa, the honeymoon suite, is furnished in rich mahogany, dark woods, and Oriental rugs.

The owners' quarters are on the fourth floor, and the entire fifth level is occupied by the extravagant penthouse. It has a bamboo ceiling, an antique oak bed, a three-sided fireplace, and, from the big deck, one of the best views in San Clemente. The crowning touch is an outdoor Jacuzzi in the corner of the deck. The penthouse is the only room that does not have a tropical theme.

The rooms are soundproofed, an advantage in an area filled with vacation crowds. Beach chairs and umbrellas are provided, and guests have free parking in a garage half a block from the hotel.

SAN DIEGO

Balboa Park Inn

3402 Park Boulevard
San Diego, CA 92103
619-298-0823

A romantic inn near Balboa Park

General manager: Ed Wilcox. **Accommodations:** 25 suites (all with private bath). **Rates:** $75–$175 1-4 people. **Included:** Continental breakfast. **Payment:** Major credit cards. **Children:** Welcome in family suites. **Pets:** Not allowed. **Smoking:** Allowed.

Four pink stucco Spanish Colonial buildings, on a corner near Balboa Park, form this complex of suites, courtyards, gardens, and terraces. Luxurious and imaginatively furnished, each suite is a world of its own. They all have refrigerators, cable TV with HBO, phones (local calls are free), and daily maid service, but each has a special theme.

In Greystoke, for example, you'll sleep in the jungle beside a painting of Tarzan; in Nouveau Ritz you'll enter the glamor of Hollywood in the 1940s; it has curved black deco couches backed by a glittery cityscape, and a bathroom in violet and black. Marianne's Southwest has a Hopi Indian motif, and Las Palmas is an exuberant splash of tropical color.

Tara is a roomy, tastefully furnished, residential-style apartment. It has an old-fashioned kitchen and a separate bedroom with a deep whirlpool tub. In the living room, a *Gone with the Wind* painting hangs on the wall. There's a wet bar, and a fire is laid in the fireplace. Tara is often used as a reception suite for groups of up to 25. It connects to the west courtyard and sun terrace. You can rent the suite alone or add the courtyard and terrace if you have a larger party.

Talmadge, on the ground floor, is a favorite of honeymooners. Off the inn's small lobby, it has white satin fabrics, a heart-shaped mirror behind the bed, a bar, a sizable kitchen with a gas stove, and a bathroom in pink.

The sun terrace has lounge chairs and a bar overlooking a lower courtyard. The service here is exemplary. You're escorted to your room, where the lights have been turned on, and shown the laundry room that guests may use. In the morning, you're served a breakfast that includes muffins, bagels, fruit, and juice, along with the local paper. Parking is on the street, with no restrictions.

Optional services are breakfast in bed, picnics to go, and private dinners by candlelight.

Catamaran Resort Hotel

3999 Mission Boulevard
San Diego, CA 92109
619-488-1081
800-288-0770 in U.S.
800-233-8172 in Canada

A casual resort on the water

General manager: Luis Barrios. **Accommodations:** 312 rooms. **Rates:** $105–$175 for 1–4 people, $15 additional person; suites $185–$250. **Minimum stay:** 2 nights on weekends in July and August. **Payment:** Major credit cards. **Children:** Under age 18 free in room with parents. **Pets:** Not allowed. **Smoking:** Non-smoking rooms available.

Polynesia comes to San Diego at the Catamaran, where the grounds are filled with palm trees, exotic birds, flowers, and streams. In the skylighted reception area, a waterfall cascades over stone into a pool of koi. A tapa cloth hangs behind the counter, and a full-size catamaran is suspended from the ceiling. The decor sets the mood for the casual atmosphere at this seaside resort, which faces a long stretch of sandy beach.

Water sports predominate. You can ride a pedal boat, take a sailboard or catamaran lesson, or rent a kayak. Two stern-wheelers cruise Mission Bay for private parties or cocktails and dancing.

The guest rooms are in two-story motel units that surround a swimming pool or edge the beach, and in a 14-story tower. Each room in the tower has a balcony with a view; the higher your room the more expansive the view of Mission Bay and the San Diego skyline. You can see the colorful sails of outriggers waiting by the pier on the beach below, and joggers and skaters on the path.

The tower rooms are furnished in a basic, contemporary style with no embellishments — nothing can compete with the glorious views. Even the penthouse suite is simple, though comfortable, with good reading lamps, textured tan walls and a crisp white bathroom. There's a kitchen suitable for cooking light meals. Drapes cover a wall of sliding glass doors that open to a balcony.

The rooms in lower buildings have balconies and patios, but their views are of the lush, well-tended gardens or the free-form pool. There's also a whirlpool spa and an equipped exercise room.

The Catamaran has several meeting rooms and is popular as a site for small conferences and seminars. You can eat well in the Atoll restaurant or on its patio, and enjoy drinks and dancing in the Cannibal Bar, one of San Diego's favorite night clubs. It has an oval bar of koa wood on one level and a large cabaret a few steps below. Complimentary hors d'oeuvres are served to hotel guests.

Horton Grand Hotel

311 Island Avenue
San Diego, CA 92101
619-544-1886
800-542-1886
Fax 619-239-3823

An updated historic landmark of old San Diego

Owner: Dan Pearson. **Manager:** Greg Pearson. **Accommodations:** 110 rooms and 24 suites. **Rates:** $109–$129, suites $159–$189. **Payment:** Major credit cards. **Children:** Welcome. **Pets:** Allowed. **Smoking:** Nonsmoking rooms available.

The Horton Grand is in San Diego's historic Gaslamp District, once a downtown core gone to seed but now prime urban property. The ornate hotel, two Victorian buildings joined by a courtyard and atrium, stands as a well-restored tribute to comforts past and present. The district is not yet the showcase planners envision, but restaurants and nightspots have sprouted, there's a new convention center, and Horton Plaza, an open-air, multilevel complex of shops and theaters, draws hordes of curious visitors. It's lively and interesting, a cultural as well as a shopping experience.

When the site for Horton Plaza was announced in the 1970s, a local developer and preservationist, Dan Pearson, realized that the oldest hotel in San Diego would be razed. So he moved the century-old Horton Grand to its present location two blocks from the Plaza and then bought another historic hotel, moved it next door, and built an atrium to connect them.

Several years and $12 million later, the Horton Grand reopened in style. Now, when you drive up to the front door, energetic young valets whisk your car and luggage away and you step into a conservatory that turns out to be the lobby. Skylights, white wicker furniture, and a cage of chirping finches create a bright and cheerful atmosphere. The clerks at the front desk, dressed in period costume, add to the turn-of-the-century ambience.

On one side of the lobby there's a small museum and gift shop of Chinese antiques. On the other is the Palace Bar, a combination parlor and saloon where renowned jazz artists play on weekends. Next to the bar is the Ida Bailey Restaurant, named for San Diego's most famous madam, whose house of ill repute was on this site during the bawdy, raucous land-boom days of the 1880s.

The rather small rooms are decorated individually, though they all have gas fireplaces and antique furniture. The best and quietest are the rooms overlooking the courtyard. The King Kalakana suite has a Hawaiian theme, while the bridal suite has a canopied antique bed. All have small sitting areas, rich Victorian draperies, lace curtains, and television sets hidden in wall niches behind mirrors.

The brick courtyard is one of the hotel's most charming features. Four floors of guest rooms surround it, their balconies overlooking white garden furniture, birds that dart among the potted ficus, and vines climbing over lattices.

One room, 309, is supposedly haunted. Guests and chambermaids have felt an unusual presence there, and some speculate that it's the ghost of Roger Whitaker, who was killed in the hotel a hundred years ago by a gambling associate. The room has been booked solid since the phenomena was investigated by psychics. "The ghost is harmless," they said. "He's really very nice."

The Horton Grand offers several special packages, such as a Jazz Special, the Victorian Grand Tradition (including afternoon tea, breakfast in bed, and a sightseeing tour on San Diego's quaint trolley), and a package "For Hopeless Romantics." There's also a third building, which provides large, deluxe suites geared to corporate travelers on extended stays.

The Pan Pacific Hotel

400 West Broadway
San Diego, CA 92101
619-239-4500
Fax 619-239-4527

A contemporary downtown hotel

General manager: Martin Astengo.
Accommodations: 436 rooms and suites. **Rates:** \$140–\$160 single, \$160–\$180 double; suites \$280–\$2,000. **Payment:** Major credit cards. **Children:** Under age 18 free in room with

parent. **Pets:** Not allowed. **Smoking:** Nonsmoking rooms available.

The Pan Pacific, which opened in 1991, is an example of the redevelopment that has sparked San Diego's urban renaissance, creating a busy district of office towers, restaurants, hotels, nightclubs, and stores.

The hotel is close to San Diego's splashy convention center, the performing arts center, Horton Plaza's shopping complex, and the Paladion fashion center. The Museum of Contemporary Art is just a few blocks away.

The glittery hotel with hexagonal towers is part of a complex that includes offices and shops. A 100-foot atrium rises from the lobby and lounge, and glass elevators soar 25 stories. The centerpiece of the atrium is "Flying Emeralds," an immense sculpture of hanging green glass. Beneath this canopy is a lounge featuring cocktails, appetizers, and piano music.

There are two restaurants: the Grill, with a Mexican and Pacific Rim menu, and Romeo Cucina, serving contemporary Italian cuisine. You can watch the cooking action at the Grill, which has an open-display kitchen, or take a table on the outdoor patio. When you want a quick, light breakfast, stop in at Creative Croissants on the corner for coffee and rolls.

The hotel has a health club on the third level, adjacent to the lap pool, Jacuzzi, and sun deck. Sauna, aerobics classes, and massage are on the fitness program. Business and corporate travelers are well-served at the Pan Pacific. They have the use of the most extensive business-support system of any hotel in the region. Secretarial and courier services, phone, fax, telex, word processing, office supplies, meeting rooms, computers, a notary public, and desktop publishing are available. There's even a law library. Ballrooms and conference facilities total 22,000 square feet.

The guest rooms start at the fourth floor and go up to the presidential suite on the 25th floor. They're furnished comfortably, in modern hotel style, and have atrium or city (and some bay) views. They all have multiline phones, TV, minibars, desks, and express check-out. Most appealing are the rooms with king-size beds and the spacious one- and two-bedroom parlor suites.

The Pan Pacific has numerous features that appeal to travelers in the city; the best one is the service. The staff is outstanding. Virtually everyone is courteous, knowledgeable, and eager to help. They're glad to recommend and provide directions to nightspots, visitor attractions, and restaurants. A courtesy van will take you to close destinations, and buses and bright red trolley cars provide more transportation.

San Diego Princess

1404 West Vacation Road
San Diego, CA 92109
619-274-4630
800-542-6275
Fax 619-581-5929

A sprawling resort complex with tropical gardens

General manager: Thomas C. Vincent. **Accommodations:** 359 rooms and 103 suites. **Rates:** $110–$195 single or double, $15 additional person; suites $215–$345. **Payment:** Major credit cards. **Children:** Under age 12 free. **Pets:** Allowed with permission. **Smoking:** Nonsmoking rooms available.

In Mission Bay, north of San Diego Bay, is a 44-acre manmade island that was formed in 1962 from marshland and developed into Vacation Village Resort. The resort's one-level bungalows, surrounded by tropical plants and lagoons and the Mission Bay beachfront, along with numerous recreational facilities, made it a favored San Diego destination.

Now it's owned by Princess Cruises Resorts and Hotels and has been renamed the San Diego Princess. Like its namesake cruise line, the hotel offers comfortable accommodations and vacation fun in the company of like-minded people.

More than half of the hotel's guests are leisure travelers, while the rest are visiting on business or staying with a group. It's an excellent choice for a group trip if you want to be near the water. The resort is a 10-minute drive from the airport and accessible by bridge from San Diego. It's convenient to the area's major attractions: Sea World, Balboa Park and the San Diego Zoo, and Old Town. Seventy golf courses are within easy driving distance, and there's an eighteen-hole putting course on the property.

You can drive or be taken by golf cart to one of the bungalows that lie along the property's curving roads. The spacious guest rooms, two to six to each white brick bungalow, have garden, lagoon, or bay views. Most have sliding glass doors to private patios or the sandy white beach that borders the island. Each room has a dressing area, refrigerator, stocked ServiBar, TV, clock radio, and air conditioning. Some rooms also contain kitchens.

There are six tennis courts, five swimming pools, a fitness center, and a new marina. You can play shuffleboard, go bicycling, jog on paths or a mile of beach, and rent sailboats and motorboats.

The suites include eight Executive Suites with movable soundproof walls, surrounding a lawn suitable for outdoor meetings, a Governor's Suite, and a grand 4,500-square-foot Presidential Bay Suite. Meeting facilities are ample and have been recently expanded with the addition of a ballroom.

The most expensive restaurant, Dockside Broiler, features seafood and a view of Mission Bay. The Barefoot Bar & Grill is more casual.

The service throughout the hotel is exemplary, with that special quality of sunny cheerfulness that seems to be a southern California trademark.

The most appealing aspect of San Diego Princess, the one that makes it different from other, similar resorts, is its beautifully landscaped grounds. Paths wind among gardens lush with palm trees, ferns, pine trees, birds of paradise, and banana trees. Many of the plantings are neatly labeled. Ducks paddle on a blue lagoon that is centered by a fountain and crossed by small, arching bridges. You can climb a high observation tower for a 360-degree view of the island, the waters around it, and the busy mainland on the other side of the bridge.

The Cottage

3829 Albatross Street
San Diego, CA 92103
619-299-1564

A secluded cottage in a residential neighborhood

Innkeepers: Carol and Bob Emerick. **Accommodations:** 1 room and 1 cottage (both with private bath). **Rates:** $49–$65 single or double, $10 additional person. **Included:** Continental breakfast. **Minimum stay:** 2 nights. **Payment:** MasterCard, Visa. **Children:** Welcome. **Pets:** Not allowed. **Smoking:** Not allowed.

The old homes and undeveloped canyons in the Hillcrest section of San Diego make it a quiet part of the city, with an unhurried atmosphere. The Cottage, built in 1913 behind the Emericks' homestead-style residence, fits with the peaceful mood and the sense of a bygone day.

Carol brings a hot breakfast from her kitchen in the morning. Fresh bread, blueberry muffins, and apple cake are a few of her specialties that accompany coffee and juice or fresh fruit.

When you arrive, Carol greets you at the front door of the main house and guides you past the herb garden and hibiscus hedge, under the rose-covered trellis, to the cozy cottage in back.

A woodstove (wood is supplied), a sofa bed, and an oak pump organ stand in the living room. An Austrian carved breakfront holds books, along with menus of San Diego restaurants, in a rack by the rocker. There's a small gas stove in the kitchen and fresh coffee beans in the refrigerator.

A king-size bed with a red quilt and white lacy pillows almost fills the paneled bedroom. Corner windows view a tiny, fenced garden. A television is hidden in a wall niche; the room also has reading lamps, a phone, and a clock radio. Travelers appreciate the padded hangers and the iron and ironing board in the closet. The immaculate blue and white bathroom, with vibrant touches of red, has a tub and a shower.

With the sofa bed, three people will fit nicely in the cottage; any more would be crowding it.

The Emericks have also opened a room in the main house to guests. The Garden Room has a private entrance, TV, and a refrigerator. If you stay in the Garden Room you'll have breakfast in the Emericks' pleasant, homey dining room. You're welcome to relax in the parlor, too, listening to the stereo and tape deck or looking through the books on opera. Other interesting items from the couple's collection include old bottles, a stereopticon, and a working player organ dating from 1875. Bob is an expert on piano and organ restoration; the pump organ in the Cottage is an example of his work.

Most of the furnishings here come from the owners' previous business as antiques dealers. Now Bob teaches sociology at San Diego State College and, with their two daughters grown and gone, Carol manages the guest house.

U.S. Grant Hotel

326 Broadway
San Diego, CA 92101
619-232-3121
800-334-6975 in California
800-237-5029 in U.S.
Fax 619-232-3626

A classic historic hotel in downtown San Diego

Manager: Joe Duncalfe. **Accommodations:** 218 rooms, 62 suites. **Rates:** $135–$155 single, $155–$175 double, $20 additional person, suites $245–$1,000. **Payment:** Major credit cards. **Children:** Under 18 free in room with parents. **Pets:** Allowed by prior arrangement. **Smoking:** Nonsmoking rooms available.

In 1985, the historic U.S. Grant Hotel underwent a four-year, $80 million restoration. The hotel had been closed for nine years, a far cry from its illustrious beginnings in 1910, when it was built by Ulysses S. Grant, Jr., in honor of his father. It had been a San Diego landmark before it fell into disrepair. The expensive restoration returned the hotel to its classic grandeur, with a soaring lobby marked by Palladian columns, 18th-century reproduction furnishings, Dutch and Venetian oil paintings, and Chinese porcelains.

In the large lobby, a concierge is on duty, prepared to procure tickets for any cultural, theatrical, or recreational event, or arrange for secretarial and other business services.

The U.S. Grant takes up a full block in the heart of San Diego's renewed downtown district, across from Horton Plaza, a multilevel shopping center. However, when you drive up to the hotel you don't enter at this front door, but at the parking lot entrance to the lobby, where a valet will take your car to the hotel garage.

A wide marble staircase leads to the meeting rooms on the mezzanine. The guest rooms, though small, are well furnished with Queen Anne mahogany two-poster beds, armoires, and wingback chairs. Each has television with cable, and movies are available. Baths of travertine marble and ceramic tile have hand-milled soaps and terrycloth robes. The suites feature decorative fireplaces and built-in bars. Their decor is comfortably traditional, if uninspired, and their casement windows open to views of the city and downtown redevelopment. There are few complaints about the service at U.S. Grant; not only is it prompt and courteous, it is given with genuine warmth.

The cocktail lounge is a congenial room with polished paneling and a fireplace. Next door is the Grant Grill, which has a classic La Broche rotisserie kitchen. Grilled entrées are served in an atmosphere of rich wood and brass, with fresh flowers on crisp linens.

Another recommended downtown restaurant is Fio's Cucina Italiana, serving award-winning Italian cuisine and reasonably priced wines. The chicken dishes are especially good, and the macadamia nut cheesecake is marvelous.

SANTA MONICA

Hotel Shangri-La

1301 Ocean Avenue
Santa Monica, CA 90401
213-394-2791

A deco hotel facing the beach

General manager: Dino Nanni. **Accommodations:** 55 rooms and suites. **Rates:** $110–$450, 1 to 4 people, $15 additional person. **Included:** Continental breakfast. **Payment:** Major credit cards. **Children:** Under 16 free in room with parents. **Pets:** Not allowed. **Smoking:** Allowed.

Like the setting for a Hollywood movie of the 1930s, the Shangri-La has an art deco motif that is beautifully accomplished. It's rare to find a theme carried through as well while keeping guests' comfort a priority.

The artfully curved, seven-story hotel stands on a busy corner in Santa Monica, directly across the street from Palisades Park and the beach. Several fine restaurants are within walking distance and a major shopping mall is close by.

The rooms on the first six floors range from studios to suites with two bedrooms and two baths. The seventh floor is reserved for two penthouse suites with sun decks. All the rooms have television, phones, and movie posters that are reminders of the period the decor evokes. Most rooms, except for those on the fifth and sixth floors, come with equipped kitchens. The open-gallery design of the building, with exterior hallways, provides cross-ventilation and ocean views.

For updated comfort with a touch of vintage L.A. in a light, bright setting by the beach, the Shangri-La is an excellent choice.

One typical studio has curved chrome chairs and a painting of pink flamingoes. There's a dressing area near the white-tile bath and a kitchen with a gas stove. At this location, and with this kind of style, $110 is not a bad price. And you get breakfast and afternoon tea, served in a pretty little breakfast room off the courtyard. A one-bedroom suite on the sixth floor will have its own wraparound deck and sleek gray furniture striped with burgundy in the spacious living room and bedroom. All rooms on the sixth floor have private sun decks facing west.

The Shangri-La has no restaurant and no recreational facilities. There's a terrace with lounge chairs in the large courtyard in back, with the only thing out of scale with the sophisticated charm here — a chunky, oversize gazebo.

Loews Santa Monica Beach Hotel

1700 Ocean Avenue
Santa Monica, CA 90401
310-458-6700
800-23-LOEWS
Fax 310-458-6761

The only beachfront luxury hotel in the Los Angeles area

General manager: Richard Cassale. **Accommodations:** 350 rooms, including 31 suites. **Rates:** $195–$245 single, $215–$265 double; suites $305–$2,500. **Payment:** Major credit cards. **Children:** Under 18 free in room with adult. **Pets:** Not allowed. **Smoking:** Nonsmoking rooms available.

Facing a broad stretch of Santa Monica sand, this eight-story hotel has a light, open atmosphere befitting its ocean-side location. Sunshine streams through Palladian windows and the skylight over a five-story atrium lobby. Couches and chairs are grouped in conversation areas in the lobby, which has a cheerful array of fountains, palms, orchids, and even a koi pond.

There are several restaurants and cafés on Third Street Promenade, a tree-lined plaza closed to traffic. Busy and festive, it has three blocks of shops, eateries, nightclubs, and theaters.

Off the lobby are United Airline and Hertz car rental counters. The hotel offers valet and self-parking, multilingual concierge service, a business center, dry cleaning, laundry, and shoeshines. Guests can rent bicycles and roller skates.

You're likely to see people in the film and television industries here; Santa Monica has become a popular site for production companies. Once the area was a getaway for movie stars. Charlie Chaplin and Mary Pickford built homes that still stand on the beach directly below the hotel. Two blocks away is the historic Santa Monica pier, with its famous restored carousel and other rides.

Most guest rooms have partial ocean views. Location makes the difference in rates; all rooms are spacious and have the same decor. They're furnished in California-casual style, with bleached rattan, wicker, and fabrics in mauve, peach, coral, and sky blue. They have narrow balconies, mini-bars, hair dryers, robes, and television with all channels. Most suites are corner rooms, so they enjoy both a pool view and full ocean view.

The pool, 30 feet above the beach, is designed for both indoor and outdoor use. Near it is the Jackson Sousa Fitness Facility. This excellent fitness center provides state-of-the-art equipment, classrooms, Jacuzzi, sauna and steam, massage, and personal training sessions.

The bewildering array of restaurants in Santa Monica — some 400 within eight square miles — makes dining choices a pleasant dilemma. In the hotel, you have two choices (plus 24-hour room service and a lobby bar that serves snacks). Riva features California-Italian cookery in an informal atmosphere, while the Coast Café offers casual meals all day on the terrace. Both are relaxing spots with ocean views.

SEAL BEACH

The Seal Beach Inn and Gardens

212 5th Street
Seal Beach, CA 90740
310-493-2416
Fax 310-799-0483

A colorful inn surrounded by flowers

Innkeeper: Marjorie Bettenhausen. **Accommodations:** 23 rooms (all with private bath). **Rates:** $108–$235 single or double, $10 additional person. **Included:** Full breakfast. **Payment:** Major credit cards. **Children:** Welcome. **Pets:** Not allowed. **Smoking:** Not allowed.

Seal Beach is a pleasant, friendly, quiet town on Highway 1, south of Long Beach. Busy in summer, it's a popular place for surfing, sailboarding, and strolling on the beach, though it doesn't have the glamour of some southern California resort areas. Go to Seal Beach to enjoy the fresh ocean breezes, some good casual restaurants, the shops of Old Town and Seaport Village, fishing off the pier, bicycle riding, and maybe a gondola ride through the canals. And while you're here, stay at the charming Seal Beach Inn, a block from the sea.

The first thing you notice about the inn is color. The brick terrace in front of the two-story inn is overflowing with bright flowers. Bougainvillea cascades over wrought-iron railings; Boston ivy climbs the walls. Blue canopies and old-fashioned red street lamps add further touches of color.

Built in the 1920s, the long-neglected inn was restored in the mid-1970s by Marjorie Bettenhausen. She created a showplace reminiscent of the inns along the Mediterranean coast of France. Antiques from her travels are in all the rooms and gardens. They include a 300-year-old French fountain, an oak fireplace mantel and altar from a historic Chicago church, a Persian tile mural four centuries old, and numerous frescoes and marble pieces. The bed from John Barrymore's estate is here, along with a French armoire that was part of a trousseau in 1839.

The rooms, named for flowers, have TVs and phones. Fourteen have kitchens and one has a fireplace. The suites have sitting areas with antiques, lacy curtains, and lots of chintz and ruffles that are almost — but not quite — too fussy for comfort. Most expensive and largest are the interior Imperial Suites, all eight of them considered honeymoon suites.

Marjorie wants contented guests, and she goes out of her way to make sure they're happy. You'll find homemade chocolate chip cookies in your room at night and a list of local points of interest. You can order a picnic basket or get a restaurant recommendation from the innkeeper or her staff.

Vienna Woods is a favorite for its elaborately carved bed from pre–Civil War Virginia. Mexican pavers form the floor and German lace curtains hang at the windows. Black and white glass tiles give the bathroom a dramatic look.

Some rooms have paneled walls and ceilings. They can be quite dark, so if you prefer a lighter atmosphere you may want to request it.

A buffet breakfast is provided in the cozy tearoom; if you're like most guests, you'll want to enjoy it by the pool or on the terrace. The fare includes homemade breads, granola, a quiche or casserole, juice, and coffee or tea. Afternoon wine and cheese are served by the fire in the dining room.

TEMECULA

Loma Vista Bed & Breakfast

33350 La Serena Way
Temecula, CA 92390
714-676-7047

A mission-style hilltop home overlooking vineyards

Innkeepers: Betty and Dick Ryan. **Accommodations:** 6 rooms (private baths). **Rates:** $95–$125. **Included:** Full breakfast. **Minimum stay:** 2 nights on holiday weekends. **Payment:** MasterCard, Visa. **Children:** Welcome. **Pets:** Not allowed. **Smoking:** Not allowed. **Open:** Year-round except Thanksgiving, Christmas, and New Year's.

When the Ryans designed Loma Vista in 1987, they chose Betty Ryan's favorite architecture: Spanish mission style, with its curved archways, red tile roofs, and cool courtyards. The interior of their imposing hilltop home is light and spacious, but the decor is more American traditional than early California, with a carpet in the living room and white and flower-patterned couches by a brick fireplace. The windows overlook the vineyards of Temecula Valley, a wine-producing region north of San Diego.

Betty and Dick are relaxed, friendly hosts who know how to keep guests happy. You'll find sherry and a basket of fruit in your room and evening wine and cheese on the patio. The champagne breakfast, served family-style in the dining room, includes hot entrées as well as sundaes made from fresh fruit, yogurt, and granola.

Loma Vista's guest rooms, named after wine grapes, are air conditioned and have queen- or king-size beds and clock radios. Each is decorated distinctively. Fumé Blanc is light and airy, with white wicker and plants; Sauvignon Blanc features the desert hues and white pine of the Southwest. Zinfandel has gracious Queen

Anne furnishings and a balcony with a view of Palomar Observatory.

The most striking room is Champagne. Though it has no balcony or view, it's a glamorous retreat with curved black lacquer furniture, a satin quilt, and framed photos of Fred Astaire and Marilyn Monroe lending a Hollywood/art deco flavor.

The Ryans will urge you to explore the historic Temecula area. The village was a stagecoach stop 150 years ago, on the Butterfield State Line between St. Louis and San Francisco, and has retained some of its Old West atmosphere. You can shop for antiques, tour the wineries, go hot-air ballooning, play golf, fish at Lake Skinner, and try the local restaurants the innkeepers recommend.

VISTA

Cal-a-Vie

2249 Somerset Road
Vista, CA 92084
619-945-2055

A country inn with a focus on fitness

Owners: William and Marlene Power. **Accommodations:** 24 cottages. **Rates:** $3,950 per person per week, European plan;

$3,250 per week American plan. **Included:** All meals. **Minimum stay:** 7 days. **Payment:** MasterCard, Visa. **Children:** Age 18 and older welcome. **Pets:** Not allowed. **Smoking:** Allowed in designated smoking rooms. **Open:** Year-round except Christmas/New Year holidays.

Forty miles north of San Diego, this exclusive spa nestles against a rural hillside like a Mediterranean village. From the tile-roofed stucco cottages the view is of citrus and avocado orchards, mountains, and blue sky. The air is clean and the climate balmy. It's an ideal setting for a retreat into self-improvement.

Throughout the year Cal-a-Vie offers women's sessions, men's sessions, and coed sessions; they begin on Sunday afternoon and end the following Sunday morning. Transportation to and from the San Diego International Airport is provided at no charge.

At Cal-a-Vie you'll find an emphasis on balance, combining the American approach to fitness with a European focus on skin and body care. Heavy exercise takes place in the mornings; the afternoons are devoted to rest, relaxation, and therapeutic treatments. The day begins with a brisk walk in the adjacent hills; then it's breakfast and a series of warm-ups, aerobics, and exercise classes. Since the spa never has more than twenty-four people at a time, each guest receives attention and instruction.

Afternoon skin and body treatments include facials, Swedish and shiatsu massage, seaweed wraps, hydrotherapy, aromatherapy, and the highlight: a one-hour Body-glo treatment that sloughs off dead skin cells and leaves you feeling rejuvenated.

In this busy schedule, time is allotted for lounging by the pool and relaxing in the gardens of oleander, lavender, and agapanthus. There's no television and no piped-in music, just the rustle of vines, the trickling of a waterfall, and bird songs. The spicy scent of eucalyptus mingles with the inviting smells of good foods baking, and you begin to think of dinner.

Three meals and two snacks a day add up to just 900 calories that don't leave you hungry. The Cal-a-Vie cuisine features fresh ingredients and a variety of spices and herbs.

Examples of the light and elegant fare are grilled swordfish with papaya salsa, mango sorbet with raspberries, Italian pear cake, and even strawberry cheesecake.

The spa provides the gear and clothing you'll need and launders it daily; all you need to pack is your swimsuit, underwear, shoes, and toothbrush. Your room, in one of the four buildings around the swimming pool, will have a clock radio, phone, armoire, a duvet on the bed, and a closet with an umbrella for the occasional rain sprinkle. All the units are the same size, with slightly different decorating schemes, and all have private patios.

Recommended Reading

22 Days in California, Roger Rapoport (John Muir Publications), $9.95. Detailed itineraries, maps, daily plans, and sightseeing highlights. Small print, no illustrations, but useful information.

Adventuring in the California Desert, Lynne Foster (Sierra Club Books), $14.00. Part of the Sierra Club series focusing on outdoor activities, camping facilities, natural history. How to best enjoy the Great Basin, Mojave, and Colorado Desert regions. A few drawings and maps. Carefully crafted, lots of information.

California: The Ultimate Guidebook, by Ray Riegert (Ulysses Press), $13.95. Riegert knows California well and is a trustworthy guide. His book divides the state by area and includes restaurants, lodging, nightlife, shopping, beaches and parks, and offbeat attractions. It covers so much ground the information is limited. Contains simple maps.

Fielding's California: The Mission Trail, San Diego to San Francisco, Lynn Foster (William Morrow), $10.95. For the history buff. Contains practical tips and suggestions for activities and explains historical events along the mission trail.

Fishing in Northern California* and *Fishing in Southern California, Ken Albert (Marketscope Books), $14.95 each. Everything you need to know about fishing California's 5,000 lakes and 30,000 miles of streams. Clear format.

Fodor's Pocket San Francisco: The Best of the City, Fodor's Travel Publications, $7.00. Pocket size, readable, covers highlights for short visits.

The Great Family Getaway Guide, Bill Gleeson (Chronicle Books), $8.95. Includes 180 California adventures — resorts, motels, theme parks, museums, and attractions with special appeal to kids. Personal, chatty style. Black and white photographs, no maps.

The Hiker's Guide to California, Ron Adkison (Falcon Press), $11.95. Detailed information on 100 hikes in the backcountry. Some maps and photographs.

Inside San Francisco, Don and Betty Martin (Pine Cone Press), $8.95. Detailed, witty, opinionated city guide. Convenient size.

Insight Guide: California (Apa Publications, Ltd.), $19.95. Grand overview of the state, with essays on its history, social fabric, ethnic cultures, and geography. Includes maps and superb color photographs.

Los Angeles Access, Richard S. Wurman (Access Press), $11.95. Divides the L.A. area by neighborhood and reviews the hotels, restaurants, and attractions in each. Color-coded and mapped. Intriguing, workable system, once you figure it out. Strong architectural focus.

Northern California Handbook, Kim Weir (Moon Publications), $16.95. Crammed with information but well organized. Contains thoughtful commentaries, maps, and some color photographs.

San Francisco Access, Richard S. Wurman (Access Press), $12.95. Divides the San Francisco area by neighborhood; color-coded (see Los Angeles Access.)

What's What

Bicycling

American River Inn, 405
Bartels Ranch and Country Inn, 90
The Bayberry Inn, 267
Beach House, 207
Blue Quail Inn, 268
Campbell Ranch Inn, 31
Carmel Valley Ranch Resort, 225
Coloma Country Inn, 394
La Costa Hotel and Spa, 486
Four Seasons Biltmore, 272
The Gingerbread Mansion, 339
The Heirloom, 411
La Mancha, 307
Ojai Inn & Country Club, 252
The Old Yacht Club Inn, 274
San Diego Princess, 561
The Sandpiper Inn, 218
Simpson House Inn, 276
The Stanford Inn by the Sea, 368

Boating

The Alisal Guest Ranch, 286
Caples Lake Resort, 418
Dana Point Resort, 497
Dockside Boat & Bed, 70
Disneyland Hotel, 472
Edelweiss Lodge, 422
Lakeland Village Beach & Ski Resort, 452
Otter Bar Lodge, 341
San Diego Princess, 561
The Stanford Inn by the Sea, 368

Business Services

The Alisal Guest Ranch, 286
The Autry Resort Hotel, 305
The Bayberry Inn, 267
The Biltmore Hotel, 528
Campton Place, 101
Carmel Valley Ranch Resort, 225
Chaminade, 283
La Costa Hotel and Spa, 486
Disneyland Hotel, 472
The Fairmont Hotel, 138
Four Seasons Biltmore, 272
Four Seasons Clift Hotel, 105
Hotel De Anza, 163
Hotel Del Coronado, 489
Hotel Nikko at Beverly Hills, 534
Hotel Nikko (San Francisco), 115
The Inn at Spanish Bay, 263
The Inn at the Tides, 15
Le Meridien San Diego at Coronado, 491
Meadowood, 93
The New Otani Hotel & Garden, 537
Ojai Valley Inn & Country Club, 252
The Pan Pacific Hotel (San Diego), 559
The Pan Pacific Hotel (San Francisco), 147
Rancho Bernardo Inn, 549
The Regent Beverly Wilshire, 483
San Ysidro Ranch, 243
Sheraton Palace Hotel, 132
Stouffer Stanford Court Hotel, 134
Surf & Sand Hotel, 519
U.S. Grant Hotel, 564
The White Swan Inn, 159

Croquet

The Alisal Guest Ranch, 286
American River Inn, 405
The Bayberry Inn, 267
Churchill Manor, 61
Circle Bar B Guest Ranch, 236
Four Seasons Biltmore, 272
Furnace Creek Inn, 298

The Heirloom, 411
The Inn at Rancho Santa Fe, 550
Joshua Grindle Inn, 362
La Jolla Beach & Tennis Club, 512
La Mancha, 307
Meadowood, 93
The Old Milano Hotel, 346
Rancho Valencia, 552
Simpson House Inn, 276
Stonepine, 230
Tenaya Lodge, 403
Ward's Big Foot Ranch, 370
Wedgewood Inn, 415

Fine Dining

Auberge du Soleil, 86
The Biltmore Hotel, 528
Campton Place, 101
Casa Madrona Hotel, 170
Chaminade, 283
Hotel Vintage Court, 120
La Mancha, 307
Madrona Manor, 48
The Majestic, 142
Meadowood, 93
Mount View Hotel, 24
The Old Yacht Club Inn, 274
Prescott Hotel, 149
Post Ranch Inn, 203
The Regent Beverly Wilshire, 483
The Sterling Hotel, 444
Stouffer Stanford Court Hotel, 134
Timberhill Ranch, 29
Ventana, 205
Villa Florence Hotel, 155
Vintners Inn, 167

Golf

The Alisal Guest Ranch, 286
Carmel Valley Ranch Resort, 225
La Costa Hotel and Spa, 486
Furnace Creek Inn, 298

The Inn at Spanish Bay, 263
The Lodge at Pebble Beach, 265
Meadowood, 93
Ojai Valley Inn & Country Club, 252
Quail Lodge, 227
La Quinta Hotel Golf & Tennis Resort, 301
Rancho Bernardo Inn, 549
Resort at Squaw Creek, 434
The Ritz-Carlton Laguna Niguel, 520
The Ritz-Carlton Rancho Mirage, 316
The Sea Ranch, 376
Silverado Country Club & Resort, 66
Wawona Hotel, 461

Historic Hotels

City Hotel, 396
Fallon Hotel, 398
The Hotel Jeffery, 400
Imperial Hotel, 391
Julian Hotel, 507
Mount View Hotel, 24
The National Hotel, 416
Sonoma Hotel, 176
The Union Hotel (Benicia), 13

Horseback Riding

The Alisal Guest Ranch, 286
Circle Bar B Guest Ranch, 236
Drakesbad Guest Ranch, 325
Furnace Creek Inn, 298
The Lodge at Pebble Beach, 265
San Ysidro Ranch, 243
Stonepine, 230
Trinity Alps Resort, 349
Wawona Hotel, 461

Kitchen/Cooking Facilities

Caboose Motel, 327
Caples Lake Resort, 418

Casa Madrona Hotel, 170
The Cottage, 563
Country Cottage, 104
Edelweiss Lodge, 422
El Encanto, 270
Gray's Retreat, 79
Holly Tree Inn, 52
Hotel Bel-Air, 532
Hotel Shangri-La, 566
Hranrad House, 361
The Inn at Rancho Santa Fe, 550
Isis Oasis, 35
Jackson Court, 125
La Jolla Beach & Tennis Club, 512
La Mancha, 307
Orchid Tree Inn, 313
Le Petit Château, 310
The Phoenix, 174
Prospect Park Inn, 516
Sandcastle, 343
San Diego Princess, 561
Scott Courtyard, 26
Sea Arch, 357
Sea Haus, 367
Silverado Country Club & Resort, 66
Sorensen's, 409
Squaw Valley Lodge, 435
Stillwater Cove Ranch, 56
Tamarack Lodge Resort, 426
Trinity Alps Resort, 349
Vagabond's House, 223

Pets Allowed with Permission

Auberge du Soleil, 86
The Autry Resort Hotel, 305
The Bayberry Inn, 267
Brannan Cottage Inn, 19
Caboose Motel, 327
Captain Dillingham's Inn, 11
Cypress Inn (Carmel), 211
Drakesbad Guest Ranch, 325
Edelweiss Lodge, 422
Four Seasons Biltmore, 272

Four Seasons Clift Hotel, 105
Golden Gate Hotel, 109
The Inn at Rancho Santa Fe, 550
Isis Oasis, 35
The Lodge at Pebble Beach, 265
Meadowlark, 22
Mountain Home Ranch, 25
The New Otani Hotel & Garden, 537
Ojai Valley Inn & Country Club, 252
Old Thyme Inn, 44
Quail Lodge, 227
Radisson Hotel Sacramento, 443
Rancho Bernardo Inn, 549
The Regent Beverly Wilshire, 483
Sandcastle, 343
San Diego Princess, 561
San Ysidro Ranch, 243
Sorensen's, 409
Stillwater Cove Ranch, 56
Tamarack Lodge Resort, 426
Trinity Alps Resort, 349
Vagabond's House, 223
Ward's Big Foot Ranch, 370

Restaurant Open to Public

The Ahwahnee, 463
Auberge du Soleil, 86
The Autry Resort Hotel, 305
Beverly Prescott Hotel, 527
The Biltmore Hotel, 528
Caboose Motel, 327
Campton Place, 101
Caples Lake Resort, 418
Carmel Valley Ranch Resort, 225
Casa Madrona Hotel, 170
La Casa del Zorro Resort Hotel, 297
Catamaran Resort Hotel, 556
Chaminade, 283
The Christiania Inn, 453
Circle Bar B Guest Ranch, 236
The Claremont Resort and Spa, 68
The Cliffs at Shell Beach, 285
La Costa Hotel and Spa, 486

Dana Point Resort, 497
The Delta King Hotel, 440
Disneyland Hotel, 472
El Dorado Hotel, 175
El Encanto, 270
The Fairmont Hotel, 138
Four Seasons Biltmore, 272
Four Seasons Clift Hotel, 105
Furnace Creek Inn, 298
Galleria Park Hotel, 107
Garden Court Hotel, 76
Harbor Court Hotel, 110
Harbor House, 332
Hill House of Mendocino, 360
Hotel Bel-Air, 532
Hotel De Anza, 163
Hotel Del Coronado, 489
Hotel Nikko at Beverly Hills, 534
Hotel Nikko (San Francisco), 115
Hotel Queen Mary, 525
Hotel Triton, 119
Hotel Vintage Court, 120
Inn at the Opera, 122
The Inn at Rancho Santa Fe, 550
The Inn at Spanish Bay, 263
The Inn at the Tides, 15
Julian Hotel, 507
Little River Inn, 355
The Lodge at Pebble Beach, 265
The Majestic, 142
Ma Maison Sofitel, 535
La Mancha, 307
Marina del Rey Hotel, 544
The Mark Hopkins Intercontinental, 145
Meadowood, 93
Mount View Hotel, 24
The National Hotel, 416
The New Otani Hotel & Garden, 537
Ojai Valley Inn & Country Club, 252
The Old Milano Hotel, 346
Pan Pacific Hotel (San Diego), 559
Pan Pacific Hotel (San Francisco), 147
The Pelican Inn, 59
Peninsula Beverly Hills, 481

Post Ranch Inn, 203
Prescott Hotel, 149
Quail Lodge, 227
Rancho Bernardo Inn, 549
Rancho Valencia, 552
The Regent Beverly Wilshire, 483
Resort at Squaw Creek, 434
The Ritz-Carlton Laguna Niguel, 520
The Ritz-Carlton Rancho Mirage, 316
The Ritz-Carlton San Francisco, 152
Rose Victorian Inn, 198
San Diego Princess, 561
San Ysidro Ranch, 243
Seal Rock Inn, 131
Sheraton Palace Hotel, 132
Silverado Country Club & Resort, 66
Sonoma Mission Inn & Spa, 17
Sorensen's, 409
Squaw Valley Lodge, 435
The Sterling Hotel, 444
Stouffer Stanford Court Hotel, 134
Surf & Sand Hotel, 519
Tamarack Lodge Resort, 426
Tenaya Lodge, 403
U.S. Grant Hotel, 564
The Union Hotel (Benicia), 13
The Upham Hotel, 278
The Villa Florence Hotel, 155
Villa Royale, 303
Vintners Inn, 167
Wawona Hotel, 461

Tennis

The Ahwahnee, 463
The Alisal Guest Ranch, 286
Auberge du Soleil, 86
The Autry Resort Hotel, 305
Campbell Ranch Inn, 31
Carmel Valley Ranch Resort, 225
La Casa del Zorro Resort Hotel, 297
Chaminade, 283
Circle Bar B Guest Ranch, 236

The Claremont Resort and Spa, 68
La Costa Hotel and Spa, 486
Dana Point Resort, 497
Disneyland Hotel, 472
El Encanto, 270
Four Seasons Biltmore, 272
Furnace Creek Inn, 298
Hotel Del Coronado, 489
The Inn at Rancho Santa Fe, 550
The Inn at Spanish Bay, 263
La Jolla Beach & Tennis Club, 512
Lakeland Village Beach & Ski Resort, 452
La Mancha, 307
Little River Inn, 355
The Lodge at Pebble Beach, 265
Meadowood, 93
Ojai Valley Inn & Country Club, 252
Quail Lodge, 227
La Quinta Hotel Golf & Tennis Resort, 301
Rancho Bernardo Inn, 549
Rancho Valencia, 552
Resort at Squaw Creek, 434
The Ritz-Carlton Laguna Niguel, 520
The Ritz-Carlton Rancho Mirage, 316
San Diego Princess, 561
San Ysidro Ranch, 243
Silverado Country Club & Resort, 66
Sonoma Mission Inn & Spa, 17
Squaw Valley Lodge, 435
Stonepine, 230
Timberhill Ranch, 29
Wawona Hotel, 461

Wheelchair Access

The Ahwahnee, 463
The Autry Resort Hotel, 305
The Babbling Brook Inn, 281
Blue Lantern Inn, 496
The Biltmore Hotel, 528
Dana Point Resort, 497
Delta King Hotel, 440
Disneyland Hotel, 472

El Dorado Hotel, 175
The Fairmont Hotel, 138
Four Seasons Biltmore, 272
Four Seasons Clift Hotel, 105
Galleria Park Hotel, 107
Holly Tree Inn, 52
Hotel Bel-Air, 532
Hotel De Anza, 163
Hotel Del Coronado, 489
Hotel Juliana, 113
Hotel Nikko (San Francisco), 115
Hotel Nikko at Beverly Hills, 534
Inn at the Opera, 122
The Inn at Spanish Bay, 263
The Inn at the Tides, 15
The Lodge at Pebble Beach, 265
Malibu Beach Inn, 543
The Pan Pacific Hotel (San Diego), 559
The Pan Pacific Hotel (San Francisco), 147
Peninsula Beverly Hills, 481
Point Reyes Seashore Lodge, 72
La Quinta Hotel Golf & Tennis Resort, 301
Radisson Hotel Sacramento, 443
Rancho Bernardo Inn, 549
Rancho Valencia, 552
Resort at Squaw Creek, 434
The Ritz-Carlton Laguna Niguel, 520
The Ritz-Carlton Rancho Mirage, 316
The Ritz-Carlton San Francisco, 152
San Diego Princess, 561
Sheraton Palace Hotel, 132
Sonoma Mission Inn and Spa, 17
Spindrift Inn, 250
Squaw Valley Lodge, 435
Stouffer Stanford Court Hotel, 134
Surf & Sand Hotel, 519
Tenaya Lodge, 403
Timberhill Ranch, 29
U.S. Grant Hotel, 564
The Union Hotel (Benicia), 13
The Upham Hotel, 278

Index

Abigail's, 437
The Ahwahnee, 463
The Alisal Guest Ranch, 286
Alpers' Owens River Ranch, 420
Amber House Bed & Breakfast Inn, 439
American River Inn, 405
Apple Lane Inn, 194
Applewood, 42
The Archbishops Mansion, 136
L'Auberge Del Mar, 499
Auberge du Soleil, 86
The Autry Resort Hotel, 305
The Babbling Brook Inn, 281
Balboa Inn, 480
Balboa Park Inn, 555
The Ballard Inn, 200
Bartel's Ranch and Country Inn, 90
The Bayberry Inn, 267
Beach House, 207
The Bed & Breakfast Inn at La Jolla, 511
Belle de Jour Inn, 46
Beltane Ranch, 36
Benbow Inn, 344
Beverly Prescott Hotel, 527
The Biltmore Hotel, 528
Blackthorne Inn, 50
Blue Lantern Inn, 496
Blue Quail Inn, 268
Blue Spruce Inn, 288
Brannan Cottage Inn, 19
Burgundy House, 182
Busch & Heringlake Country Inn, 448
Caboose Motel, 327
Cal-a-Vie, 572
Campbell Ranch Inn, 31
Campton Place, 101
Caples Lake Resort, 418
Captain Dillingham's Inn, 11
Carmel Valley Ranch Resort, 225
Carter House, 336
Casa Arguello, 102
Casa Madrona Hotel 170
Casa del Mar, 179
Casa Tropicana, 554
La Casa del Zorro Resort Hotel, 297
Catamaran Resort Hotel, 556
The Centrella, 254
Chaminade, 283
Chalfant House, 393
Château du Lac, 522
Checkers, 530
The Christiania Inn, 453
Churchill Manor, 61
Circle Bar B Guest Ranch, 236
City Hotel, 396
The Claremont Resort & Spa, 68
The Cliffs at Shell Beach, 285
The Coloma Country Inn, 394
La Costa Resort and Spa, 486
The Cottage, 563
Country Cottage, 104
Country Rose Inn, 234
Creekside Inn & Resort, 40

Cypress Inn (Carmel), 211
Cypress Inn (Miramar), 58
Dana Point Resort, 497
Deer Run, 92
Deetjen's Big Sur Inn, 202
The Delta King Hotel, 440
Disneyland Hotel, 472
Dockside Boat & Bed, 70
El Dorado Hotel, 175
Doryman's Inn, 546
Drakesbad Guest Ranch, 325
Dunbar House, 1880, 428
East Brother Light Station, 83
Edelweiss Lodge, 422
Eiler's Inn, 517
An Elegant Victorian Mansion, 334
Elk Cove Inn, 329
El Encanto, 270
The Fairmont Hotel, 138
Fallon Hotel, 398
Featherbed Railroad Company, 371
Foothill House, 20
Four Seasons Biltmore, 272
Four Seasons Clift Hotel, 105
The Foxes Bed and Breakfast Inn, 457
Furnace Creek Inn, 298
The Gables, 165
Gaige House, 38
Galleria Park Hotel, 107
Garden Court Hotel, 76
Garden House Inn, 474
Gate House Inn (Jackson), 413
Gatehouse Inn Bed and Breakfast (Pacific Grove), 255
The Gingerbread Mansion, 339
Glendeven, 351
The Golden Door, 500
Golden Gate Hotel, 109
Grandmere's Bed & Breakfast Inn, 430
Gray's Retreat, 79
The Green Gables Inn, 257
Greenwood Pier Inn, 331
Happy Landing Inn, 213
Harbor Court Hotel, 110
Harbor House, 332
Hartley House, 442
The Headlands Inn, 358
The Heirloom, 411
Heritage House, 353
Highlands Inn, 214
Hill House of Mendocino, 360
Holiday Harbor, 373
Holly Tree Inn, 52
Hope-Merrill House, 33
L'Horizon, 309
Horton Grand Hotel, 558
Hotel De Anza, 163
Hotel Bel-Air, 532
Hotel Del Coronado, 489
Hotel Griffon, 112
The Hotel Jeffery, 400
Hotel Juliana, 113
Hotel Nikko (San Francisco), 115
Hotel Nikko at Beverly Hills, 534
Hotel Queen Mary, 525
Hotel Shangri-La, 566
Hotel Sheehan, 117
Hotel Triton, 119
Hotel Vintage Court, 120
Howard Creek Ranch, 382
Hranrad House, 361
The Huntington Hotel, 140
Imperial Hotel, 391
The Inn at Depot Hill, 209
Inn at the Opera, 122
The Inn at Rancho Santa Fe, 550
The Inn at Saratoga, 168
The Inn at Shallow Creek Farm, 375
The Inn at Spanish Bay, 263
The Inn at the Tides, 15

The Inn at Union Square, 124
The Inn on Mt. Ada, 476
Isis Oasis, 35
The Jabberwock, 245
Jackson Court, 125
Jasmine Cottage, 80
La Jolla Beach & Tennis Club, 512
Julian Hotel, 507
Joshua Grindle Inn, 362
The Knickerbocker Mansion 484
Korakia Pensione, 306
Lake Arrowhead Hilton Resort, 524
Lakeland Village Beach & Ski Resort, 452
Little River Inn, 355
Llamahall Guest Ranch, 450
The Lodge at Pebble Beach, 265
Loews Coronado Bay Resort, 493
Loews Santa Monica Beach Hotel, 567
Loma Vista Bed & Breakfast, 571
The Lost Whale Inn, 378
MacCallum House, 364
Madrona Manor, 48
La Maida House, 503
The Majestic, 142
Ma Maison Sofitel, 535
Malibu Beach Inn, 543
Mammoth Mountain Inn, 424
La Mancha, 307
Mangels House, 196
The Mansion at Lakewood, 181
The Mansions, 143
Marina del Rey Hotel, 544
The Mark Hopkins Intercontinental, 145
The Martine Inn, 259
Meadowlark, 22
Meadowood, 93
Le Meridien San Diego at Coronado, 491
Monterey Plaza Hotel, 247
Mount View Hotel, 24
Mountain Home Ranch, 25
The National Hotel, 416
New Davenport Bed & Breakfast Inn, 232
The New Otani Hotel & Garden, 537
The Nolan House, 127
Northstar at Tahoe, 459
Oasis Water Resort Villa Hotel, 312
Ojai Valley Inn & Country Club, 252
The Old Milano Hotel, 346
Old Monterey Inn, 249
Old Thyme Inn, 44
Old World Inn, 64
The Old Yacht Club Inn, 274
Oleander House, 184
Orchid Tree Inn, 313
Otter Bar Lodge, 341
Oyama Wildflower Barge, 172
The Palms at Palm Springs, 314
The Pan Pacific Hotel (San Diego), 559
The Pan Pacific Hotel (San Francisco), 147
Pelican Cove Inn, 488
The Pelican Inn, 59
The Peninsula Beverly Hills, 481
Petite Auberge, 128
Le Petit Château, 310
The Phoenix, 174
Pigeon Point Lighthouse Hostel, 161
The Pillar Point Inn, 84

La Playa Hotel, 216
Point Reyes Seashore Lodge, 72
Post Ranch Inn, 203
Prescott Hotel, 149
Prospect Park Inn, 516
Quail Lodge, 227
La Quinta Hotel Golf & Tennis Resort, 301
Radisson Hotel Sacramento, 443
Rainbow Tarns Bed & Breakfast, 402
Rancho Bernardo Inn, 549
Rancho Caymus Inn, 88
Rancho Valencia, 552
Red Castle Inn, 432
The Red Victorian, 150
Reed Manor, 366
The Regent Beverly Wilshire, 483
La Residence Country Inn, 63
Resort at Squaw Creek, 434
Rick's Lodge, 338
The Ritz-Carlton Huntington, 547
The Ritz-Carlton Laguna Niguel, 520
The Ritz-Carlton Rancho Mirage, 316
The Ritz-Carlton San Francisco, 152
Robles del Rio Lodge, 229
Rockwood Lodge, 407
Rose Victorian Inn, 198
Roundstone Farm, 74
San Diego Princess, 561
The San Remo Hotel, 130
San Ysidro Ranch, 243
Sandcastle, 343
The Sandpiper Inn, 218
Scott Courtyard, 26
Sea Arch, 357
Sea Haus, 367
The Sea Ranch, 376
The Seal Beach Inn and Gardens, 569
Seal Rock Inn, 131
Seven Gables Inn, 261
Shadow Mountain Ranch, 509
Sheraton Palace Hotel, 132
The Sherman House, 153
Silver Rose Inn, 28
Silverado Country Club & Resort, 66
Simpson House Inn, 276
Sonoma Hotel, 176
Sonoma Mission Inn & Spa, 17
Sorensen's, 409
Spindrift Inn, 250
Squaw Valley Lodge, 435
St. James's Club and Hotel, 539
St. Orres, 348
The Stanford Inn by the Sea, 368
The Sterling Hotel, 444
Stillwater Cove Ranch, 56
The Stonehouse Inn, 220
Stonepine, 230
Stouffer Stanford Court Hotel, 134
Strawberry Creek Inn, 506
Sundial Lodge, 222
Sunset Marquis Hotel and Villas, 504
Surf & Sand Hotel, 519
Sutter Creek Inn, 455
Tamarack Lodge Resort, 426
Ten Inverness Way, 54
Tenaya Lodge, 403
Thirty-Nine Cypress, 82
Timberhill Ranch, 29
Travelers Repose, 300
Trinidad Bed & Breakfast, 380
Trinity Alps Resort, 349
U.S. Grant Hotel, 564
The Union Hotel (Benicia), 13

The Union Hotel (Los Alamos), 238
The Upham Hotel, 278
Vagabond's House, 223
La Valencia Hotel, 514
Ventana, 205
Victorian Garden Inn, 177
Victorian Inn on the Park, 157
The Victorian on Lytton, 78
Victorian Mansion, 240
The Villa Florence Hotel, 155
Villa Rosa, 280
Villa Royale, 303
Villa St. Helena, 97
The Village Inn, 495
Vintners Inn, 167
Vizcaya, 446
Ward's Big Foot Ranch, 370
Wawona Hotel, 461
The Webber Place, 185
The Wedgewood Inn, 415
Westwood Marquis Hotel and Gardens, 540
The White Swan Inn, 159
Windy Point Inn, 501
The Wine Country Inn, 95
Zane Grey Hotel, 478
Zinfandel Inn, 99

Best Places Report

Authors of the Best Places to Stay series travel extensively in their research to find the best places for all budgets, styles, and interests. However, if we've missed an establishment that you find worthy, please write to us with your suggestion. Detailed information about the service, food, setting, and nearby activities or sights is most important. Finally, let us know how you heard about the place and how long you've been going there.

Send suggestions to:

The Harvard Common Press
Best Places to Stay Suggestions
535 Albany Street
Boston, Massachusetts 02118

NAME OF HOTEL ______________________________

TELEPHONE ______________________________

ADDRESS ______________________________

______________________________ ZIP ____________

DESCRIPTION ______________________________

____

____

____

____

____

____

YOUR NAME ______________________________

TELEPHONE ______________________________

ADDRESS ______________________________

______________________________ ZIP ____________